TANZANIA

A Political Economy

D1561801

TANZANIA
A POLITICAL ECONOMY

BY

ANDREW COULSON

CLARENDON PRESS · OXFORD
1982

Oxford University Press, Walton Street, Oxford OX2 6DP
London Glasgow New York Toronto
Delhi Bombay Calcutta Madras Karachi
Kuala Lumpur Singapore Hong Kong Tokyo
Nairobi Dar es Salaam Cape Town
Melbourne Auckland
and associates in
Beirut Berlin Ibadan Mexico City Nicosia

Published in the United States by
Oxford University Press, New York

British Library Cataloguing in Publication Data
Coulson, Andrew
Tanzania
1. Tanzania—Economic conditions
2. Tanzania—Politics and government
I. Title
330.9678 HC557.T3
ISBN 0-19-828292-3
ISBN 0-19-828293-1 Pbk

Library of Congress Cataloging in Publication Data
Coulson, Andrew
Tanzania
Bibliography: p.
Includes index.
1. Tanzania—Economic conditions. 1. Title
HC885.C68   330.9678   81-14034
ISBN 0-19-828292-3 (Oxford University Press)
ISBN 0-19-828293-1 (Oxford University Press : pbk.)
AACR2

Typeset by Syarikat Seng Teik Sdn. Bhd., Kuala Lumpur.
and Printed in Great Britain
at the University Press, Oxford
by Eric Buckley
Printer to the University

PREFACE

The first outline for this book was written in 1971 when the author was working for the Ministry of Agriculture in Dar es Salaam. The details began to be filled in during four busy years (1972–6) lecturing at the University of Dar es Salaam, and the research was completed in the library of Rhodes House, Oxford, and at the University of Bradford.

The plan was to write a history of colonial Tanganyika that would shed light on contemporary Tanzanian decision-making. As the work progressed it became inevitable to extend it back to the years before colonial rule, and meanwhile time did not stand still. The strengthening of the bureaucracy in 1972 was followed by the compulsory movement of the rural population into villages in 1974–5. The country was rescued from food and foreign exchange shortages by the World Bank and western governments, and the Tanzanian army invaded Uganda and drove out Idi Amin. The study of economic history and colonial policy enabled these and other events to be interpreted as more than isolated aberrations by individuals, or the results of bad weather or luck.

The book that results is clearly in the interdisciplinary tradition that flourished at the University of Dar es Salaam in the 1970s, and is still continued today. Much of this writing is quoted in references or in the bibliography, and there is a sense in which the whole book is a synthesis of the work of those writers, although (and perhaps for that reason) no one of them would agree with all that is included.

Several friends read chapters in draft. Their suggestions greatly improved what was written, although in no case did I accept all the advice I was offered. I would like to express my gratitude to Henry Bernstein, Brian Bowles, Debbie and Ian Bryceson, Steve Curry, Michaela von Freyhold, Noreen and Ralph Ibbott, Finn Kjaerby, and Abdul Sheriff.

While writing the book I wrote several papers which were published elsewhere. I am grateful to Macmillans for permission to incorporate material from an article which appeared in Judith Heyer, Pepe Roberts, and Gavin Willams (eds.), *Rural Development in Tropical Africa*; to Heinemann Educational Books for permission to use material from my article in *Industrialisation in Africa* (edited by Martin Fransman); and to the Tanzania Publishing House for permission to use part of an article which appeared in *Workers and Management* (edited by Henry Mapolu). My friend Robert Hutchison encouraged me to start work, Lionel Cliffe assisted in the publication of a volume of readings which preceded this book, Pauline Greenwood typed the manuscript, and Andrew Schuller and Phoebe Allen of Oxford University Press converted the typescript into a book. My wife Judy allowed many plans to be disrupted so that the book be written. I am grateful to all of these, and to countless civil servants, students, academics, and farmers without whose insights the book could not have been written. The responsibility for the inevitable errors and misinterpretations is mine.

ANDREW COULSON
Bradford
October 1980

CONTENTS

List of Maps   ix
List of Tables   ix
List of Abbreviations   xii
A Note on Currency   xv

PART I: INTRODUCTION

1 Nyerere's Tanzania   1
2 Tanzania and the International Economy   6

PART II: DEVELOPMENT AND UNDERDEVELOPMENT BEFORE 1900

3 The Interior   15
4 Zanzibar and the Coast   21
5 The German Conquest   27

PART III: THE COLONIAL SYSTEM

6 The German Colony   33
7 Agricultural Production under the British   43
8 Agricultural Marketing and Co-operatives   60
9 Non-industrialization   70
10 Education and Ideology   81
11 Indirect Rule   95

PART IV: THE NATIONALIST TAKE-OVER

12 The Nationalists   101
13 The Independence 'Struggle'   109
14 The Peaceful Transition   118

15 Zanzibar 123

PART V: THE FRUITS OF INDEPENDENCE

16 The Early Years 135
17 Agricultural Policy 1961–1967 145
18 Industry before the Arusha Declaration 168
19 The Arusha Declaration 176

PART VI: HARSH REALITIES

20 Production and Income Distribution 185
21 Social Class and Social Services 202
  Appendix 1 The University of Dar es Salaam 224
  Appendix 2: The Great Uhuru Railway 231
22 Ujamaa and Villagization 235
  Appendix: The Ruvuma Development Association 263
23 Parastatals and Workers 272
  Appendix 1: The State Trading Corporation 1967–1972 290
  Appendix 2: The Mwananchi Engineering and
          Construction Company 295
24 Development Strategy and Foreign Relations 299
25 The Tanzanian State 317
Notes 332
Further Reading 351
Bibliography 360
Index 383

MAPS

		Page
1.	Tanzania in Africa	3
2.	Relief and physical features	7
3.	Rainfall probability	8
4.	Distribution of cattle and principal export crops	9
5.	Communications and main towns	153

TABLES

		Page
7.1	Tanganyika: Agricultural Exports 1913 and 1938	44
7.2	Wage Rates by Province 1927 and 1940	46
7.3	Imports of (a) Cotton Piece Goods and (b) Boots and Shoes, 1925–1937	47
7.4	Conscription of Labour 1941–1945	49
7.5	Tanganyika's Exports 1913–1961	56
8.1	Cotton Production in the Lake Region 1951–1960	67
8.2	Numbers of Registered Primary Cooperative Societies 1959	68
9.1	Industrial Establishments in Tanganyika 1914–1945	72
9.2	Duties on Selected Goods Imported into East Africa 1935	74
9.3	Tanganyika's Trade with Kenya and Uganda 1951 and 1958	75
9.4	Net Output and Employment in Manufacturing Industries 1958	79
10.1	Numbers in School 1926–1956	85

10.2 Tanganyikan Africans in Education 1956 90
10.3 School Attendance by Age Groups 1957 and 1962 91
10.4 Employment in Selected Professions by Race 1962 91
12.1 Urban Population Growth 1948–1967 102
12.2 Cost of Living and Wage Indices: Dar es Salaam 1939–1955 105
15.1 Zanzibar: Population by Race 1948 124
15.2 Land Ownership on Zanzibar and Pemba 1948 127
15.3 Zanzibar Election Results 1961 and 1963 131
16.1 Registered African Trades Unions in Tanganyika 1956–1963 138
16.2 Average Cash Earnings of Wage Labour 1956–1963 139
17.1 Production of Main Export Crops 1960–1968 145
17.2 Cost per Ton of Cooperative Societies by Size of Society 1967 150
17.3 Economics of Maize Fertilizer Trials near Iringa 1972/3 and 1973/4 155
18.1 Gross Profit Outflows and Net Inflows of Private Capital 1961–1968 174
20.1 Balance of Trade (Tanzania Mainland) 1965–1977 187
20.2 Finance of Trade Deficits (Tanzania Mainland) 1970–1977 187
20.3 Gross Material Product at Constant Prices 1965–1977 188
20.4 Gross Domestic Product at Constant Prices 1965–1977 189
20.5 Production of Major Export Crops 1966–1978 190
20.6 Production in Selected Industries 1966–1978 191
20.7 Composition of Imports 1967 and 1977 192
20.8 Sources of Government Income 1967/8, 1973/4 and 1976/7 193
20.9 Allocation of Government Expenditure 1967/8 and 1976/7 194
20.10 Standard of Living of Wage Earners in Dar es Salaam 1966/78 195
20.11 Urban Employment and Unemployment, 1969 and 1975 196
20.12 Standard of Living of Rural Producers 1966–1975 197

20.13 Malnutrition among Children in and outside Dar es
      Salaam   199
20.14 Production and Export of Cloves 1960–1978   200
21.1 Recurrent Expenditure on Curative and Preventive
      Medicine   208
21.2 Imports of Baby Foods 1973–76   210
21.3 Household Possessions 1969   212
21.4 Urban Housing Conditions 1967   213
21.5 Numbers in School 1965–1975   216
22.1 Registered Ujamaa Villages 1969–1974   241
22.2 Net Cereal Imports 1974–1977   260
22.3 Food Aid 1974–1977   261
23.1 Growth of Parastatal Assets 1964–1971   279
23.2 Regular Wage Employment 1969 and 1974   279
23.3 Friendship and Mwanza Textile Mills   282
24.1 Commitments of External Public Loans and Grants
      1967–1975   302
24.2 World Bank Lending Programme in Tanzania up to
      June 1978   304
24.3 USAID Projects under Implementation 1977   305
24.4 Tanzania's Trade with Kenya and Uganda 1962–1977   308
24.5 Aid Donors involved in Regional Planning 1975/7   314

ABBREVIATIONS

ASP	Afro-Shirazi Party (of Zanzibar), amalgamated with TANU on the mainland to form the CCM in 1977.
ASU	Afro-Shirazi Union (of Zanzibar), which became the ASP in 1957.
BCU	Bukoba Co-operative Union.
BRALUP	Bureau of Resource Assessment and Land Use Planning (a research department at the University of Dar es Salaam).
CCM	*Chama cha Mapinduzi* (Party of the Revolution). The new party formed from TANU and the ASP in 1977.
CIA	The US Central Intelligence Agency.
COSATA	Co-operative Supply Association of Tanganyika. (An ill-fated co-operative wholesale company.)
EAPH	East African Publishing House (Nairobi).
ENI	Ente Nazionale Idrocarburi (the Italian state-owned oil corporation).
ERB	Economic Research Bureau (of the University of Dar es Salaam).
FAO	Food and Agriculture Organization (of the United Nations).
IBRD	International Bank for Reconstruction and Development ('The World Bank').
IDA	International Development Association (the 'soft loan' branch of the IBRD).
ILO	International Labour Organization (of the United Nations).
INTRATA	International Trading Association of Tanganyika. (An ill-fated co-operative import–export company.)

IPS	Industrial Promotion Services/(Tanzania) Ltd. (an investment bank).
KNCU	Kilimanjaro Native Co-operative Union.
KNPA	Kilimanjaro Native Planters' Association (the fore-runner of the KNCU).
MECCO	Mwananchi Engineering and Construction Company. (A nationalized construction company.)
MNC	Multinational corporation.
NBC	National Bank of Commerce.
NDC	National Development Corporation.
NHC	National Housing Corporation.
NIC	National Insurance Corporation.
NMC	National Milling Corporation.
NUTA	National Union of Tanganyika Workers. (The sole trade Union after 1964.)
OAU	Organization of African Unity.
RDA	Ruvuma Development Association (a group of villages in the south-west of the country).
STC	State Trading Corporation.
TAA	Tanganyika African Association (the precursor of TANU).
TANU	Tanganyika African National Union.
TAZARA	Tanzania Zambia Railway Authority.
TDFL	Tanganyika Development Finance Company Ltd. (an investment company).
TFL	Tanganyika Federation of Labour.
TIB	Tanzania Investment Bank.
TNR	*Tanzania* (previously Tanganyika) *Notes and Records* (a journal).
TPH	Tanzania Publishing House.
TRDB	Tanzania Rural Development Bank.
TYL	TANU Youth League.
UPE	Universal primary education.
USAID	United States Agency for International Development.
UTP	United Tanganyika Party (the opposition party, 1955–9).

UWT   *Umoja wa Wanawake wa Tanzania* (Union of Tanzanian Women), the TANU women's organization.

WHO   World Health Organization (of the United Nations).

ZNP   Zanzibar Nationalist Party.

ZPPP   Zanzibar and Pemba People's Party.

A NOTE ON CURRENCY

Tanzanian currency is based on the shilling, divided into 100 cents. Its foreign exchange value is tied to the value of Special Drawing Rights issued by the International Monetary Fund, and consequently fluctuates in terms of other currencies. At the end of 1980 one US dollar was worth approximately 8 shillings, and one UK pound approximately 19 shillings, but in August 1979 a UK pound would have purchased only about 15 shillings. During the British period and up to 1967 20 shillings (or one East African pound) exchanged for one UK pound. From 1905 to 1914 one German mark was equivalent to one shilling in Kenya or Uganda, and 20 shillings equalled one East African or British pound. Before 1905 the Germans used rupees, Indian currency also used on Zanzibar. The value of rupees fluctuated in terms of marks, until it was fixed in 1905 when three rupees were exchanged for four marks.

PART I: INTRODUCTION

1 NYERERE'S TANZANIA

> We have been oppressed a great deal, we have been
> exploited a great deal and we have been disregarded a
> great deal. It is our weakness that has led to our being
> oppressed, exploited and disregarded. Now we want a
> revolution . . .
>
> THE ARUSHA DECLARATION (1967)[1]

The mainland part of Tanzania became independent in 1961
under the leadership of a politician and philosopher called Julius
Nyerere. The handover was peaceful, and twenty years later
Nyerere remained in power, unrivalled within the country, re-
spected as the leader who brought independence, and the *mwalimu*, or teacher, who interprets current events and creates new
policies. In 1967 the only legal political party on the mainland,
TANU (the Tanganyika African National Union), accepted the
Arusha Declaration, which lowered the salaries and lessened the
fringe benefits of civil servants and politicians, and was accompanied by the nationalization of the banks and the biggest importing houses; the state also took majority shareholdings in several
subsidiaries of multinational corporations and a majority of the
sisal plantations. The slogan of the Declaration was 'socialism
and self-reliance', and later the same year Nyerere wrote papers
exploring the implications for education (*Education for Self-
Reliance*) and in the rural areas (*Socialism and Rural
Development*).[2] The objective was *ujamaa* [socialist] villages:

Our Agricultural organization would be predominantly that of co-operative living and working for the good of all. This means that most of our farming would be done by groups of people who live as a community and work as a community. They would live together in a village; they would farm together; market together; and undertake the provision of local services and small local requirements as a community. Their community would be the traditional family group, or any other group of people living according to ujamaa principles, large enough to take account of modern methods and the twentieth century needs of man. The land this community farmed would be called 'our land' by all the members; the crops they produced on that land would be 'our crop'; it would be 'our shop' which provided individual members with the day-to-day necessities from outside; 'our workshop' which made the bricks from which houses and other buildings were constructed, and so on. (Nyerere 1976d: 351.)

For some years after 1967 Tanzania was the country in Africa most noticeably committed to socialist principles. Nyerere became a world figure, a spokesman for the 'poorest of the poor', demanding a New International Economic Order that would give them a greater share of the world's wealth, and trying to ensure that the non-aligned countries acted as a trade union, merging some of their individual interests to campaign on a common programme.

Nyerere willingly admitted that much of what passed in Tanzania was imperfect, often drawing a distinction between his policies and the failure of his ministers and civil servants to implement them. He did not claim that the country was socialist; but he did claim that the worst excesses of capitalism had been tamed, and that the country was moving in the direction of greater equality of treatment for all its people, with the state in control of the economy.[3]

Yet Nyerere's Tanzania was full of paradoxes. Western governments were so impressed by the commitment to 'self-reliance' that they were willing to overlook the nationalizations that followed the Arusha Declaration, with the result that Tanzania became a major recipient of Western capital, much of it on concessionary terms. Freedom of expression was confined within narrow bounds, and for many years the country was high on Amnesty International's lists of political prisoners; the largest numbers were detained in 1972 following the assassination of Vice-President Karume, the leader of Zanzibar, the off-shore island which merged with the mainland, Tanganyika, a few months after its independence in December 1963, to form the United Re-

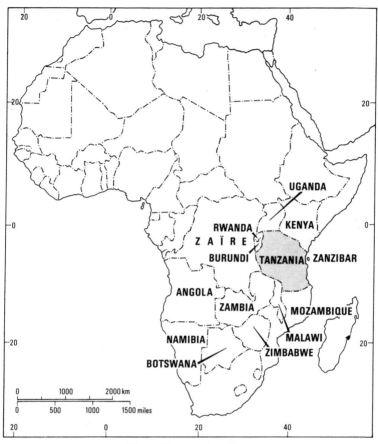

MAP 1 Tanzania in Africa
(Based on Berry 1971)

public of Tanzania. Contrary to Nyerere's statements in 1967 and 1968 that ujamaa must be voluntary, the move between 1973 and 1975 of a large proportion of rural population into 'planned villages' of 250–300 families was compulsory.[4] Democratically elected individuals gradually lost their power to new arms of the bureaucracy; the right to strike, and even to speak out against oppressive managements, was removed from workers' organizations; elected local government was replaced by civil servants appointed in Dar es Salaam; marketing co-operatives were disbanded in favour of corporations with top management appointed by the President; Parliament was downgraded to a point where it had little function; and within the Party and in the villages appointed officials became more powerful than elected representatives.

Economically there were few successes and many failures. Production of the important export crops hardly rose between 1968 and 1978, while most of the country's foreign exchange reserves were spent on food imports in 1974 and 1975. There were falls in production in several important industries, and the nationalized corporations became heavily indebted to the nationalized banks. Neither in industry nor in agriculture was there much sign of the economic miracle that one would expect to find in a socialist state moving forward with the enthusiasm of the people.

The present volume attempts to explain these paradoxes. This can only be done in a historical context, for Nyerere and TANU did not inherit a blank sheet; in 1961 they took over a running business, an economy organized to produce raw materials for capitalist markets. Moreover, it was a business which could not run without outside help: serious training of senior African administrators had started only six years earlier (Pratt 1976: 18), and at independence there were hardly any Tanzanian African engineers, accountants or architects, and very few doctors and agriculturalists. There was no quick way of changing the inherited economic structure.

But it would be wrong to write a study of Tanzania purely in terms of a dependency theory which explains underdevelopment in terms of loss of surplus in a colonial or neo-colonial economy. The strength of Issa Shivji's pioneering *Class Struggles in Tanzania* is that his *bureaucratic bourgeoisie*, or ruling class, comprised of the top officials, managers, judges, politicans, etc., is treated as a class within the Tanzanian social formation which does have some power at home and abroad. The weakness of that book is that it is so preoccupied with class struggles that it omits any discussion of Nyerere's writing and his role as a creator of ideology for the ruling class. The Arusha Declaration, for example, is interpreted exclusively as a means for that class to gain a property stake in the commanding heights of the economy (Shivji 1975: 64, 79, 85–99). To take this line is to fail to discuss most of the policies that make Tanzania attractive to socialist sympathizers in other countries, the work of the most influential thinker and writer on the African continent, and the ideas which the Tanzania ruling class has internalized to greater or lesser extent.

Romanticizing Nyerere and writing a history of Tanzania around a biography of him, is even less illuminating. A reader of Cranford Pratt's *The Critical Phase in Tanzania 1945–1968: Nyerere and the emergence of a Socialist Strategy*, the result of many years' thought about Tanzania, comes away with an impression of Nyerere as a far-seeing superman who can do little that is wrong. But this does not square well with the 'villagization', the increasing power of the officials, and the 1978 expulsion of more than 400 students from the University of Dar es Salaam. Nyerere was informed about these, and contradicted several of his earlier ideological statements. And therein lies the clue to his position: for as well as being an active executive President, he is a creator of ideology for the new ruling classes in Africa (Nellis 1972). Not all that he says is internalized; prescriptions that are too demanding are dropped, and he is not the only source of ideology. But for a clear understanding of Tanzania—and indeed of Africa today—it is necessary to separate Nyerere the producer of ideology from Nyerere the President of Tanzania.

And that is the excuse for this book. For those who know little about the country, it will serve as an introduction, combining a historical outline, statistical information, and advice on where to read more. Those who are familiar with Nyerere and his writing may benefit from an attempt to interpret the underlying, historically determined, economic position. Only in this way can one avoid being either romantic or dismissive about Tanzania. Noone who reads this book will be left in any doubt that those struggling for a better existence for the masses in Africa and elsewhere can learn much from Tanzania's experience—even if many of the lessons are negative.

2 TANZANIA AND THE INTERNATIONAL ECONOMY

> The penetration of the interior by modern transport technology, tax-demanding colonial officials, and immigrant settler-farmers, merchants and traders and mining companies fashioned the economic base of most of Africa's contemporary nation states. Subsaharan Africa's politico-economic units became integral components of the global capitalist economy and shared its erratic progress through the disruption of two World Wars and the contractions of the inter-war depressions before reaching the more settled and expansionary period in world trade and investment after 1945.
>
> J. FORBES MUNRO (1976: 208–9)

Tanzania possesses the most varied ecology of any country in Africa.[1] There is a belt of tropical forest along the coast and on the islands of Zanzibar and Pemba. Most of the land area is covered by rolling grassland, thorn scrub, or tsetse-infested acacia woodland. But there are also highland areas, including several of volcanic origin, where rainfall is high, the soil fertile, and the climate cool, so that temperate crops can be grown. The west comprises a plateau, about 1000 metres above sea-level, where the rainfall averages more than 750 millimetres a year. There are also great lakes: Lake Victoria, shared with Uganda and Kenya; Lake Tanganyika, forming the border with Zaire: and Lake Nyasa, along the border with Malawi in the south-west. There are rivers—the Rufiji and its tributaries draining one-fifth of the land area of the country; the Pangani and Wami in the north; the Kagera, Malagarasi, and Kiwira in the west; and the Ruvuma forming the border with Mozambique in the south—with the potential to produce hydroelectric power, and the possibility of irrigation farming if ways can be found to combat the threats of salinity and flooding.

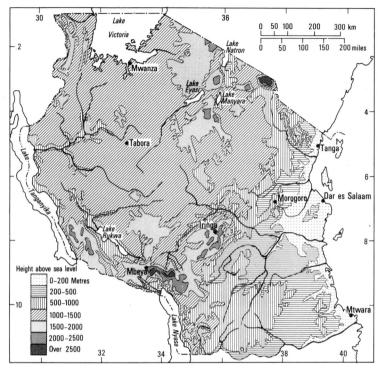

MAP 2 Rainfall and physical features
(Source: Berry 1971)

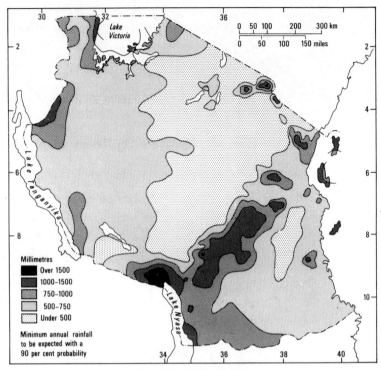

MAP 3 Rainfall probability
(Source: Berry 1971)

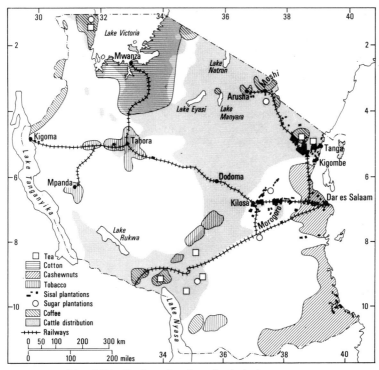

MAP 4 Distribution of cattle and principal export crops
c. 1967 (Source: Berry 1971)

Virtually every crop known to agriculturalists will grow in one or more of these areas. Wheat, coffee, tea, potatoes, and pyrethrum grow in the cool mountains. On the inland plateau grow maize; rice; sorghum; varieties of millet; cotton; and tobacco, as well as sisal—a cactus from which string is made, and until recently the country's most valuable export. Coconuts, cashewnuts, rubber, cocoa, cloves, and a wide variety of spices grow on the coastal strip or on Zanzibar and Pemba. Each ecological unit produces its own fruits and vegetables.

The grasslands are suitable for cattle-keeping, but this is difficult in most of the acacia woodland areas owing to the presence of tsetse fly. There are true pastoralists, such as the Maasai, who depend entirely on cattle for their livelihood, but most of the cattle-keepers are semi-pastoralists who both keep cattle and tend crops.

The human population density has never been high. Even today with a population of eighteen million, the average density is only about 20 people per square kilometre (Thomas 1979). There is considerable doubt about population levels in the past, but estimates for Africa south of the Sahara for the year 1800 vary from about three people per square kilometre to about six. Western Europe at the same period had a density of between twenty and thirty (Munro 1976: 20–3). There are few towns. Before the colonial period the largest were ports such as Kilwa, with a population of several thousand as early as the fifteen century. Up to the First World War, Dar es Salaam, the present capital, had a population of only about 20 000. Today about 800 000 people live there, but the second-largest urban centre, Mwanza, has a population of less than 100 000, and in the country as a whole only about 10 per cent of the population live in urban areas.

The present volume tells the story of the incorporation of this land area and these people into the world capitalist system. It is convenient to divide the story into five periods—the precapitalist centuries before AD 1500; the period of mercantile capitalism (1500–1800); early industrial capitalism (1800–70); maturing industrial capitalism (1870–1945); and the present period of a gradually more integrated world capitalist economy (Munro 1976: 11–16).

Before 1500, for at least two thousand years, the East African coast was in contact with civilizations in the Persian Gulf, India, and even China, to which it was linked by sea trade across the Indian Ocean. In relation to these, the East African coastal towns and islands were periphery areas,[2] sources of luxury items:

ivory (especially for India), mangrove poles (for house building in the Arabian peninsula), some slaves, and small quantities of several other products. From about AD 1200 gold from Zimbabwe (in present-day Zimbabwe) began to be taken overland to ports in present-day Mozambique, and then up the East African coast by sea, giving prosperity to the coastal ports, especially Kilwa. Apart from this trade in gold, there is litle evidence (in the early period) of contact between the interior and the coast. Food was grown on the flood-plains of the Rufiji and Pangani rivers and along the coastal strip, ivory could be obtained near the coast, but other products from the interior could not stand the high cost of head transport to the coast.

In the period of mercantile capitalism, from about AD 1500, West Africa came under very direct influence from Europe in the form of the slave-trade. The slaves were used in America and the Caribbean initially to dig for gold (most of the indigenous population having been killed by fighting or disease) but later to grow sugar, cotton, and tobacco on plantations. The East African coast was controlled by the Portuguese, whose ships were the first to round the Cape of Good Hope. They took over the trade in gold, and sacked Kilwa, the largest town. But they were more interested in India than East Africa, and the ports north of present-day Mozambique gradually broke free. Kilwa in particular regained some of its lost prosperity and began to trade with the interior, importing textiles (from India), arms and ammunition, and salt, and exporting ivory, gum, and (from about 1730) slaves, mainly destined for French sugar plantations on the Indian Ocean islands of Mauritius and Réunion.

Between 1800 and 1870 an industrial revolution took place in Britain. Textile production was mechanized, coal was mined and used to drive steam-engines and to make steel, which was used for shipbuilding, railways, and machines of many sorts. There were booms in construction as farmers were driven from the land to become wage-workers in the new towns and cities, where they produced rapidly increasing exports of textiles, but needed imports of food, cotton, wool, and other raw materials. In the Americas slavery was replaced by a system of 'free' labour which left the ex-slaves (and their children) little alternative but to produce the same commodities as before for very low wages. In West Africa the slave-trade gave way to 'legitimate commerce', in which the local population supplied oil-palm products or groundnuts in exchange for textiles and other manufactured goods.

In East Africa the effect of the industrial revolution was indirect.[3] Ivory prices at Zanzibar doubled between 1820 and 1850, and then trebled between 1850 and 1890, owing in the main to increasing demand for knife handles and piano keys in the west. The ivory had to come from farther and farther away. Caravans to bring ivory to the coast were organized by the Nyamwezi and other inland tribes, and later by Arabs and other residents ('swahili') from the coast, until East and Central Africa became a vast hunting-ground for ivory. The ivory was taken to Zanzibar, an island off the Tanzanian coast that was effectively colonized by Arabs from Oman in the Persian Gulf at the beginning of the nineteenth century. Sultan Seyyid Said moved his capital from Muscat to Zanzibar in 1840. Initially most of the ivory went to India (from where some of it was resold to Europe). In exchange, textiles from India were imported into Zanzibar, and from there into the interior. The trade was financed by Indian merchants on Zanzibar, joined later by merchants from Europe and America, and was increasingly direct to and from those countries. In addition to textiles, the traders sold arms and ammunition. On Zanzibar the Arabs planted a new crop, cloves, which was picked with slave labour. Slaves were also exported to Mauritius and Réunion, and to the Arabian peninsula, but the greatest numbers were retained on the islands of Zanzibar and (later) Pemba for the clove plantations, and on the mainland opposite, where they grew food. Towards the end of the century, ivory was becoming scarce, and firearms had become widespread in the interior. Warrior chiefs extended their territorial claims, and growing numbers of their subjects were sold into slavery, though probably not sufficient to prevent population increase in the country as a whole.

European Powers were increasingly involved. The industrial revolution in Britain was copied, and improved upon, in Germany, France, and Belgium, and in the United States. By the last quarter of the nineteenth century, these countries had industrialized behind protective tariffs, and were competing for markets for their industrial products. The desire for secure sources of raw materials, the possibility of wealth if gold, diamonds, or copper were discovered, but, above all, the fear that competitors might secure protected markets for their industrial products led to the colonization of Africa at the end of the nineteenth century. Railways were built, civil administrations were installed, and taxes were imposed, to be paid in money or labour. Zanzibar became a British Protectorate; slavery was slowly abolished, and the declining importance of its port, following the construction of new ports at Dar es Salaam and Mombasa, left it almost totally dependent on cloves, now picked mainly by 'squatter' labour, freed slaves with no easy alternative livelihood. The East African mainland was divided between German East Africa and the British colony of Kenya until the First World War, after which German East Africa was itself divided, under mandates from the League of Nations, between Tanganyika, administered by Britain, and Rwanda-Urundi, under Belgian administration. During the German period cotton, coffee, sisal, and other crops were produced by plantation companies, white settlers, and by small-scale African farmers, and these three means of production were continued in Tanganyika under British rule. Even the depression of the 1930s, when raw material prices fell, was not allowed to stimulate industrialization, which began, under settler initiative, in neighbouring Kenya. By 1945 Tanganyika and Zanzibar were incorporated into the world capitalist system as suppliers of raw materials and importers of manufactured goods.[4]

But by 1945 world economic power had shifted decisively to the United States, which was nearly self-sufficient in raw materials, and did not depend on colonies. It dominated its competitors through its multinational corporations (which had the resources to buy up or create subsidiaries in other countries whenever the conditions of production made it profitable to do so) and through its influence over the international lending agencies (notably the World Bank and the IMF). Chemical substitutes were produced (mainly from oil) for cotton, sisal, rubber, and other agricultural raw materials, which became less important. Oil and food grains became the strategic primary products, and neither was exported, in the main, from colonies. Britain and France could see no economic necessity to retain colonies, while the United States, itself an ex-colony that had successfully fought for independence, encouraged nationalist movements. In quick succession countries in the Indian subcontinent, south and southeast Asia, and most parts of Africa, were given independence.

The Korean War boom of the early 1950s was the last occasion when the traditional raw material exports were in short supply. Consumer goods were also difficult to obtain and import substitution was therefore begun or continued in many countries. But thereafter given quantities of most of the traditional export crops would purchase less and less in terms of manufactured goods. The newly independent states in Africa had little chance of competing successfully in export markets for manufactured goods, and they had no capital goods sectors, so they were forced to import machinery, inputs for their newly created industries, and many consumer goods, and to seek capital from overseas if they were to make many new investments.

Tanzania, formed by the union of Tanganyika and Zanzibar in 1964, was in a particularly weak position, for Kenya had forty years' start in industrialization and a much wider range of skills, and Nairobi had emerged as the 'natural' centre for import substitution in East Africa. The first five years of independence showed that financial incentives alone would not persuade many multinationals to invest in Dar es Salaam; industrialization could only take place if the state took the risk, as it did following the nationalizations of 1967. It was never easy to be competitive in such a big, poor, and underpopulated country, and the effect of the much increased parastatal investment from 1967 on was to raise the prices of industrial products (and transport) and so to make agricultural production (on which the economy relied) less and less rewarding for the farmers. As the situation deteriorated in the 1970s, following the oil price rises, Nyerere and TANU turned more and more to state intervention in an attempt to guarantee production. The result, as we shall see in later chapters, was an increasingly powerful bureaucracy which tried to tell the farmers what to do, often disregarding the prerequisities for efficient agricultural production. In the face of foreign exchange crises it increasingly depended on capital from the World Bank, the IMF, and capitalist governments. Criticism from workers or students was no longer tolerated. The paradox was that, in order to earn the foreign exchange to pay back the loans, and to feed the cities, there was little alternative but to persuade farmers to grow the traditional crops and workers to lower their living standards. The country continued to import its machinery and many key manufactured goods, while exporting primary agricultural products; in that sense Tanzania in the 1970s remained a neo-colonial state.

PART II: DEVELOPMENT AND UNDERDEVELOPMENT BEFORE 1900

3 THE INTERIOR

> In south Pare also, it seems that, around 1700, population growth provoked attempts to provide more effective forms of political control, based on territory rather than kinship: a crucial step, which was taken in Ufipa at about the same period. So too in Usambara, the Kilindi conquest in the eighteenth century was possible mainly because there was already a need for a more centralised system: more organised defence was necessary in the face of raids by the Masai.
>
> ROBERTS (1968: xii)

> All the traditions agree that chiefs and chiefs' sons were foremost in the organising of long-distance porterage to the coast.
>
> SHORTER (1973: 45)

Before 1800 the most advanced inland societies were in mountainous areas where a food surplus could be gained by the cultivation of cooking bananas. Bananas reached East Africa from South-East Asia about two thousand years ago, in the ships of traders from India. Their cultivation was associated with the introduction of iron tools which eased the task of clearing the thick trees of the tropical rain forests.

Varieties of the grain crops millet and sorghum had been domesticated locally, and were grown in areas of lower rainfall where the trees could be cleared by burning.[1] They were nutritious and drought-resistant, but relatively low-yielding. Today they are still grown on the central plains, but they have been joined by maize, cassava (manioc), and sweet potatoes, all crops brought to Africa from South America by the Portuguese, and rice, grown in valley bottoms and on flood plains, which came from Asia and was taken inland along the caravan routes.

Cattle and goats were herded both in the plains and in mountainous areas. Livestock provided the people with many different forms of security. The zebu and ankole cattle could survive for several months without rain, and if rain came at an unseasonable time of year they could make good use of it. Cattle were sources of calories, fats, vitamins, and salt, as well as proteins—through milk and blood as well as meat. They produced manure which could be used to improve crops. Last but not least they were means of storing wealth for use in the future—a means which in addition produced 'interest' in the form of milk and calves.[2]

Chieftainship emerged first in the mountain areas because there a surplus which was worth defending from attack could be produced from relatively limited areas of land. The longest lines of chiefs recorded by oral historians go back to about 1700 and come from these banana-growing areas. The chieftainship was often associated with possession of economically valuable skills, such as iron working (which produced means of defence as well as of agriculture), weather forecasting ('rain-making' in anthropological terms, also of economic value), or special skill in hunting (Roberts 1968: x–xii).

In return for organizing the defence of an area a chief received either a proportion of the crop or free labour on his own farm. Chiefs therefore had an incentive to innovate. The complex irrigation systems at Engaruka near Arusha (irrigating 2000 hectares, and begun at least 250 years ago), on Mount Kilimanjaro and in the Usambara and other mountain areas were probably built by communal labour organized by the chiefs;[3] so were the soil conservation works, which involved the construction of stone walls and terraces in the Usambaras. Oral tradition specifically associates the chiefs with one of the most remarkable achievements of all—the transport of thousands of tons of grass from flood-plains to slightly higher ground that succeeded in building up the fertility of small areas of land around villages which today make up the coffee-banana-growing areas of West Lake Region (Kjekshus 1977: 45).

The detailed arrangements could vary. For example in Ngoni society, the *inkosi*, or 'head of administration',

controlled a considerable portion of the wealth of the society. All booty taken in plundering belonged to him, to be distributed as he wished. Most of the cattle in the society were entrusted to him as head of the state, though many in the community helped care for, and eventually benefited from, these herds. His fields were among the largest and to work in them he could demand labour on a much larger scale than other people. In the judicial realm he was the final arbiter. . . . He decided national policies towards neighbouring states. . . . In a word, he had the final say in most matters that were of importance to the society. (Redmond 1972:90)

In Bukoba, where robusta coffee had been grown for many years before the Germans started exporting it to Europe, 'Coffee trees belonged to the chiefs alone, and such coffee trees as were found in individual native gardens had been planted by the chief's orders, were regarded as his property, and were maintained by the occupier of the plot for the chief's use' (Jervis 1939: 51).

During the nineteenth century most cultivators in the interior came under the allegiance of a chief.[4] The trend was accelerated by trade with the coast. Before 1800 it is likely that only the Yao traders at Kilwa had regular contact with the coastal towns. Inland trade had, however, been taking place for a thousand years, but it was a short-distance trade. Iron and salt were obtainable from a relatively small number of places, and so iron hoes or salt were exchanged for food or pottery in a series of small markets. After several transactions the hoes might finish up a long distance from where they were produced, without any one trader having carried them more than a few miles.

The difference between this and the nineteenth-century trade with the coast was not in the quantities—the quantities of hoes and food traded before 1800 were no doubt greater than those of ivory or slaves later on—but in the goods that were traded. Firearms and ammunition, in particular, had an important influence and could be purchased at the coast. Their use led to a more ruthless hunting of elephants for ivory. It also affected the skirmishes between tribes and the hunting of slaves. Small isolated clans who cultivated far from anyone else in the bush were forced to ally themselves with some chief or other for protection. The chiefs profited directly from the long-distance trade. It was common for one of the tusks of every elephant killed to be the property of the chief, while the other belonged to the man who killed it (Shorter 1973: 45; Redmond 1972). Some chiefs, such as the Nyamwezi, organized their own caravans to the coast. But if this was not possible, they could still get some benefit from the passing caravans, by charging tolls (*hongo*) or simply raiding them. Thus trade led to centralization, and by the time the Germans came, almost the whole of the country was divided between a small number of tribal empires with organized armies and administrations, based on possession of firearms.

The centre and south was divided between the Gogo, the Nyamwezi, the Hehe, the Kimbu, the Sangu, and the Ngoni. To the north-east lay the Maasai. Apart from the Maasai, all these tribes produced great warrior chiefs; but the process came late. Oral historians have seldom been able to find lineages going back before 1800, while the Ngoni ruling clans only entered the country in the 1840s. Fundikira created the Nyamwezi empire at about the same time, and after his death in about 1860, another great chief, Mirambo, continued the systematic export of ivory. Mirambo allowed the chiefs he conquered to stay in power provided they paid him the ivory; but Nyungu ya Mawe, who broke away in 1871 and founded the Kimbu empire to the south, used what amounted to a salaried civil service (Shorter 1973: 49–50, and articles by Kimambo and Roberts, in Kimambo and Temu (eds.) 1969). The Hehe kingdom, built by Munyigumba who ruled between about 1855 and 1878, and continued by his son Mkwawa who led the most prolonged resistance against the Germans, also used appointed civilians to rule the empire. The Ngoni empire was not strongly established till the 1850s but it quickly brought under its control almost all the inhabitants from the coast at Lindi right across southern Tanzania to Lake Nyasa.

Most of the chiefs lived in large fortified villages. They received tribute in the form of food from their widely scattered subjects, and were able to tax (the Gogo, for example, charged in hoes as late as 1891), or raid, passing caravans, but they also grew a lot of their food in permanent fields near their settlements. This was made possible by agricultural innovation: the use of iron hoes in place of wooden ones, the cultivation of new crops such as maize or rice, the use of both cattle manure and green manure, and advanced systems of inter-cropping, crop rotation, and irrigation (Kjekshus 1977: 26–50).

They also kept large herds of cattle, in areas where today this would be impossible because of tsetse fly. The fly was probably present, but its danger was known, and the density of the fly population was kept down by the relative absence of game animals and thick bush. The presence of cattle and of food reserves maintained by chiefs for their subjects meant that the nineteenth-century inhabitants of these areas were better protected against famine and other calamities, and probably also better fed, than their successors today, although the margin between life and death was not great, and there were destructive famines from time to time, as Bryceson rightly reminds us (Kjekshus 1977: 51–68; Bryceson 1978: 8–11).

The increase in the size of the political units during the nineteenth century encouraged specialization in industrial or craft skills. The task of selecting ores and other ingredients, and of building kilns with which to make iron from them, was complex, and confined to the relatively few places where ore was available. The blacksmith's craft of beating the iron into implements, or repairing existing implements, was more widely dispersed. In 1860 Burton reported that there were blacksmiths who could make hoes, spears, arrowheads, axes, daggers and knives, sickles, razors, rings, bells, pipes, pincers, and a great variety of ornaments (Kjekshus 1977: 81–2). By 1900 they could, with difficulty, repair muzzle-loading rifles. The over-all size of the iron industry was sufficient to supply the needs of the whole country: an observer in 1892 estimated that 150 000 iron hoes were sold each year on the Tabora market alone (Kjekshus 1977: 90).

There was also a textile industry, probably based on varieties of cotton which reached the country between AD 1000 and 1500. The cotton was spun by hand. The oldest cotton spindles have been found by archaeologists at coastal sites such as Kilwa, from where the technique spread very slowly inland. By 1900 the 'fixed heddle loom' for weaving could be found almost everywhere, and yellow and black dyes were being made from forest plants (Kjekshus 1977: 105–9).

Other crafts were the tanning of leather, boat-building, the manufacture of fishing nets, traps, and sails, bows and arrows, pottery, and baskets. Of particular importance was the manufacture of salt. At the coast salt was extracted by evaporation from sea water. Inland there were some important salt lakes, but also the salt springs of Uvinza and Ivuna in the west. Archaeological excavation has shown that the Uvinza spring, still Tanzania's principal source of salt, was being worked a thousand years ago, although production probably only reached its peak around the time of the German conquest (Kjekshus 1977: 92–105).

The economies of late nineteenth-century Tanzania cannot be described as advanced, even for their day: little or no use was made of the wheel; stone was not used in building; and virtually all firearms and ammunition had to be imported. They did possess craft skills; but too much labour time was spent on procuring food, on transport, and on warfare for a large surplus to be extracted and ploughed back into improving security and living conditions.

They were certainly not static. New crops, such as maize, rice, cassava, and cotton, spread quickly, and many improvements were made in the techniques of agricultural husbandry. Forms of decentralized administration were experimented with, as were different types of diplomacy with the explorers, missionaries, and traders who passed through. At least four chiefs—Kimweri of the Shambaa, Merere of the Sangu, Rindi of Moshi, and Mirambo's successor Mpandashalo—recognized the importance of writing, and hired Arab or Swahili clerks to assist them.

To develop further these societies would have needed a long period of non-exploitative contact with the rest of the world. This could not be, for the forces that were making for centralization were coming from outside—represented by the slave and ivory traders promoted by the Sultan of Zanzibar and financed by Indian merchants on Zanzibar, described in the next chapter. Moreover, by 1800 an industrial revolution was taking place in Britain, and by 1900 the military/industrial strengths of Britain, Germany, and the United States bore no relation to those of the Tanzanian chiefs. From the points of view of the industrial capitalists of the West, the untouched parts of the world were too important, both as sponges to absorb surplus production and as sources of raw materials, to be left alone. There was no way in which the trading contacts between them and Africa could be equal.

4 ZANZIBAR AND THE COAST

The addition of ivory to the indigenous trade goods of
central and western Tanzania led to the formation of a
vast long-distance trading network which linked the
coast with the far interior, as the pattern of regional
trade came to support the operation of this international commerce.

ALPERS (1969: 51)

Trading contacts between East Africa and the Red Sea go back
at least two thousand years, although the oldest archaeological
sites at the coast are only half that age. Trade in the Indian
Ocean was made possible by the pattern of the winds, which
allowed voyages from India to Africa during six months of the
year, while the return journey could be made during the other six
months. From about AD 750 there was some migration from the
Persian Gulf to Zanzibar and Pemba, while from AD 1200 Muslim
influence has been found at all the coastal sites that have been
excavated.[1]

Several of the most important sites were on islands—
Kilwa Kisiwani, Zanzibar, Pemba, Mafia, and, further south,
Mozambique Island. Around AD 1200, one of these islands, Kilwa, whose rulers apparently came from Shiraz on the Persian
Gulf, gained control of the trade in gold. Gold was mined in
Zimbabwe, taken overland to the port of Sofala in Mozambique,
and from there carried north by ship to India and the Persian
Gulf. Ivory was also exported from a very early date, especially
to India, and mangrove poles were taken to Arabia where they
were used in building the ceilings of houses. In the other direction came textiles and porcelain, some from as far away as China.

In 1498 the first European, Vasco da Gama, sailed to India
round the Cape of Good Hope, and in 1505 the Portuguese sacked Kilwa and Mombasa and gained control of the trade in gold.
The Europeans possessed warships with guns mounted on the

decks which gave them a decisive advantage on the sea, though they were as yet not strong enough to penetrate inland in either Africa or Asia. They eventually controlled the whole Indian Ocean, including Muscat (taken in 1580); they built Fort Jesus at Mombasa from 1593, and established small settlements in India. But the Portuguese did not have the resources to control what they had conquered, and many of the East African coastal settlements managed to continue a semi-independent existence. Kilwa in particular, previously the richest state on the coast, managed to find a new role: by 1600 Yao traders from inland were exchanging ivory and beeswax for textiles and beads, and so linking the coast with the trading network inland.

Muscat, the capital of Oman, at the foot of the Persian Gulf, was equipped with a small fleet of naval ships and broke free of the Portuguese in 1650. The Omanis proceeded to drive the Portuguese south, becoming in the process the strongest naval power in the Indian Ocean. In 1652 they drove the Portuguese out of Zanzibar, and in 1699, after a three year siege, Mombasa. However, in 1741 the local rulers in Mombasa broke away, and it took almost a hundred years for the Omani sultans to reassert their authority. In those hundred years, having lost their stronghold on the coast, the Omanis developed Zanzibar as the most important outpost of their empire. It was less than 50 kilometres from the mainland, and had plenty of water, a pleasant tropical climate, and could easily be defended. It soon became apparent that its agricultural potential could be exploited in its own right through the cultivation of food crops, coconuts, and (from 1810) cloves, and its easy access from the sea made it an ideal centre from which to expand the import and export trade with the mainland.

From their base in Zanzibar, the Omanis gradually annexed the other trading settlements. Kilwa was taken in 1784, Pemba in 1822, and Mombasa, after several unsuccessful attempts, in 1837. The potential of Zanzibar was particularly recognized by Sultan Seyyid Said who became Sultan of Oman in 1806 and ruled for fifty years. In 1828 he signed an agreement with the Mwinyi Mkuu, or chief of the Hadimu people of Zanzibar, under which he colonized the island. No doubt influenced by the sight of the Omani fleet standing off Zanzibar harbour, the Mwinyi Mkuu, in return for cash payments, agreed to share his sovereignty, to cede tax collection and foreign relations to the Arabs, to allow the Arabs to take over land, to impose a head tax, and to provide regular supplies of labour for the Arabs. By 1840 Seyyid Said had moved his capital to Zanzibar, and made only a few return visits to Oman.

Zanzibar's power was based initially on trade, including the trade in ivory and slaves, but also and increasingly on its production of cloves. It quickly became clear that the western half of the island provided the ideal environment for cloves. The first trees were planted in 1810; by 1834 trees at Kizimbani and Mtoni were mature and yielding a profit of 1000 per cent per year on the cost of planting them. Sheriff describes the 1840s as years of 'clove mania', as clove trees were planted in all suitable areas. A relatively small number of Arab families, including that of Seyyid Said himself, took over most of the best land in the western half of the island, and the Hadimu were confined to the less fertile eastern half (Sheriff 1971: 171–200).

After the conquest of Pemba in 1822, cloves were planted there too. They grew well on the steep valley sides which are a feature of that island; this meant that they could be planted almost anywhere, in contrast to Zanzibar where cloves grew well only on the western half of the island. Thus Africans as well as Arabs were able to start plantations, although a more common arrangement was crop sharing, between an Arab who owned trees, and an African who picked them. The fact that economic power on Pemba was less polarized was to have important consequences in the years immediately before independence.

Ivory was, however, the most important commodity traded, and at no time was the export value of slaves or cloves anywhere near as high as that of ivory. At the beginning of the nineteenth century, the trade was mainly with India. India produced most of the textiles, and, since Indian women were expected to wear ivory bangles which were buried with them when they died, it also provided the greatest demand for ivory. For many centuries Indian merchants had visited Zanzibar, but from about 1810 they started to settle. In 1819 there were 214; fifty years later there were at least 5000 Indians on the island. They came because of the possibilities of trade with India; but when the trade declined they quickly adapted to meet the new demands from Europe and America (Sheriff 1971: 112–28; 343–58).

In Europe and America industrial revolutions were creating new bourgeois classes, and new trading patterns for both necessities and luxuries. The demand for ivory was for luxury goods, inlaid items, serviette rings, mathematical instruments, combs, knife handles, billiard balls, and piano keys, to name but a few. In return textiles were easily provided from the factories of the industrial revolution. Ivory exports to Britain alone doubled from approximately 135 tonnes per year between 1800 and 1820 to about 270 tonnes per year in 1830s; in 1859 220 tonnes of ivory were exported through Zanzibar, worth £146 666 (the next most valuable export was cloves, worth £55 000), and on average around 180 tonnes of ivory was exported per year until the 1890s (Sheriff 1971: 209–12; Beachey 1967: 287).

Elephants were hunted in lands further and further from Zanzibar itself. The effects of this on some inland tribes are described in the next chapter. The collection and transportation of the ivory was a major undertaking, carried out initially both by trading chiefs from the interior and by Arabs or others from the coast. But the Sultan of Zanzibar charged higher rates of customs duty on caravans organized from the interior, with the result that caravans were increasingly organized from the coast. The Arabs set up permanent staging settlements inland, at which ivory could be collected. The first of these, founded in 1845, was near Tabora; another was built at Ujiji on Lake Tanganyika in the 1860s. Credit for the loads of textiles, beads, guns, and other goods was provided by Indian merchants who settled in Zanzibar. Some of these also tendered for the right to collect the customs duties for the Sultan of Zanzibar. The rates were fixed on a sliding scale, with ports distant from Zanzibar (which might have been tempted to trade elsewhere) paying lower rates. From 1827 the tenders for the whole coast were taken by one family, that of Jairam Sewji. Sewji became the most powerful man on Zanzibar, and many foreign merchants, and even the Sultan himself, borrowed from him. In 1861 the Indian community controlled three-quarters of the immovable property on the island.

Foreign traders from America, Germany, and Britain came to Zanzibar. The most active were Americans from the small port of Salem near Boston, who began to arrive in the 1820s, and whose rough cotton cloth called *Merikani* (after 'American') had, by the 1840s, become the standard trade good in the interior. The Americans began by lending money to the Indian merchants; but the roles were soon reversed, and American influence declined after 1860. German and British trading companies established branches in Zanzibar in the 1830s. The British Government's first concern was to minimize French and Portuguese, and later German, influence. The Indian merchants were technically citizens of British India, and the British used this as an excuse to justify their intervention in Zanzibar. They also acted to limit the power of the Sultans, notably through their campaign to abolish the slave-trade.[2]

For many years slaves from Africa had been taken to Arabia

and the Persian Gulf. But Chittick has shown that before the Omani period these slaves came from present-day Somalia, rather than from further south. There was also a small demand for slaves in India; Sheriff has estimated that before 1800 the total demand from areas north of Zanzibar did not exceed 2000 slaves per year, and that it reached perhaps 3000 a year in the 1830s. The coast north of Mozambique never supplied large numbers of slaves to the Caribbean or the American mainland because of the long distances involved. The first European-induced demand for slaves was for the Indian Ocean islands of Mauritius and Réunion where the French established sugar plantations from 1735 onwards. These slaves were mainly taken from Mozambique, though perhaps 2000 a year came from Kilwa and Zanzibar in the 1780s. The plantations were disrupted by the Napoleonic Wars between 1804 and 1814, and the Moresby Treaty of 1822 which outlawed the trade from Zanzibar to any Christian country effectively ended the trade to the south. The trade to Arabia and the Persian Gulf was prohibited by another treaty signed in 1845. There remained only the trade from the mainland to Zanzibar and Pemba, and back to other parts of the mainland, such as the hinterland of Lamu in present-day Kenya. This in its turn was limited by an agreement signed in 1864 which outlawed the trade between the months of January and May (the most convenient as far as the winds were concerned) until it was finally abolished in 1873. Sheriff estimates that the peak of the trade was in the 1860s, when about 20 000 slaves a year were brought to Zanzibar, about half being retained on Zanzibar to assist in clove cultivation, while the rest were re-exported to Pemba or to various parts of the coast.

These figures, based on a careful study of shipping records, imply that, while the slave-trade undoubtedly had a serious effect on some parts of Tanzania, especially in the south, overall it did not prevent population growth on the mainland. Sheriff argues that the *export* of slaves was not of unique importance to the Sultans of Zanzibar; they were prepared to limit it in 1822, 1845, and 1864 because the legal trade in ivory, cloves, and textiles was much more important to them. But Sultan Barghash was only persuaded to allow the abolition of the *import* of slaves into Zanzibar in 1873 when the British navy blockaded Zanzibar port. British officials, and the historians who followed them, exaggerated the extent of the trade, especially after 1873. Since sea captains 'Dhow-chasing in Zanzibar Waters' were paid a price for every slave they liberated, and the officials were trying to show the British public that slavery was indeed being abolished, they had every incentive to go chasing innocent dhows.

Sultan Seyyid Majid died in 1870. One of the enterprises of his last years was to build a new city in a natural harbour on the mainland opposite Zanzibar. This was the port of Dar es Salaam, laid out on a scale suitable for a capital. If Majid had lived he would probably have tried to preserve the commercial empire by moving his capital to the mainland. His successors, however, were less far-sighted and the new city stagnated until the Germans chose it as their capital in 1891 (Sutton 1970: 4–10). Meanwhile in 1872 a hurricane blew down most of the clove trees on Zanzibar. It was the last opportunity to move to the mainland, but instead Sultan Bhargash devoted all his energies to replanting the clove trees on Zanzibar and establishing new clove plantations in Pemba.

The Europeans were closing in. In 1885 Bismarck claimed a large part of the mainland as the protectorate of German East Africa, and in 1890, concerned to keep the Germans out, the British forced the Sultan to declare Zanzibar and Pemba a British protectorate. British civil servants were appointed to key positions, and in 1893, when the Sultan died, the British reorganized 'the least intractable' of several contenders for the throne, on condition that he accept the authority of the Queen of England. Although Zanzibar's trading position continued to be important for some years, it had no long-term future in the face of competition from Dar es Salaam and Mombasa. Zanzibar and Pemba were gradually left dependent on cloves. They had a near monopoly of the world market but the quantities produced fluctuated by a factor of eight, with prices falling in good years and rising in bad ones (Sheriff 1971: 197). It had become an archetypal colonial economy, utterly dependent on the fortunes of one crop.

5 THE GERMAN CONQUEST

> The reign of the tsetse fly in Tanganyika is a recent,
> twentieth century phenomenon that followed the
> breakdown of the man-controlled ecological system
> that Burton and others witnessed.
>
> KJEKSHUS (1977: 5)

Contact with the world outside undermined and then reversed
most of the achievements of the tribal societies of the interior.
Trade turned agriculturalists and craftsmen into porters; disease
wiped out most of the cattle; and the fighting and turmoil between 1890 and 1920 depopulated large areas of the country.

There is, of course, an ambiguity in this position. Contact with
the coast at the beginning of the nineteenth century had been one
of the main causes of the political centralization which had made
possible innovation in agriculture, warfare, and other spheres.
Moreover, the societies in the interior could have used many of
the skills available at the coast. But they were not strong enough
(either in consciousness or in military strength) to resist the chal-
lenges from the coast with anything like equality.

The earliest contacts were encouraged by the existence of markets at the coast. The leaders of tribes such as the Yao or the
Nyamwezi realized that ivory or slaves had commercial value,
and that they could be exchanged for textiles and firearms. In the
long run neither the imports nor the exports did much for the
Yao or the Nyamwezi; for the commercial policy of the Sultan of
Zanzibar turned them into the porters, rather than the financiers
or entrepreneurs, of the caravans to the coast.

The imports displaced local production of textiles, iron, and
salt, the three most important industrial products of the interior
up to that time. As early as 1860 cotton weaving was dying out in
Zanzibar, as mass-produced Indian textiles poured in. By 1880
the local textile industry in the Nyamwezi area was in decline,
while in the 1890s textile production in Bukoba, which was still in

its infancy, was forced out by imports from the coast. Salt production at the coast largely ceased when imports from India and the Persian Gulf started arriving in the 1880s. Iron production survived longer: in remote areas like Sumbawanga the remains of the industry could still be found in the 1920s, but elsewhere this too had been destroyed (Kjekshus 1977: 80–110).

In their place came hunting of elephants for ivory, the capture of slaves, and the provision of food for the plantations on Zanzibar and elsewhere. Elephant hunting was certainly a skill, but hardly a foundation for economic growth. Large areas were hunted right out of elephant, and the ivory had to come from farther and farther away. Up to 1850 Nyamwezi controlled more of the trade than Arabs and Swahili, and up to 1860 there were still elephant around Tabora; but by 1870 the caravans were no longer Nyamwezi, and to find ivory they had to go as far as Karagwe or Uganda, in the north, or to cross Lake Tanganyika into the Congo basin. It was for this latter purpose that an Arab settlement was established, around 1860, at Ujiji, near Kigoma on the shore of Lake Tanganyika (Sheriff 1971: 385–401).

The early Nyamwezi caravans went to the coast during the dry season, when there was little agricultural work to be done, and returned home in time to cultivate the crops (Sheriff 1971: 378, quoting Burton in 1872). But long journeys from the coast to the centre of Africa and back took a whole year, and required semi-permanent porters. In the 1890s more than a third of adult Nyamwezi males were away at the coast, and increasing numbers were not returning for the main agricultural seasons (Roberts 1967: 129). By 1910 the labour-intensive agricultural techniques that enabled permanent cropping to take place in Tabora had been replaced by 'shifting cultivation' in which land was cultivated for a few years and then left fallow for several years to regain its fertility (Kjekshus 1977: 157–60).

In 1890 the Germans crushed the first revolts against their rule, but more devastating in the short run, and arguably more deleterious in the long run, was the outbreak of rinderpest (a disease of cattle similar to tuberculosis in humans) reported for the first time that year. Within five years it wiped out 90 per cent of the cattle in most parts of the country. Only a very few isolated pockets escaped. Human beings were not affected directly, but they died of hunger, exacerbated by severe attacks of red locusts in 1893 and 1895. In the west whole kingdoms disappeared, including that of Karagwe, and the Uzinza kingdom in present-day

Geita. In the north the Maasai lost their economic and military strength and a large proportion of their human population; much of their grazing land in the rift valley or on the slopes of Mount Kilimanjaro was eagerly claimed as 'uninhabited' by the German or British settlers who arrived during the following years. Over the remainder of the country the loss of cattle meant for the inhabitants the loss of wealth (it was as if all the banks in the country had gone bankrupt), the loss of a potential source of income, and the loss of vital source of food when grain supplies failed (Kjekshus 1977: 126–32).

Rinderpest was not the only disease to attack in the 1890s. Smallpox appears to have been absent for at least a generation, but now it returned with considerable loss of life. Jiggers, or sand-fleas, lay their eggs on the feet or under toe-nails; if the eggs are removed quickly the recipient comes to no harm, but if they are left they fester and can easily cause lameness or death from gangrene. Jiggers arrived in southern Africa for the first time in 1872 on a ship from Brazil, and spread quickly. Smallpox was transmitted by the caravans working inland from the coast. Rinderpest was introduced and taken as far south as Khartoum by the British army under General Gordon in 1884–5, and perhaps also by the Italian army in Somalia in 1889. All three diseases are thus linked with outside intervention in Africa (Kjekshus 1977: 132–6).

In the 1890s they were accompanied by loss of life from the fighting that accompanied the German conquest. The outcome of this disastrous combination was the worst famines that anyone alive at the time could remember—in 1899 a German doctor estimated that three-quarters of a million people had died in the previous five years. Later on, comparable famines were to follow the Maji Maji in 1905–7 and the First World War in 1919–20—two more wars covering large areas of the country, but in particular the south, in which Europeans were involved (Kjekshus 1977: 137–53).

The Germans did not win control of the country easily. Kjekshus's list of fifty-four conflicts between 1889 and 1896 gives a clear indication of the extent of the resistance, and of how the Germans destroyed the power of the chiefs one by one. The earliest resistance, between 1889 and 1890, was on the coast itself, led by Bushiri, an Arab plantation owner, and Bwana Heri, a Zigua who collected the tolls from the caravans that passed through the town of Muheza inland from Tanga. In open fighting, or the storming of a fort, the German breech-loading rifles, supported by a few machine-guns, provided overwhelmingly superior fire-power compared with the muzzle-loading rifles, spears, and bows and arrows of their adversaries. But both Bushiri and Bwana Heri used guerrilla tactics, hiding in thick bush and firing their muzzle-loaders one by one, or attacking the porters. The Germans replied with a scorched-earth policy, destroying crops, confiscating cattle, burning crop stores and villages. It was hunger that forced Bwana Heri to surrender at Sadani in 1890, just as it was hunger that ended the Maji Maji resistance fifteen years later (Kjekshus 1977: 145–51, 186–90).

Bwani Heri came close to uniting the inland tribes to fight the Germans. When he surrendered, Arabs, Indians, slaves, Zigua, Nyamwezi, and other tribes surrendered with him; 600 warriors from Tabora were on their way to reinforce his army, and he had made an alliance with the Ngoni. But his surrender gave the Germans control of the lower parts of the Pangani valley, and of the Usambara mountains, and these areas were quickly made available for white settlement. Meanwhile the Germans attacked the inland tribes one by one. Their next effort was to subdue the Hehe, then under Mkwawa the strongest inland tribe, and to press on up the Pangani valley towards Kilimanjaro. In 1891 the Hehe ambushed a German column a few miles above the Ruaha gorge on the present main road from Dar es Salaam to Iringa, and it was not till 1898, when Mkwawa took his own life rather than face capture, that Hehe resistance was finally ended.

To the north of Hehe territory lay the Nyamwezi and the Gogo, while to the south and west lay the Ngoni. With only a small number of soldiers, the Germans had the luck to succeed in besieging Siki, the Nyamwezi chief, in his fort near Tabora in January 1893. Rather than face capture Siki blew himself up in his ammunition store: had the explosion come a few minutes later many Germans would have died too. Nyamwezi resistance thus ended in 1893, and the Gogo were subdued later the same year. The Ngoni did not fight. They had been willing to ally with their traditional enemies, the Hehe and the Nyamwezi, but the Germans acted before the necessary diplomacy was completed. The Germans then completed their conquest of the north by defeating the Chagga and the various tribal groupings around Lake Victoria; but here much of their work had been done for them by the rinderpest which had decisively weakened the Maasai, the Zinza, and the people of Karagwe.

By 1896 there were German forts and administrative stations covering most parts of the country, and a hut tax of 3 rupees was being collected wherever possible. Overall the resistance had been very costly in terms of African life and German time; it would have been even more successful if the tribes had combined more quickly. As it was, some chiefs, such as Merere of the Sangu or Rindi of Moshi, actually worked with the Germans in an attempt to ensure their independence from near-by tribes who threatened them.

The resistance did not, however, end in 1898. In July 1905 the Maji Maji rebellion broke out near Kilwa, and quickly spread until nearly all the tribes in the south were involved in what was probably the most widespread resistance to the imposition of colonial rule in Africa. Several thousand warriors who tried to storm the fort at Mahenge were killed by the fire of the German machine-guns. This time the Ngoni ruling clans decided to fight, but the Hehe did not, which meant that the German garrison at Iringa was able to relieve its comrades besieged at Mahenge and Songea. The Germans followed up with two punitive expeditions, aimed at destroying crops as well as men, and by May 1906 most of the warriors in the west had been killed. In the east fighting continued till August 1907, when it ceased with the onset of famine. In two years 75 000 people may have died, and the war was followed by three years of famine. The Ngoni population was reduced to perhaps a third of its previous level, and the areas involved are depopulated to this day (Iliffe 1979: 168–202 and 1969b: 17–26; Redmond 1972: 222–82).[1]

For the six years of the First World War, 1914–20, a German army remained undefeated, pursued by numerically much larger British armies, and living almost entirely without supplies from Europe. By the end of the war most of the troops on both sides were African, and were living off the land, buying or stealing crops as best they could. Quite predictably, the years at the end of the war were again years of famine, the climax of all that had gone before.

In 1920 the people were probably more backward than they had been in 1850. They were worse fed, industrial and agricultural skills had been lost, there were many fewer cattle, and large areas of the country had been depopulated. Above all, the tsetse fly had started to invade areas where cattle had previously roamed. In depopulated areas thick bush spread unimpeded, and game populations supporting tsetse fly increased. The German map of 1913 shows approximately one-third of the country infested by the fly; a British map of 1937 shows approximately two-thirds (Kjekshus 1977: 164–5). The presence of fly made cattle-keeping impossible, and presented a small risk to the human population. Colonial and post-colonial writers assumed that the tsetse had always been there; but it had probably been confined to small areas. The tsetse fly advanced because of the devastation caused by the colonial intrusion; and the colonial policy of removing the human populations from these areas had the worst possible result; it allowed the game animals which support the tsetse fly to multiply. Today most of these areas are tsetse-infested game parks; before 1920 most of them supported large, and relatively prosperous, human and cattle populations.[2]

It is clear that underdevelopment was associated, directly or indirectly, with the penetration of the country by traders, missionaries, and colonizers, pursuing avenues of profit opened up by the industrial revolutions in Europe. This is not to say that the European conquest could have been avoided, or that, if it had, the inland chiefs would have been able to import Western technology and eventually confront the European capitalist ruling classes with a measure of equality. There is little point in speculating about what might have been. What in fact happened was that the Europeans also developed the productive forces. They built roads, railways, and cities, developed formal education, and eventually handed over most of what they had created to Africans. What needs emphasis, since it was so often neglected by colonial historians, is the cost—the loss of life, the loss of reliable and nutritious sources of food, and, more generally, the loss of many of the skills with which the inhabitants had learnt to turn their harsh environment to their advantage.

PART III: THE COLONIAL SYSTEM

6 THE GERMAN COLONY

> We have not gone to East Africa to found plantations
> for 300–400 people, but to make a vast country
> bloom, to find raw materials and create markets for
> German trade and German industry.
>
> COLONIAL SECRETARY DERNBERG, 1908[1]

For most of his life Bismarck argued that colonies would bring
more trouble to Germany than advantage, and refused to have
anything to do with them. In the 1880s, however, he suddenly
changed his position.

Historians have argued over why this happened. There was a
colonial lobby in Germany which resented the fact that many
Germans were migrating to the United States and so being lost to
Germany, and hoped instead to find space for settlers in Africa.
Then there were economic arguments: Germany had no secure
source of raw cotton in a period of increased protectionism, and
the interior of Africa promised mineral wealth, and a captive
market for industrial products. There were also strategic considerations: colonies could provide the excuse for occupying key
coasts and harbours, and with the opening of the Suez canal,
East Africa became important as a base from which the new
trade route to India might be controlled. A colonial policy could
also be a diversionary tactic—it was one of the few issues which
could unite influential elements of the organized German working class with bourgeois and petty bourgeois interests; Bismarck's

change of policy helped him win the German election of 1884. He also hoped that a policy of competitive colonialism would divert his rivals, the French, into investing money and energy in Africa, and so to ignoring more important considerations at home.[2]

These explanations need to be understood in the light of the economic situation faced by Bismarck and by the capitalist economies in Western Europe. The years 1873 to 1896 form the period of the 'Great Depression', a period of consolidation when profits were generally low, and the industrialized powers were competing with each other. One consequence of this was a search for new markets; another was increased pressure to introduce protection. In Germany and America the competitive pressure led to the formation of monopolies and cartels—the start of the era of 'monopoly capitalism'. The industrial working classes became increasingly organized and socialist parties began to threaten the capitalist states.

Bismarck changed his policy from the moment—in 1882—that he feared Germany would be excluded by France and Britain from trade with West Africa. King Leopold of Belgium was already creating an empire in the Congo, and so between 1884 and 1885 Bismarck convened a conference of the European Powers that laid down 'spheres of influence' for each in Africa. Germany promptly claimed four 'protectorates': 'German East Africa' was claimed the day the Berlin Conference ended.

The basis for this was twelve treaties with chiefs in East Africa obtained by an adventurer called Karl Peters who in 1884 formed a *Gesellschaft für Deutsche Kolonisation* ('Society for German Colonization'), travelled secretly to East Africa, and in only six weeks walked 100 miles inland and collected his treaties according to which local chiefs ceded their territory and rights to the society. The chiefs cannot have realized what they were doing. Much of what they signed away was in any case the concern of the Sultan of Zanzibar, who promptly protested to the British about the loss of his rights. But in 1885 the British were threatened by the Russians in Afghanistan, and were trying to extricate themselves from the Sudan and to secure Egypt following General Gordon's death at the siege of Khartoum; they could not afford yet another dispute. So when Bismarck sent five warships to Zanzibar, the British persuaded the Sultan to accept the German presence.

In 1886, without consulting the Sultan, the European powers reduced his rights on the mainland to a strip of coast opposite Zanzibar 10 miles wide but excluding the harbours of Dar es Salaam and Witu. In 1888 the Germans purchased their part of this strip for 400 000 Marks. Meanwhile Peters went on more expeditions, and came back with claims for more territory, including much of what was later to be Uganda. But in 1890 Britain and Germany agreed the borders of German East Africa as those of present-day mainland Tanzania plus Rwanda and Burundi. This time the British were less hard pressed elsewhere, and determined to prevent the formation of a German colony controlling the headwaters of the Nile. They struck a tougher bargain, granting Bismarck only Helgoland, a small island of strategic importance off the German Coast, in return for the German claims to Uganda. Clearly even at this late stage, Bismarck did not rate the economic potential of his new colonial acquisitions very highly.

He certainly did not want the expense and complication of maintaining a colony, and so in 1885 Peters was encouraged to set up a limited company, the 'German East Africa Company', to administer the colony. But the company proved unable even to win the country militarily. The wars of conquest were long, difficult, and destructive (Chapter 5), and as early as 1889 the German government was forced to assist. In 1891 it took over full administrative responsibility from the company.

As soon as a chief submitted, the Germans imposed taxation in his area, usually a hut tax of 3 rupees per hut. For many peasant farmers this did not mean much change, for they had previously paid tribute to feudal warlords, such as Chabruma of the Ngoni, or Mkwawa or Mirambo. But for the chiefs and their families it meant much more than a loss of income: the fact that instead of receiving tribute they paid tax to the Germans demonstrated that they were a subject people. The Germans preferred the tax to be paid in money. The alternative was forced labour, used to build roads or the forts with which the Germans held the country militarily. Figures from Songea show how quickly the transfer to a cash economy was made. In 1899, the first year in which tax was collected, 1651 rupees were paid in cash, 706 rupees in kind, and 21 209 rupees, representing the labour of more than 7000 men, were paid in labour. By 1903 the cash payment was 38 045 rupees (Redmond 1972: 186–7).

The people could raise money in either of two ways: they could sell something—food, or an animal, or a crop such as cotton or coffee grown specifically to earn the cash—or they could work as labourers.[3] Some labouring work was available locally, with mis-

sions, settlers, or the government. But the majority of those who
earned the tax money by paid employment had to travel long
distances, often on foot, to the sisal or rubber plantations around
Tanga or Morogoro.

As far as production of raw materials was concerned, the Germans used three means of organizing African labour: white settlers, plantation companies, and small-scale African farmers. In
areas with suitable soil, climate, and transport connections to the
coast they encouraged both white settlers and plantations. As
early as 1891 they started building a railway inland from Tanga
along the Pangani valley, in the direction of Mount Kilimanjaro,
opening up the most promising areas for white settlement. Progress was very slow, and this railway did not reach Muheza, thirty
miles inland and the main point of access to the East Usambara
mountains, till 1893. But then a large area of land was purchased,
for nominal sums, from a member of the chief's family, and divided up among settlers for coffee cultivation. A similar development took place in the West Usambaras when, in 1905, the railway reached Mombo. In the mountain areas most of the land
that was not given to settlers was declared forest reserve, so that
the people had little alternative but to move out of the area or
work for the settlers. The coffee succeeded initially, but the top-
soil was quickly washed away, and yields declined. As the railway
pressed on towards Kilimanjaro, other settlers started occupying
land there, or purchasing it, mainly from the Maasai. On the
volcanic soil they could get yields of coffee five times those in the
Usambaras, but transport was still a problem; it was not till 1907
that the railway from the coast was close enough to persuade
large numbers of settlers to go to Kilimanjaro, and it was not till
1911 that it reached Moshi.

Coffee was also grown by African farmers. In Bukoba, west
of Lake Victoria, robusta coffee had been grown and traded by
chiefs long before the colonial conquest. It was first exported to
Europe in 1898, using the steamer service across Lake Victoria
to Kisumu in Kenya, and the railway to Mombasa. Thereafter,
exports rose rapidly, but production by settlers failed: the crop
only grew well on village sites where fertility had been built up
over many years by manuring and by transporting grass to feed
cattle.

On Kilimanjaro some of the settlers introduced arabica coffee
cultivation to Africans. By 1909 Chief Marealle had planted
15 000 trees, and, as a contemporary writer explained, an increasing number of 'the more intelligent propertied classes—

chiefs, akidas, and the like' were growing the crop with support from German officials (Iliffe 1979: 154).

The hot, malaria-infested lowlands enjoyed a much lower rainfall, and were less attractive than the mountain areas to settlers. Inland from the coast at Tanga, the first crops to be tried were cotton and rubber. For many years Africans had tapped rubber from trees growing wild in the forest: in 1899 exports of wild rubber were worth 1.3 million rupees, and in 1905 they were worth 2.5 million rupees. This success encouraged settlers to plant the crop. They used the drought-resistant 'manihot' variety; 250 planters were growing the crop by 1910, and in the years before the First World War they made a lot of money. The crop was, however, already doomed, for the varieties being planted in the rain forests of Malaya and the Philippines were easier to tap, higher-yielding, and gave a better quality product than the low-rainfall Tanganyikan estates could ever produce. When the price collapsed in 1913, the Tanganyikan planters could not compete and the plantations never revived after the First World War (Iliffe 1969b: 100–1; Henderson 1965: 152; Raum 1965: 191–2).

An almost perfect crop for the environmental conditions of much of the lowlands was, however, already in the country. This was the cactus sisal, from whose leaves a tough fibre could be extracted for use as rope, string, or agricultural twine. The Tanzanian crop was propagated from only sixty-two plants which survived the long (illegal) journey from Brazil in 1892. By 1910 there were fifty-four plantations exporting about 20 000 tons a year (Hitchcock 1959: 5). Although the price fell somewhat before the First World War, sisal because the most valuable export product; a position that was to be reinforced in the 1920s and 1930s, and to survive till independence.

Sisal was grown mainly on plantations owned by companies in Europe and run by salaried managers. This was because of the large investment required for the purchase of the decortication machinery and for transport, and because of the three-year wait from planting before the first harvest. The agricultural operations were, however, labour intensive. In order to minimize labour costs the plantation companies used migrant labour. It was originally planned that the labourers would come from the surrounding areas, and for this reason areas of 'native reserve' were left between the plantations in the Pangani valley. But the plantations did not grow their own food, and most of the farmers in these reserves found that by growing and selling food they could make sufficient money to pay tax without submitting to irksome conditions on the estates. So instead migrants came from far away—initially from the Nyamwezi area, later (in British times) from Kigoma, Songea, and from the neighbouring countries of Burundi, Rwanda, and Mozambique (Iliffe 1971: 12–18).

Sisal decortication required plentiful supplies of water and easy transport communications to the coast. The railway from Tanga towards Kilimanjaro was built along the Pangani valley, and within a few years the strip of land between the river and the Usambara and Pare mountain ranges was turned into a long line of sisal estates. At the same time another railway, the Central Line, completed as far as Morogoro in 1907 and Kilosa in 1909, opened up other large areas for sisal growing in and around Morogoro.

One of the aims of the German colonization had been to provide Germany with a reliable source of raw cotton. Cotton was eventually to become Tanganyika's second most important export, but most of the initial attempts to grow it failed. Soil and weather variability made it difficult to grow reliably near the coast: even the most expensive investment in irrigation and steam ploughs failed. By 1911 both Baron Otto, near Kilosa, and the Leipzig Cotton Spinners at Sadani, near the coast, had given up, and these much publicized failures discouraged other plantation companies.

The early attempts to persuade Africans to grow cotton also failed. In 1902 the Germans compelled the inhabitants of each village in the Rufiji and some other coastal areas to work for twenty-eight days a year on small communal crops of cotton. Yields were low, and the price was low. In 1905 the Maji Maji revolt broke out in these cotton-growing areas. It was suppressed with such brutality that there was a reaction in Germany against the whole colonial administration. In trying to understand why the revolt broke out when and where it did, many Germans, including Governor Rechenberg who arrived in 1906, concluded that one of the main causes was the compulsory cotton scheme (Iliffe 1969b: 54–5).

They compared the situation at the coast with that around Lake Victoria, where the construction of a railway from the Kenyan port of Mombasa to Kisumu, on the Kenyan shore of Lake Victoria, had stimulated peasant production for export in parts of Tanganyika near the Lake. The export of peasant-produced robusta coffee from Bukoba was already rivalling that of the settlers in the Usambaras; and in Mwanza, where cotton had been introduced by a settler and then taken up by some of the chiefs, with the encouragement of the missionaries, and promoted by the German government, the crop was being grown with enthusiasm and production was rising.

Rechenberg quickly decided that he wanted to base agricultural policy on peasant production. There was already a plan to bring illiterate German-speaking peasants to Tanganyika, hoping that they would work on small plots without hiring labour. This failed but Rechenberg continued to promote the idea of an African yeoman peasantry. There were strong arguments in his favour. From the government's point of view it was cheap, almost riskless, quick, and of seemingly unlimited potential. Settlers needed credit, took time to develop their farms, often lost money, and in any case most of the land areas where they wanted to settle were already being farmed by Africans. Peasant agriculture was self-financing, in the sense that all that it required was for the world prices to be passed on to the farmers through a reasonably efficient marketing system, and for tax to be paid in cash. In response to changes in prices, the peasants would increase or decrease production; if prices fell too much, they could stop altogether and wait for better times: settlers would demand subsidies and could create far more trouble politically. Finally, and this consideration was not lost on the German government shocked by the violence of the Maji Maji, it was a policy that was relatively popular with the African population. Peasants were expected to walk long distances to the sisal plantations, and they disliked the discipline and low wages; they preferred to stay at home and sell part of their own produce.

In order to create an efficient marketing system. Rechenberg encouraged the Indian merchants at the coast, including many who had made their money in Zanzibar, to set up branches inland. The most active of these merchants, Allidina Visram, has been described as 'perhaps the most important individual in the economic development of East Africa' (Erlich 1965: 408; Mangat 1969: 51–3). He was born in India in 1865 and came to Bagamoyo as an employee of a Zanzibar firm in 1877. A few years later he set up his own business, and opened stores in almost every German or British administrative centre in East Africa, supplied initially by head caravan, although Visram was one of the first to realize the potential of the railways. He opened his first branch in Uganda in about 1896, and around the turn of the century moved his head office to Mombasa. The diaries of administrators and missionaries show how much they appreciated the services he provided.

The numbers of Asian traders grew rapidly. Some of the Asians who came to East Africa as labourers on the Uganda railway stayed on and became traders. The large organizations, such as Visram's, tended to break down, as traders up-country found it convenient to deal with more than one agent at the coast. The large German trading companies, and later British ones too, were there, but there were also many smaller import/export houses and produce merchants.

In order to create an efficient transport system Rechenberg wished to extend the Dar es Salaam railway line from Kilosa to Tabora, and on to Kigoma on Lake Tanganyika. He justified his proposal on the grounds that it would pay for itself out of increased tax revenue arising from the production of groundnuts. There was also a military aspect: a railway right across the centre of the country would prove invaluable if there was another outbreak of the Maji Maji. With considerable difficulty the German parliament was persuaded to advance the money, and the railway was built. It reached Tabora in 1912 and Kigoma in 1914, just as the First World War broke out (Iliffe 1969b: 73–6).

Rechenberg had already left, and most of his policies were being reversed. The colony had after all been created by settlers and now many of them had found profitable crops, coffee on the slopes of Mount Kilimanjaro and rubber and sisal on the plains. From 1904 onwards they controlled the advisory 'Governor's Council', and the government was increasingly implementing tax and labour policies to suit them. In 1913 there were 5336 Europeans in the country, more than in Kenya at that time. Of these 882 were adult male settlers and 1 per cent of the land area had been allocated to them (Taylor 1963: 21; Henderson 1963: 155). However, the largest areas of land under European Council were sisal or rubber plantations which had not displaced large populations, and the peasant sector had considerable vitality, exporting rubber, coffee, beeswax, cotton, groundnuts, and other crops in increasing quantities, and selling livestock and food to the cities and to the plantation workers. Whether in fact African agriculture would have been suppressed in favour of settlers, as in Kenya, had it not been for the First World War, remains an interesting speculation. As it is, the coexistence of peasants, plantations, and large-scale capitalist farming continues to this day (Iliffe 1969b: 202–4).

The last ten years of German rule, from 1905 to 1914, also saw the creation of most of the rest of the colonial infrastructure that was to be handed over to the nationalists in 1961. There was

considerable investment. Maps were drawn, roads were built,
towns were laid out, the country was explored for minerals,
schools and hospitals were opened, and important advances were
made in medical and agricultural research.

In view of its size, and the fact that they had to start from
scratch, the mapping of the country was no small achievement;
some of the German maps were still in use in the 1950s. They
were drawn for military and tax-collecting purposes, and to assist
in the construction of roads and railways. The layout of much of
the present-day road network, and of the main towns, dates from
German times; the Germans also built feeder roads for use by
ox-carts into many remote highland areas. Their geological ex-
ploration was also thorough: only one significant mineral discov-
ery (the Williamson Diamond Mine) was made during the British
period.

German rule created a demand for literary skills, for there was
no possibility of the Germans in the country running all its institutions without some other source of semi-skilled labour. The
building and upkeep of the mission stations themselves required
craftsmen, and some of the mission schools provided training in
carpentry and building, and also metal working, shoe-making,
and printing. At the coast and in the main administrative centres,
the government opened its own schools. By 1914 there were 60
primary schools, and 9 post-primary establishments, mainly
teaching craft skills, although one of them, Tanga School, had
four German teachers on its staff, and 500 students, and offered
a more literary education designed to produce African administrators. But since the mission and government schools could not
meet the demand for semi-skilled and skilled labour the government also recruited from India, especially for the more technical
jobs such as the repair and driving of steam-engines on the railways (Cameron and Dodd 1970: 55–9, 108–10; Hornby
1962: 148–50 and 1964: 83–90. For a contrasting view see Hirji
1974).

Africans were used to fill middle-level administrative posts,
since, for example, there were never more than 79 European
administrative staff in the districts. Initially the Germans simply
took over the Sultan of Zanzibar's officials: *liwalis* in the main
towns, *akidas* under them, and *jumbes* or headmen responsible
for tax collection at the local level. But gradually the Germans
replaced the *liwalis* by German officials, and appointed younger
men as *akidas* and *jumbes*, mainly graduates from the secondary
school at Tanga. Since they used the bureaucracy of the Sultan of

Zanzibar, the Germans also used his language, swahili. It was already understood by people living along the trade routes and at the coast. By 1914 the Germans were using it in the courts and in administrative correspondence. They thus contrived, by accident as much as design, to give Tanzania a national language (Taylor 1963: 21; Iliffe 1979: 208–10).

German agricultural and medical research was based at Amani, in the Usambara mountains. A wide range of crops and trees were brought into the country; there have been no significant introductions of new crops since. On the medical side, the first doctors were surgeons who treated the wounded in the fighting with Abushiri in 1888. In the 1890s a network of hospitals was established along the coast, and at Morogoro, Bumbuli, and Kilimanjaro, all important areas of German settlement. Medical research was of a high order. As early as 1891 locally grown quinine was introduced as a prophylactic to control malaria (it was later to make a vital contribution to the German campaign in East Africa during the First World War). Dr R. Koch identified sleeping sickness and its bovine version, trypanosomiasis, with the tsetse fly, and 'tick fever' and East Coast Fever (another cattle disease) with the tick. The fact that he and his fellow doctors were veterinarians as well as human doctors enabled them to produce a smallpox vaccine using local cows—four million doses had been used by 1914. Health regulations were introduced to prevent the spread of intestinal diseases. The last Annual Report before the war showed 70 000 patients, more than 90 per cent of whom were African, treated in twelve general hospitals, a sanatorium, and a lunatic asylum, while 750 000 vaccinations were administered (Titmuss et al. 1964; Koch 1898).

The economic structure laid down by 1914 was in all but detail that handed over in 1961. Lines of communication, towns, and land areas alienated to settlers or plantations did not greatly change during British rule. Few new crops were grown, either by plantations or by peasants. It had been established that there were no mineral resources of huge value in the country. Above all, the mechanisms by which African labour was 'persuaded' to work had been pioneered, as had the need for African education. The history of the British period was to be closely tied to this, as Africans realized that with European education they had the means to a secure job, and, eventually, to political power.

7 AGRICULTURAL PRODUCTION UNDER THE BRITISH

> The first object of the Government is to induce the
> native to become a producer directly or indirectly,
> that is, to produce or to assist in producing some-
> thing more than the crop of local foodstuffs that he
> requires for himself and his family.
>
> GOVERNOR CAMERON (1926)[1]

By 1914 a balance had been achieved between plantation agriculture, white settlers, and small-scale African farmers. Sisal had
become the main plantation crop, grown along the railways running inland from the coast, and depending on migrant labour.
There were nearly 1000 settler families in the country, but they
had not been able to control sufficient land to force the majority
of Africans to work for them, as in the 'White Highlands' of
Kenya. Most Africans continued to grow their own food and paid
their taxes by selling small quantities of crops or livestock. Neither the wages paid to migrant labourers nor the returns to small-
scale farming, were sufficient to support a man and a family: both
systems depended on women growing food to feed themselves
and their children, and the absence of migrants had particularly
adverse effects on the environment in their home areas, where
dry-season tasks such as soil conservation, maintenance of irrigation systems, or house building were neglected (this provides an
explanation for the backwardness to this day of areas such as
Kigoma or Songea) (Kjekshus 1977: 157–60).

The variety of crops grown is clear from the export statistics
(Table 7.1). In terms of value the largest export was sisal; it was
followed by rubber, by this time grown mostly by settlers, but
suffering severe competition from production in South-East Asia;
then came hides and skins, copra from coconut plantations near
the coast, and then cotton, groundnuts, and beeswax, all largely
produced by peasants, with coffee some distance behind. These

TABLE 7.1
Tanganyika: Agricultural Exports 1913 and 1938

Produce	1913			1938		
	Quantity ('000 tons)	Value (£'000)	Percentage of total value	Quantity ('000 tons)	Value (£'000)	Percentage of total value
Sisal	20.9	536	30	101.4	1 425	38
Rubber	1.3	309	18	—	—	—
Hides and Skins	3.4	275	15	3.0[a]	160	4
Copra	5.5	117	7	4.0	32	1
Cotton	2.2	98	5.5	9.1	380	10
Groundnuts	9.0	96	5	3.6	31	1
Beeswax	0.6	71	4	0.7	55	2
Coffee	1.1	47	3	13.8	386	10
Sesame	1.5	20	1	5.3	53	1
Rice	0.8	9	0.5	8.2	91	3
Sugar	—	—	—	4.0	40	1
Others[b]	n.a.	200	11	n.a.	1 055	28
Total	46.3[c]	1 778	100	152.7[c]	3 708	100

[a] Hides only.
[b] Mainly minerals and forest products; gold accounted for 16% of total exports in 1938.
[c] Excluding 'others'.
Source: Annual Reports of the Department of Agriculture (adapted from Leubuscher 1944: 204).

figures do not take account of the production of foodstuffs for local consumption, including sales of cattle, maize, and groundnuts for feeding the cities and the plantation labour forces.

The British governed from 1916 or 1917, in most parts of the country, till 1961. This period was dominated by events on the international stage; the economy had barely recovered from the First World War when it was plunged into the depression of the 1930s; the prices of all its products fell, and the effects were still being felt up to the outbreak of the Second World War. This time there was no fighting on Tanzanian soil, but the economy was required to contribute to the British war effort, and for a short time the iron fist that underlay the velvet glove of colonialism was more perceptible than usual. Only during a very short period in the 1920s, and the last fifteen years of colonial rule, was there much investment in the colony.

From 1920 to 1946, Tanganyika (present-day mainland Tanzania) was administered by Britain under a mandate from the League of Nations. The mandate made it clear that the colony was to be administered in the interests of 'the material and moral well-being and the social progress of its inhabitants'.[2] But no time-scale was laid down for the local population to take over, and the British acted as if independence was a long way off. After the Second World War the country become a 'trusteeship territory' of the United Nations. The Trusteeship Committee was more effective at prodding the British than the Permanent Mandates Commission had been; yet, as we shall see, by this time the more far-sighted British officials recognized that independence was inevitable with only the timing in question.

THE INTER-WAR YEARS

In the 1920s the British followed inconsistent policies in East and Central Africa. They were torn between a 'West African solution', which would have meant economies largely dependent on peasant production, and a 'South African solution' with political power in the hands of settlers. In the end they allowed Kenya and Southern Rhodesia to be dominated by settlers, while Uganda and Nyasaland became largely peasant economies. Northern Rhodesia was organized around its copper mines, while Tanganyika maintained the balance between peasants, settlers, and plantations inherited from the Germans (Iliffe 1969b: 201–10).

During the First World War, the British confiscated German property. The estates and plantations were auctioned in 1922. Germans were not allowed to bid, and many of the smaller farms were taken by Greeks or Asians. But within a few years Germans were permitted to return, and did so in such numbers that by the end of the 1930s there were more German settlers than British in the country and a real possibility that it might be handed back to Germany as part of a policy of appeasing Hitler.

Sisal recovered quickly after the war to become overwhelmingly the most important export. There were about 150 growers, including some settlers, but the biggest plantations were owned by European companies and run by salaried managers. Wages remained low (Table 7.2). As late as 1940 an unskilled labourer might earn only 5 shillings per month, and a skilled man 15 or 20 shillings. Since tax was approximately 10 shillings per head per year, it is not surprising that most plantation workers returned home with only a few possessions more than they took away with them, and a month or twos' wages in cash.[3] The terms of service were given legal backing by the Master and Servant Ordinance of 1923, designed among other things to ensure that 'the workman shall carry out the service he has agreed to perform'. It was amended in 1926 to incorporate the *kipande* or 'ticket' system,

TABLE 7.2
Wage rates by province 1927 and 1940
(shillings per month)

Province	1927	1940
Unskilled labour		
Northern	10–30	7–15
Lake	6–24	6–20
Western	7.5–24	5–12
Central	10–18	5–12
Eastern	15–30	6–21
Southern	10–26	8–15
S. Highlands	5–15	6–12
Tanga	15–30	9–18
Semi-skilled labour		
Northern	18–30	15–30
Lake	10–30	9–50
Western	12–40	9–50
Central	15–45	10–30
Eastern	20–60	10–60
Southern	15–40	9–60
S. Highlands	10–45	10–30
Tanga	24–50	10–35
Skilled labour		
Northern	30–80	30–100
Lake	40–120	30–200
Western	20–150	23–80
Central	30–100	20–99
Eastern	20–180	30–100
Southern	25–90	15–100
S. Highlands	30–105	20–150
Tanga	40–120	20–200

Note: The rates for 1927 include an allowance for payment of rations in kind. In 1940 an amount varying from 3 shillings per month to 15 shillings should be added to make the figures comparable.

Source: Annual Reports of the Labour Department 1927 and 1940.

under which the worker did not get his full pay until he had completed his 'task'; the task was intended to take thirty days, but the worker was paid provided he completed it within fifty. Those recruited from a distance signed a contract to complete 6 *kipandes*. During the depression this was extended to 9 *kipandes*, and after the Second World War contract periods were lengthened again, so that many workers even from within Tanganyika had two-year contracts, while workers from outside were recruited on three-year contracts (Baker

1934: 56; Lawrence 1971: 111–13).

The next crop to expand production after the First World War was coffee. Settlers on the slopes of Kilimanjaro and Meru were planting more and more of the crop, taking advantage of the link with the Kenyan railway to Mombasa, which had been constructed by British soldiers during the war. But Africans in those areas were also planting coffee as quickly as they could, and in the process were turning the communal grazing areas on the mountain slopes into coffee farms: in 1923, with encouragement from British administrators and agriculturalists, 300 000 seedlings were planted by Africans. Between 1922 and 1925 the settlers tried to prevent African planting, as in Kenya. They failed, because African cultivation was too successful to be stopped and had the support of influential British administrators. By 1927, when Cameron issued a circular to discourage the growing of arabica coffee in areas where it was not already established, it was too late: the next year's Annual Report of the Moshi District Agricultural Officer stated that 'the area of native coffee in Arusha is increasing against all the discouragement it is possible for my department to give'. By 1933 there were about six million African-owned coffee bushes, about one third of the families on Mount Kilimanjaro was growing coffee, and more than half of the coffee produced in the country was grown by Africans (Iliffe 1979: 274–8).

Cotton cultivation, carried out almost entirely by small African farmers living to the south of Lake Victoria, also increased, until by 1938 cotton rivalled coffee as a source of foreign exchange. Marketing was facilitated by the opening, in 1928, of a railway line from Tabora northwards to Mwanza on Lake Victoria. Even

TABLE 7.3

Imports of cotton piece-goods and boots and shoes 1925–1937

	Cotton piece-goods		Boots and shoes	
	Value ('000 000 shillings)	Volume ('000 000 yards)	Value ('000 000 shillings)	Volume ('000 pairs)
1912	13.2			
1925	18.1	27	0.2	44
1931	8.9	28	0.3	203
1937	14.3	46	0.6	397

Sources: Tanganyika *Trade Reports* and *Die Deutschen Schutzgebiete* 1912–1913 (following Leubuscher 1944: 206, with 1 Deutschmark put equal to 1 shilling).

so the returns were low—a hectare of cotton in 1931, on the basis of an average yield of 150 kg of seed cotton per hectare, would have yielded only 20 shillings. There is evidence that in these areas cotton growing had been compulsory for several years before the war. The range of minor exports also extended, supplemented at the end of the 1930s by minerals, mainly gold from a brief gold rush in the Lupa gold-field.

The 1930s were dominated by the effects of the world depression, which exposed Tanganyika's dependence on world markets for primary products. Growers' prices fell, for sisal estates as well as for African farmers. The prices of imported goods fell too —especially textiles, as the country was flooded with cheap imports from Japan. Thus the quantities of textiles and shoes imported did not fall (Table 7.4; see also Brett 1973: 149–56), but sisal wages were cut by half, and fewer workers were employed. The poll-tax was not reduced, so peasant producers had to increase the volume of crops sold in order to pay their taxes. In fact both the sisal plantations and the African farmers managed to increase their production even though the prices had fallen, much to the delight of the colonial officials. The officials devised 'Grow More Crops' campaigns from 1930 onwards, which involved considerable use of force (such as minimum acreages of cotton to be cultivated, or threats of conscription for those who could not pay tax). It was during these campaigns that many agriculturalists became concerned about the long-term effects on the soil of this non-voluntary effort; hence the use of force for soil conservation and rehabilitation works that was such a prominent feature of post-war agricultural policy. Another cause for alarm was the lack of attention being paid to food production. The response to a series of local famines was more coercion, which included by-laws stipulating the cultivation of minimum acreages of cassava or other famine reserve crops. Farmers were also planting maize, a higher-yielding crop than the traditional sorghum and millets, and one requiring less labour per acre, but a crop that failed if the rains were poor. When it failed, the government had to bring in 'famine relief': hence the insistence on famine reserves. The 1930s thus show an increasing dependence of small-scale producers both on the world markets for their sales of cash crops and on the government for their food in years when the maize crop failed (Bryceson 1978: 24–7).

THE SECOND WORLD WAR

During the Second World War the British Government planned

agricultural production in entirely new ways. Certain crops were regarded as being of strategic importance. Sisal and rubber were classified as of strategic importance, especially after the capture of Indonesia and the Philippines in 1941. Cotton, on the other hand, was non-strategic, since there was a large stockpile in the United States. Food production, necessary to feed the sisal plantation work-force, to avoid importing if possible, and even to export to troops in Kenya and the Middle East, was also strategic, especially the production of wheat (Bowles 1974: 4–5).

Sisal production was assured initially by the negotiation of a long-term contract with the British Ministry of Supply, at a favourable price; in order to meet this contract the government organized the conscription of labour (Orde-Browne 1946: 10–15). Some figures on numbers involved are given in Table 7.4.

TABLE 7.4
Conscription of labour 1941–1945

1941	960
1942	2 495
1943	13 500
1944	30 500
1945	26 200

Source: Orde-Browne 1946: 10

Cotton, on the other hand, was demoted: in 1942 it was allotted a low price (22 cents per kg.), while rice and groundnuts received increased prices of 10 cents and 22 cents per kg. respectively. These prices were calculated on the basis of 35 cents for a day's work: on that basis cotton should have received 47 cents per kg. Not surprisingly production of rice and groundnuts rose, while that of cotton fell; it rose only slowly after the war, despite the change in priority (Bowles 1974: 7).

Settlers were expected to produce large quantities of food. Generous guaranteed prices were given for wheat, maize and beans, provided these could be produced in new bags and in large quantities. Planting subsidies were also granted, to guarantee a return of almost 250 shillings per hectare (100 shillings per acre) to anyone who planted a large area. The conditions could, with few exceptions, only be met by Europeans; a similar arrangement for small-scale producers would be unthinkable even today (ibid.).

The State itself also embarked on wheat production. The first large-scale state farming operation was the Northern Provinces

Wheat Scheme which started in 1942 on approximately 8000 hectares of land on the plains between Moshi and Arusha, near the present Kilimanjaro International Airport. It was mechanized: the experts wanted crawlers, but had to make do with metal-wheeled tractors. Yields were low (the average was about 6 bags per hectare) but given the high prices the scheme made only a small loss and 'saved the cost of two shiploads of wheat'. Its relative success was one of the reasons for the uncritical reaction of the Director of Agriculture when he received the next proposal for mechanized state-farm agriculture, the post-war Groundnuts Scheme.[4]

THE POST-WAR YEARS

The years after the war saw the continuation of the policies that had been used before and during it: conscription to supply sisal estate labour as necessary; guaranteed prices and other inducements to encourage settlers; the use of force to direct African peasant production; and state farming in the form of the Groundnuts Scheme.

The mechanized production of groundnuts was first suggested in 1946, by the General Manager of the United Africa Company, as a means of dealing with the post-war shortage of edible fats and oils. The Tanganyika Director of Agriculture prepared the first outline plan. More detailed proposals accepted by the British Labour Government a few months later meant that the government took all the risk, while the United Africa Company became one of a number of subcontractors on cost-plus contracts. The project was to cost £24 million (including a new harbour and 150 miles of railway) and the target was three million acres of groundnuts. When the scheme was wound up less than ten years later, £35 million had been spent, and what remained was little more than three large areas of cleared bush.[5]

The mistakes were exposed in detail in the British press. It transpired that the planning had been rushed: only nine weeks had been spent in field reconnaisance, and much of this was from the air. No detailed mapping of soils or topography had been carried out, and there was a marked lack of information about rainfall patterns or likely crop yields (Frankel, 1950).

The scheme failed for the following reasons:

1. The rainfall at the largest site was insufficient for groundnuts. This site had been approved on the basis of only seven years of rainfall readings at a station which was later shown to receive slightly more rain than the land actually cleared. When

the distribution between months was taken into account it could be concluded that groundnuts would not do well in more than three years out of five (Overseas Food Corporation, 1956: 31).

2. Some chemical tests of the soil were made, but no mechanical analysis. This would have shown up a clay content which ensured that the land set hard in the dry season, effectively confining agricultural operations to periods when the soil was wet. It would also have identified an abrasive content in the soil which led to rapid wear of implements (Wood 1950: 179–81; OFC 1956: 31–2).

3. The mechanical equipment was untried in the conditions. Many of the bulldozers had seen service in the Second World War, and some were actually converted tanks. Other machinery, such as groundnut harvesters designed for American farms, could not operate on rough, recently cleared land. Some machines, such as the root removers, were designed specially for the project; but they were produced on a large scale before they had been tested on the site, and often required expensive and time-consuming modification (Wood 1950).

4. Even with new machinery there were problems with spare parts and maintenance, made worse by difficulties with inexperienced drivers and delays in clearing goods through the congested ports of Dar es Salaam and Mombasa.

5. Where groundnuts grew—as they did (briefly) at Urambo and Nachingwea—they were attacked by rosette disease, and at the start of the project there were no varieties resistant to this disease (OFC 1956: 35–5).

6. Sites for headquarters at Kongwa and Nachingwea were built before adequate water supplies had been found. This would have made it impossible to switch to more labour-intensive production methods, if this had been thought desirable (Frankel 1950: 151–2).

Most of this was obvious to technicians in the field by the end of 1948, but policy changes were not made until well into 1950. This was partly because responsibility was shared between a Board of Directors in London, a headquarters organization at Kongwa, and two leaders on each site (the second for the firms of contractors who were hired for the land-clearing operations). The London officials were particularly unwilling to believe that all was not well (Wood 1950: 147–50).

The most experienced agricultural officers in Tanganyika were involved in this project; and yet, of the six reasons for failure, five were agricultural considerations of a most elementary kind.

Rosette disease was identified as a major constraint on groundnut production in the literature produced by the Ministry (such as the handbook for extension workers (Rounce 1946), or the 1931 Annual Report). The possibility of soil compaction making cultivation difficult in the dry season is commonplace in tropical agriculture. The vegetation at Kongwa was typical for a marginal rainfall area, and the difficulties with supplies and untested machinery should have been predicted by those who had served in the war. Their faith in machinery and in large-scale operations organized by government led the most experienced agriculturalists of the day to use £35 million on a project that had so many flaws that if it had not failed for one reason it would still have failed for several others.

From the mid-1930s to the mid-1950s it was believed that force was necessary to make small farmers change their agricultural techniques. In 1937 the Native Authorities Ordinance was amended to allow by-laws to be passed for the enforcement of soil-conservation measures and other agricultural practices; this meant that anyone who 'offended' could be taken to a Native Authority Court, at which the chief presided, and be fined or imprisoned. Behind the chiefs lay the power of the European colonial administrators: one district commissioner, questioned in 1942, explained that he enforced the cultivation of 1 acre (0.4 hectare) of cotton per adult male, 1 acre of groundnuts and a quarter of an acre of rice per household, and in addition he expected to find every 'able-bodied African' working in the fields during normal hoeing hours (Cliffe 1964: 17–24; Bowles 1974: 6).

At the end of the war new legislation was passed which allowed the government to control the production and marketing of virtually every crop. This legislation, applied almost everywhere, was to have the effect of discrediting both the chiefs (who were clearly exposed as the stooges of the British) and the agricultural staff (who were forced to act as policemen and prosecutors in the chiefs' courts): this aspect is considered further in the Chapter 11.

The most systematic application of this approach to agricultural change was in a small number of large 'schemes' which combined attempts to prevent soil erosion with other agricultural aims. In 1947, Sukumaland, the area south of Lake Victoria, was selected by the Colonial Office as one of two areas in the British Empire where cotton cultivation should be increased (Maguire 1969: 26–42). The 'Sukumaland Development Scheme' had been conceived by the agriculturalists before the war, and was financed largely from the surpluses obtained by the government from paying low prices to cotton farmers during the war. It involved reopening large areas of Geita District which had been depopulated since the 1890s, by constructing roads and providing water supplies; but in the 'old' cotton areas along the railway line, where it was felt that there was no room for more cattle or people, an incredibly wide range of by-laws was enforced:

By 1953 or 1954 the Sukuma peasant felt that he was being pushed around .... Everywhere new rules, regulations and taxes seemed to require this, prohibit that, or take a few shillings yearly from his pocket. He had to tie-ridge and manure certain portions of his fields, plant specified minimum acreages of cassava (as an antifamine measure) and cotton, plant at certain times and pull out cotton stalks by certain dates for burning after harvest, refrain from cultivating near gullies, cutting trees, or transporting cattle without a permit, have his cattle dipped or innoculated against disease, slaughter or sell a certain percentage of his cattle each year and produce on request certificates indicating sale or attesting that the hides from the slaughtered beasts had been seen by the appropriate government officer. These were just a few of the more salient ... natural resources measures which had begun to accumulate by 1952. (Maguire 1969: 30–1).

Two of the schemes concerned livestock specifically. The Mbulu Development Scheme involved a cattle census followed by compulsory reductions in the numbers of animals; it was eventually subverted by the big stock-owners who had most to lose from it (Meek 1953: 158–66). The Iringa Dipping Scheme involved compulsory dipping of cattle—for a small fee to be paid each time—and was understandably resented.

Finally, there were schemes intended to protect the soil on the steep slopes of the Uluguru, Usambara, and Pare mountains, where the peasants were forced to build bench terraces. Here the by-laws were extremely unpopular: in the Uluguru mountains an African was shot dead by a white policeman in July 1955, and by 1956 the colonial government realized that it was not possible to enforce the laws. As soon as they were relaxed, the terraces were broken down, the manuring and tie-ridging ceased, and it was obvious that a moral victory had been won over the colonial state (Young and Fosbrooke 1960: 166–7; Molloy 1971: 60).

Paradoxically, it is now clear that the agricultural and economic logic behind many of the rules was wrong, so that the farmers were absolutely correct in opposing them. The rules for terracing in the Uluguru and other mountain areas were under suspicion even before the schemes were abandoned. It was discovered that in one demonstration area 'terraces were completely sterile', and the 1956 annual report of the Uluguru Scheme concluded that 'rice yields are frequently better on untreated land than on terraces'. These conclusions were subsequently confirmed by research which also revealed that the most serious threat to the soil in the Ulugurus was from landslides, the likelihood of which was greatly *increased* by the type of bench terraces forced on the peasants in the 1950s (Temple 1972: 110–23).

In Sukumaland, tie-ridging has been questioned because, while it undoubtedly results in soil and water conservation and so raises yields in dry years, it is intensive in its use of labour at a critical time of the year, and therefore reduces the total area that can be cultivated by a given labour force (Collinson 1963: 30; De Wilde and others 1967: Vol. 2, 429–30). The same principle affects ridging, and so it too is only economic in certain situations (Rotenhan 1968: 69–70). Saylor (1970a: 27) showed that farmers who accepted the recommendation for cotton spacing suffered losses varying from 55 kg per hectare in Mwanza District to 85 kg per hectare in Shinyanga District; he also found (in 1969 at least) that it made no significant difference in which month cotton was planted—quite contrary to the recommendations of the extension service to plant early.

The difficulties arising from attempts to improve the cattle economy are similar. Dipping is beneficial if it can be carried out regularly, for the whole life of the animal; but if dipping ceases (as well it may if the distribution of chemicals and the maintenance of the dip and water supply depend on government bureaucracy) then the animal will be more susceptible to disease than if it had never been dipped and had achieved a resistance (Kjaerby 1980: 16–19). Destocking is of no benefit to an individual if grazing is communal, unless all stock-owners destock together: even then the poor suffer proportionally more than the rich. Thus Parkipuny (1976: 147–8) is probably right when he claims that destocking will never be acceptable until there is a more or less even distribution of cattle—and in most parts of Tanzania this would mean revolutionary changes.

In retrospect, it is even questionable whether the crisis in soil fertility was not itself exaggerated. This is not to deny that there is soil erosion, or misuse of land, in many parts of Tanzania. But in the twenty years following the end of the schemes, livestock numbers and cash-crop production both more than doubled without a dramatic crisis of soil erosion. Ridging was becoming popular in parts of Sukumaland even before the Scheme, and the 1938 report of the Agriculture Department played down the dangers in other parts of the country (pp. 7, 32). Just as with the Groundnuts Scheme, much of the agricultural advice was technically wrong. But the complaints were ignored, and the peasants were given no choice; and so 'Bench terraces were dug to order in the knowledge that they were useless; the Luguru deliberately chose sterile sites in order to avoid damaging fertile land.' (Temple 1972: 118).

RURAL CAPITALISM

By the mid-1950s it was clear that mass compulsion was counterproductive. A new policy had, however, already been tried out in a few areas. This was an open espousal of differentiation: it was to concentrate resources on relatively rich farmers and/or villages who could be expected to increase their marketed production by the use of machinery and fertilizer, and by hiring labour. The policy change was the central statement in the 1956 Annual Report of the Department of Agriculture:

Agricultural extension work in Africa frequently finds itself up against a brick wall of peasant conservatism, sometimes strengthened by political misconceptions. ... It becomes necessary to withdraw the effort from some portions and to concentrate on small selected points, a procedure which has come to be known as the 'focal point approach'. Under this method limited areas or progressive individuals are chosen for the initial attack ... Once success has been achieved and appreciated at these points, it is then a comparatively simple matter to spread outwards from them. (p. 1.)

Farmers who refused to accept 'modern methods' were described as stubborn, lazy, ignorant, conservative, unco-operative, etc. There was little or no recognition that logic often lay in the refusal to do what the extension staff advised.

It was the intention to increase inequality. In the words of an economist a few years later: 'Extension officers are ... expected to approach the interested and the important ones in a village and to group them together as progressive farmers ... The grouping together of the progressive farmers can be called an attempt to establish rural elites with progressive attitudes ...'(Ruthenberg 1964: 65).

These selected individuals were to be given credit, 'a reputa-

Table 7.5
Tanganyika's Exports[a] 1913–1961

Year	Sisal[b] ('000 tons)	Coffee ('000 tons)	Cotton ('000 tons)	Groundnuts ('000 tons)	Cashewnuts ('000 tons)	Tea ('000 tons)	Hides and calf skins ('000 tons)	Skins and fur skins (nos. '000)	Diamonds ('000 carats)	Total value ('000 000 shillings)
1913	21	1.1	2.2							
1919	17									
1920	17									
1921	8	3.8	1.1							
1922	10	4.3	1.5	12.5			1.4	0.14		26
1923	13	4.0	1.5	16.5			1.9	0.17		34
1924	18	5.3	2.5	18.7			2.4	0.19		52
1925	18	6.0	4.5	9.1			2.4	0.29		58
1926	25	6.5	4.9	15.9			1.3	0.30		60
1927	33	6.6	3.9	14.1			2.4	0.36		66
1928	36	10.4	4.9	10.6			2.8	0.48	23.3	78
1929	46	8.9	4.9	7.8			2.1	0.47	13.3	74
1930	50	11.5	3.7	17.3			1.7	0.36	7.8	52
1931	56	9.3	2.4	3.1			2.0	0.17	1.4	32
1932	61	11.4	3.2	15.9			2.6	0.10	1.4	44
1933	70	12.7	5.1	19.2		—	3.9	0.26	1.2	50
1934	73	14.8	5.6	8.0		—	3.1	0.31	1.4	52
1935	83	18.6	10.0	16.4		—	3.1	959	1.4	68
1936	81	12.1	11.3	22.8		—	3.1	1571	2.7	90
1937	91	13.6	11.5	22.3		0.1	3.2	1572	3.2	100
1938	101	13.7	8.9	3.8		0.1	3.0	1157	3.6	74
1939	93	16.6	11.6	4.5	0.9	0.2	3.5	1151	3.4	86
1946	112	10.0	4.0	0.5	3.2	0.6	2.6	1408	119	222
							2.4	1790	92	

Year										
1951	142	16.6	8.3	8.5	8.2	0.8	2.5	1.51	9	480
1952	158	18.6	11.1	9.4	11.5	1.0	3.1	0.83	332	810
1953	171	15.2	14.8	1.1	11.4	1.1	4.4	1.09	171	948
1954	168	19.4	12.1	2.5	16.3	1.6	4.5	1.22	330	708
1955	174	18.5	20.4	5.6	18.2	1.7	3.8	1.12	323	746
1956	186	21.6	27.9	15.1	16.7	2.0	3.5	1.07	358	758
1957	182	18.5	27.2	16.1	33.7	2.2	3.6	1.08	373	940
1958	198	22.2	32.1	12.6	31.3	2.3	3.6	1.23	515	828
1959	209	19.6	30.7	12.1	33.2	2.7	4.5	1.35	555	886
1960	205	26.2	32.0	14.6	55.3	3.7	n.a.	n.a.	n.a.	958
1961	198	19.2	33.0	3.4	28.0	4.4	n.a.	n.a.	n.a.	n.a.

[a] The quantity figures are for domestically produced exports to all destinations up to 1948, but from 1949 exclude exports to Kenya and Uganda. The total value figures apply to domestic exports to all destinations, including Kenya and Uganda, throughout the period shown.

[b] Exports of sisal were less than one ton in 1898 and 1899, reached 15 tons in 1901, jumped to 225 tons in 1902, and thereafter increased very rapidly to the nearly 21 000 tons shown for 1913.

Sources: International Bank for Reconstruction and Development (1961: Table 3) for years up to 1959, and United Republic of Tanzania *Economic Survey* 1965–6 (in Smith (ed.) 1966: 55) Table V, for 1960 and 1961. Based on trade statistics from the East African Statistical Department.

tion through high-ranking visitors, newspaper reports, etc.' and encouraged to hire labour (ibid.). Labour-hiring peasants, or small capitalist farmers, or *kulaks*, the word often used in literature on Tanzania, could soon be found in every part of the country. Some were from chiefly families, who could claim large areas of good quality land. Others had made some capital in trade or as migrant labourers. In a review of the relevant literature, published in 1974, John Sender showed that almost every rural survey carried out in the years immediately before and after independence demonstrated the existence of these larger farmers (Sender 1974: 2–17).

In two areas they played a particularly conspicuous role. One was in Ismani, not far from Iringa town, where the forest was cleared for maize growing from the early 1950s. Yields were very high in the early years, enabling some of the first entrants to purchase tractors and to weed farms of 100 hectares or more using hired migrant labour from Njombe. Research completed in 1972 showed that 9 per cent of the farmers held 53 per cent of the land under cultivation, and owned 96 per cent of the capital equipment; they contributed nearly 70 per cent of the maize that was marketed, and this in its turn was a substantial proportion of the total maize marketed in the country (Awiti 1972a: 61 and 75).

The other area that came to be dominated by large-scale African farmers was Mbulu, where African wheat farmers began by hiring tractors and combine harvesters from settlers, then purchased second-hand equipment themselves, and finally new equipment. By the end of the 1960s about 150 African farmers were not only cultivating large areas of wheat, but were also providing an efficient hire service for about 4000 households in the area, most of whom grew some wheat (Raikes 1972: 20).

The 1950s also saw new marketing policies: farmers' prices were raised, and—at last—co-operative marketing was encouraged. These changes are the subject of Chapter 8, where it will be seen how they formed part of the same policy of increasing differentiation—by removing the controls which hindered unrestrained capitalist accumulation. The earlier theory that production would rise only if prices fell, so that farmers were forced to grow more to pay tax and finance essential needs, died slowly. But from the colonial point of view the new policy exceeded all expectations, as Table 7.5 shows: from 1954 to 1959 the tonnage of cotton exported rose 2½ times and cashewnut production doubled, while coffee production rose by 40 per cent between

1955 and 1960 despite the departure of many settlers as independence approached. In the eleven years up to 1961 there was a total trade surplus of about £77 million, most of which was invested on the London market. There was just one cloud on the horizon: in seven of the ten years between 1945 and 1954 and again in 1961 and 1962 maize was imported (Bowles 1976a: 81–2).

8 AGRICULTURAL MARKETING AND CO-OPERATIVES

> The [Co-operative] Union was popular mainly because it ended the Asian monopoly of the purchasing of coffee. It helped to arouse the consciousness of peasants to turn against this group of exploiters... But some 'black' leaders are also exploiters... The leading group has tried to solidify itself and done its best to keep the ordinary peasant member out of leadership positions. This has prevented the peasants from developing into a social force capable of challenging the dominant businessmen and progressive farmers for the local leadership. Thus the co-operative union as an economic agent has contributed to the material welfare of the new elite who have taken the leadership from the traditional aristocrats.
>
> RWEGOSHORA (1976)[1]

The conditions under which crops can be marketed largely determine what is produced for sale. A colonial government had three means of collecting produce from dispersed small farmers: it could allow private agents to do this more or less uncontrolled, hoping that competition would ensure fair prices; it could persuade the farmers to market their crops themselves through co-operative marketing organizations; or it could create its own bureaucracy (i.e. a marketing board) to purchase and subsequently sell the crops.

The Germans used the first method, as we saw in Chapter 6. They also established the precedent that most of the local traders would be Asians. Importing, exporting, and shipping were arranged by import/export houses at the ports; they included branches of European trading companies as well as Asian merchants. No one company dominated: by the end of the colonial period the biggest importer controlled only 5 per cent by value of imports, in contrast with Nigeria in which the United Africa

Company imported 34 per cent of imports by value, and was strengthening its position by diversifying into assembly and manufacture (Hawkins 1965).

Even in German times it was difficult for Africans to enter trade, other than at the lowest level, since Asian traders were already established in most towns. The British actively discouraged Africans from any sort of commercial operation—the Credit to Natives (Restriction) Ordinance of 1931 insisted that an African must have specific government permission before he could even request a bank to lend him money. So, from the start, when Africans involved themselves in trading they sought some means of protection, such as a co-operative which might be given a local monopoly for buying a certain product. In this they were sometimes supported by the British. In 1925 it was Charles Dundas, previously an official in Moshi, but by then posted to Dar es Salaam, who made possible the registration of the Kilimanjaro Native Planters' Association, the first co-operative organization, formed to market African-produced coffee on Kilimanjaro.[2] The leading African was Joseph Merinyo, an educated member of a chiefly family, who had been taught coffee cultivation by a German settler and who, as Secretary of the Native Authority Treasury, had toured the mountain with Dundas, persuading the farmers to plant coffee and pay their taxes.

The KNPA was formed by representatives from the main coffee-growing areas of Mount Kilimanjaro, and it later expanded to include Mount Meru (around Arusha) and the Pare mountains as well. It charged a subscription of one shilling a year, in return for which it provided spraying and marketing services for its members. It negotiated better terms for the sale of its coffee to Europe and so raised the growers' incomes. Not surprisingly its membership expanded, to exceed 10 000 by 1926.

The young, mission-educated, coffee growers of the KNPA became spokesmen for the Chagga, and its mass meetings provided a forum in which grievances from all over the mountain could be aired. By 1927 it was in conflict with the settlers (still trying to follow their friends in Kenya, and ban the growing of coffee by Africans), the chiefs (since the KNPA was taking over their function as spokesmen for the Chagga), and the local Provincial Commissioner (whose sympathies lay with the settlers and the chiefs). In that year Cameron issued a circular ordering the agricultural staff to discourage the growing of coffee by Africans. In 1928 local administrative staff in Moshi were ordered not to help the KNPA, and an attempt was made to wind it up and hand over its assets to a Council of Chiefs; this was only prevented by an appeal to Dundas in Dar es Salaam. But the next year the officials insisted that it compete directly with Asian traders: the traders fought with each other to buy the coffee regardless of quality, and the KNPA drifted into a financial crisis. Finally it was destroyed in 1931 when the Provincial Commissioner arrested Merinyo and most of the committee on charges of fraud. The main charge was never proved and may well have been invented by the Provincial Commissioner himself to discredit the Association.

But the *idea* of African marketing co-operatives had support in high places, not least in London where the Fabian socialist Sydney Webb (Lord Passfield) was Colonial Secretary. In 1931 a colonial adviser, C.F. Strickland, visited Tanganyika and explained how useful co-operatives were proving to the British in India and Ceylon. His book *Co-operation for Africa*, published in 1933, commented favourably on the Moshi experience (p. 40).

In 1932, with Strickland's advice, a Co-operative Ordinance was passed, designed to ensure government control over the movement. Under this ordinance a new co-operative, the Kilimanjaro Native Co-operative Union, was registered to market African coffee on Kilimanjaro. The government took responsibility for auditing and supervising the accounting, and a European was appointed as manager. The Union itself was broken down into many small primary societies, each registered separately under the Ordinance, so that any society which broke the rules, including rules that outlawed political activity, could be deregistered by the Registrar of Co-operative Societies. The Union was nominally controlled by elected representatives of the primary societies; since these were frequently chiefs (the primary society boundaries corresponded to those of the chiefdoms), there were no more mass meetings, and the Union was effectively confined to crop marketing.

In 1934 it was allowed a 'compulsory marketing order', making it the only legal purchaser of African-grown coffee on the mountain. This ended competition with the Asians, and made possible a stable organization. Yet the colonial government was reluctant to register other co-operatives. The next was the Ngoni-Matengo Co-operative Marketing Union, registered in Songea in 1936 to market fire-cured tobacco.[3] This co-operative was created by the government in order to constitute a body that could borrow money:

Until 1935 officials of the Department of Agriculture controlled the industry. In this capacity, they supervised the crop's production, and handled its purchase, processing and sale. By 1935, the industry had grown too large to be handled competently by the Department, which had limited resources in men and finances. Accordingly, the government [*sic*] decided to establish another body to run the industry. Some consideration was given to handing over the industry to a private company and giving it monopoly rights. However, no company or individual was judged sufficiently interested in, and capable of, taking over. Finally, it was decided that a co-operative movement be formed to control the industry. The decision to form a co-operative appears to have been made by the government alone, as no evidence was found to show that the people of Songea had any say in its formation. The government decided on the co-operative for economic reasons. Capital was needed to sustain and increase the growth of the industry. The government was unwilling to provide money. However, a co-operative could obtain needed capital. Indeed, in 1935, the Colonial Development Fund offered to lend 2000 pounds to the new movement. (Redmond 1976: 66).

Expatriates ran the Union, with 'considerable influence or control over the industry' (Redmond 1976: 68). Chiefs or their appointees often headed the primary societies until as late as 1952 (p. 72). But fire-cured tobacco production did not rise substantially until compulsion was reintroduced in 1964, after independence. The Union failed to grow, because fire-cured tobacco production was not profitable, which meant that a class of commercial African capitalist tobacco growers was not easily able to take control from the chiefs and the (in this case largely ineffective) expatriates.

A similar reluctance is well illustrated by the refusal in 1937 to register a coffee co-operative in West Lake. This was largely the initiative of Klemenz Kiiza, who had worked as a clerk in the local tax office under the Germans, and in 1920 started a 'Native Trading Company' in Bukoba, with government approval. In 1924 he became the first leader of the Bukoba Bahaya Union, whose members, mainly a younger generation of clerks and traders, pressed for more education, especially literary education, and for an end to the semi-feudal *nyarubanja* land tenure system under which the chiefs got much of the benefit from coffee production. In 1928 Kiiza purchased a mechanical coffee huller, and in 1931 he acquired the land to start a coffee-curing factory. But in order to open this factory he needed a licence from the government, and government permission to borrow money from the banks. In 1935, still supported by the Local Provincial Commissioner, he organized 700 growers into a co-operative to supply coffee to his factory. But in 1937 the Registrar of Co-operative Societies refused to register it, on the grounds that the proposed society was really a business run by Kiiza. At the same time the government tried to enforce new rules concerning coffee growing, which would, among other things, have outlawed the traditional practice of planting coffee bushes in the shade of banana trees, thereby making coffee growing almost impossible for small farmers. Riots broke out. Some members were imprisoned. Kiiza's licence was withdrawn, and he spent most of the war years trying to sell his factory. It was not till the 1950s that co-operatives were allowed in Bukoba and Mwanza (Iliffe 1969a: 139–40).

The riots were not confined to Bukoba: there were similar disturbances on Kilimanjaro, directed against the chiefs and the KNCU.[4] The response of the government was, in 1937, to create a new body, the Moshi Native Coffee Board, which was prepared to take over the marketing of African-produced coffee should the government find it necessary. In the case of Kilimanjaro coffee, that power was not used till 1945.[5] But for coffee in Bukoba, and for the wartime 'strategic' crops elsewhere (see Chapter 7), the government intervened much earlier, curtailing the Asian traders, or replacing them with marketing organizations of its own. In other words, at a time of crisis, the colonial government used its third alternative for marketing crops—it set up its own organizations to do it.

In 1941, for example, the Bukoba Coffee Control Board (expatriate dominated) was established as the monopoly buyer of coffee (which was sold to the British Ministry of Food), while the Bukoba Native Coffee Board (consisting mainly of chiefs) began enforcing rules for coffee cultivation. Similar boards were set up to market cotton and African-produced tobacco—and also food crops, notably oil-seeds, wheat, and maize. Other boards were set up to market crops grown on estates or plantations—sisal, tea, sugar, and pyrethrum. In 1942 the constitution of the wheat board was changed to give a dominant say to settlers. But even the cotton board, marketing a crop grown only by Africans, was controlled by expatriates. These boards purchased the crops from the farmers at prices arranged with the government, and sold them to the British Ministries of Food or Supply. The cotton price to growers in particular was held down (cotton was not, at the beginning of the war, a priority crop) with the result that nearly half a million pounds had been accumulated by the board by 1945. Profits were also made from the sale of coffee grown in Bukoba; but in Moshi the KNCU operated a system under which the benefits of any sale at higher than anticipated prices were passed back to the farmer as a 'second payment'.

After the war the effectiveness of this bureaucratic structure as a means of creaming off surplus from peasant farmers became apparent. In 1947 the two Bukoba coffee boards were combined, and the new board signed a seven-year fixed-price contract with the British Ministry of Food. Seven Asian exporters were appointed agents, on a 5 per cent commission. Since the coffee was sold below the world price, the main benefit of this went to the British purchasers (to the British economy if the coffee was re-exported); even so the various Bukoba coffee boards made a profit of over 25 million shillings in the period 1945–52.

The profits on cotton trading came to nearly 160 million shillings between 1943 and 1952. They were made by purchasing the lint cotton, from Asian-owned ginneries, at fixed prices (farmers' prices were also announced) and then selling on the world market at much higher prices, particularly between 1949 and 1952 (Bowles 1974: 14).

In contrast, during this whole period the KNCU system of second payments succeeded in keeping somewhat more of the world price for its members, making them the best-off farmers in the country, approximately as well off from their coffee earnings as workers earning a minimum wage. It enabled them, for example, to levy a special additional tax in 1943 to finance Chagga education (discussed further in Chapter 10): this would have been impossible in Sukumaland at that time when many farmers' total annual cash income only just paid the government tax.

But it also made it inevitable that Africans elsewhere should demand similar co-operatives, and in this they were supported by Colonial Secretaries in the British War Cabinet and in the post-war Labour governments of 1945–51, and by the advisers these people sent to Tanganyika. In 1949 a new general ordinance allowed for boards to be set up 'to control and regulate' any crop, but these boards were to be transitional arrangements pending the establishment of African co-operatives. Brian Bowles has pointed out that this legislation was in part a frightened reaction to serious riots over coffee prices in Uganda earlier in the year.

In Bukoba the decision to allow co-operatives was taken in 1950. The arrangement was extraordinary: farmers were given a huge financial incentive to register themselves as co-operatives:

The Member for Agriculture and Natural Resources in Dar es Salaam, had, as a result of a meeting with the Registrar of Co-operative Societies in August 1949, told the chairman of the B.N.C.B. that the Government relied upon boards to promote co-operative societies since co-operative societies were a means to the voluntary participation of growers in improving production. The financial interests of the growers should be enlisted (with the implication that this had not previously been a motive of British policy); yet the B.N.C.B. was withholding profits from them. It was delaying the formation of co-operative societies; it had only to publish the existence of surplus funds, announce that these would be distributed to co-operative societies and co-operative societies would spring up. . . . Little happened until early 1950, when the Ministry of Food doubled its price for robusta coffee from £65 a ton to £132 a ton. The Board then decided that 24% of the increase should be passed on to the growers, a further 37% to growers who were members of co-operative societies, the rest to be retained by the Board for the expenses of developing co-operative societies together with an agricultural development programme. This decision resulted in the formation of forty-nine co-operative societies by the end of the year, the formation of the Bukoba Co-operative Union, and a decision that part of the previous years' profits should also be paid over to members of the co-operative societies. (Bowles 1979: 9).

Even after this the co-operatives were not allowed much power. The Board had signed seven-year contracts with Asian buyers, and until these expired in 1954 the Union was merely allowed to become the zonal agent in one of the seven zones into which the area had been divided. In the other six zones the Union had no marketing function, but a lot of money to distribute. Even that was lessened by colonial order: when the surpluses were distributed, the poll-tax in the area was raised from 15 shillings to 25 ' shillings, the Board levy on coffee was doubled, and fresh powers were taken to prevent smuggling to Uganda.

In the cotton-growing areas the government did not accept co-operatives till 1952; they had already created a marketing system in these areas which met their essential aims, and they were reluctant to dismantle it. The 1937 Cotton Ordinance had limited the numbers of traders licensed to supply each ginnery, and during the war the government had created an organization to buy the ginned crop, which in years of rising prices made the profits mentioned earlier.

African resentment of this system was concentrated on the Asian buyers who purchased the crop and who frequently cheated the growers. The farmers were sufficiently concerned to be prepared to pay a small fee for an independent weighing before the official sale. It was from this beginning that Paul Bomani created the Victoria Federation of Co-operative Unions.[6]

Bomani's early career bears some resemblance to that of Klemenz Kiiza some thirty years before: his father was a Lutheran pastor, and when Paul left school he started work in the accounts office at the diamond mine at Mwadui, a hundred miles south of Mwanza. He left this job in 1947 to become the accountant in the Mwanza African Traders' Co-operative Society, a group of African traders in Mwanza town. Bomani soon became their secretary, but then recognized the problems of competing with the Asians in retail trade, and the more promising possibilities offered by cotton marketing. He organized the independent weighing scheme, and petitioned the administration to be allowed to register a co-operative union. The government delayed the process but, eventually, in 1952 sent an able co-operative officer and allowed the Union to register. It grew rapidly, assisted by loans to its primary societies from the Lint and Seed Marketing Board. In 1953 its 38 primary societies purchased 12.5 per cent of the crop, in 1954 65 societies purchased 32 per cent. By 1958 there were 275 societies purchasing 83 per cent of the crop. Since the marketing of cotton depended on ginneries, it was logical for the Union to purchase or build its own ginneries. This was accepted by the colonial government, and the Union was allowed to borrow money to buy its first ginnery in 1956. By 1959 it was buying effectively the whole cotton

TABLE 8.1
Cotton production in the Lake Region 1951–1960

Year	Total production ('000 bales (lint))	Area ('000 hectares)	Number of cotton growers ('000)	Percentage of crop handled by co-operatives
1951	40	—	—	—
1952	70	67	—	—
1953	39	36	—	13
1954	91	87	159	32
1955	109	—	—	44
1956	121	136	219	63
1957	151	—	268	70
1958	152	162	248	83
1959	183	170	—	100
1960	161	—	—	100

Source: Ruthenberg (1964: 55).

TABLE 8.2
Numbers of registered primary co-operative societies 1959

Province	African marketing co-operatives	Other types of co-operative	Total membership
Lake	324	1	130 382
West Lake	76	1	80 402
Southern Highlands	55	2	31 945
Northern	54	4	47 575
Southern	31	—	15 440
Eastern	27	7	9 522
Tanga	6	2	9 412
Central	—	1	116
Western	—	1	200
Total	573	19	324 994

Source: Annual Report on Co-operative Development, 1959.

crop, and could boast a turnover which was probably greater than that of any other non-government African-owned business on the continent. And yet in a sense it was a very powerless organization. It purchased the crops at prices approved by the government, and sold to a reformed marketing board with its head office in Dar es Salaam, which was run by expatriates until several years after independence. Government accountants and auditors and the 'advisory' staff of the Co-operative Development Division were always watching over what it did.

As more co-operative unions were recognized, so the local marketing boards were disbanded or ignored, with the exception of the Lint and Seed Marketing Board (marketing cotton) and the Coffee Board. In 1955 the Grain Storage Department, the marketing organization for buying and (if necessary) importing food crops, purchased a record crop of maize. It was unable to store it, and forced to export at a loss of more than £1 million. The following year it too was abolished, along with the special prices and subsidies it gave to large-scale farmers. The colonial government was no longer prepared to make special favours for settlers, and for the next few years food-crop marketing, considered too risky for co-operatives, and uncontrolled—i.e. it returned to the hands of private traders.

But in all the export crop areas co-operative societies were registered (Table 8.2) and production rose to an extent unforeseen even by the most optimistic agricultural officers before the war

(Table 7.5, p. 57). On the whole this rise was not achieved by improvements in techniques, although African farmers did take steps to improve the soil, so that the experts' worries about soil erosion proved unfounded, at least for the short run. The rise was achieved without compulsion. As explained in the previous chapter, the cost was in terms of equality: a large part of the marketed surplus came from a minority of farmers who employed labour and hired or purchased machinery. We can now see, in addition, the role of the co-operative movement in this.

First, it enabled the farmers to receive higher prices. Second, it was a means of channelling power and influence to the larger growers. Third, it was a way of involving ambitious, educated Tanzanians in crop production. The decision to disband the boards appears to have been conscious: its aim was to increase capitalist production for the market. Bowles compared the logic with that used to argue for abolition of the slave-trade, or the repeal of the Corn Laws. The last word in this chapter can be left to him:

A major element in co-operative policy in Tanganyika appears to have been the desire for social control on the part of the colonial government. Social control was not of course purposeless or neutral . . . The context was an economic policy of increasing the production of cash crops; within that context the administration might have decided to use direct force. Co-operative policy was the alternative. Its cost was believed to be cheap, it had the added bonus of channelling produce into easily identifiable and controllable outlets and it capitalised on anti-Indian feeling among the producers. But whether and where it should be applied appears to have depended upon the extent of control of the growers already achieved. In Moshi co-operative policy was invented to deal with a crisis in the 1930s. In Bukoba it was applied only after considerable division within the colonial administration itself, for the local administrators believed they had achieved control of coffee-growing. In Mwanza co-operative policy was applied only after pressure from the growers themselves.

The result can be and indeed has been interpreted as a nationalist victory, that is, that co-operatives were imposed upon the British government by Africans. This interpretation appears both to exaggerate the extent to which a co-operative organisation is a liberating agency, and the extent to which the British colonial administrators opposed co-operatives . . . . One should ask the same question about co-operatives as about Independence: to what extent did they liberate and to what extent were they against British interests? (Bowles 1979: 14–15).

9 NON-INDUSTRIALIZATION

It was undesirable to accelerate the industrialisation
of East Africa which must, for many years to come,
remain a country of primary produce.
THE SECRETARY OF STATE FOR THE COLONIES, QUOTED BY
THE GOVERNOR OF TANGANYIKA IN 1935[1].

By 1920 competition from mass-produced imports had destroyed most of the traditional craft skills in Tanzania. By the
same date most of the minerals known about today had been
discovered—the large coalfields near the shores of Lake Nyasa
in the south-west, the iron-ore deposit at Liganga (medium in
size, easy to mine, but including titanium and manganese in the
ore, and therefore requiring special treatment before smelting),
exploitable deposits of phosphates and smaller deposits of copper, lead, tin, nickel, and sulphur, as well as salt from brine
springs and the sea, and soda from Lake Natron.

The agricultural potential was also known fairly accurately.
There were a few important mountain areas where high-quality
volcanic soil was combined with adequate rainfall, so that a
wide range of crops could be grown; most of this land was in
use by 1920, either by peasant farmers or by coffee planters. In
other mountainous areas the rainfall was adequate but the soil
poor in nutrients; in some of these, white settlers had taken over
much of the land, but found it hard to make money. Most of
the rest of the country was rolling savannah, acacia woodland,
or semi-desert, much of it without reliable water supplies and infested with tsetse fly, which made it almost impossible to keep
cattle. In most of these areas, settler or plantation agriculture
was not viable and there was little alternative but to depend on
peasants producing with little investment other than their
labour.[2]

Overall, the resource base was sufficient for a balanced industrialization. Coal and water-power could have provided the

energy base. Coal, sulphur, and salt could make the foundation of a chemical industry. Steel could be produced provided the demand was there—e.g. for a continuing programme of railway building. A whole range of agro-industries could have been created to process food products such as tea, sugar, meat, and fruits, as well as leather, twine, cotton, and (at a price) rubber.[3] Yet in the 1920s the decision was taken not to industrialize. Industry would bring ruin to the tribal society that Cameron and his team of administrators were trying to rediscover or retain. The African worker 'detribalized' in the towns was dangerous: his place was in the village or working for short periods on European plantations.

In 1921 the list of industries in Tanganyika included 12 cotton ginneries, 4 flour mills, 6 soap or oil mills, 14 jewellery manufacturers, 2 printers, 2 furniture makers, 3 soda-water factories, 1 tobacco factory, 2 manufacturers of salt, 1 of pottery, and 2 of lime, a total of 49 factories in all. Some coffee processing, and 8 sisal factories should probably be added to the list, but by any standard the industrial sector was minute. Although the tobacco factory employed 102 workers, and the two salt-works 300 between them, these were exceptional. Most of the 49 factories were no more than small workshops, the majority of which (for example the 14 jewellers and the 3 soda factories) were owned by Asians. Almost all had been in operation before the First World War.

During the war itself a greater degree of self-reliance had been shown:

Spinning wheels and looms were constructed . . . After several trials the roots of a local tree were found to produce the best dye, of a brownish yellow colour similar to khaki. Rubber gathered by planters was vulcanised with sulphur and make-shift tyres for automobiles and bicycles were produced . . . A group of planters successfully produced a motor fuel of sorts, similar to benzol, from coconuts. Candles and soap were made out of tallow and wax. Bags for grain and other produce were made from palm leaves. Cigars and cigarettes were manufactured from locally grown tobacco. Rum and whisky (ninety-two per cent proof) were distilled . . . Boots were made from the skins of cattle and game; tanning materials from mangroves . . . Cloth, rope and string (from pineapple and sisal) were being made at Morogoro. Fruit juices and jams were produced at Dar es Salaam. (Gardner 1963: 58–9.)

Small-arms ammunition, mines, and artillery shells were also produced, as were eleven varieties of spice, blankets, spinning-

TABLE 9.1
Industrial Establishments and Manufacturers in Tanganyika
1914–1945

	1914	1921	1931	1939	1945
Agricultural processing for export					
Cotton ginneries	n.a.	12	29	34	35 (3937)
Sisal decortication	n.a.	n.a.	9	120	126 (n.a.)
Tea factories	—	—	1	4	6 (n.a.)
Coffee curing	—	—	—	10	11 (n.a.)
Rubber factories	—	—	—	—	12 (n.a.)
Meat products	—	—	1	—	—
Agricultural processing for internal use					
Flour mills	4	4	32	55 ⎱	103 (1314)
Rice mills	—	—	17	24 ⎰	
Oil mills/soap factories	4	6	27	27	72 (590)
Copra drying	—	—	—	3	5 (100)
Sugar/jaggery	—	—	5	3	21 (n.a.)
Creameries/ghee factories	—	—	—	77	312 (1721)
Tannery	—	—	—	—	1 (310)
Bacon curing	—	—	1	1	3 (69)
Manufacture for local market					
Salt	2	2	7	6	10 (1084)
Cigarette & tobacco factories	1	1	1	4	4 (325)
Bakeries	—	—	—	38	44 (190)
Ice and soda-water	3	3	46	46	30 (133)
Beer	—	—	—	1	1 (130)
Sawmills	—	—	18	22	29 (1696)
Furniture makers	2	2	22	48	30 (210)
Fibre board factory	—	—	—	—	1 (300)
Lime burning	1	2	13	11	14 (732)
Pottery	—	1	—	—	— —
Jewellers	14	14	17	7	10 (20)
Printers	2	2	10	10	11 (75)
Miscellaneous					
Power stations	—	—	—	6	6 (201)
Others	—	—	12	26	8 (218)
Total	33	49	269	583	905

Note: The figures in brackets show numbers of employees. For the factories with figures available, the average number of employees in 1945 was 18.4.
Source: Adapted from *Tanganyika Territory Blue Books*, 1921, 1931, 1939, 1945.

wheels and important drugs and vaccines, including enough quinine (from cinchona) to protect the German troops throughout the war. Some of the quantities produced were considerable: for example 15 000 bottles of whisky and 10 000 tons of soap.

This impressive range of production ended when the Germans were driven out, and was not equalled till the 1960s, after independence. Moreover, during the intervening forty years the Kenyan capital, Nairobi, and its port, Mombasa, established themselves as the leading centres of industrial growth in East Africa.

During German times and in the early years of British rule, Tanganyika imposed a small general tariff on imports for the purpose of raising revenue. It was too small to provide much protection to infant industries in the territory. However, as early as 1923, Kenya 'adopted the principle of fostering suitable industries as the foundation of her policy' and imposed protective tariffs on wheat and flour, sugar, cheese, butter, bacon and ham, tea, ghee, ale, beer, and stout. The Government of Tanganyika was persuaded to impose the same duties, and to abolish duties at the Kenya/Tanganyika border, and in 1927 Tanganyika formally joined the customs union which already operated between Kenya and Uganda.[4] Effectively there were no tariffs on the Kenya/Tanganyika border, from 1923 right up to 1967 when they became a major matter for negotiation in the Treaty for East African Co-operation. Throughout this period, Tanganyika suffered because of the greater degree of industrialization in Kenya: it was calculated that, as early as 1931, the loss of revenue to Tanganyika caused by the absence of duties at the Kenyan border was 1.2 million shillings, and the figures must have been higher thereafter (Armitage-Smith 1932: 23).

By the late 1930s industrialists and financiers in Britain and the settlers who influenced policy in Kenya saw that they would benefit from a more general industrialization, since imports of textiles and other consumer goods from Britain had largely been replaced by imports from Japan. They therefore gave encouragement and protection to a wider range of import substitution and export processing industries (Brett 1971: 298–9). In 1935 the effective duties were as shown in Table 9.2. But not until after the Second World War was the Tanganyikan government willing to encourage industries. As a result, while Kenyan industrialists were investing in import-substitution industries, in 1945 in Tanganyika the only factory of any size depending on imported inputs was the beer factory started in the 1930s by a German capitalist. Most of the other industries were either processing agri-

TABLE 9.2
Duties on selected goods imported into East Africa 1935

	%
Blankets	22
Boots and shoes	56
Woollen goods	51–60
Cotton piece-goods	44–50
Umbrellas	59
Bicycles	45

Source: Leubuscher (1944: 107).

cultural products that could not otherwise be exported (35 cotton ginneries, 126 sisal decorticators, 6 tea factories, 11 coffee-curing factories, 12 rubber estates, and a tannery) or they were processing for the local market on a very small scale (there were 103 grain mills for a total urban population of less than 150 000, 72 oil mills and soap factories, 312 milk-processing centres spread around the cattle-keeping areas and operating for a few months each year, 44 bakeries, 29 sawmills, and 30 furniture factories or workshops). There were also 6 power stations, 30 ice and soda-water manufacturers, 4 cigarette or tobacco factories, 14 lime burners (no cement factories), 10 salt-works and the brewery. Excluding the sisal, tea, and rubber plantations, the statistics for which do not separate the agricultural workers from those working in the factories, the labour force totalled less than 15 000 in 761 establishments (Table 9.1). Even the Second World War had very little impact on industrial development in Tanganyika: goods that could no longer be imported from Britain or Japan were imported from Kenya instead; Tanganyika's imports from Kenya and Uganda rose from 7.5 million shillings in 1939 to nearly 25 million in 1945 (Honey, 1974: 65), while its exports to those countries decreased in value, and by the end of the 1950s the trade was even more unbalanced (Table 9.3).

The railways contributed to the growth of Nairobi and Mombasa as industrial centres at the expense of Dar es Salaam, Tanga, Moshi, and Arusha. The railway line from Mombasa to Nairobi continued to Kampala, the capital of Uganda. There were branch lines from this main line to Moshi and Arusha in northern Tanzania and Kisumu on the Kenyan shore of Lake Victoria, from where a steamer service served the Tanganyikan ports of Musoma, Mwanza, and Bukoba on the east, south, and west of the lake respectively. Railway tariffs discriminated against Tanganyika in two ways. Firstly, they gave the lowest rates per ton to manufactured goods and to certain crops, not-

TABLE 9.3

Tanganyika's trade with Kenya and Uganda 1951 and 1958

('000 000 shillings)

	1951	1958
Exports		
Tobacco, unmanufactured	2.5	8.8
Coconut oil	2.4	5.1
Wood, lumber and cork	2.8	(2.0)
Beans and peas etc.	1.2	2.3
Hides, skins and fur skins	1.8	0.1
Electric energy	n.a.	1.4
Sugar and sugar preparations	—	0.1
Other	12.4	32.4
Total	23.0	52.1
Imports		
Cigarettes	25.8	61.8
Beer	2.2	11.1
Wheat flour	7.0	11.3
Clothing and footwear	5.7	11.4
Manufacture of metals	n.a.	n.a.
Tea	2.9	7.4
Sugar and sugar preparations	4.3	9.1
Cement	—	11.3
Other	24.6	n.a.
Total	72.5	180.8

Note: Exports are for use in Kenya and Uganda and imports for use in Tanganyika.
Source: International Bank for Reconstruction and Development (1961: 474).

ably wheat and maize, grown by settlers. The crops produced in Tanganyika were nearly all transported at high rates. Secondly, rates along competing routes were equalized. Thus the rate from Mwanza to Dar es Salaam was the same as the rate from Mwanza to Mombasa via the Lake ferry to Kisumu, and the rate from Moshi to Mombasa equalled the rate from Moshi to Tanga. Since fewer ships called at Dar es Salaam or Tanga than at Mombasa, there was a strong incentive for the export produce from northern Tanganyika to be routed through Mombasa; this was the main reason why the railways within Tanganyika ran at a loss during the 1930s. It also gave trading companies and industrial investors an even greater incentive to locate new processing or import-substitution factories in Mombasa rather than Dar es Salaam or Tanga (Armitage-Smith 1932: 81–90; Brett 1973: 91–9; Leubuscher 1944: 112f).

As soon as the Tabora to Mwanza railway was opened in 1928 it became obvious that the railway rating system discriminated against Tanganyika, and that the failure to raise a tariff at the Kenya/Tanganyika border caused a loss of revenue to the Tanganyikan government, while making it difficult to industrialize within Tanganyika. Sir Sydney Armitage-Smith was a colonial financial adviser who came to Tanganyika in 1932 to advise the government on the economies it should make during the world depression. Many of his proposals were reactionary: in particular the cuts in the government education budget that were made following his report were bitterly regretted twenty years later. But on the issue of customs duties he had no illusions: 'Tanganyika should take steps forthwith to levy customs import duty at the same rates on foodstuffs from Kenya and Uganda as those chargeable on foodstuffs imported from foreign parts, and should cease to deplete her revenue and impoverish her citizens by protecting the products of her neighbours' (Armitage-Smith 1933: 25). He also recognized that the Tanganyikan railways 'fail to profit by the haulage of the bulk of the exports of the Territory', and suggested a pooling system that would have given them some of the revenue received by the Kenyan system from goods from northern Tanganyika exported through Mombasa (ibid, p. 84).

Governor Cameron was informed in the 1920s of the damage that could be caused by the customs union with Kenya.[5] He spent much of his energy fighting to avoid a political union which would have given the Kenyan settlers control over Tanganyika and Uganda. But he nevertheless signed the customs union agreement in 1927, and neither he nor his successors renegotiated it. He may have regarded it as the price for political independence; more likely he was simply against industrialization.

The only exceptions were agricultural processing industries. Thus, for example, in 1926 the government supported a firm called Meat Rations Ltd., owned by a group of Kenyan settlers. The company had a capital of £30 000, more than half of which was a loan from the Colonial Development Fund. The government gave it a 5000-acre farm at Maswa near Mwanza, a monopoly of meat processing in the Lake area, and a guaranteed return on its investment of 10 per cent for five years. Armitage-Smith commented acidly in 1932 that this was justified 'not as a commercial proposition but as a most valuable experimental plant in relation to the problem of overstocking and utilization of cattle products', i.e. it provided an outlet for old and sick beasts sold off during destocking campaigns (Armitage-Smith 1933: 13, 14, 15). It made a profit on its sales of meat extract, but other by-products proved less satisfactory, and, when losses rose to almost £6000 in 1935, the company was wound up (Austen 1968: 241; Brett 1973: 276).

In contrast, a Japanese firm which in 1928 opened a match factory in Tanga received no help from the government, even though at that time matches were being imported. As soon as the idea of the factory was suggested, a group of British industrialists persuaded the Tanganyika government to inform the company that if the factory was built, the government would impose an excise duty equal to the import duty on imported matches, and this forced the factory to close (Brett 1973: 269–70).

A few years later, in the depths of the depression, a factory to make twine from sisal was set up by the Tanganyika Cordage Company. The money was British, prominent British business men were on the Board, and the idea was to take advantage of imperial preferences which allowed colonial produce to be imported duty-free into Britain. In 1934, 750 tons were exported, and over 2000 tons in 1936. British processors in Dundee and Belfast feared for their loss of business. The British government was lobbied, and threatened to impose a prohibitive tariff on the imports unless a voluntary agreement to limit the imports could be reached with the British Rope, Twine and Netmakers Federation. During a debate in the British Parliament (Brett 1973: 270–3) the Minister at the Board of Trade changed the rules of the game: 'It is obvious that manufacturing countries like ours could not afford to provide free or assured markets for manufactured goods in competition with their own.' In other words imperial preferences only existed so long as they were not actually used. Racialism was confirmed the following year, when the Secretary of State added that the duty would apply only to the produce of *colonies*, and not to *dominions* such as Australia or South Africa. A few months later an agreement was negotiated, but since it prevented the Tanganyikan factory from selling its product below the price offered by its British competitors, it was impossible to break into the British market. Production fell and the factory closed in 1938.

The government attitude was clear: it was to discourage industrialization unless it was an essential part of some agricultural production programme, and to discourage non-British investors, even if it meant that what they would have produced had to be imported from Kenya. This opposition even extended to Asians who wanted to start factories, such as a group who tried to start a clove-oil factory on Zanzibar in 1924 (Honey 1974: 62–3) or the owners of the smaller cotton ginneries who were squeezed out in favour of British firms such as the Tanganyika Cotton Company in the 1930s.

It is understandable that this should be the British government attitude, but less understandable that the Permanent Mandates Commission, which was supposed to be ensuring that Britain acted in the interests of all the inhabitants of Tanganyika, should have allowed it to continue. The Commission was certainly aware of the issues, through reports such as those of Armitage-Smith. Charlotte Leubuscher suggests that it was simply not interested or competent when it came to questions of economics: it spent more time discussing whether Tanganyika, Kenya, and Uganda should be allowed to have common postage stamps than on this issue (Leubuscher 1944: 119).

Import substitution started after the war. The British Labour Government encouraged its colonies to prepare ambitious development plans. The plans for Tanganyika published in 1944 and 1946 did not allocate money specifically for industries.[6] However, the general rise in spending, and not least the Groundnuts Scheme of 1946–50, demonstrated the shortage of locally produced goods. Peasants received higher prices for their crops, and rapidly increased their production, so that the value of agricultural production increased five times between 1946 and 1952, and with it the demand for basic consumer items such as textiles, bicycles, cooking utensils, agricultural implements, all means of transport, and cigarettes.[7]

Even so the industrialization was slow, and dependence on Kenya continued to increase. The main difference between the list of factories at the end of 1955 and that of ten years earlier lies in the number of 'factories' (over 300 employing ten workers or more) concerned with the maintenance and repair of lorries, cars, agricultural machinery, and boats.[8] These were mostly powered by petrol or diesel engines which were imported in large numbers as road transport began to compete with the railways. By 1955 there were twenty power-stations. In the manufacturing sphere the most significant development was three interdependent factories, planned together and encouraged by the colonial government, and built by three different British multinational corporations. These were a tin-can manufacturing plant (Metal Box) employing 218 workers, a paint-mixing plant (Robiliac) employing 51 workers, and a meat-packing plant, Tanganyika Packers, built by Liebigs in Dar es Salaam to can beef for export to Britain, and employing some 800 workers. At the end of 1955 the textile industry consisted of a dyeing works and a small weaving factory, each employing only 28 workers. Cotton spinning was entirely absent despite the fact that Tanganyika had exported cotton since German times, with exports rising to over 30 000 tons per annum by 1958. The number of concerns involved in agricultural processing—mainly large-scale operations for export, and small-scale ones serving the local market—had increased. Many small-scale operations, including jewellery, shoe-making, sawmilling, and woodworking, continued to be the preserve of the Asian community. The first large-scale sugar factory, on irrigated land south of Mount Kilimanjaro, had just been opened by a Danish company. By 1958 there were still only about 300 enterprises with more than five employees in manufacturing (as distinct from processing for export), with just under 20 000 workers, mainly in the food and furniture business (Table 9.4).

TABLE 9.4
Net output and employment in manufacturing industries 1958[a]

Industry	Number of employees[b]	Net output ('000 000 shillings)
Food, drink, tobacco, milling, etc.	6 396	89.7
Carpentry, furniture, and sawmilling	8 079	32.0
Clothing and footwear	448	4.0
Motor vehicle repair and general engineering	2 691	17.4
Brick-, block-, and tile-making	893	3.0
Other	1 194	6.2
Total	19 701	152.3[c]

[a] Preliminary estimate.
[b] African employees only.
[c] Includes indirect taxes, estimated at £790 000.
Source: International Bank for Reconstruction and Development (1961: 230).

So, although industrialization speeded up slightly in the years immediately before independence, for most of the colonial period it was effectively non-existent. The result had consequences for employment: most of those who were employed either worked in agriculture or in the service sector, which included the

government, the railways, and the docks. The majority of those
in agriculture, and many in government service, were on short-
term contracts of three to six months. Thus the trade-union
movement began among workers in service industries, notably
the dockers. Once the migrant workers on the sisal estates were
organized, in 1958, the power of the unions was an extremely
strong force in favour of independence. But it was not predominantly an *industrial* working class, since there were so few industries. The independent country would have to arrange most of its
own industrialization in the highly competitive world markets of
the 1960s and 1970s, starting from a virtually non-existent base.

10. EDUCATION AND IDEOLOGY

> Subjectively, the missionaries might have considered
> themselves as being on a 'civilizing mission on the
> dark continent'. But objectively their role was to pre-
> pare the ideological groundwork for the subsequent
> imperialist penetration. It was missionary education
> which facilitated the separation of the African from
> his traditional society for absorption into the colonial
> socio-economic system. HIRJI (1973: 3)

The first opposition to colonial rule was military—the wars of
conquest and the Maji Maji. It was organized by some (not all)
of the chiefs—the ruling classes of pre-colonial Tanzania. It was
defeated because the chiefs had no answer (not even the fanatic-
al spirit inspired by the Maji Maji oath) to the machine-guns of
the Germans or their willingness to destroy food stores, crops in
the fields, and cattle. By 1907 further military resistance was out
of the question. Chiefs who might have opposed the Germans
were replaced, while those who had collaborated were given
more responsibility. A 'comprador class', resigned to German
interests, was created.

The next opposition was very different. It came from the petty bourgeoisie—i.e. from the minority of Africans who found
their hopes of advancement as traders, clerks, or junior civil servants blocked by the colonial system. It was not till the 1950s
that this opposition took an openly political form, but the roots
of the political movements of the 1950s can be traced back to
the beginnings of 'European' education.[1]

Even before the formal imposition of German rule there were
chiefs who welcomed Islamic teachers or Christian missionaries
—there were Islamic teachers at Kimweri's court in Usambara
in 1848. This Islamic teaching should not be underestimated; it
involved arithmetic, and reading and writing taught from the
Koran in Arabic script, and, for example, enabled the Sultan of

Zanzibar to collect his customs, to build palaces and ships, and to mount sea voyages to Europe (Jiddawi 1951: 25–31).

The first Protestant missionaries arrived in the 1850s; the first Catholics in 1868. The missions established bases at the coast, and then worked inland along the trade routes. Since they arrived about twenty years before colonial military occupation, they were entirely dependent on the goodwill of the local chiefs. The chiefs initially underestimated the threat that the missions posed to their traditions. Some, such as the Nyakyusa, valued the employment possibilities and trading contacts with the outside world which followed the establishment of a mission. Others welcomed the missionaries for diplomatic or even military reasons, for example the Bondei around Muheza who hoped that the mission at Magila would secure their independence from their much stronger neighbours, the Kilindi; or the Nyamwezi under Mirambo who wanted a counterweight to the Arab presence at Tabora. Merere of the Sangu welcomed the missionaries for the same reason that he later fought on the side of the Germans—as a means of ensuring his independence from the Ngoni and the Hehe (Oliver 1965: 66–71; Iliffe 1969a: 127; Roberts 1968: 136.)

Both Protestant and Catholic missionaries recognized that 'Africans would only be converted by Africans',[2] so they started schools to train African catechists or evangelists. Before long there was a network of 'bush schools' around each mission station, where the catechists taught reading and writing, and from which the best students proceeded to primary schools, usually with boarding places, at the mission stations themselves. Many early converts were freed slaves who had no other 'home' than the mission.[3] Others, especially inland, were the sons, or other close relatives, of chiefs, sent to the mission schools as part of the arrangements for establishing the mission, or because the chief realized that this might be a way to secure his son's succession.

The early missions were never very secure. Several of their hosts turned against them, and they had no military power. Roland Oliver described them as 'small independent states', with their rules and regulations, their farms and gardens on which work was compulsory three days a week, and even their own police forces for defence and the enforcement of their internal rules and regulations. They expanded in German times, especially in the years after the Maji Maji. By 1912 there were 171 mission stations in mainland Tanzania, with 616 European and

1694 African staff, including the catechists and teachers who ran 1119 schools for about 100 000 pupils (Smith 1963: 107), although the effective number of pupils may have been less than this, perhaps 60 000 (Hornby 1964: 87–8).

It soon became apparent that the missions threatened many of the traditional institutions of the tribes. They opposed dancing, the ceremonies surrounding births, marriages, and deaths, traditional styles of clothing, polygamy, and initiation ceremonies. Tribal education was a lifelong process in which more and more wisdom was acquired by instruction from elders as a man or woman grew older. Initiation at puberty was an important part of this education. The 'syllabus' was relevant to the life of the tribes: it covered the skills required for good agriculture, for health and child-rearing, and for survival in times of famine or disaster, as well as tests of bravery and stories about the origins and history of the tribe (Raum 1940; Castle 1966: 39–45).

Mission education differed in at least three important respects. First, much of its relevance was indirect, such as the skill of reading which depended for its usefulness on suitable written materials being available. Secondly, whereas traditional education had always been for all, since the tribe could not afford to have uninitiated members, mission education was for a highly select minority. Moreover, it contained a strong ideological element: the Christian religion and all the time devoted to inculcating 'a liking for order, cleanliness, diligence, dutifulness and a sound knowledge of German customs and patriotism' (Cameron and Dodd 1970: 56). Finally, the skills imparted could easily be put to individual advantage outside the tribal setting. Any boy (there were hardly any places for girls) who had passed through a mission primary school could become a teacher or a catechist, or get a job in a government office, and so receive a regular salary, though not a high one, without the need to do manual work. Mission education, with its combination of reading, writing, arithmetic, and Christianity, was the ideal means of creating a new class of literate officials, cut off from their tribal origins, different in important ways from their tribally-educated cousins, and with loyalties to those who had educated them and so given them the chance of a new life.

The British took the decision to continue using Swahili as the language of administration and of the courts. They re-employed many of the younger German-trained civil servants, the products of the old Tanga School, but were reluctant to entrust them with responsibility. Instead they preferred the graduates of schools run by English missionaries, such as Kiungani, a school founded by Anglican missionaries on Zanzibar in 1869 which drew its students from Anglican missions on the mainland and offered a four-year education in Swahili and English (Iliffe . 1969a: 154–6).

After the First World War, the re-establishment of education was by no means the government's first priority. As late as 1922 there were only two expatriates in the government educational service. In 1923/4 the financial provision for education was only 263 000 shillings, about 1 per cent of the government budget. This rose to 2 440 000 shillings, 8 per cent of the budget, in 1931/2, only to be cut sharply back in the years which followed, to less than four per cent of the budget in 1936 and 1937. In 1938 total government revenue was over 40 million shillings, but expenditure on education was still less than 2 million (Listowel 1965: 112–13).

The British were not only mean; they also allowed three parallel education systems to develop, one for each of the three races. In 1933 there were places for 51 per cent of the Europeans of school age (most of the rest were in boarding-schools in Kenya or England, where their fees were paid by the government), 49 per cent of the Asians, and only 1.84 per cent of the Africans (Listowel, p. 113). The Director of Education pointed out privately in 1925 that separate Asian and African systems were maintained as part of a deliberate policy of divide and rule:

At present we have a . . . growing race-consciousness among the Africans and a growing feeling of resentment that the Asiatics get so many of the 'plums.' In my opinion coeducation might conceivably weaken this healthy and natural rivalry and eventually lead to making common cause for political ends . . .
(Rivers-Smith, then Director of Education.[4])

Asian schools were at first started privately by groups of parents, but in 1925, as part of a general policy of supporting schools started by 'Voluntary Agencies', they began receiving government grants for maintenance. The government also began to open its own schools for Asians, including, in 1930, a postprimary 'central' school. By 1945 there were more than eighty government-supported Asian schools, with a total of just under 8000 pupils; by 1956 more than 20 000 Asians were in school, 5586 of whom were in years 7–12 (Table 10.1). Morrison

TABLE 10.1
Numbers in School 1926–1956

	European			Asian			African			
	Years 1-6	Years 7-12	Total	Years 1-6	Years 7-12	Total	Unassisted Years 1-4	Government assisted Years 1-6	Years 7-12	Total
1926	580	—	580	1 360	—	1 360	162 806	5 843	—	168 649
1936	725	—	725	3 742	293	4 035	191 061	30 570	26	221 657
1946	599	—	599	7 277	1 547	8 824	n.a.	115 516	1 446	n.a.
1956	1 929	464	2 393	14 461	5 586	20 047	84 300	345 014	13 857	443 171

Source: Morrison (1976: Tables 2.1, 2.2, and 2.3, pp. 45 and 46).

(1976: 51–2) points out that in 1956 in years 9–12 there were still more Asians in school than Africans, while in the population as a whole there were 100 Africans for every Asian. There were also by this time places for more than 2000 European children, the majority in years 1–6 since the colonial government still paid the fees for older European children to attend boarding-schools in Kenya or England. In 1961 12 million shillings was spent on Asian education, more than 9 million on European, but only 72 million on African.

Marjorie Mbilinyi has highlighted the ambivalence of the British towards education for Africans. Government officials were aware, from a very early stage, that a class of educated Africans would become a threat to them; they therefore tried to plan African education so that only the numbers required by the economy would be educated, and to concentrate, as far as possible, on the sons of chiefs, headmen, or influential town-dwellers. On the other hand the missions wanted to give a basic education to as many potential converts as possible. They were suspicious of post-primary education, since many of those who received it left them and took jobs in towns. They wanted their education to be 'practical'—i.e. related to the agriculture of the area, and not aimed at preparing students for more education in secondary schools. This view was cogently argued by the Phelps-Stokes committee, financed by an American missionary foundation, whose reports in 1922 and 1925 influenced educational thinking in all British African colonies. After the Second World War, this type of thinking was incorporated into the 'middle school' syllabus, and it was only at the end of the 1950s, with independence in sight, that the 'practical' parts of the syllabuses were dropped—the nationalists felt that practical skills were a waste of time, the most important education being book-learning in order to get the paper qualifications needed for jobs previously held by Europeans. Many aspects of Nyerere's 1967 paper *Education for Self-Reliance* implied a return to the policies of the mid-1950s[5].

Up to the 1940s few Africans received more than three years' schooling, and in the depression of the 1930s it was post-primary education that was most drastically cut back: as late as 1940 only five schools offered a complete secondary education—i.e. ten years' schooling—to Africans. The overwhelming majority had no opportunity to go to school at all. Those that did go to school —and there were less than 200 000 places until well into the 1930s—went mainly to mission schools where they paid fees that covered the costs. A much smaller number—about 15 per cent of the total—went to mission schools that were assisted by the government.[6]

This colonial education was class-biased as well as mean and racialist. At the top of the pinnacle was Tabora School, created as a school for chiefs and the sons of chiefs in 1924.[7] Tabora Girls' School followed in 1929. Tabora School was modelled on an English public school, but with a syllabus adapted to include the practical training thought to be necessary for African leaders. Discipline was maintained through a prefect system; the pupils were divided into 'houses' on tribal lines, though this was dropped in 1934 when pupils refused to accept orders from prefects from other tribes; the school was accommodated in imposing buildings with cloisters, leaving no doubt that it was an élite school. The syllabus combined a 'literary' education, in English in the higher forms, with 'practical' training in agriculture, crafts, 'native administration' (i.e. a knowledge of the working of Native Authority courts), and even at times road-building. But from 1935 these 'practical' subjects were dropped, almost all the teaching was given in English, and the school was opened to commoners, with entrance by competitive examination. This enabled it to take promising pupils from all over the country, and to maintain its status into the 1950s and 1960s. For a number of years it was the only school whose graduates could go directly to Makerere College, in Uganda, which took its first Tanganyikan students to read for teachers' certificates in 1934, and from 1949 offered the only opportunity in East Africa to read for a London University degree. It is no coincidence that a high proportion of Tanzania's present leadership attended Tabora School in the 1950s.

Native Authority Schools were founded by chiefs. Some were schools which pre-dated the First World War and were reopened before a British educational administration was set up. Others were founded very quickly after 1925 when the chiefs were made responsible for collecting tax for the British, but allowed to keep a proportion of this tax for 'development projects': one of the most popular 'projects' was founding schools, and native authority schools were better equipped and staffed than ordinary primary schools, and (not surprisingly) gave preference to the sons, and sometimes the daughters, of chiefs and headmen. The government at first treated them as voluntary agency schools, providing financial assistance with the running costs, but they were reluctant to lose control, and by 1937 it was accepted that native authority schools were government schools, with the government providing trained teachers and teaching materials, and frequently much of the cost of teachers' salaries and boarding as well (Cameron and Dodd 1970: 65–6; Listowel 1965: 94–7).

There were only a tiny number of 'central schools'—never more than twenty-six—which offered four more years of education on top of the two or three years in mission or government primary schools. But even then there were differences in the syllabuses for children of different kinds of parents, as can be seen from a 1924 report on Bukoba Central School:

Two broad divisions have been made in the school, forming a 'General side' and a 'Special side'. The first consists chiefly of sons of Sultans, Chiefs and wealthy land owners who receive a general all-round training consisting of academic subjects such as English, Mathematics, Geography, Hygiene and practical subjects such as Agriculture, Animal Husbandry, Elementary Carpentry and Tailoring, and Native Handicrafts (such as Drum-making etc.). The second will consist of apprenticeship to various trades, carpentry, tailoring, etc.[8]

For the rest, there was either no school at all—there were places for fewer than 10 per cent of the children of school age before the Second World War—or just two years in a mission or government 'village school', often little better than a German 'bush school' of twenty years earlier. The syllabus emphasized arithmetic and reading, but much time was spent on the school farm. A typical school had four classes—two in the morning and two in the afternoon—and only two teachers, each teacher responsible for two classes.

When world prices and government revenue fell in the years of the depression in the 1930s, the British government insisted on a balanced budget, which meant that government expenditure had to be cut. Education was, it appeared, expendable. The budget was cut by a third: the grants-in-aid paid to voluntary agency schools were cut by almost half, fourteen of the twenty-six post-primary institutions training Africans were closed, and the number of teachers paid for by the government was reduced by 40 per cent. The result was extremely slow Africanization and continuing dependence on Asians: in 1937 14 out of 18 clerks in the Secretariat were non-African, as were 37 out of 39 in the Treasury, and 100 out of 114 customs officials.[9]

Paradoxically, the situation improved during the Second World War. Money was available under the Colonial Development and Welfare Act, and government expenditure on education more than doubled between 1939 and 1945. There was a 43 per cent increase in over-all enrolment with a 250 per cent increase in enrolment in government-assisted schools. Even so, in 1945 there were only about 1000 primary schools in the country: 200 government or native authority schools, 300 voluntary agency schools assisted by the government, and 500 registered but unassisted. These now offered a four-year course. There were then eighteen secondary schools (eight government and ten assisted) offering a further four years, and twenty-four small teachers' training colleges, mostly run by the missions. There were only twenty-seven Tanzanians in residence in Makerere College (Cameron and Dodd 1970: 61, 71. Compare Table 10.1).

During the depression it had been suggested that Native Authorities might finance all primary education in their areas by levying a special tax for the purpose. This had been opposed by the missions, partly because they distrusted the 'pagan' Native Authorities, but perhaps more because they knew that many of the areas in which missions were strongest were poor in terms of income from cash crops. There was, however, one particular area which could benefit from such an arrangement—Mount Kilimanjaro where the 'second payment' system of the Kilimanjaro Native Co-operative Union meant that the farmers received more than half of the world price for their coffee. In 1943—during the war—the Chagga Council was allowed to levy a special welfare tax on coffee grown on Kilimanjaro, most of the money to be used on the building of schools. Once they were built, the government paid 85 per cent of the teachers' salaries. This arrangement enabled the people of Kilimanjaro to build and staff primary schools, and later secondary schools, all over the mountain. Universal primary education was effectively achieved during the 1950s, and there was a period in the 1960s when a high proportion of the students in the University of Dar es Salaam came from this one tribe. By comparison, tribes in the coastal areas and in the south who had embraced the Muslim faith received little help: missionary opposition prevented the recognition by the government of Muslim schools (with the exception of the Aga Khan schools of the Asian community). Thus, while there was nearly universal primary education on Kilimanjaro, in other areas it was almost impossible to get a

Western education if one did not wish to be associated with the Christian missions. The effects of this are visible to this day (Cameron and Dodd 1970: 67–8).

After the war, with pressure from African parents and politicians as well as the United Nations Trusteeship Committee, investment in education continued under the government's Ten-Year Development Plan. The missions also rapidly expanded their involvement. In 1947 83 000 boys and 30 000 girls, about 10 per cent of the children of primary-school age, attended school. By 1956 the proportion had risen to nearly 40 per cent, and there were almost 2500 students in secondary schools, including 204 girls—in 1947 there had not been a single female student above Standard VIII. There were more than 2000 teachers in training, and more than 800 students were in various forms of vocational training. But only 20 students were studying for degrees, with another 59 in a variety of non-degree courses at universities or professional institutes. It was a tiny number from which to draw the high-level manpower to run a country (table 10.2).

TABLE 10.2
Tanganyikan Africans in education 1956

Level	Number of institutions	Enrolment
Primary (years 1–4)	2 589	336 079
Middle (years 5–8)	357[a]	32 845
Secondary (years 9–10)	24	2 119
(years 11–12)	4	290
Higher	1[b]	
Advanced secondary		80
Non-degree professional courses		59
Degree courses		20
Other[c]		8
Teacher training courses		
Post Standard VII	26	2 072
Post Standard X and XII	4	182
Vocational courses	2[d]	832

[a] Includes 90 'district schools' giving only Standards V and VI and 10 secondary schools giving Standards VII and VIII.
[b] i.e. Makerere University College. Statistics for students studying at the higher level outside East Africa were not published.
[c] Includes students taking post-graduate diplomas, in the School of Art, and on special-entry general courses.
[d] Ifunda Trade School and Tengeru Natural Resources School. Private agencies and some government departments ran other institutions.
Source: Morrison 1976, Table 2.4, based on data from Department of Education Annual Reports.

Even in 1962 less than fifteen Tanganyikan Africans graduated from Makerere, and the small numbers in anything beyond
the first four years of primary education can be seen in Table
10.3, while Table 10.4 shows the extent to which the professions
were still dominated by Europeans and Asians.

TABLE 10.3
School attendance by age groups 1957 and 1962

Year		Lower primary	Upper primary	Secondary I–IV	Forms V and VI
1957	Population	895 000	792 000	720 000	338 000
	Enrolment	364 024	41 290	5 931	28
	Percentage	40.7	5.2	0.8	0.008
1962	Population	976 000	864 000	785 000	365 000
	Enrolment	443 799	75 936	13 690	485
	Percentage	45.5	8.8	1.7	0.1

Source: Pratt 1976: 94.

TABLE 10.4
Employment in selected professions by race 1962

Profession	Total	African	Asian	European
Architects	11	0	2	9
Civil engineers	84	1	22	61
Mechanical engineers	52	0	6	46
Surveyors	94	1	1	92
Physicians	184	16	60	108
Lawyers	57	2	11	44
Veterinarians	45	9	1	35
Geologists	41	0	0	41
Zoologists	12	1	0	11

Source: Pratt 1976: 93.

But to end a discussion of colonial education with statistics
would be to neglect the ideological impact: education was the
most powerful weapon in the battle for the minds of the colonized. At the beginning of this chapter, we considered the impact of mission education on tribal society, and in particular the
way it created a petty bourgeois class of Tanzanians who could
earn their living by working for wages, and who had different
interests from their cousins, who remained peasant producers.
We have also seen how, during the colonial period, this process

was continued: education comprised special schools for the sons of chiefs, headmen, and rich townsmen and farmers, with either nothing at all or a brief two years of 'practical' training for the children of agricultural producers.

The British frequently feared that their legitimacy would be challenged by this emerging petty bourgeoisie—as indeed it was. In an attempt to stem the tide, from the beginning they imbued their education with nationalist ideology, first German then British. When, in the 1950s, this was undermined by African nationalism, they drew on another ideology, created by American political theorists, as a means by which the educated could be convinced that they were different from, and better than, the masses: this was the ideology of 'modernization theory', or 'dualism', which distinguishes between the 'modern' and the 'traditional': everything 'modern' (or Western) is good, while the traditional is bad. These ideas pervaded educational reports and still influence policy today.[10] An interesting example is a book by two ex-colonial educators, published as late as 1970:

The traditional is, for this day and age, wasteful, destructive, outmoded, and static. Traditional agriculture is based on a system of land tenure in accordance with 'native law and custom'. Ownership of land is largely communal . . . There are advantages in this situation, such as keeping land out of the hands of money-lenders, but the disadvantages are great. No cultivator can be encouraged to spend capital on land which is only his or his family's to use. No small plots can be consolidated. No pioneering can be done without the approval and support of the community. Single-minded individual enterprise is therefore often stifled. (Cameron and Dodd 1970: 18–19.)

This of course reflects the views of the East African Royal Commission of 1955 and the Kenyan Swynnerton Plan, and, as we shall see, a similar ideology underlies the Tanganyikan First Five-Year Development Plan of 1964; empirically there is little support for it, as Chapter 7 has shown. The first sentence of the quotation above suggests that 'development' must involve rejection of the past; from there it is but a small step to the view that the poor hopeless peasant can only be rescued by an enlightened educated élite: 'How to overcome *the destructive conservatism of the people* and generate the drastic agrarian reforms which must be effected if the country is to survive is one of the most difficult problems *the political leaders* of Tanzania have to face.' (Ibid., p. 19, my emphasis.)

This ideology enables the educated to think of themselves collectively (i.e. as a class) as the bearers of all things modern and good. Even though they have been almost totally divorced from direct involvement in production, they feel that they alone can tell others what to do. It is no wonder that they often find it hard to admit that the peasantry may have been better off in the past than they are today, and that peasants might be able to increase production and labour productivity without having to be told how to do so by educated bureaucrats and teachers. The paradox was that the same ideology contained the seeds of the process that was to undermine formal colonial rule. For the Christian religion, and the philosophical writings of Adam Smith and John Stuart Mill, contained the ideas of individualism, liberalism, and equality, and however much schools were told to 'teach less of the dangerous doctrine of brotherhood and equality and give all instruction in practical tasks' (advice given by Count Pliel in 1886 and quoted in Smith 1963: 99) there were always a few teachers who were prepared to discuss liberal ideas.

Colonial education put the petty bourgeoisie in a somewhat better economic position than most of the indigenous population, yet the colonial system was incapable of satisfying the aspirations of this class which were the result of this very process of education. Being placed in the colonial state apparatus, the petty bourgeoisie were, in a sense, nearest to the seats of political power, but being under the direct domination of the colonizer, they became conscious of their powerlessness, of their inability to do anything by or for themselves. Or, in other words, by this inability they acquired a consciousness of themselves as a class 'for itself' much more readily than any other oppressed class in the society. Thus, given the global anti-colonial struggles and the sharpening of the contradictions betwen the colonizer and the colonized, it is not surprising that the petty bourgeoisie successfully led the struggle for independence. (Hirji 1973: 5)

11 INDIRECT RULE

> From the viewpoint of British Indirect Rule policy,
> the maintenance in power of the largely ineffective
> *bakama* [the ruling clan of the Haya, the tribe on the
> west of Lake Victoria] could only be regarded as a
> sham... For the Haya themselves, the only channels
> of political expression still open were intrigue within
> an increasingly irrelevant Native Authority structure,
> or accommodation to an authoritarian, if essentially
> benevolent, European government. Eventually a
> third possibility would present itself—the aspiration
> towards total control of the European machinery—
> but for this there was not yet sufficient daring or
> strength.
>
> AUSTEN (1968: 232)

In 1920 Britain was given responsibility for Tanganyika under a
League of Nations mandate. The British had controlled most of
the land area since 1917, and Sir Horace Byatt, who headed the
civilian administration during the war, became the first British
Governor in 1920. On the surface, the mandate was clearly intended to be temporary—for 'peoples not yet able to stand by
themselves under the strenuous conditions of the modern
world'[1]—and the country was to be developed and governed in
the interests of its African inhabitants. Byatt's first concern was
to repair the infrastructure damaged during the war, and to start
collecting taxes. Since most of the plantations and estates had
been confiscated as German property, and had fallen into disre-
pair, initially there was little alternative but to encourage
peasant production (Iliffe 1979: 262–3; Bates 1957: 43–75).

Sir Donald Cameron, who succeeded Byatt in 1925 and stayed
for six years, is remembered for his passionate belief in 'indirect
rule'.[2] This was an attempt to rule the country through chiefs,
or at least to give the chiefs an appearance of ruling the country. They were allowed to hold their own courts, and to keep

part of the tax revenue they collected for use in development projects. But sitting behind them were the British Provincial and District Commissioners. Chiefs were expected to do what the British told them, and those who took too independent a line were replaced, regardless of the legitimacy of their claims to be chiefs.

Cameron has been described as 'the first great governor', and Nyerere himself, in 1956, singled him out as the only governor up to that time who had not ruled the country as if it were a British colony (Listowel 1965: 75; Nyerere 1966: 41). This view, however, is too generous to Cameron, and unjust to Byatt, under whose administration most of what is commonly attributed to Cameron was begun. One of the most careful studies of the period describes Cameron as 'a professional bureaucrat fighting to preserve the structure that had nurtured him'—in other words to create an impression of indirect rule while leaving the real power with the British (Austen 1968: 152). We can see this process at work by examining Cameron's attitude to the various problems with which he dealt.

Cameron made it clear when he arrived in Tanganyika, and many times thereafter, that he was ruling on behalf of the African population, but he also made it clear, for example when laying the foundation stone of Tabora School in 1925, 'that Tanganyika was definitely and for ever embodied in the framework of the British Empire' (quoted by Mbilinyi 1975: 4). While he certainly did not want political power in the hands of settlers, he took steps to encourage them. In 1927, in response to settler pressure, he attempted to limit the growing of coffee by Africans. He had seen from his experience in Nigeria that the 'West African' or 'Ugandan' system of exploitation—i.e. encouragement of African farming—could work, and he promoted it; yet he was not prepared to risk alienating settlers (Iliffe 1979: 277–8; Rodgers 1974: 97–8).

The Kilimanjaro Native Planters' Association, the first African co-operative, was established before Cameron arrived—and was made possible by Charles Dundas, the first of two Secretaries for Native Affairs who served under Cameron (the second was Philip Mitchell, later Governor of Uganda and Kenya) (Dundas 1955: 123–8). No new co-operatives were accepted during Cameron's six years in Tanganyika. Nor can he be said to have encouraged a rapid promotion of Africans in the administration. In 1923, Philip Mitchell, at that time District Officer in Tanga, decided to run the Tanga government office entirely with

African staff. The most senior African, Martin Kayamba, whose story is told in the next chapter, was by any standards a remarkable man. Yet when asked why no Africans were appointed to the Legislative Council, Cameron replied that there were no Africans in the country with sufficient understanding of English —and when the Permanent Mandates Commission pointed out that Kayamba was more than able to understand English, Cameron replied evasively that this was not the only requirement.[3]

Cameron is often credited with fending off the movement for 'closer union', or federation, with Kenya and Uganda which seemed likely to occur when he arrived in 1925, and which would have allowed Tanganyika to be dominated by the settlers who already controlled the Kenyan state. Yet, as we have seen in Chapter 10, he failed to prevent economic dependence on Kenya, as regards both import duties and railway rates. Since the policy in Tanganyika was not to industrialize, there was no justification for protecting goods produced in Kenya. This was pointed out by the Permanent Mandates Commission, but the British made no effort to change the policy.

A case can therefore be made against Cameron that, while he was well-intentioned, and in some ways politically enlightened, when it came to economics he was uninterested; he put his faith in a utopian political philosophy, and hoped that economics would look after itself. This is a temptation for the economically weak: a not dissimilar criticism has been made of President Nyerere after 1967 (Nellis 1972: 186–96).

It remains to consider the effectiveness of the basic policy of indirect rule, that of ruling through chiefs. The evidence suggests that it was almost totally ineffective. In northern Nigeria and in Buganda there were long-established and powerful chieftainships. In Tanganyika the same degree of centralization had never been achieved. There were, in large areas of the country, many small chiefdoms which, at times, in the past had paid tribute to overlords such as Mirambo or Mkwawa, but also claimed an independence of their own, and had broken free during the German conquest and rinderpest outbreaks of the 1890s. Moreover many chiefs had been killed or banished by the Germans. The search by British administrators for the 'legitimate' chief was often fruitless; or if such a person was found, he might be uneducated and opposed to much of what they were trying to implement; in such cases the British found ways of amalgamating the chieftainships, or they simply deposed the 'legitimate' rulers and replaced them with nominees of their own, preferably young, educated, and easy to influence. In any case the amount of real power held by the chiefs was never great—the expatriate Provincial Commissioners and District Commissioners were always at their side. In short it was a transparent attempt to disguise the reality of foreign rule. It began to break down in the 1930s as soon as the British tried to use the chiefs to enforce unpopular agricultural measures, a process that was completed, as we have seen in Chapter 7, in the 1950s. The chiefs quickly lost the confidence both of their people and of their British masters (Iliffe 1979: 330–4).

The British always recognized that sooner or later they would be threatened by a class of educated Africans. Lord Lugard discussed this in his book *The Dual Mandate in British Tropical Africa*, first published in 1921. He was paternalistic and patronizing about Africans in general:

The virtues and the defects of this race-type are those of attractive children, whose confidence when once it has been won is ungrudgingly given as to an older and wiser superior . . . Perhaps the two traits which have impressed me as those most characteristic of the African native are his lack of apprehension and inability to visualise the future, and the steadfastness of his loyalty and affection. (Lugard, 4th edn. 1929: 70.)

But he also wrote (pp. 80–1) about 'Europeanised Africans'—the educated who he claimed were more cut off from their people than the colonialists:

advancement in self-government must depend on the extent to which the educated class is in sympathy with, and capable of representing, the illiterate sections of the people. In this respect the claim of the African intelligentsia is . . . very weak (p. 84.)

Lugard, despite his blimpish paternalism and racialism, criticized earlier British policy, argued for accelerated promotion of African administrators (p. 88), and even gave qualified praise to the Pan-African Congress of 1919 (p. 83). In contrast, Cameron advocated a deliberate policy of divide and rule: he foresaw a time when 'the educated native' would 'seek to gain possession of the machinery of Government and run it on Western lines', but his answer to this was to aim at 'indirect administration through the appropriate Native Authority—Chief or Council'; in this way he could claim that he was administering the country

'through the people', while at the same time hoping that he
would 'have the Native Administration on our side rather than
on the side of those who desire to destroy them' (i.e. the
educated).[4]

We have seen how this idea of an alliance with the chiefs
failed, at least in Tanganyika's case. But there was another possibility, and this was an alliance with the educated, in some suitable institutional form. In the 1920s and early 1930s there were
British politicians and officials who argued that this could be
achieved through *co-operatives*, which they saw as a logical extension of indirect rule. Lugard himself argued this position, in
the foreword to C.F. Strickland's book *Co-operation for Africa*,
to which we referred in Chapter 8:

The fundamental principle of the [co-operative] system is identical with
that of 'Indirect Rule'—which could be better named 'Cooperative
Rule'—the essential aim of both being to teach personal responsibility
and initiative . . . (Lugard 1933: vii.)

The illiterate and very conservative agricultural majority is apt to regard with some distrust the trousered and Europeanized African as a
townsman ignorant of the things that matter most. But as education
spreads, the influence of the Europeanized native and of the press
which he owns and controls and reads to village audiences tends to increase, and the peasant population becomes 'politically-minded'—a
phase already reached in India, and already becoming visible in Africa.
This changing outlook constitutes in my view one of the major problems of Africa today. The *intelligentsia* have the opportunity in this era
of transition and adaptation to be of inestimable service to their country, or to clog the wheels of progress by causing racial animosities and
preaching doctrines as yet impossible of realisation. Work in connexion
with co-operative societies . . . will, as Mr. Strickland points out, create
new openings for the educated African. By engaging in such work he
will no longer 'deprive the countryside of the mediation which he . . .
might provide between the old dispensation and the new' . . . (pp. viii–
ix.)

Not the least attractive feature of this movement is that perhaps no
other system offers better prospects of producing leaders from among
the people. (pp. x–xi.)

Lugard expected the co-operatives in Africa to avoid politics:

It will go far to disarm misgivings and assure support for the cooperative movement that Mr. Strickland . . . is able to tell us that in no coun-

try whatever—with the exception of Great Britain . . . —has this movement taken part in politics or agitation. Of the many thousands of societies known to him in India only one assumed a political attitude by adopting 'Non-Co-operation', and thereby ceased to exist. (p. x.)

And he also insisted on close government control in the form of a 'Registrar' with the power to 'set up societies and if need be to liquidate any which do not obey the rules'. The Registrar could thus decide the size of societies, and employ a cadre of inspectors and auditors to ensure that the societies were run in the interests of their members (pp. xii–xiii).

It was, however, to be twenty years before the possibilities opened up by this alliance were recognized. For, as we saw in Chapter 8, after 1932 the colonial government refused to treat seriously African co-operatives that were not directly controlled by chiefs or expatriates. It was not till the Victoria Federation of Co-operative Unions was accepted in 1952 that the penny dropped. As more and more co-operatives were registered with colonial approval (and supervision) so the alliance between the educated and the colonial state was legitimized. Without the co-operative movement, with its apparent demonstration that Africans could be successful in business, but in reality almost total control by central government, it would have been much harder to transfer power in 1961.

PART IV: THE NATIONALIST TAKE-OVER

12 THE NATIONALISTS

> The 'African Assocation' has a membership of less
> than 100 ... *Kwetu*, which was started in 1938 ... has
> a circulation of about 1000 copies ... Up to the pre-
> sent, the only central institution of government in
> which Africans are represented is the Advisory
> Council on Native Education ... African interests are
> represented on the Legislative Council by a European
> missionary.
>
> Alien rule must in time have something of the same
> result in unifying African sentiment as Mill held that
> it had possessed in other parts of the world.
>
> Lord Hailey (1942)[1]

The growth of nationalist consciousness was a consequence of
the provision of education; it was also linked with the growth of
towns.[2] In 1914 Dar es Salaam had a population of 20 000; by
1931 this had risen to 24 000 and by 1948 to nearly 70 000, while
by 1958 it was nearly 130 000. Tanga, Tabora, Mwanza, Dodoma, Lindi, and Morogoro, the six biggest towns outside Dar es
Salaam in 1948, had a population of only 70 000 between them,
while all the remaining urban areas (excluding Zanzibar) totalled only another 60 000 (Table 12.1).

TABLE 12.1
Urban Population Growth 1948–1967

	Census figures			Annual Growth Rate (%)	Projections	
	1948	1957/8	1967		1975	1985
Dar es Salaam	69 227	128 742	272 515	7.8	497 000	1 053 400
Tanga	20 619	38 053	60 939	4.8	88 700	141 800
Mwanza	11 296	19 887	34 855	5.8	54 700	96 400
Arusha	5 320	10 038	32 348	12.4	82 300	264 900
Moshi	8 048	13 725	26 969	7.0	46 400	91 400
Morogoro	8 137	14 507	25 263	5.7	39 300	68 400
Dodoma	9 414	13 435	23 569	5.8	37 000	65 000
Iringa	5 702	9 587	21 946	8.6	42 200	96 100
Kigoma/Ujiji	—	16 255	21 369	2.8	26 600	35 100
Tabora	12 768	15 361 .	20 994	3.2	27 000	37 000
Mtwara/Mikindani	—	15 266	20 414	3.0	25 800	34 700
Musoma	2 962	7 207	15 415	7.9	28 200	60 300
Lindi	8 577	10 315	13 351	2.6	16 500	21 200
Mbeya	3 179	6 932	12 469	6.0	19 900	35 600
Bukoba	3 274	5 297	8 186	4.4	11 600	17 800
Others	23 503	39 474	67 182	5.9	103 000	176 200
TOTAL	197 266	364 081	677 784	6.4	1 146 200	2 295 300

Source: Adapted from *A Strategic Grain Reserve for Tanzania* (Marketing Development Bureau, 1974), Vol. II, pp. 45, 46, based on Census data.

In each of these towns could be found a variety of African organizations: tribal societies, dance clubs, football clubs, organizations of traders, and many more. Three types of organization were to prove particularly important in the development of nationalist consciousness: clubs for African civil servants and teachers, from one of which the first political party, TANU, was eventually to be formed; trade unions; and co-operative societies.

The senior African civil servants, educated at Kiungani or Tabora School, regarded themselves as an élite. The most urbane, and the most highly promoted, was Martin Kayamba.[3] He was a member of a remarkable family. His grandfather was a son of Kimweri of the Shambaa who was placed by Kimweri to rule over the Bondei people. In 1877, not long after Kimweri's empire broke up, his son, Kayamba's father, walked into the newly founded Anglican mission at Magila to become one of the first Christian converts in Tanganyika. In 1883, well before the German conquest, the mission sent him for two years to a public school in England. When he returned, he became a teacher at Kiungani, where Martin was born in 1891. Martin's own son, born in 1911, was sent for secondary education to Alliance High School in Nairobi, and became, in 1929, the first Tanganyikan to study at Makerere.

Martin Kayamba was an able student, but he insisted on leaving Kiungani and worked for short periods in a variety of jobs in Kenya, Uganda, and Zanzibar. He returned to German East Africa in 1914, intending to set up as a trader. He was interned by the Germans during the war, but by February 1917 he was court interpreter in Tanga, not long after its liberation from the Germans. When in 1923 Philip Mitchell, District Officer in Tanga, decided to run his office entirely with African staff, Kayamba was given the senior post. In 1929 he was appointed to the only government committee on which Africans were represented, the Advisory Committee on Native Education, where he argued for more education for Africans, especially more secondary education, for greater use of English, and for girls' education. He saw no reason why the secondary schools in Tanganyika should not be improved so that they could send students direct to Makerere College. In 1931 he was selected— again by Philip Mitchell, then Secretary for Native Affairs in Dar es Salaam—to travel to London with two other Tanganyikans to present the African view to a Parliamentary Committee which was considering the question of closer union in East Africa; there he argued for an 'African Council' involving representatives of the educated and the chiefs, which would give Africans 'a channel for airing the view of every section of the community'. The following year he was promoted to become Philip Mitchell's assistant in Dar es Salaam, and in this capacity he travelled all over the country, talking to the educated and the chiefs, and trying to interpret their aspirations to the colonial government.

Kayamba's personal position was made clear in a short book which he wrote in 1938.[4] He was against industrialization, against the emergence of large African-owned land holdings, and argued for a return to 'a life of peaceful and contented peasants, living in their own world', which could be achieved if they lived in planned villages. The comparison with Julius Nyerere's thought a generation later is instructive: Kayamba was the most distinguished product of Kiungani School, Nyerere the product of a similar education at Tabora; both men had visions for the future of their people which in certain respects were remarkably alike.

In 1922 Kayamba was a founder member and first president of the Tanganyika Territory African Civil Service Association, a club formed to unite Christian and Muslim civil servants in Tanga and to help them improve themselves. A branch was soon formed in Dar es Salaam, and it was members of this branch who in 1929 were encouraged by Governor Cameron to found the African Association, which was open to all Africans. Twenty-five years later, in 1954, Nyerere and his friends used this organization to create the political party TANU.

From 1936 onwards, the African Association had a rival: the African Welfare and Commercial Association.[5] This was originally founded as a welfare society for African traders without tribal links in Dar es Salaam. In 1936 it widened its membership, and also its purpose, as its proposed by-laws (quoted by Iliffe 1969a: 148) made clear:

Since the Africans are not represented in the Legislative Council, this Association, as the central body, looking after the welfare of all Africans in Tanganyika Territory, would always watch carefully any laws proposed by the Government which may affect Africans, and after proper consideration, would make such representations to Government, and Members of Legislative Council, as the Association consider proper in the interests of Africans . . . Every African is bound to obey the Association, whether he is contributing or not, just as he obeys the Government.

There were by this time many tribal societies in Dar es Salaam, whose members visited their compatriots in hospital, collected small subscriptions to support their families, and, if one of them died, arranged his or her funeral. But this society, beginning as a welfare society for those with no tribal links, was turning itself into a national political organization. Its founder was Erika Fiah, a Ugandan shopkeeper who came to Dar es Salaam during the First World War. He read the works of British and American socialists and in 1937 started the newspaper *Kwetu* (the homeland) which campaigned not only for more educational facilities for Africans and for political power, but also against the élitism of the African Association and of individuals like Kayamba. From 1939 Fiah spent most of his time with the Dar es Salaam dockers and neglected the Welfare Association, which did not survive for long without him. The African Association was less dependent on one man, and, though it stagnated during the war years, it was revived later, as we shall see in the next chapter. But Fiah's work with the dockers was almost as significant, for out of it grew the trade-union movement.

For many years the docks had been the biggest employers of labour in Dar es Salaam and Tanga. Conditions of work were poor, so it is not surprising that the docks were the first places where the working class became conscious of its power. In 1937 there was a dock strike in Tanga and forty dockers formed a trade union. The first large-scale strike on the docks in Dar es Salaam, in 1939, was a strike by the casual workers who wanted not only more money but also some of the fringe benefits enjoyed by the permanent workers, and it failed because the companies were in a position to recruit a new unskilled labour force. In 1941 the companies that ran the lighterage and unloading in the port (which were mainly subsidiaries of international shipping lines) negotiated a cost-plus contract with the government, under which wage increases would automatically be passed on in higher prices. In 1943, during the war, when inflation had caused a rise in prices and wages had fallen behind, there was another strike. Eight hundred men were involved, and this time the permanent, and more skilled, workers joined in, making it much harder for the companies to break the strike by recruiting a new labour force. The government therefore invoked the defence regulations, 142 men were arrested, and the strike was

TABLE 12.2

Cost of living and wage indices: Dar es Salaam 1939–1955
(1 September 1939 = 100)

Date	Cost of living index	Dock daily rate, casual labour	Estimated dock take-home pay, casual labour
1 Sept. 1939	100	100	100
Feb.–Apr. 1940			154
June 1940		120	
Sept. 1942	122		
Jan. 1944	167		
Jan. 1946	184		
Mar. 1947	187	153	
Sept. 1948	247	260	
Oct. 1950	299	260	
Dec. 1951	351	273	
Dec. 1953	418	303	
Dec. 1954	400	367	554
Dec. 1955	393	467	940

Source: Iliffe (1970: 123), based on a variety of government documents, including Annual Reports of the Labour Department 1942–55.

broken after twelve days. A tribunal was set up during the strike, and, as a result of its report, the wages of the skilled workers were raised; even so, the unskilled labour force was still probably worse off than it had been in 1939. Despte a promise that no one would be victimized, five workers were dismissed, including three who had given evidence to the tribunal.[6]

By 1947 prices had risen even higher (Table 12.2), and shortages of goods made living conditions in Dar es Salaam very difficult. In September, after fruitless negotiations, the dockers struck again, and the strike quickly spread to other groups of workers. On the third day railway workers joined, and started spreading the strike up-country. On the fourth day there were pickets all over Dar es Salaam, and by the sixth even the African teachers in two secondary schools had joined. In Dar es Salaam the strike ended on the twelfth day, when a tribunal under G.W. Hatchell was appointed. The tribunal was influenced by the degree of discontent revealed by the strike, and recommended wage increases of 40–50 per cent, which made the dockers better off than they had been in 1939, and a gradual end to the use of casual labour in the docks. The government and private employers soon brought their wages into line. Upcountry the strike continued for a month, involving workers at the Mpanda lead mine, the Uvinza salt-works, and various small firms in and around Mwanza.

As Iliffe (1970: 134) observed:

The 1947 award made the dockers a privileged group among Tanzanian workers, the best paid, most formidable, labour force in the country. It was won by the first real exercise of African power since the end of Maji Maji—an exhilarating and enlightening experience, no doubt, for those who participated. But the award had to be implemented. Hatchell himself had recognised this by insisting that 'the workmen shall appoint accredited representatives of each category of workmen who shall be allowed to represent the workmen and to discuss with the employers any matter arising out of the employment'. Thus encouraged, and with the experience of victimisation in 1943 to guide them, the dockers now formed their first permanent organisation. Action had created consciousness; now consciousness was institutionalised in a trade union.

The Dockworkers and Stevedores Union was formed in October 1947 without assistance from the government. But the government soon seconded an officer 'to render all assistance to the union', with the idea, if possible, of securing a moderate leadership. An agreement covering terms of service, which included a phased decasualization of the labour force, was signed in November 1948. But when in 1950 this agreement was used by the employers to sack workers, there was another strike. The employers immediately brought in blackleg labour, and the result was the greatest outbreak of violence before independence: a European and an Asian policeman were critically injured and two Africans killed. The Union was dissolved by High Court order, its assets were confiscated, and almost all the permanent workers left or were sacked, so that eleven years' experience of working-class organization was lost.

This was to have important consequences for the character of the trade union movement. Five years later national unions of unskilled workers were still not encouraged, although the government was prepared to register small local craft associations. Tom Mboya, the American-influenced Kenyan unionist, visited Tanganyika in 1955, and argued that 'responsible' educated union officials should establish trade unions from the top downwards. The government and the employers accepted this because they realized that it was in their interest to create a well-paid, permanent (i.e. non-migrant) labour force (Sabot 1979: 208 – 9, 224 – 8).[7] In the month after Mboya's visit, the government accepted the registration of the Tanganyika Federation of Labour (TFL), a body to co-ordinate all other unions. The positions of leadership were taken by officials of the African Commercial Employees Association, the Tanganyika African Government Servants' Association, and the Tanganyika Railway African Union, all unions with a high proportion of clerical staff among their members. Leadership was no longer in the hands of unskilled or semi-skilled workers, such as the dockers. The new union leaders—Kawawa, Kamaliza, Mpangala, and later Tandau—had been to secondary schools, but they had not worked in factories or on the land.[8]

The trade unions were not supposed to be involved in politics. Nyerere and Rashidi Kawawa, the first General Secretary of the TFL, later to be Prime Minister, were friends; but there could be no open co-operation between TFL and TANU, at least up to 1957. Similarly, the co-operatives were supposed to be for marketing, and any which were thought to be dabbling in politics ran the risk of having their registration cancelled by the Registrar of Co-operative Societies. Just as the co-operatives were watched over by officials from the Co-operative Development Division, so the unions were watched over by Labour

Officers from the Department of Labour.

Clearly neither the co-operatives nor the unions were productive, in the sense of adding to the production of goods and services. They were essentially parasitic, depending on the government to fix agricultural prices which gave them sufficient margin, or to underwrite wage agreements reached with the employers.[9] Their leaders were 'petty bourgeois'—not peasants, not manual workers, and too dependent on the state to be described as a capitalist bourgeoisie. We shall see in the next chapter how they played a decisive role in the independence campaign—the unions by organizing strikes and boycotts in the towns and on sisal plantations, the co-operatives by promoting the expansion of African cash-cropping in the rural areas and by seeming to demonstrate African ability in business. The nationalist politicians (whose roots were in the co-operatives, the unions, among the civil servants and clerks of the African Association, or who joined the Party as paid officials on leaving school) were ambitious but their instinct was not to invest to expand their capital and control of markets; they were more likely to think first of more expenditure on consumer goods or social services. Moreover, co-operatives and the unions had expanded with the patronage of the state, and when faced with problems they instinctively turned to the state for help—in the form of controlled cost-plus pricing, guaranteed markets, subsidized credit, and—eventually—state ownership. The character of the parastatal sector which was to dominate post-Arusha Tanzania owes much to the fact that those who took control of the state in 1961 were not capitalists.

13 THE INDEPENDENCE 'STRUGGLE'

> The Tanganyika African National Union was born in July 1954, and modern political development in Tanganyika really begins from that date. But it would be absurd to imagine that this organization, which gathered strength so quickly and so quickly achieved its preliminary goal of independence, sprang out of thin air. Nor is its triumph attributable to any special abilities or virtues of the people of this part of Africa. The fact is that historical circumstances favoured Tanganyika . . .
>
> NYERERE (1966)[1]

This chapter is concerned with Tanganyika's achievement of independence. Today even Nyerere realizes how limited that independence was, and talks about 'flag independence', implying that real independence is something connected with economic development, and still to be fought for.

At the time, however, it seemed a glorious struggle for an outcome that was far from certain (Pratt 1976: Chapter 2). When TANU was founded in 1954, no one foresaw that within five years the British would agree to go. Many, including Edward Twining, Governor for the ten years from 1949 to 1958, would have liked to stay longer, and did all they could to obstruct the nationalists. But it was a struggle that they had no chance of winning. Internally everything was in TANU's favour: the growing group of educated Tanganyikans realized that the colonial state was holding them back; and the co-operative movement, the trade unions, societies such as the African Association and TANU itself, gave those educated Tanganyikans the opportunity to organize an effective political campaign. The power at their disposal was shown positively in the ability of the co-operative movement to market rapidly increasingly volumes of African-produced crops, and negatively in the way the trade

unions could bring important parts of the economy to a standstill. As Nyerere pointed out, history had been kind in other
ways: there were no strong vested interests who might have
more to gain from an alliance with the colonists than from independence; tribal groupings were such that no particular tribe
could expect special favours; and Swahili provided a national
language understood by almost all the men in the country.

Externally also there was much in TANU's favour. Influential
British civil servants had realized that retention of colonies was
not an economic proposition. The pro-nationalist 'Africa Group'
in the Colonial Office in London was influenced by Lord
Hailey. Hailey had spent most of his life in India, but in 1939,
at the request of the wartime government, he was asked to visit
Britain's African colonies to recommend political changes that
would be needed during or immediately after the war. Hailey
realized that many of the raw materials produced in colonies
were no longer strategic; indeed, the one raw material that was
strategic in the post-war world, oil, had largely to be imported
from countries which were not colonies. Administration and
economic development were expensive. From 1943 onwards,
Hailey was prepared to speculate publicly about the forthcoming
independence of Britain's African Colonies (Hailey 1943: 27–
34, 62–3 and 1952: 181–3).

He also compared colonies with depressed areas of advanced
countries, for which Keynes had shown that government investment was needed to bring about growth. He argued in favour of
production in traditional African agricultural systems, against individual land tenure, and for African representation on 'all
schemes which impose restrictions on African producers'. He
recognized the weakness of Cameron's style of indirect rule,
based on chiefs, and pointed out that this method of administration left no place for 'the middle classes'—the traders, employees of trading firms, farmers employing labour, money-
lenders, lawyers, schoolteachers, editors, doctors, chemists, lorry and bus operators, and shopkeepers. Finally, Hailey realized
that strong and persistent nationalist movements were inevitable, and that in order to secure the co-operation of these 'middle classes', the British would need to develop local institutions,
and to recruit Africans into the upper levels of the civil service
(Hailey 1942: 9–13, 62).

After the war these arguments were supported by administrators such as Andrew Cohen (shortly to become Governor of
Uganda), politicians such as Fenner Brockway and Iain Macleod,

Oxford academics such as Marjorie Perham and Thomas Hodg-
kin, and periodicals such as *African Affairs* and the *Journal of
Administration Overseas*. Their position was strengthened by
Mau Mau in Kenya between 1952 and 1956, which showed how
expensive it was to hold down a nationalist movement by force.

They were also supported by the United Nations Trusteeship
Committee. The Permanent Mandates Commission had been an
ineffective body, easily satisfied with the British government's
justifications for its actions. But both the Soviet and the American delegates on its post-war successor, the Trusteeship Committee, wanted independence quickly. The reports of the visiting
missions which came to Tanganyika every three years from 1948
onwards were therefore widely publicized political documents,
which the British had to take seriously.[2] They called for greater
educational provision for Africans, constitutional changes to
bring Africans into the administration, protection of African
rights to land, and they were quick to condemn economic or social policies which they felt were not in the interests of Africans.
The Trusteeship Committee itself sat semi-permanently in New
York, and so provided an international forum for nationalist
views. In 1952 Kirilo Japhet and Earle Seaton used it to raise
the Meru Land Case.[3] In 1955 Julius Nyerere gained an international hearing for TANU's claim for independence.

In the years after the war, Twining played into the hands of
the nationalists by attempting to implement a number of inflammatory and racialist policies. First and foremost, he encouraged another wave of white settlement. As long as the settlers
were given land previously farmed by Germans, or taken from
the edges of forest reserves around Mount Kilimanjaro, there
was little that Africans could do. But in 1951 the government
moved Africans from their land at Nanyuki, between Mounts
Kilimanjaro and Meru, to make way for expatriate diary farmers. The Meru Citizens' Union was quickly formed to fight the
evictions, and it managed to lobby the 1951 visiting mission of
the Trusteeship Committee before the evictions had actually
taken place. In 1952 Kirilo Japhet and Earle Seaton, representing the Meru Citizens' Union, but with money for their air tick-
ets raised by a tour of the country under the auspices of the
African Association, addressed the Trusteeship Council in New
York. A few months later, the case was taken to the Security
Council. The British changed their policy: there were no more
evictions, and from then until independence they were so sensitive over all questions of land that they frequently could not

even get the land to implement their own government projects.[4]

Secondly, Twining played into nationalist hands with his agricultural policies, the 'land development and soil conservation' schemes described earlier. Not only were the rules and regulations themselves unpopular, but the nationalists were able to claim, with justice, that they were applied to African holdings but not to European settlers farming similar land. By 1957 the rules were unenforceable, and the schemes abandoned. The longest-lasting effect had been to discredit the chiefs as stooges of the British, since they had supported and tried to enforce the rules, and so leave the path open for TANU. In 1955 Nyerere, the Party Secretary, Oscar Kambona, and Joan Wicken (an expatriate who was raising money for the Party training centre, Kivukoni College) started touring the rural areas and immediately received an overwhelming response.

Thirdly, Twining upset educated Africans by various aspects of his economic policy. The 'Ten-Year Development Plan' for the years 1947–56 was based on documents prepared during the war, and its total planned expenditure of £19 million was far more than the British had ever before spent on the colony, though still small beside the £35 million spent on the Groundnuts Scheme during just four years of that period. But no Africans, of any description, had been consulted in the preparation of the Plan. When they saw it, they were unhappy with the section on education which put the emphasis in African education on primary and middle schools and on agricultural education, while expanding secondary education for Europeans and Asians. This was confirmed in practice: the full quota of places at Makerere College was not taken up, while from 1949 onwards bureaucratic hurdles were created to prevent Africans joining the administrative grades of the civil service (Listowel 1965: 131–3; Pratt 1976: 18).

Finally, and perhaps most important of all, Twining gave himself away with a series of constitutional changes put forward in response to pressure from the UN and the Colonial Office. In 1951 a 'Committee on Constitutional Development' proposed a Legislative Council with forty-three members: the Governor himself, twenty-one members appointed by the Governor, and another twenty-one made up of seven representatives of each of the three racial groups. There were more than a hundred times as many Africans as Asians, and more than 400 Africans for every European; yet Europeans, Asians, and Africans were to be given equal representation, and the Governor and his nominees would have had an over-all majority (Pratt 1976: 29–34).

This proposal was clearly far removed from the Trusteeship Agreement's commitment to develop the country 'towards self-government or independence', or to 'develop the participation of the inhabitants of Tanganyika in advisory and legislative bodies and in the government of the Territory, both central and local, as may be appropriate to the peculiar circumstances of the Territory and its people'. It looked suspiciously like the multiracial arrangements that Britain had instituted elsewhere, and which in the Central African Federation gave political control to the white minority. The suspicion was confirmed in 1955 when Twining suggested replacing the Native Authority Councils by District Councils. The District Councils would be African, but they would report to multiracial 'Provincial Councils'; it was a completely new innovation to introduce European and Asian representation into local government, which, as part of indirect rule, had been entirely African. So when, from 1957 onwards, Twining tried to implement this policy, Africans correctly saw it as an attempt to preserve white rule. Cranford Pratt (1976: 31–5) suggests that this, more than anything else in the last years of colonial rule, persuaded Africans to support TANU.

In 1939 the African Association was in poor shape, especially in Dar es Salaam, not least because the government insisted on transferring members who spoke out to jobs up-country. It was revived by its Zanzibar and Dodoma branches, which in 1939 and 1940 arranged 'interterritorial conferences'. The 1940 conference took an explicitly nationalist line, resolving 'that His Majesty's Government should consider the possibility of forming Provincial and Inter-Provincial Boards, where Africans could represent their own country. In a word, we are now claiming for a voice in the Government...'[5] In 1945, echoing resolutions of the Manchester Pan-African Congress of that year, it set out to build a mass political organization with branches in every district and town.

After the war, the Dar es Salaam branch received recruits from two important sources. One was Makerere University College, where the students, whose natural leader was Julius Nyerere, had themselves formed a branch in 1944. The other was the army: soldiers who had fought with the King's African Rifles during the Second World War campaigns in Somalia, Madagascar, Burma, and Thailand returned to Dar es Salaam. On their travels they had seen India on the brink of independence, and met Africans from West Africa where political move-ments were much more advanced (Listowel 1965: 121, 186–92). In 1950 these younger groups of nationalists took over the lead-ership and presented a memorandum to the Constitutional Com-mittee set up by Governor Twining in which they pressed for one man one vote. During the following year the Meru were evicted, and in 1952 the Association[6] was involved in raising the money to send Japhet and Seaton to the Trusteeship Council. In April 1953 Nyerere was elected President, and almost at once prepared to turn the Association into a political party. Almost simultaneously, Twining started making life difficult: he passed an order forbidding civil servants to join it, and in 1954 he pass-ed a 'Societies Ordinance' which required every public organ-ization to be registered and to supply a registrar with a list of members and a copy of its constitution. On 7 July 1954 the Association turned itself into TANU, the Tanganyika African National Union, the first political party in Tanganyika. Three months later, after redrafting its constitution, it was accepted by the Registrar of Societies (Pratt 1976: 36–7).

It was already clear that TANU's leader was an exceptional man.[7] Nyerere was born in 1922 in a village in Mara Region, east of Lake Victoria. He was a younger son of a chief whose rule at the time covered no more than 5000 people. He did not go to school until he was twelve years old (in 1934), but then within three years he won a place at Tabora School, where he distinguished himself in debating. From Tabora he went to Mak-erere College in 1943, to read for a teaching diploma. Twice he won first prize in the East African Literary Competition, the second time for an essay which applied John Stuart Mill's ideas on the subjection of women to tribal society (Edgett-Smith 1973: 46). On leaving Makerere he refused a chance to work in a government school, and instead took a teaching job in a Ro-man Catholic secondary school in Tabora. He became secretary of the local branch of the African Association, and his presence in Tabora during the years 1945 to 1949 meant that he knew most of those who passed through Tabora School during that period, a group which included many who were later to become cabinet ministers or top civil servants. In 1949 the Roman Catholic mission arranged a scholarship to Britain; Nyerere was clear in his own mind that he would follow a political career as soon as he came home, and wanted the broadest possible educa-tion; he was fortunate in being allowed to study history, econom-ics, and philosophy at Edinburgh University. In Britain he came into contact with Fabian socialists, and wrote an essay on the race problem in East Africa, intended for publication as a Fabian pamphlet (Listowel 1965: 199–208). He returned to Tanganyika in 1952 and took a job in another Roman Catholic school, this time twelve miles outside Dar es Salaam. Since he was not a civil servant, he was free to be involved in political activity. He was still a teacher in 1954, when TANU was formed, but in 1955 he resigned his teaching job in order to concentrate full-time on political work.

Twining continued to be obstructive: for three years between 1955 and 1958 TANU was a prohibited organization in the Lake Province, and it was also banned for a period in Tanga Region. In 1955 he passed an Incitement to Violence Act, which included a clause making it difficult to speak publicly in favour of an African state; and the same year an amendment to the penal code made it an offence 'to print, publish or . . . make any statement likely to raise discontent amongst any of the inhabitants of the Territory'. This clause could be used to outlaw any form of political activity (Pratt 1976: 37).

Twining also promoted a rival political party, the United Tanganyika Party, which was formed around a number of chiefs sympathetic to the British, and white settlers (Iliffe 1979: 521–2). It was, in fact, the UTP which first proposed general elections based on a common roll composed of everyone in the country who could claim an income of 3000 shillings per annum or education at secondary level. Each voter would then vote for three candidates, one of each race, and the UTP expected to gain control by winning the Asian and European seats. An election was held on this basis in September 1958, with only 60 000 eligible voters in the whole country. But between 1954 and 1957 TANU grew rapidly, from 15 000 members (mostly transferred from the African Association in 1954) to more than 200 000 at the end of 1957, and before the 1958 election Nyerere managed to persuade his executive committee that TANU was strong enough to win if African voters supported sympathetic European and Asian candidates as well as African candidates. He was proved triumphantly right when TANU-supported candidates won all but one of the seats that were contested (Listowel 1965: 303–11; Pratt 1976: 41–2).

At the same time as the Party was growing, so were the co-operatives and the trade unions. In 1952 there were 188 co-operative societies with 153 000 members; by 1957 these figures had already risen to 474 and 305 000 respectively. By 1959 there were 617 societies, and the co-operatives were effectively marketing all the cotton produced in the country, the coffee produced by African farmers, much of the paddy and cashew-nuts, and were beginning to make inroads into the marketing of maize and oil-seeds. Their membership had risen to 325 000 out of a population of approximately two million farm families, which, although still only a minority, included most of the prosperous kulak farmers who were rapidly increasing their production of export crops in the 1950s.[8]

The story of the growth of the trade unions in the last half of the 1950s is the more dramatic because it brought them into a series of confrontations with the government which almost certainly had much to do with the decision of the British to depart gracefully. As we saw in the previous chapter, the Tanganyika Federation of Labour was formed in July 1955, after the three-day visit by Tom Mboya. Its General Secretary until he became a cabinet minister in 1960 was Rashidi Kawawa. Kawawa was born in 1930. His father was a game scout. He passed the examination to go to Tabora School, but refused to go on to Makerere because he wished to support the education of the rest of his family, and instead became a clerk in the government. He joined the Tanganyika African Government Servants' Association, and was quickly elected to the executive committee; in 1952 he became Assistant General Secretary, and in 1954 President. But meanwhile he had changed his civil service job, and become a social worker. He had also taken a leading acting part in three government propaganda films, and been placed in charge of the welfare of the Kikuyu interned in two government camps during the Mau Mau.[9]

The TFL's objective was strong national unions, with educated leaders, created from on top. Three such unions were registered in 1955, and three more in 1956.[10] In December 1956 the Local Government Workers Union organized a strike to coincide with a visit of Princess Margaret to the capital. About 10 000 other workers downed tools in sympathy, and there would have been a general strike had it not been for the intervention of two British trade-unionists who happened to be in Dar es Salaam at the time. The result was the first legally backed minimum wage in Dar es Salaam.

In 1957 six more national unions were registered, and Kawawa started organizing on the sisal plantations; a national union of plantation workers was registered in 1958. But meanwhile there was a bus strike in Dar es Salaam in 1957: Asians and

Europeans drove the buses, which ran virtually empty, since TANU had organized a boycott by the bus users. The result was another victory for the strikers. In 1958 there was a strike at the breweries. Again European and Asian employees ran the factory, while TANU organized a boycott of beer. Kawawa was arrested and tried for intimidating two strike-breakers, and Nyerere attended the trial. The TFL and TANU were openly working together, presenting the government with the prospect of never-ending non-violent resistance in the towns (Tordoff 1967: 137–41). Since in the rural areas the peasants had broken down the terraces they had been forced to build, and refused to dip or destock their cattle, it was clear that the government's legitimacy was threatened. When the General Election of September 1958, fought on the UTP's system, produced fifteen TANU-supported candidates from fifteen seats, there was really nothing the British could do but leave. But by this time Governor Edward Twining had given up; it was left for his successor, Richard Turnbull, to announce in October 1958 that Tanganyika would develop as an African state. Thirty-eight months later it was independent.

14 THE PEACEFUL TRANSITION

> The British gave up the idea that they could retain final authority for another decade in Tanganyika. They hoped that by that decision they would be able more effectively to secure a continuation of the economic policies initiated by the colonial government, a British predominance in the civil service for a long transitional period and, more generally, a continuing close association with Britain.
>
> R. Cranford Pratt (1976)[1]

By October 1958 the British recognized the strength of the nationalist movement, and it was only a matter of time before they handed over power. But at the end of 1958 neither they nor the nationalists thought that independence would come within three years.

Nyerere realized that to achieve independence quickly, his best strategy was to collaborate with the British, especially when they provided a governor as flexible as Turnbull. The British, for their part, sought to avoid inflammatory policies. They promoted the idea of elected African local government; they permitted the formation of national trade unions with moderate leaderships, which could negotiate wage agreements between workers and employers and then ensure that their members honoured them; and above all they encouraged the co-operative movement, as a means of involving progressive farmers and ambitious educated Tanganyikans in a form of administration, just as Lugard had argued was possible twenty years before.[2] This support of the co-operatives complemented their agricultural policy: for the rules and regulations were abandoned, and the policy was to encourage 'progressive farmers' to take loans, to hire labour, and to use modern methods to produce crops for sale. The success of these co-operatives made it possible for Turnbull to argue that the people were ready for independence.

But exactly when this would be was unclear till the last minute. In March 1959 Turnbull appointed five ministers from amongst the members of parliament who had been elected. Originally, he proposed three only, a European, an Asian, and an African. Nyerere insisted on an African majority, and eventually Chief Fundikira, George Kahama, Solomon Eliufoo, Amir Jamal, and Derek Bryceson were appointed. Fundikira was the chief of a large tribe, the Nyamwezi, who had been trained in agriculture at Makerere and Cambridge, the first chief to commit himself to TANU in 1957. Kahama was the head of the Bukoba Co-operative Union, and had served on the Legislative Council since 1957. Eliufoo was a secondary school teacher, soon to be elected leader of the Chagga. Jamal was one of the first Asian business men to support the nationalists, while Bryceson was a white settler who had come to Tanganyika as late as 1951, but who had been nominated to the Legislative Council in 1956, from where he had supported nationalist positions. On the other hand, Kawawa, the leading trade-unionist, was not included, nor was Oscar Kambona, the Secretary-General and fund-raiser for the Party, or Edward Barongo and Saidi Maswanya, both former policemen, or indeed any of the more 'populist' wing of professional politicians.

It was not until December 1959 that Turnbull conceded that a majority of ministers should be elected Members of Parliament, which meant that the British had decided to leave as quickly as they could. A general election was held in August 1960, in which TANU won seventy out of the seventy-one seats. Nyerere was appointed Chief Minister and, acting on his advice, the Governor then appointed nine elected members as ministers: this time Kambona and Kawawa were included, as well as Paul Bomani, the founder of the Victoria Federation of Co-operative Unions, and Nsilo Swai, another schoolteacher. But he also reappointed Sir Ernest Vasey as Minister for Finance. Vasey had come to Tanganyika in February, from Kenya where he had also been Minister of Finance. He stayed till January 1962, and in that period he and C.M. Meek, Nyerere's Principal Secretary, exercised considerable influence over economic policy.

As soon as Nyerere took office, he made it clear that independence by the end of 1961 was his aim. There were no problems. The final round of talks was held in Dar es Salaam in March 1961, after which it was announced that Tanganyika would have internal self-government in May and independence in December. The British Colonial Secretary was Iain Macleod, who was extremely flexible; following Macmillan's 'wind of change' speech in February 1960, the British had decided to give independence to their colonies as quickly as they could, and Tanganyika was to be the test case, the first in which the steps to independence that had been followed in India or Ghana were speeded up.

The British did what they could, however, to ensure the continuation of their policies. In 1959 there were only seven Tanganyikans out of 299 administrative officers in the civil service. If, as the independence agreement implied, the existing institutions were to be maintained, the country would be dependent on manpower from overseas for many years to come; thus special provisions were made to persuade serving British civil servants to stay on after independence, and gradually hand over to Tanzanians.

The country also lacked financial resources, and would continue to be highly dependent on foreign capital if it was to implement an ambitious investment programme. The British tried to minimize their initial commitment; in July 1961 they offered only £10 million as an 'independence settlement', of which £3 million was earmarked for paying the pensions of retired British officials. Nyerere—and Vasey—had expected at least twice as much. The British increased their offer somewhat, but Tanganyika was still left in the position of having to beg if it was to finance its development plans.

Finally, the departing British left behind a series of reports on virtually every aspect of the economy, which were to continue to influence policy years after they left. The best-known, and the most influential, was *The Economic Development of Tanganyika*, produced by a World Bank team in 1960 and published in 1961.[3] Much of this report was devoted to agricultural policy, where it distinguished between the 'improvement approach' and the 'transformation approach'. The improvement approach described the agricultural policies of the late 1950s—agricultural extension and co-operatives, focused particularly on the richer, more progressive, labour-employing farmers. The report implied that this was good for the time being, but not for ever, and not if Tanganyika really expected to develop her agriculture quickly. The team therefore recommended the transformation approach, which meant the use of machinery and irrigation, large capital expenditure, a total transformation of traditional agricultural systems rather than their improvement.[5]

There was also a report on industrial development financed by the United States Agency for International Development. This was carried out by Arthur D. Little consultants, and also published in 1961.[4] After a review of Tanganyika's raw material resources, it concluded that there was considerable scope for agricultural processing for export, and some scope for import substitution, provided that suitable incentives for foreign firms (protection against competition, tax holidays, government money, and even subsidies and guarantees against nationalization) could be provided. This and the World Bank report formed the foundation of the Three Year Development Plan, 1961–4, prepared by Vasey and largely consisting of a 'shopping list of projects' for which it was hoped that foreign capital would be forthcoming.[6]

In 1962 *A Survey of Wholesale and Retail Trade in Tanganyika* by the Economist Intelligence Unit was published.[7] Its analysis demonstrated the dominant role of non-African traders (i.e. Asians and Arabs), but it advised the government to think carefully before intervening. For, as the report more than once pointed out, 'Tanganyika has a low-cost distribution system'. At the time the co-operative movement was contemplating a much greater involvement in the wholesale and retail trade: to them the message was a clear 'keep out'.

There were a number of reports on the civil service. Probably the most influential, produced by a team headed by the Ghanaian civil servant A.L. Adu, defined the terms of employment in the civil service and, while making clear that African civil servants could not expect to enjoy all the privileges enjoyed by Europeans, recommended civil service salary scales comparable with those in other ex-colonial countries. In addition two reports financed by the Ford Foundation argued for a rapid Africanization of the civil service, with crash training programmes, and accelerated promotions for Africans.[8]

This reports, and that of the 1961 Raisman Commission, which proposed a continuation of the East African Common Market and the East African common services (railways, airline, tax collection, etc.),[9] defined in outline most of the policies that were to be followed from 1960 to 1966. They were orthodox policies, based on the assumption that continuity would be maintained and the country run by the civil service rather than TANU (Pratt 1976: 90–8, 103f.). British judges, civil servants, and schoolteachers were persuaded to stay, as well as engineers, agriculturalists, doctors and technical 'experts' of every kind. Industrialization would be undertaken mainly by foreign private companies, responding to suitable incentives. There was little thought about socialism, beyond a general commitment which was brought into the Party constitution when it was revised shortly after independence in 1961. As far as the British were concerned, between 1960 and 1964 Tanganyika was a model state, with an enlightened leader, pursuing non-racial but essentially orthodox economic policies.

15 ZANZIBAR

> When assuming direction of state affairs in the 1890s,
> the British, understandably, regarded Zanzibar as an
> Arab state, directed by an Arab dynasty ruling over
> Arab, African and Indian inhabitants. . . . They per-
> sisted in perceiving Zanzibar as divided into perma-
> nent ethnic divisions.
>
> BENNETT (1978: 267–8)

Zanzibar and Pemba up to the end of Zanzibar's 'commercial
empire' in 1890 formed the subject of Chapter 4. The present
chapter deals with the seventy-three years in which the islands
were ruled by the British, until they left rather abruptly at the
end of 1963, and concludes with a discussion of the revolution
of January 1964 which preceded the union with the mainland.

The British regarded Zanzibar as a tiny Arab sultanate,
suitable for the growing of cloves, but for little else. They were
not particularly interested in continuing the commercial activities of the nineteenth century, which inevitably declined in importance once the natural harbours were developed on the
mainland at Mombasa and Dar es Salaam. British influence over
the Arab sultans gradually increased, and in 1890 the Germans
recognized Zanzibar as a British protectorate; in 1891 the British took over tax collection and began to appoint their own
administrators, and in 1896 they used their navy to ensure that a
pro-British candidate became Sultan. The Sultans were the leaders of a small group of no more than a hundred Arab families
who dominated the production of cloves, especially on Zanzibar
where most the land suitable for clove production on the western side of the island was owned by them. On Pemba clove
trees were owned by Africans as well as Arabs; indeed, seventy
years earlier the African leaders on Pemba had requested the
Arabs to rid them of their rulers, at that time the Masrui from
Mombasa; and when, a few years later, cloves were planted,

Africans as well as Arabs secured suitable land, although the former often had to contribute labour to the latter in order to be allowed to farm (Clayton 1976: 12).

Nominally the British ruled at the request of the Sultans, but in practice their administration differed little from that in other colonies. British colonial civil servants, who reported to the British Resident, took most of the important decisions, and controlled the finances, the judiciary and the police force, while British missionaries ran schools.[1]

There were other Arabs on the islands, who were not outstandingly wealthy, and did not own land or grow cloves. Many of them arrived during the colonial period and set up small shops in remote parts, and soon dominated the retail trade in imported items such as textiles. The over-all racial balance in 1948 is seen in Table 15.1.

TABLE 15.1
Zanzibar: population by race 1948

Race	Zanzibar Island		Pemba Island		Total	
	No.	per cent	No.	per cent	No.	per cent
African	118 652	79.3	81 208	70.9	199 860	75.7
Arab	13 977	9.3	30 583	26.7	44 560	16.9
Asian	13 107	8.8	2 104	1.8	15 211	5.8
Comorian	2 764	1.8	503	0.4	3 267	1.1
Goan	598	0.4	83	—	681	0.3
European	256	0.2	40	—	296	0.1
Other	221	0.2	66	—	287	0.1
Total	149 575	100.0	114 587	100.0	264 162	100.0

Source: Zanzibar Protectorate *Notes on the Census of the Zanzibar Protectorate, 1948* (Zanzibar: Government Printing Press, 1953), p. 2 (from Lofchie 1965: 71).

There was also a wealthy Asian community, concentrated in Zanzibar town. Although many of the more far-sighted Asian merchants moved their headquarters to the mainland, others stayed. They had good reason to do so: much of their wealth was tied up in buildings in Zanzibar town, and they had lent heavily to Arab plantation owners and so gradually they too came to own clove plantations. In the 1930s it was a major concern of British colonial policy to prevent the Arab plantation owners losing control of their land to the Asians to whom they had become indebted (Lofchie 1965: 104–26).

The Asian community also invested in schools, and was thus in a position to supply middle-level manpower—clerks, and various kinds of technical labour—to the colonial government. Special opportunities for advancement in the civil service were given to the children of the rich Arab families, so that when the British began to withdraw in the 1950s, posts in the civil service were largely filled by Arabs and Asians.

The African population was excluded from economic and political power. It derived from three sources: the original inhabitants of the islands, freed slaves, and migrant labourers from the mainland who started coming to the islands to help with the clove harvest as soon as the slaves began to be freed, and who settled on the island in large numbers in the 1920s and 1930s.

The treaty of 1828 signed between Sultan Seyyid Said and the leader of the Hadimu people enabled the Arabs to take over as much land as they wanted for clove growing, and even to receive forced labour from the Hadimu people to clear land for cloves. The Hadimu were forced into the less productive eastern half of the island, where they developed peasant agricultural systems similar to those found on the mainland opposite. These involved fishing and the cultivation of coconuts and cassava. They also had to pay colonial taxes. But in addition they had to work on the clove plantations: initially this was achieved through brute force, in that headmen (*masheha*) were themselves sent to Pemba if they could not produce sufficient labourers—between 7000 and 10 000 clove pickers were recruited in this way in 1911 (Sheriff 1976: 12).

But the effect of the depression, taxation, and the direct use of force by the government was to turn the Hadimu peasantry into a labour 'reserve army' for the clove areas of Pemba and Zanzibar. In 1931, a good year, 15 000 clove pickers went from Zanzibar to Pemba; in a poor year many fewer labourers were needed, and the wage rates were much lower. The peasant reserve army could supply labour as and when required, and in years when it was not required could still subsist: the colonial government could always provide a few bags of maize as 'famine relief' if it was needed to keep the labour force alive (Sheriff 1976: 12–17).

The next-largest population grouping on Zanzibar was the freed slaves. Anyone born on Zanzibar after 1890 was free, and a decree of 1897 prevented any new enslavement and allowed the existing slaves to apply to the government for a 'certificate of release'. For this their former owners received a small amount of compensation, but nothing at all was paid to the freed slaves. Partly for this reason, the procedure worked very sowly. By 1907 fewer than 15 000 slaves, out of perhaps 75 000, had been released. Slavery as such was not outlawed till the 1920s and there is evidence that it continued surreptitiously after that.

Those released were often worse off than those who remained as slaves. A few returned to the mainland, but many had been on Zanzibar too long to have maintained contacts on the mainland, and in the inter-war years it was not easy to arrive penniless in Dar es Salaam or Mombasa and find' work. The freed slaves found it difficult to move to the eastern half of the island, because the Hadimu had devised land tenure arrangements to prevent any more land being taken away from them by the Arabs, and these arrangements also kept out most of the freed slaves. Some did succeed in moving to Pemba, but after a time it was not easy to get land there either. For most of the freed slaves there was only one alternative, to come to terms with the master who had just freed them. This suited the British and the plantation owners, who otherwise could not have continued to harvest the cloves. Various arrangements were arrrived at, and are referred to as 'squatting', since the land continued to belong to the Arab plantation owners. The most common was for the squatter to be allowed to grow food and annual cash crops between the Arab's clove trees, but not to grow cloves or any other tree crops. In return he worked for the Arab for a few days each week, usually for a minimal cash payment. A less common arrangement allowed the squatter to cultivate fruit trees as well as annual crops, and a very few earned enough money to purchase small plots of land and plant cloves (Clayton 1976: 16–17).

The Hadimu and the squatters together did not supply sufficient labour to bring in the clove harvest, and migrant labour was therefore brought over from the mainland. Clayton estimates that from the turn of the century till the 1930s between 3000 and 4000 migrants arrived each year, of whom about half settled permanently on the islands. Many of these migrants went to Pemba; others worked in manual jobs in Zanzibar town, providing crews for boats, working in the Zanzibar docks, in road gangs, or in transport by hand-cart and human-powered rickshaw. The migrants who undertook these jobs had to be physically strong; and in the inter-war period they became a sort of élite. It was among this group that leaders like Abeid Karume were involved in starting the first trade unions, as well as the 'African Association for Immigrant Workers' which had links with the African Association on the mainland (Clayton 1976: 23).

In 1948 more than 75 per cent of the population of 264 000 was African. Yet not a single African owned more than 3000 clove trees, but 165 Arabs and 75 Asians did. Two hundred and fifteen Africans, compared with nearly 600 Arabs or Asians, owned 1000 or more trees (Table 15.2).

TABLE 15.2
Land ownership on Zanzibar and Pemba 1948

Number of trees owned	Arabs	Asians	All Africans[a]	Total
3000 or more	165	75	—	240
1000 to 2999	320	35	215	570
250 to 999	1 885	190	1 690	3 765
50 to 249	1 990	35	11 675	13 700
0 to 49	1 640	10	8 600	10 250

[a] Includes Comorians.
Source: Lofchie (1965: 87).

The economy was dependent on cloves: they provided at least 80 per cent of the foreign exchange earnings. Four-fifths of the cloves were produced on Pemba, and labour had to be found to harvest this crop. In a good year there were problems getting in the harvest; in a bad year there was much less employment and considerable poverty. While the British ruled in connivance with the rich Arab plantation owners and the Asian business men, the only response available to the divided African population was passive resistance, striking, or (above all) rioting (Bowles 1976b: 12).

The year 1948 saw the most effective challenge to the colonial government in the whole pre-independence period, the General Strike. It was not the first challenge: in 1928 and 1929 attempts had been made to organize a boycott of the payments of ground-rent to Arab and Asian landlords by Africans who had built huts outside Zanzibar towns (Clayton 1976: 22). But after the war conditions in Zanzibar were very bad, as they were on the mainland. Prices had risen faster than wages, and there were shortages of food, and black-marketing. In 1946 and 1947 the poverty was increased by poor clove harvests, and many trees were attacked by 'sudden death' disease. In 1946 there had been a dock strike at Durban, and in January 1947 the Mombasa dock-workers went on strike, to be followed later that year by the Dar es Salaam dock-workers. In Zanzibar also it was the dockers who started the strike, on 20 August 1948, demanding wages comparable with those secured by their friends in Dar es Salaam. The government immediately took steps to recruit a new labour force, making the strike very bitter; but they also began making concessions over pay. The strikers were able to prevent ships unloading, and after a fortnight food was becoming scarce. On 2 September there was a riot, a moral victory for the strikers, since the police kept it under control only by releasing two men they had arrested earlier in the day. By this time most of the African workers in the town were on strike, including those working for the government, for commercial firms, and the great majority of house servants. Food supplies were not reaching the markets. On 3 September there were rumours that the strikers were about to attack the police armoury, and a platoon of reinforcements was called in from the mainland. Despite this, and increasing confidence on the government's part as many workers became short of food, the strike continued for another week—it lasted for three weeks in all. In the aftermath considerable wage increases were given to almost all wage-workers in Zanzibar (Clayton 1976: 26–43).

The strike was important because effectively the whole African work-force was involved. The women showed their support by boycotting the purchase of *khanga* (a type of cloth) for the duration of the strike. The strike was started by immigrant workers, whose position was threatened by the decline in the importance of Zanzibar port, but it spread to include all African workers. It is reasonable to suppose that if there had been a more effective trade union organization at the time, it would have had more lasting results. Nevertheless it was the first warning to the British and to some of the more far-sighted Arabs of what was to come.

After the General Strike the British reconsidered the long-term future of their protectorate. They conducted a population census and commissioned a social and economic survey from a professor of anthropology at the University of Cape Town (the result was published in 1949, in 21 volumes).[2] But in 1948 the creation of representative political institutions had hardly begun. Rule was by Decrees, signed by the Sultan but passed by a Legislative Council which from 1926 consisted of sixteen members:

eight British officials and eight 'non-official' members nominated by the Sultan on the advice of the British. From 1947 the eight 'non-officials' were a European, three Arabs, two Asians, and only two Africans; before 1946 there had been no Africans at all. But in 1956 a commission on constitutional development headed by Sir Walter Coutts proposed democratic methods of choosing these 'non-official' members.

Some of the younger Arabs, notably Seif Hamoud, a committee member of the Arab Association, and Ahmed Lemke and Ali Muhsin, had already begun to create non-racial institutions (such as the Zanzibari Association which Lemke organized among students and workers in London betwen 1951 and 1953). Muhsin edited a newspaper, *Mwongozi* [The Guide] which published in Swahili, Arabic, and English. In order to create a political party which would be sufficiently broadly based to attract African votes, they joined, as ordinary members, the *Hizbu l'Watau l'Riaia Sultan Zanzibar* [the National Party of the Subjects of the Sultan of Zanzibar]. This was a small society started by Africans in Kiembe Samaki village, four miles from Zanzibar town, where African farmers had a grievance because they had lost their land (with inadequate compensation) for the extension of Zanzibar airport. They also suffered what they felt was interference from the veterinary department in their livestock keeping; animals that contracted rinderpest were slaughtered, and from 1949 they had to pay for compulsory dipping. Finally, in 1951 some of them refused to let their animals be innoculated against anthrax, and this led to a boycott of government activities, the arrest of eighteen villagers, and a riot when the remaining villagers, having captured a van taking eleven of the accused to prison, tried to storm the local gaol and release the rest; the police opened fire and five people were killed. The villagers had recognized the potential of a worker/peasant alliance, and shown up the weakness of the colonial state: they had released eleven men and nearly broken into the prison, reinforcements took some time to arrive from the mainland, and one of those who was subsequently convicted following the riot was an off-duty policeman. But it was not till 1955 that they formed their party. The Arabs joined it in 1956, and were quickly elected to the executive posts. The name was changed to the Zanzibar National Party. The original African leaders remained as president and vice-president and a number of other Africans joined the Party, notably a group in contact with socialist countries who organized a youth wing and started trade unions (Lofchie 1965: ch. V; Bowles 1976b: 17–18).

In 1956, following the report of the constitutional commissioner, it was announced that elections for six seats on the Legislative Council, on an extremely limited franchise, would take place the following year. The 'mainland' Africans were less well organized than the ZNP, and their leaders at first opposed the elections. But in February 1957 an 'Afro-Shirazi Union' was formed. It was a loose alliance between the African Association, on Zanzibar, and the Shirazi Association on Pemba, both of which could trace their origins back to the 1930s, but which hitherto had functioned as social clubs rather than political parties.[3] The model was TANU, which had also been created by organizing branches of the African Association into a political party, and then publicizing workers' and peasants' causes in order to build up mass support. From the start Nyerere and the ASU leaders were in contact, and in the elections of July 1957 their candidates won five of the six seats, and the sixth was taken by an Asian. After the election the ASU became a more formal party, the Afro-Shirazi Party (ASP). The ZNP did not win any seats at all, but because of the ten members who were nominated by the British, the Africans were still in a minority on the Legislative Council (Lofchie 1965: 175–80).

Between 1957 and 1961 it became clear that independence was not far away, even though violence and racial bitterness were increasing. In 1959 the Pemba wing of the Afro-Shirazi Party (i.e. the members of the old Shirazi Association) broke away and formed the Zanzibar and Pemba People's Party (ZPPP). Meanwhile the ZNP arranged social services for its members, expanded its youth wing (under Abdulrahman Babu) and a trade union on the dockside which rivalled that of the ASP. It even organized groups of its supporters (mainly indigenous Africans) to replace mainlanders (who mostly supported the ASP) on the clove plantations. In January 1961 there was another election, this time with 22 seats; the ZNP won 9, the ASP 10, and the ZPPP 3. When two of these last three decided to support the ZNP and one the ASP, there were just eleven MPs on each side, and deadlock. So another election was arranged for June, with one extra constituency. This time the ZNP and ZPPP agreed not to compete with each other, and together they won 13 out of the 23 seats, with 10 going to the ASP (Lofchie 1965: 183–201).

Since the ZNP was the most organized party, expressed loyalty to the Sultan, and could claim support from Africans as well as

Arabs, this result suited the British, and they prepared to hand over power. There was just one doubt: in the June 1961 election the ASP had won 50 per cent of the votes—as many as the other two parties together—and had ended up with fewer seats only because of the way in which the constituencies were chosen. Before independence, the British wanted one more election. This was held in June 1963. Shortly before it, Babu and the youth and trade union wings of the ZNP broke away to form the Umma Party with a socialist philosophy; but even so the ZNP/ZPPP alliance won 18 seats, and the ASP 13, although yet again the ASP took more than 50 per cent of the votes (Table 15.3). On 10 December the British left, and one month later, on 12 January 1964 came the Zanzibar revolution, which left the ASP in power at last (Lofchie 1965: 201–20, 257–74).

TABLE 15.3
Zanzibar election results 1961–1963

		January 1961	June 1961	July 1963
ASP	seats:	10	10	13
	votes:	36 698	45 172	87 085
	% of votes:	40	50	54
ZNP	seats:	9	10	12
	votes:	32 724	31 724	47 950
	% of votes:	36	35	31
ZPPP	seats:	3	3	6
	votes:	19 451	12 411	25 609
	% of votes	17	14	16
Total seats:		22	23	31
Total votes:		88 873	89 307	160 644

Source: Based on J. Mosare, 'Background to the revolution in Zanzibar' in Kimambo and Temu (eds.) (1969: 235).

From the 1948 General Strike onwards, Zanzibar had become increasingly violent. Those who backed the ASP had several grievances. They were kept out of civil service posts by lack of education; and in all four elections held before independence they gained the most votes but no political power. The years 1952–4 and 1957–64 were also poor years for cloves—which meant unemployment and depression in all parts of the economy. Violence was directed against the government—as in the

1948 strike and in the 1951 Kiembe Samaki riots. But it was also directed increasingly against Arabs, not so much the rich few as the much more numerous 'Manga' Arabs who kept the small shops dispersed over the island. The most serious grievance in the rural areas, which led to a widespread boycott of Arab shops and the death of sixty-eight Arabs during the 1961 elections, was squatter evictions, in which 'mainlanders' (i.e. migrants and some freed slaves), who squatted on the clove plantations and sold food in Zanzibar town, were expelled to be replaced by African supporters of the ZNP.

The level of violence was never so great on Pemba, where the majority of Africans disliked the aggressive and often disorganized ASP and voted for ZPPP or ZNP candidates. They seem to have realized that their interests as owners of clove trees rather than pickers of cloves were likely to be better served by the ZNP than by the ASP; as Bowles has pointed out, those who called themselves 'Shirazi' were not describing their nationality so much as the fact that most of them were medium-scale clove producers and employers of labour.[4]

The actual details of the revolution are obscure even today; the present account follows an article by Michael Lofchie written in 1967. Zanzibar in 1964 was ripe for revolution. The grievances of mainland Africans in the docks (where the employers began to give preference to the members of the ZNP trade union) and on the plantations (where squatters were being expelled) had already led to violence which the British had shown that they could not control. The defection of Babu and the trade unions from the ZNP in 1963 had created the possibility of a united African opposition—Babu's Umma Party and the ASP merged immediately after the 1964 revolution. The ZNP passed legislation to make life difficult for those who opposed them, including a Control of Societies Act under which virtually any political organization could be banned, and there was every likelihood that they would move to a one-party state if they could. Their main fear was the police force, which was all that the British had left them for defensive purposes; but it had mainly British and Asian officers and was partly staffed by Africans from the mainland and from other British colonies, notably Kenya and Malawi. One of the first decisions after independence in December 1963 was to retire many of these policemen from the mainland. But since the police were the only armed force on the islands, the retired policemen were a potential revolutionary force.

Before dawn on Sunday 12 January 1964, a group of about forty men, including several retired police, stormed the main police armoury, the radio station, and then a second armoury. With its supply of arms lost, the regime was powerless. 'For all practical purposes, the revolution was successfully completed by daybreak' (Lofchie 1967: 34). The Sultan and his family were lucky to escape by small boat to the mainland, and eventually (with Nyerere's assistance) to England. The remaining Arabs, especially the shopkeepers, were not so lucky, and at least 5000 were massacred in the days which followed.

It is probable that the revolution was planned and led by John Okello, a Ugandan who had had contact with the Mau Mau in the Kenyan forests in the 1950s, and had come to Pemba in 1959, where he worked as a labourer and builder. He moved to Zanzibar in 1963 and organized his plot.[5] Probably two other groups were plotting at the same time: the official ASP leadership, under Abeid Karume, very likely with Nyerere's support, and the Umma group led by Babu, possibly with Chinese assistance. But Okello got in first, and within a few days a 'Revolutionary Council' under his chairmanship had been created to run the islands. But Okello could rely on no political organization, and during the two weeks following the revolution made trips to Pemba and the mainland. While he was away, Karume and Babu got together, took control of the police, and when Okello returned from another trip to the mainland he was simply refused entry at Zanzibar airport and sent back to the mainland. Abeid Karume, an ex-merchant seaman, by then a boatman in Zanzibar harbour and trade-unionist, who had been involved in Zanzibar politics since the 1930s, and whose party, the ASP, had maintained links with TANU since its foundation, became President of Zanzibar. Within a few weeks he was negotiating a union with the mainland. 'The United Republic of Tanzania' was announced to the world on 23 April 1964.[6]

PART V: THE FRUITS OF INDEPENDENCE

16 THE EARLY YEARS

This plan is a challenge to the nation—as big a challenge as that which we faced to achieve Uhuru.

NYERERE, 8 June 1965[1]

Between 1961 and 1965 Nyerere and the TANU leadership made the adjustment from being a successful party in opposition to becoming the leaders of a party in power. They recognized that their freedom was limited by the structural dependence of the economy and the shortage of trained Tanzanians, and began to lower the aspirations of those who thought that independence meant immediate prosperity, or even African control of the economy. As they suppressed organized groups, notably the trade unions, who tried to use these issues to create their own power base, so they consolidated their own position (Pratt 1976: Ch. 7).

As part of the process of transition, in January 1962, only one month after the triumphant handing-over of power, Nyerere resigned as Prime Minister, 'to act as a bridge between the people and the new government by demonstrating in practical terms the importance of the Party'.[2] Rashidi Kawawa became Prime Minister; Richard Turnbull remained as Governor-General, appointed by the Queen of England, and in theory appointing the Prime Minister and his cabinet.

Cranford Pratt suggests that Nyerere's motives for resigning can best be seen by examining how he spent his time (Pratt 1976: 114–21). He did not build a strong party bureaucracy that would rule the country in place of, or alongside, the civil service; nor did he set out to create some new mass organization. Instead he returned to his home village, Butiama, to think and to write. The result was four pamphlets: the well-known *Ujamaa— the Basis of African Socialism*, which was rewritten five years later to form the basis of agricultural policy after the Arusha Declaration, the lesser known *Tujisahishe* or 'Let us Correct Ourselves' about self-criticism, *TANU na Raia* about race and citizenship, and a paper on imperialism called 'The Second Scramble'.[3] Then he began to travel widely within the country, explaining to enthusiastic audiences that independence was only the first step to full liberation, which could be achieved by self-help and hard work. He was becoming more and more the *mwalimu*, the far-seeing moral teacher, who knows what is right for his subjects, and is himself never wrong.

Nyerere's resignation cleared the way for Kawawa to take a series of tough measures (Pratt 1976: 121–6). Sir Ernest Vasey, the Minister of Finance, and C.M. Meek, the Prime Minister's principal secretary, were sacked, as were the British officers in charge of the police. The new cabinet gave more weight to the political leaders of the independence campaign: Kambona and Lusinde were promoted, while Maswanya and Kasambala were included in the cabinet for the first time. A crash training programme for civil servants was begun, with the promise of accelerated promotion to follow. In the regions, the two fundamental institutions of Cameron's indirect rule were abolished—Native Authorities were replaced by elected District Councils, while the chiefs lost all official power, most of which passed to Regional and Area Commissioners, political appointees responsible for the implementation of party policy in their areas.[4] Kawawa's cabinet also 'nationalized' agricultural land, in the sense of converting all titles to land into 99-war leases; in this they resisted pressure for an immediate take-over of settler farms, while giving the settlers an indication that they could not expect to stay in the country indefinitely.[5] They also ensured that co-operative societies and unions were registered in all parts of the country. Finally, as we shall see, Kawawa, the founder of the Tanganyika Federation of Labour, and the most experienced trade-unionist in the country, took steps to limit the powers of the trade unions.

Kawawa's government passed a new constitution, replacing the Queen as Head of State by a President. In December 1962, a year after independence, Nyerere was elected President of the Republic of Tanganyika under this constitution. In January 1963 he announced that TANU membership would now be open to all races (hitherto only one or two exceptional Europeans and Asians had been allowed to join) but that Tanganyika would become a one-party state. There had been virtually no opposition to TANU in the 1958, 1959, and 1960 elections, but Nyerere made it clear that when the next election was held, probably in 1965, only candidates who had been pre-selected by the Party would be allowed to stand. Since more than one individual would generally be allowed to contest each seat, he claimed that this would still be democracy, in that it would allow the people to reject individuals they did not like—as indeed happened in 1965 when two ministers, nine junior ministers, and, in all, half the sitting elected MPs were rejected in one way or another.[6]

But this is to anticipate; in May 1963 Nyerere travelled abroad for the first time as President, to the inaugural meeting of the Organization of African Unity in Addis Ababa, where he pledged 1 per cent of Tanganyika's budget for the liberation struggle. In June he visited Kenya and Uganda, in July the United States, Canada, and England, and in November he addressed the FAO in Rome and visited Scandinavia. The *mwalimu* from Tanganyika was fast becoming a spokesman for Africa on the international stage.

At home the government continued to clamp down on the trade-union movement. To appreciate how much was at stake, it is necessary to go back to 1958, by which time the unions had shown themselves to be the force most immediately threatening the colonial government. Although there were still less than 50 000 unionists, they had organized successful boycotts of the buses and the brewery, achieved wage increases for more than half Tanzania's 400 000 wage workers and the first legal minimum wage in Dar es Salaam, and caused widespread disruption on the sisal estates as they tried to get recognition. Towards the end of 1958 the sisal workers had been allowed to form a national union, and by 1961 the government estimated that 136 000 workers were members of the Plantation Workers' Union, out of about 200 000 union members in the country as a whole (Tordoff 1967: 137–41; Friedland 1969: 52, 161).

In 1959 Christopher Tumbo was elected General Secretary of the Tanganyika Railway African Union. This union had begun

TABLE 16.1
Registered African trade unions in Tanganyika 1956–1963

Membership	Number of unions			
	1956	1958	1961	1963
more than 20 000	—	—	1	1
10 000–19 999	—	—	1	3
5000–9999	—	5	5	3
2500–4999	1	3	1	1
1000–2499	4	3	3	3
500–999	2	3	1	—
50–499	6	4	2	1
Number of unions with 50 members or more	13	18	14	12
Total Union Membership	12 891	44 850	199 915	147 177

Source: Annual Reports of the Labour Department.

as a staff association for clerks, with a moderate leadership, but Tumbo was more militant. In February 1960 he led a strike which lasted eighty-two days, easily a record. The strike was for more pay, but was also directed against the arrogance and racialism of many white employees of the railways. The strikers feared that if co-operative or federal arrangements continued, these men would stay on in positions of power after independence in Tanganyika (all the railways in East Africa were operated by the East African High Commission, with headquarters in Nairobi, and Kenya was still some years from independence). There were similar fears in the postal service, which was also run by the East African High Commission, and there too the African workers struck. Both strikes were ineffective, since European and Asian employees were able to maintain the services. The railway strike dragged on despite the efforts of two visiting unionists from the International Confederation of Free Trade Unions to end it, until at the end of April the Government of Tanganyika put pressure on the railway management, who made some concessions over pay, so that a settlement could be reached (Friedland 1969: 224–32).

The strike did not succeed in breaking the co-operative arrangements within East Africa. Both Nyerere and Kambona were in favour of East African co-operation, and in June 1960 Nyerere was even willing to consider delaying Tanganyikan independence by twelve months if that would allow Kenya and Uganda to become independent simultaneously, so that the

three countries could federate from the day they became independent. Until 1963 he would have been willing to lead Tanganyika into an East African Federation, provided the other
East African leaders were equally committed (Nyerere 1966: 96;
Pratt 1976: 177–8).

By 1962 many of the moderate union leaders—such as Kawawa, Namfua, and Kamaliza—were cabinet ministers. Those
elected in their places not only embarrassed the government
over the future of the East African High Commission services,
they also campaigned for immediate nationalization of the sisal
industry, and for a much more rapid Africanization of the civil
service. Nyerere's deal with the British made all these impossible; yet the unions had the power to bring vital sections of the
economy to a standstill.

The result was the suppression of the movement. In 1962 three
Acts were passed, one limiting the right to strike, another preventing civil servants from joining unions (though they were
allowed to join the Party), and a third giving the Tanganyika
Federation of Labour increased powers over its constituent
unions. Its General Secretary, Kamaliza, was brought into the

TABLE 16.2
Average cash earnings of wage labour 1956–1963
(shillings per month)

	July 1956	June 1958	May 1960	June 1962	June 1963
Agriculture, forestry, hunting and fishing	34	36	55	80	112
Mining and quarrying	57	60	96	141	171
Manufacturing	67	71	91	143	174
Construction	79	87	103	128	165
Electricity, gas, water and sanitation	75	97	134	139	193
Commerce	80	87	82	154	199
Transport (excluding railways), storage, and communications	121	139	187	221	277
Services (excluding domestic and government)	70	100	107	160	235
Government, E.A. High Commission (incl. railways) and Local Authorities	88	102	122	166	216
Total	57	62	80	122	165

Source: Annual Reports of the Labour Department

cabinet as Minister for Labour, and in September 1962 a Preventive Detention Act was passed, soon to be used against trade-unionists. At the same time, the minimum wage was increased, so that the average earnings of those in wage employment doubled between 1960 and 1963 (Table 16.2). In 1963 Christopher Tumbo, the leader of the railway union, was arrested by the Kenyan police in Mombasa, and handed over at the Tanganyikan border; he remained in preventive detention (i.e. without trial) for four years; at about the same time the leader of the Plantation Workers' Union, Victor Mkello, was confined by government order to a remote part of the country (Pratt 1976: 185–6).

In January 1964 the army mutinied, over essentially the same issues: the men wanted more pay and the replacement of their British officers by Tanganyikans. The mutiny sparked off similar disturbances in the Kenyan and Ugandan armies, and shocked the country and the world. Nyerere went into hiding for several days and Dar es Salaam was at the mercy of the mutineers. But they had no plan to take over the state, and, four days after the mutiny began, were only beginning to negotiate with the more militant trade-union leaders. When this was reported to Kambona and Nyerere they called for British help. The mutiny was over thirty minutes after sixty British marines landed by helicopter on the hockey pitch at Lugalo barracks outside Dar es Salaam (Listowel, 1965: 430–40; Edgett Smith 1973: 109f.).

After the mutiny the army was rebuilt; an almost completely new rank and file was recruited, and the British officers were replaced by Nigerians, Canadians, and Tanganyikans. More than 500 people were detained, including all the trade-union leaders in Dar es Salaam and up-country who were thought to be against the Party. Under a National Union of Tanganyika Workers Act only one trade union was to be allowed, affiliated to TANU and with its General Secretary appointed by the President. Membership of this new union, NUTA, was made compulsory for workers, and it was given a guaranteed income of more than 500 000 shillings per annum through compulsory deductions by employers from every wage or salary paid.[7]

Six weeks before the mutiny Zanzibar and Pemba had been given independence, and the revolution on Zanzibar took place one week before the mutiny. Three months later, in April 1964, Nyerere flew to Zanzibar and signed 'articles of union' with Abeid Karume, the leader of the Afro-Shirazi Party, under which Tanganyika and Zanzibar combined to form the United

Republic of Tanzania. Nyerere has consistently defended this merger as a working example of African unity, showing how a small country can unite with a large one without being dominated or swallowed up by it. But it is also probably true that he exerted considerable pressure to get it agreed quickly because he wanted to influence what happened on the island, and in particular its foreign relations. The British, and following them the Americans and the other West European powers, were slow to recognize Karume's government. They disliked the way he had seized power, were unsure whether this power extended to Pemba as well as Zanzibar, and did not wish to be associated with the violence which followed the revolution. On the other hand, within ten days ten communist countries recognized Zanzibar, and three in particular (the Soviet Union, China, and East Germany) made trained experts available and promised financial assistance. The terms of the Union made foreign policy a 'union' matter—i.e. one decided in Dar es Salaam rather than Zanzibar. Other 'union' affairs were to be defence and security, citizenship, civil aviation, posts, harbours, customs, trade, and the monetary system, including the management of foreign reserves. All other powers were kept by the Zanzibar Revolutionary Council. Karume became First Vice-President of the United Republic (Kawawa became Second Vice-President), and forty MPs from Zanzibar, nominated by the Revolutionary Council, were added to the mainland parliament (Edgett-Smith 1973: 122f.; Pratt 1976: 138–9).

In mid-1964 Nyerere launched the First Five-Year Plan, the first Plan that Tanzanians could call their own (the Three-Year Plan 1961/2 to 1963/4 had been largely prepared by Sir Ernest Vasey before independence). Even so, it was prepared by an expatriate team, headed by the French planner M.J. Faudon who worked in the Ministry of Development Planning. Implementation was to be overseen by a Directorate of Planning in the President's Office. In the course of preparing the Plan, policy positions were prepared by each ministry, the summaries of which formed the substance of Volume 1 of the printed document—and effectively of the plan as a whole, since the detailed proposals and estimates for projects in Volume 2 were soon overtaken by events. The policies, discussed in the three chapters which follow, appeared to be a determined attempt to break away from the inherited structural dependence. They involved a positive commitment to industrialization, notably import substitution, an attempt to divert resources into a 'transformation approach' in the rural areas, designed to make the best use of mechanization and irrigation, and manpower planning which determined that for the time being most of the investment in education should be in the secondary and technical fields (Pratt 1967).

The spending estimates of the Plan proved to be optimistic. The price of sisal, the country's biggest source of foreign exchange at the time, fell from approximately £100 per ton in 1964 to £60 per ton in 1967. But the Plan had also assumed a successful 'mobilization' of foreign capital, and in 1965 diplomatic disputes were to lead to the freezing of aid from Tanzania's three largest aid donors. The dispute with West Germany was a consequence of the union between Tanganyika and Zanzibar (Pratt 1976: 139–41). East Germany had been one of the first countries to recognize Zanzibar, to provide technicians, and to offer financial assistance. West Germany was the third-largest donor to the mainland, following the UK and the USA. West Germany, however, operated a rigid policy of refusing recognition to any country that recognized the existence of East Germany. Thus the union of Tanganyika and Zanzibar created a diplomatic problem: the Zanzibaris had no wish to lose their East German aid and technical assistance, yet, if East Germany was recognized, the mainland would lose its West German aid. Nyerere's attempts to force a compromise on Karume and on both sets of Germans were either not understood or not appreciated by the West Germans: he allowed the East a consulate in Dar es Salaam, but no embassy or ambassador, and refused offers of East German aid for the mainland. After much fruitless diplomatic activity, in February 1965 the West Germans withdrew their military personnel (who were training air-force and naval staff following the mutiny) and their offers of financial aid; Nyerere promptly ordered other German technical assistance staff to leave too, bitterly resenting the threat of economic blackmail in the West German actions. The effect of this episode was to refine Tanzania's policy of non-alignment. It became clear that aid would be accepted from anyone who gave it on fair terms and without political strings—and that just as an aid donor was not expected to agree with every Tanzanian policy, so acceptance of aid by Tanzania did not imply approval of every policy of the donor. It was on these lines that Nyerere defended increasing involvement with China: the first interest-free untied loan was signed in 1964, and in 1965 Nyerere visited Peking and the Chinese first offered to build a railway from Dar es Salaam to

Lusaka in Zambia, a project which had been turned down by the World Bank and the governments of the US, Britain, Japan, and the Soviet Union the year before. A similar defence was invoked to justify the existence of Chinese and Soviet arms and experts on Tanzanian soil involved in training guerrilla armies for Mozambique, Angola, Zimbabwe, and Namibia (Pratt 1976: 152–6, 161–6).

The second dispute, with the United States, did not lead to a formal break in diplomatic relations, although relations 'had been marked by such recurring mistrust as to make any major dependency on American aid most improbable' (Pratt 1976: 141–2, 152). Its immediate cause was the credence given by Kambona and Nyerere to various letters which claimed that the US was recruiting mercenaries to overthrow Nyerere and his government; Kambona used the letters to suggest that the CIA was about to do in Tanzania what it had previously done in the Congo or what it was in the process of doing in Vietnam. In December 1964 Nyerere admitted that the documents were forged, but he did so in a way that was not designed to encourage the continuance of close relations between Tanzania and the US.

The third dispute arose from Tanzania's distrust of British policy in Zimbabwe (Pratt 1976: 147–52). Ian Smith proclaimed UDI in November 1965. In December the Foreign Ministers of the Organization of African Unity passed a resolution to break diplomatic relations with Britain if steps to crush Ian Smith were not taken at once. No such steps were taken, and five countries, including Tanzania and Zambia, broke off diplomatic relations. In response the British froze a £7.5 million loan which had been agreed in principle but not yet signed. Existing agreements were allowed to run on until they expired—which meant that British technical assistance staff continued to be recruited until 1968, after which all forms of official British assistance ceased.[8] From a close dependence on Britain in 1961–4, culminating in the military assistance provided by Britain to crush the 1964 mutiny, Tanzania was now in a position in which it would have to manage without British money and experts.

It was in this situation that the first general election under the new 'One-Party State' constitution took place in October 1965. Two Ministers (Bomani and Kasambala, both with backgrounds in the co-operative movement) were defeated, along with nine junior ministers and six other MPs (Cliffe *et al.* 1967: 300). If account is taken of MPs who chose not to stand or who were not selected by their constituency party branches, or who were rejected as unsuitable by the National Executive Committee of the Party, more than half the elected members were new. The election was a diplomatic success, being hailed by students of politics all over the world as 'One-Party Democracy'. The non-democratic aspects tended to be glossed over—the detention of most of the trade-union leaders, and the lack of real power in parliament, as distinct from the party committees where policy was debated before it ever came to parliament. Much was made of the defeat of Paul Bomani, which was at least partly a vote of no-confidence in the co-operative movement with which the Bomani family was closely associated in the Lake area. Not much notice was taken of the economic uncertainties—the non-appearance of foreign aid (though in important ways this was an advantage), the failure of the agricultural settlement schemes, the slowness of industrial projects, and élitist attitudes that were emerging in the secondary schools and at the university. To these we now turn.

17 AGRICULTURAL POLICY 1961–1967

> The basic difference between Tanzania's rural life
> now and in the past stems from the widespread intro-
> duction of cash crop farming. Over large areas of the
> country peasants spend at least part of their time . . .
> on the cultivation of crops for sale . . . And in many
> places our most intelligent and hard-working peasants
> have invested their money (or money advanced
> through public credit facilities) in clearing more land,
> extending their acreage, using better tools, and so
> on, until they have quite important farms of 10, 20 or
> even more acres.
>
> NYERERE, *Socialism and Rural Development* (1967)[1]

At independence, the Tanzanian nationalists inherited a thriving
capitalist agriculture, based on plantations, settlers, and an expanding class of African capitalist farmers. In the following six
years, roughly up to the Arusha Declaration of February 1967,
sisal production was static but the main export crops produced
by small-scale African farmers continued to expand—cotton at

TABLE 17.1
Production of main export crops 1960–1968
('000 tonnes)

	1960–2 average	1966–8 average	Growth rate per annum (%)
Sisal	202.3	197.5	−0.5
Coffee	23.6	48.1	12.5
Cotton	33.5	70.0	13
Cashewnuts	45.1	74.3	9
Tea	4.0	6.4	8
Tobacco	2.2	3.8	10

Sources: Tanzania, United Republic of, *Background to the Budget 1967–8*, p. 18; *Economic Survey 1970–1*, p. 21.

13 per cent per annum, coffee at 12.5 per cent, and cashewnuts at 9 per cent (Table 17.1). The non-monetary agricultural sector grew more slowly, but even so gross domestic product grew at 4.8 per cent per annum in real terms between 1961 and 1966, and there were balance of payments surpluses.

But the nationalists, Nyerere in particular, were not happy with the structure of the agriculture they inherited. Settler farms and plantations were owned by foreigners. The settlers showed their distrust of the new government by leaving in large numbers from 1960 onwards, taking much of their capital with them —at least £3 million;[2] the plantation companies were suspected of making unreasonably large profits during the Korean War boom of the 1950s.

Nyerere was not much happier with the trend towards inequality which was associated with African capitalist farming. As early as 1958 he argued against freehold land tenure and a free market in land:

If we allow land to be sold like a robe, within a short period there would be only a few Africans possessing land in Tanganyika and all the others would be tenants . . . If two groups of people were to emerge—a small group of landlords and a large group of tenants—we would be faced with a problem which has created antagonism among peoples and led to bloodshed in many parts of the world.[3]

His 1962 paper *Ujamaa—the Basis of African Socialism* is an attack not just on individual land tenure but on capitalism as a system, which is contrasted unfavourably with an idealized version of 'African socialism' in some unspecified pre-colonial time and place. But it was not till 1967, in *Socialism and Rural Development*, that Nyerere explicitly attacked the peasant who expands his farm to 10 or 20 acres as the enemy of equality and a fair system of agricultural production.

The coming of independence meant that settlers virtually abandoned large parts of the country: the Southern Highlands, the Usambara mountains, and much of the area to the north of Arusha. They stayed on productive wheat land in West Kilimanjaro, and Oldeani 70 miles west of Arusha, and on maize/coffee/dairy farms near Arusha town. Part of the abandoned land was taken over by Africans, but much of it returned to bush.

Sisal production was less affected by the departure of settlers than by the dramatic decline in the world price between 1964 and 1967. The result was a rapid fall in employment in the industry; from 110 000 in 1962, 83 000 in 1964, to only 34 000 in 1967.[4] Production was maintained, as the fields already planted were harvested, but replanting stopped completely on many plantations, and many more were unable to repay loans they had received from the commercial banks.

Given such fundamental change in the settler and plantation sectors, it was inevitable that the government should be cautious in its policies towards small-scale African farmers, however much Nyerere disliked the implications. Government policy took two forms: firstly, there was an attempt to make available to a wider range of farmers the institutions and services under which capitalism had prospered during the colonial period. Thus the co-operative movement was expanded, with little control of registrations, in all parts of the country; the agricultural extension service was given increased budgets for training programmes, in order to offer the services which the colonial government had given to selected 'focal points' to a much wider range of farmers; credit was made available to small farmers, though large farmers still got the greater share; and the Department of Community Development was expanded, in order to influence sections of the peasantry (particularly women) who were so resistant to capitalist influence that they refused to give up traditional agricultural practices or diets. All these policies together were described—by the World Bank in 1960—as 'the improvement approach'. The First Five-Year Plan (1964–9) accepted most of the World Bank's logic and emphasized that these policies would not require large injections of capital.[5]

The same could not be said about the 'transformation approach', the second strand of rural policy. It was proposed in the World Bank Report, accepted uncritically in the First Five-Year Plan, and seemed to offer a version of capitalist farming under government control.[6] It could take many forms. The World Bank Report described the (Kenyan) Swynnerton Plan, in which peasant holdings were reorganized and mapped so as to give each farmer a single plot, as an example of the transformation approach; it also recognized that there were few areas in Tanganyika where this could be applied. A more applicable form was the creation of settlement schemes on unoccupied land, where farmers would be given land on condition that they followed rules and regulations that defined 'modern' agricultural techniques. The First Five-Year Plan proposed more than sixty pilot settlement schemes to be established by 1970, with the hope that 200 would be established by 1980. Each was to com-

prise 'about 250 comprehensively planned, economically profitable individual farms which will be encouraged to work on a co-
operative basis and which will justify the investment in economic and social overheads of about £150 000 per settlement'.
A third form of the transformation approach, given almost as
much money to spend in the First Five-Year Plan, was the development of Tanganyika's river basins for planned irrigation
farming. The World Bank mission had been struck by the apparent agricultural potential of the flood plains, particularly that of
the Rufiji river, its tributary, the Kilombero, and the Pangani
river running from the foothills of Mount Kilimanjaro to the
coast near Tanga. The United Nations was commissioned to
produce feasibility studies of the potentials of these river basins
for irrigation farming on a large scale. The Five-Year Plan
accepted the World Bank target of 25 000 acres to be newly irrigated each year from 1970 onwards. If this target had been
achieved, 10 per cent of the agricultural land area in the country
would have been irrigated by 1980. Since there was no tradition
of large-scale irrigation, completely new agricultural systems
were to be established by the government, on a settlement-
scheme basis. Overall, out of £28 million to be invested in agriculture during the Plan, £19 million were to be spent on the
transformation approach in one form or another.[7]

Both the improvement approach and the transformation
approach were attempts to escape from some of the implications
of colonial capitalism. Both, however, were only half thought
out. The improvement approach attempted to spread capitalism
so that everyone became involved; but it is hardly surprising,
given the nature of capitalism, that it failed to stem the growing
inequality. The transformation approach was itself based on individualistic farming, and, if it succeeded in gaining a return on
its heavy capital investment, could only do so by increasing inequality. In that sense both approaches were utopian, and it is
to their failure that we now turn.[8]

The improvement approach involved three main policies: government promotion of co-operative unions and societies, increased emphasis on agricultural extension, and community development.

THE CO-OPERATIVES

The extremely rapid growth of the co-operative movement between 1955 and independence was described in Chapter 8. It
was concentrated in the areas which produced coffee and cotton

for export, although there were also co-operatives marketing
fire-cured tobacco in Songea and paddy in Mbeya. It was a
movement of marketing co-operatives—little attempt was made
to organize co-operative production. It expanded in the 1950s
at least partly because the government enabled the co-operatives
to offer higher prices. But in the 1960s much of the expansion
was based on compulsion—once the government allowed a
'compulsory marketing order', the co-operative became the only
legal purchaser of particular crops, and frequently there was no
other outlet of any description (small quantities were smuggled
to towns, or to Kenya and Uganda). Food crops such as maize
could be sold legally in the District where they were grown, but
it was an offence to move them across District boundaries without permission. At certain times of the year private traders
would have paid much higher prices than the co-operatives, and
the margins between the co-operative buying and selling prices
were obvious to the farmers, since cereals could be purchased
from the co-operatives, as well as sold to them. The differential
between the two prices quickly widened; 'single channel marketing' of maize probably meant that the consumers' price rose by
50 per cent in the period 1964–9, while the producers' price
stayed constant (Kriesel et al. 1970: 36–7).

Thus in the food crop areas co-operatives had to be imposed. This was done after independence:

When Tanganyika achieved independence in 1961 some important decisions were taken by the Government vitally affecting the movement. It
was decided to embark on a crash programme for the organisation of
co-operatives in vast sections of the country which until then were
largely untouched by the movement: the central and coastal parts,
Mtwara and Ruvuma in the south, and the western areas. It was decided that the co-operative form was well suited to the African setting
and to the achievement of independence in the economic sense: control
of the economy by the indigenous people rather than by expatriates
and others non-African in origin.

Thus ... the number of registered co-operatives increased from 857
in 1961 to 1533 at the end of April 1966 ... To help bring about this
great expansion the Co-operative Societies Ordinance was changed in
1963 so that the Registrar of Co-operative Societies no longer had the
final power to refuse to register a co-operative because he was not satisfied as to its viability ... The political pressures were considerable.
Societies were organised from 'on top', without genuine local demand
or even understanding, but in their enthusiasm in the first flush of freedom, people went along.[9]

The result was inefficient, corrupt and undemocratic co-operatives. The Special Committee reported in 1966 that losses averaged around 2 per cent of turnover in a sample of 300 societies. The farmers were aware of these situations, but unable to do anything about them because of the lack of democratic control at Union level.[10]

TABLE 17.2

Cost per ton of co-operative societies by size of society 1967
(shillings)

	cashew societies	cotton societies	coffee societies	maize societies
Volume handled per year (tons)				
more than 2000	22	48	47	14.5
1000–1200	27	53	52	22.5
200–400	105	140	90	73
100–200	—	—	140	—

Source: Kriesel *et al*, 1970, Table 5.2.

Many primary societies were too small to be efficient (Table 17.2), but even then the committee-men—often themselves the more successful 'progressive farmers' of the focal-point approach—benefited. They received generous allowances. Migot-Adholla (1969a: 237–8) studied one particular society in which each committee-man received nearly 700 shillings per year just for attending society meetings. The opportunities for fraud increased as the number of societies grew faster than the supervisory staff of the Co-operative Development Division. When the co-operatives became the main vehicle for government credit schemes for small farmers, the committee-men were usually the first to receive the credit, and often avoided repayment.

But Migot-Adholla concluded that most of the committee-men made their largest earnings from illegal transactions connected with the co-operative tractor schemes. In 1964 and 1966 the co-operatives were persuaded by the government to take responsibility for two large fleets of tractors. The accounts showed that on average each tractor ploughed only 125 acres per year and the fleets operated at a substantial loss until the schemes were abandoned in 1969. Unofficially they often stopped on the way home and did some private ploughing, for which the driver and the committee member split the earnings. Migot also documents the stories of mechanics and mechanization field officers who were able to increase their incomes by using government facilities and spare parts to repair private tractors (Migot-Adholla 1969a: 238–9, 246–9).

Thus by the mid-1960s the position of the co-operatives was highly ambiguous. John Saul could see both positions: on the one hand he defended the co-operative movement, from a nationalist position:

The marketing of all peasant produced export crops and of an increasing proportion of internally-disposed food-crops in Tanzania is now handled by co-operatives generally under compulsory marketing orders which rule out alternative channels for selling one's crop. Every region has at least one co-operative union and some of the better-off districts have had two or three, to which will be affiliated anything from a handful to some 30 or 40 primary societies. The co-operatives are thus key bodies in the development process, affecting the price and, therefore, the material incentives which are made available to the farmer ... In addition to their marketing functions *per se*, they have the potential to play a wider development role. Theoretically they provide a network of grass-roots contacts, and a structure well-suited to the channelling of new forms of rural credit, which can sustain programmes for providing agricultural advice and for making available fertilizers, insecticides, and other inputs. Similarly, they can, and sometimes do, act in the spheres of research, transportation, processing and the like ... In brief, it is tempting to see the co-operatives as a major agency for carrying out many *initiatives* relevant to the development effort. (Cliffe and Saul 1972: 314–5.)

But in 1970, commenting on the reorganization of the Victoria Federation of Co-operative Unions the previous year, he described their weakness:

The combination of inefficiency, corruption and opportunism remains a great problem. Produce losses have remained substantial, for example, and the whole process of financing and purchasing the crop has presented some familiar problems. The absence of tractors and the foreclosing of loopholes in the credit system have reduced the leeway for corruption but even at the Union level the elected committee-men have, from the early post-reorganisation period, reasserted their claim for increased *posho* [allowances] and prerequisites ... Once again, this continues in part because the general apathy of the growers has not been basically challenged or uprooted. (Saul 1970b: 219)

Saul, like most writers in the 1960s and early 1970s, was unwilling to admit the extent to which the co-operatives were the

creation of central government, and therefore an open encouragement to imaginative entrepreneurs to benefit personally
from whatever patronage was available from the government.
The manner in which their salaried officials were appointed
made the unions essentially undemocratic, and it was at union
level that the power to take policy decisions lay. Union officials
had a large say in the appointment of the salaried staff (co-
operative secretaries) of the primary societies, while those who
were elected by the primary societies to union committees were
liable to be corrupted by the opportunities for earning allowances, or getting credit. With no effective democracy at the
primary society level, there could be no control over the unions,
and probably there could have been no effective local democracy without more emphasis on co-operative *production*, instead
of just co-operative marketing. So the co-operative movement
after independence in no way reduced differentiation; on the
contrary, it allowed the strong to get stronger while taxing the
poor through its deductions and cesses on the value of their
crops.[11]

THE EXTENSION SERVICE

Before 1956 the 1500 or so extension workers had been, in
effect, rural policemen who arrested and prosecuted farmers
who did not follow the Native Authority rules and regulations.
Most had only a few weeks' agricultural training and many were
related to, or appointed by, chiefs. But the impressive gains in
production in the late 1950s were obtained without the use of
this kind of force, and there was a reaction against it.

The new emphasis on 'modern' agricultural technology justified a more highly trained extension service. The first two-year
certificate courses were started in the early 1950s, and agricultural officers were sent abroad for diplomas or degrees. By 1960
about 800 certificates had been awarded, while more than 200
officers had received higher education in agriculture (Ruthenberg 1964: 49).

In the 1960s this supposedly revitalized extension service was
studied several times, with depressing conclusions. The evidence
suggested that it was having little or no impact, except on some
of the larger farmers, or in a small number of crops (such as tea
and tobacco) for which the extension officer's approval was
needed if farmers were to get credit (most of this credit derived
from World Bank loans to Tanzania). The studies showed,
firstly, the extent to which extension workers and other govern-

MAP 5 Communications and main towns
(*Source*: Heyer, Roberts, and Williams 1981)

ment staff associated with each other, and with the richer farmers (Thoden van Velsen 1973: 159–162; Sender 1974: 42–5),
and, secondly, that most extension workers visited an extremely
small number of farmers. Hulls (1971: 6) found that in a year
the average extension worker visited only 73 households (some
of them more than once). The 'Rural Development Research
Committee' of Dar es Salaam university employed students who
accompanied extension workers during a week of their working
lives. They discovered that the average extension worker worked a 32-hour week, of which about 9 hours were spent on farmers' farms. The time spent on other types of agricultural work
(meetings, credit applications, inspection of stores, showing officials around, and in schools) totalled nearly as much (Cliffe
et al. 1968: 3–5).

But thirdly, the studies showed the limited extent to which
the farmers were actually following extension recommendations:
Hulls (1971) found that only 38 per cent of the cotton in his
sample taken across Sukumaland was planted during the recommended period (p. 11); the average plant population per acre
was about half of that recommended (p. 16); only 3 per cent of
the sample used fertilizers or insecticides (p. 18), and 40 per
cent did not know why it was good to uproot and burn cotton
stalks at the end of the season (p. 23). He concluded:

There seems to be no valid reason for altering the conclusions that the
Extension Service in Sukumaland is at present having no measurable
influence on the cotton husbandry standards of the vast majority of
farmers in Sukumaland. Since the major extension effort has been concerned with cotton production it seems extremely unlikely that such extension effort as there has been with other crops has been any more
effective. In short, the failure to communicate modern agricultural
technology to the vast majority of the farmers of Sukumaland appears
to have been almost total. (Hulls 1971: 30.)

Finally, many studies found that much of the advice given by
extension workers was not appropriate to small farmers. The
clearest case of this concerned inter-cropping. Even today extension workers are still trying (with little success) to persuade farmers to plant their crops in pure stands—but meanwhile the
advantages of inter-cropping (planting more than one crop in a
field) have been realized by agricultural economists, and research stations are proving that a given field inter-cropped will
frequently yield more than the same field divided into two
halves, with each half planted with the pure stand (Finlay 1974).

Belshaw and Hall (1972: 55) give nine reasons why inter-cropping can benefit farmers. These include agro-economic reasons, such as plants with different types of roots not competing for nutrients, labour savings (e.g. in weeding), and minimization of risk if one of the crops fails. As far back as 1963, Beck (1963: 18) established that the low yields of many coffee bushes on Mount Kilimanjaro were not due to the presence of bananas, and Collinson (1963b: 18) discovered that addition of groundnuts to a crop of maize did not lower the yield of maize. A recent study of Bukoba coffee brings out the complexity of the issues, and the potential dangers of disturbing a farming system established over centuries:

In the major coffee-growing areas of the Region, coffee is grown inter-planted with bananas, as it was in the pre-colonial period. This arises both from land shortage and from the nature of the husbandry system on the very poor and infertile soils of coastal Bukoba. These have been characterised by one agronomist as little more than a rooting medium and though this is an exaggeration, there is no doubt that they are very poor in plant nutrients. This was overcome by the Haya and their predecessors in the area by planting permanent banana *Bibanja* [groves]. . . on which fertility was gradually built up by manuring and mulching with manure and crop residues, banana leaves, grass and manure from cattle grazed on the poor *Rweya* grazing land. In this way, soild nutrients from a relatively large area were concentrated upon the *Kibanja* in which beans, coffee and various other annual crops were inter-planted with bananas. . . . Thus even if land was available, to produce pure-stand coffee would have required turning over part of the permanent food plot, on which fertility had been laboriously built up over generations and whose size would in most cases be tailored to family subsistence requirements.
    Nevertheless, for the past 40 years, the agricultural extension service has been encouraging farmers to plant pure-stand coffee and considering this practice the *sine qua non* of modern farming. . . . It is scarcely surprising that the extension service has had minimal success. (Raikes 1976a: 2–3.)

Belshaw and Hall give other instances where the researchers who produced extension recommendations failed to put themselves in the shoes of small farmers. For example, if land is available in plenty, a farmer wanting to increase production has the choice of intensifying his production (by use of chemical inputs) or of expanding extensively (by using more land). But often there is more risk in the former, even if he gets his inputs on credit. In 1975 a conference of extension and research officers recommended the use of fertilizer on maize; but their own figures (Table 17.3) showed that the average gain in income from using fertilizers was only 50 shillings per acre—in a bad year a farmer who used fertilizer could easily be worse off. A series of trials subsequently showed that fertilizer on improved varieties of maize does pay in some parts of the country, but not in others, such as Tanga Region (Sperling 1976). But the extension service continues to advocate use of fertilizers almost everywhere.

TABLE 17.3

Economics of maize fertilizer trials near Iringa 1972/3 and 1973/4 (shillings)

	No fertilizer	Medium rate of fertilizer	High rate of fertilizer
Income per acre	852	1295	1534
Costs per acre	470	862	1106
Margin per acre	382	433	428
Additional income from using fertilizer	—	51	46

Assumptions: large-scale farming and chemical weed-killers
Source: Research/Extension seminar, Iringa, February 1975.

Similar problems are found in the choice of crops recommended. Often these are not the best-paying crops in the area. Collinson demonstrated this with regard to a long campaign in parts of Tabora Region to grow aromatic tobacco when flue-cured tobacco was far more profitable (Collinson 1970). In parts of Ruvuma Region as late as 1968 each farmer was being compelled to grow one acre of fire-cured tobacco, a crop that gave an extremely low return for the labour involved. Cotton continues to be recommended for the coastal areas, even though it is not the best-paying crop, and is very susceptible to insect damage (Coulson 1977c: 51–3). In 1974 the government made Dodoma one of the centres for its World Bank financed 'National Maize Programme'; by the following year it was recommending millet and sorghum—but sequences involving a few years of government promotion of maize (the crop with the greatest average yield), until there is a famine, followed by some years of promotion of millet and sorghum (the crops with the greatest yields *in poor years*) can be found during the colonial period (von Freyhold 1979: 12–14). The farmers are under-standably confused by such changes in policy.

Finally, we can get an idea of the virtues of the extension ser-vice by looking at the projects claimed as success stories. In 1964 Ruthenberg published a well-researched defence of exten-sion, and as examples of success he gave the expansion of coffee growing, and of pyrethrum, higher cotton yields in Kilosa, 'cat-tle/coconut schemes' in Tanga, and the introduction of ox-drawn equipment (Ruthenberg 1964: 69–77). Today, with the possible exception of coffee, these cannot be regarded as successes. The increase in coffee production has been shown to be due more to increased acreages than to new methods (Saylor 1973). Pyrethrum production subsequently declined, as did cotton pro-duction from the whole eastern zone, including Kilosa. The Tanga cattle/coconut schemes collapsed not long after Ruthen-berg wrote (Groeneveld 1968), and encouragement of ox-cultivation has had to start almost from nothing in every five-year plan.[12]

Later the smallholder tea schemes in the Usambara moun-tains, in Bukoba, and in the Southern Highlands were described as success stories (Moody 1970; Luning and Venema 1969). But recent research found that yields in the Bukoba smallholder tea project were only 50 per cent of those anticipated, while only half the planned acreage had been planted (Raikes 1976c: 7). A similar story can be told about tobacco production in the Tabora area (Boesen and Mohele 1979).

In the period of the focal-point approach, production certainly rose. The evidence summarized above suggests that the role of the extension service in producing this increase can easily be ex-aggerated. President Nyerere had more research supporting him than perhaps he realized when he said that 'even if he was to sack all agricultural officers, agricultural production would in no way be affected, because the experts confined themselves to sta-tistics and report writing anyway'.[13] He would have been even more precise if he had added that when they did meet farmers, it was usually the richer, educated, commercially-minded farmers—and that even they frequently rejected the advice offered.

COMMUNITY DEVELOPMENT

The idea of community development was to soften up tradition-al communities who were resisting the cash economy—i.e. the extension of capitalist relations of production. In the words of the First Five-Year Plan (Vol. 1, p. 34): 'Especially in rural areas, even greater reliance will be placed on the Community Development staff to prepare the ground for the reception of the advice and instruction of the technical services by, for example, overcoming apathy and attachment to out-dated practices.'

Much of the community development effort was complementary to extension and co-operative policies: according to the Plan the Community Development Department would give 'the most efficient agricultural producers ... the honorific title of Pioneer Farmers', and advise farmers on the value and use of co-operative societies as means of marketing their crops and obtaining government credit (p. 35).

But there was one important difference. At least half the community development staff were women, and much of their activity was directed towards introducing peasant women to Western ideas about child-rearing, cooking, eating, and health. This type of work was too obviously manipulative to be very successful, and a separate Ministry of Community Development ceased to exist after 1967.[4] The obituary was written by Michaela von Freyhold;

the 'community development officer' ... was sent to foster among peasants a desire for higher standards of living and to teach them how they might achieve this out of their own resources, despite backward agricultural technology and low prices for their products. ... originally the idea of this paternalistic institution appears to have been to send a sufficiently 'Westernised' person to the rural areas so that some of her knowledge and habits in child-care, nutrition, sanitation and home-crafts would somehow rub off on the villagers. ... The struggle against ignorance and disease was thus presented as one against old traditions and for a more 'modern' way of life whose incarnation was the European. This worked to some extent in areas where mission influence was strong ... In areas outside the mission orbit people had their reservations against the foreign ideas. It was still felt that worrying about nutrition, sanitation and disease prevention was for Europeans while they themselves had neither the means nor the calculating mind (which peasants think is necessary) to improve their health and living conditions in any substantial way. In order to attempt the laborious task of eradicating disease and malnutrition despite private and public poverty the peasants would first have to believe that they can succeed and that their health is important. Short of a cultural revolution which attacked the self-neglect of peasants as part of the lack of self-assurance which colonialism had caused, the community development officer was charged with a hopeless task. (von Freyhold 1979: 39–40.)

THE TRANSFORMATION APPROACH

The first settlement schemes had been started in the early 1950s on the land originally cleared for the Groundnuts Scheme at Urambo and Nachingwea. The deliberate aim was to create 'yeoman farmers', who would learn 'modern agriculture' on relatively small holdings, but then graduate to 30- or 50-acre farms, which they would own on leasehold, and farm with hired labour and machinery (Overseas Food Corporation 1956: 159–63; Lord 1963; Ruthenberg 1964: 80–9). At Urambo the main cash crop was flue-cured tobacco, a crop whose price reflected the assumption that it could only be grown by European settlers. The crop was certainly more complicated to grow profitably than other crops grown by peasant farmers, and it required credit for fertilizers, for curing barns, and for labour. In order to qualify for credit the farmers depended on the recommendation of the extension workers. But the returns far exceeded those in the ordinary agriculture of the area and the scheme prospered (Scheffler 1968: 275–305). At Nachingwea there were plans for mechanized production of groundnuts, soya beans, and maize. Here prices were similar to those available to peasants growing the same crops, and fees were deducted to cover the overhead costs of the scheme. Settlers left the scheme as fast as they came in (Ruthenberg 1964: 82). These were the models for the settlement schemes in the First Five Year Plan. Thus in 1963 one could not claim that settlement schemes were viable: there were as many failures as successes.

The 1963/4 schemes, with the exception of some tobacco projects established by the British-American Tobacco Company and the possible exception of one scheme for which the main crop was wheat, were complete failures. The policy was officially abandoned in April 1966 (Kawawa 1966), with financial loss of about 20 million shillings. Very little surplus had been marketed, and the settlers had simply exploited the credit made available by the government. Since the schemes were to be 'modern', everything was of the best: houses were built for the settlers, tractors were provided, and so were large quantities of food. There was no need for them to produce, or even to work. The result was summarized by President Nyerere looking back after six years:

When we tried to promote rural development in the past, we sometimes spent huge sums of money on establishing a settlement, and supplying it with modern equipment, and social services, as well as often providing it with a management hierarchy. In other cases, we just encouraged young men to leave the towns for a particular rural area and then left them to their own devices. We did these things because we recognized that the land is important to our economic future, but we acted on the assumption that there was a short cut to development in these rural areas. All too often, therefore, we persuaded people to go to new settlements by promising them that they could quickly grow rich there, or that Government would give them services and equipment which they could not hope to receive either in the towns or in their traditional farming places. In very few cases was any ideology involved; we thought and talked in terms of greatly increased output, and of things being provided for the settlers . . .

In effect, we said that capital equipment, or other forms of investment, would lead to increased output, and this would lead to a transformation in the lives of the people involved. The people were secondary; the first priority was the output. As a result, there have been very many cases where heavy capital investment has resulted in no increase in output—where the investment has been wasted. And in most of the officially sponsored or supported schemes, the majority of the people who went to settle lost their enthusiasm, and either left the scheme altogether, or failed to carry out the orders of the outsiders who were put in charge—and who were not themselves involved in the success or failure of the project. (Nyerere 1968c: 66–7.)

The irrigation projects fared little better. There were long delays in completing the preliminary work, and at the two largest schemes, Kahe (near Kilimanjaro) and Mbarali (not far from Mbeya), no outside donor was willing to pay for the work. By the time engineering work on the Kahe scheme was completed in 1970, a United Nations project set up specifically to advise what crops should be grown had failed to come up with any concrete proposals, and there was already evidence of salinity appearing in the 4000 hectares of cleared land. The government attempted to turn it into a kenaf plantation—with conspicuous lack of success. Mbarali did not cover even its running costs till the mid-1970s when Chinese management was brought in. A smaller scheme at Kalenga, near Iringa, designed and built by North Koreans, achieved lower yields than farmers growing the same crop (paddy) on the swamps outside the scheme, but without the heavy costs of irrigation works, and was eventually abandoned. Another small scheme at Mombo was used to grow annual crops of maize, which could have been grown without the irrigation. By 1975, apart possibly from a Chinese state farm at Ruvu outside Dar es Salaam (though there were reports that this had major problems of flood control), two expatriate-run sugar plantations, and some supplementary irrigation on set-tler coffee farms, there was not a single successful irrigation pro-ject in the country (Boeree 1972). Moreover no attempt was being made to persevere with the settlement scheme idea: those that continued to function had either been abandoned to peasant farmers or were being run as state farms.

MODERNIZATION IDEOLOGY

All the institutional policies discussed in this chapter—co-operatives, extension, community development, and settle-ment—were justified by an appeal to modernization theory. The view that peasants are primitive, backward, stupid—and gener-ally inferior human beings—dominates the rural chapters of both the 1961 World Bank report and the Tanganyikan First Five-Year Plan. We have already linked it, in Chapter 10, to education and class formation: it is obviously ahistorical, but powerful because it provides ideological support for an other-wise insecure class of the educated, causing them to believe that they, rather than workers or peasants, have the answers to the problems of development. Quotations from the First Five-Year Plan illustrate these attitudes and class positions:

The greater part of Tanganyikan peasant agriculture continues to be characterized by primitive methods of production and inadequate equipment. Yet significant inroads have been made into the conserva-tism of the rural population who, as they become organized into co-operatives, respond encouragingly both to the technical advice provided by Government staff and to cash incentives in the form of semi-durable and durable consumer goods. (p. 19.)

(Note the condescension with which the peasants are treated.)

Attitudes will evolve through social emulation, co-operation and the expansion of community development activities. Where incentives, emulation and propaganda are ineffective, enforcement or coercive measures of an appropriate sort will be considered. (p. 19.)

(The underlying threat of force.)

Community Development techniques will be concentrated in areas wherein a change in individual attitudes of peasant farmers has to be brought about in order to gain a response to technical advice. (p. 20.)

(The rationale for community development.)

...a change in emphasis is to be found in the relative shares of expenditure... devoted to the more radical transformation agricultural programmes... it is these programmes which, although long-maturing, bring about a relatively abrupt transition of the people concerned to modern techniques with regard to land use, land tenure and patterns of agricultural production, and economic attitudes. (p. 21.)

(The transformation approach as yet another way of breaking 'traditional' agriculture.)

A clearer exposition of the rationale for the transformation approach is given in the 1961 World Bank report:

When people move to new areas, they are likely to be more prepared for and receptive of change than when they remain in their familiar surroundings. And when people are under pressure to move or see the advantage of doing so, they can be required to abide by the rules and to adopt new practices as a condition of receiving new land. (IBRD 1961: 75.)

In all these quotations the objective is the same—increased production of cash crops. It is to be achieved by manipulation; the peasants are dehumanized, treated as objects out of which production is to be squeezed. The achievements of pre-colonial agriculture are ignored (see Chapter 3); it is not recognized that the colonial peasant was often correct to resist the technical advice he was given; and these quotations grotesquely underestimate the difficulties of transferring the technology of irrigation farming and mechanization to African conditions, problems illustrated by the failures of the settlement schemes. The transformation approach can be understood as a desperate reaction to peasant resistance: if there was no other way of making the farmer grow more crops, then the last hope was to take him right away from his 'traditional' surroundings, to settlement schemes on which, in return for land, he could be made to follow the instructions of the agricultural staff.

CAPITALIST AGRICULTURE

It remains to explain how, if the government policies failed—cooperatives, extension, community development, settlement schemes—agricultural production continued to rise up to 1967. For rise it did, at least as regards the main export crops. Some of the data have already been presented in Table 17.1. Between 1960–2 and 1966–8 coffee and cotton production grew at more than 12 per cent per annum—despite the departure of settler coffee farmers and falls in farmers' prices for cotton. The growth rate for production of cashewnuts and tobacco was around 10 per cent per annum. There are no reliable statistics for the most important food crops, but marketed wheat production rose at more than 20 per cent per annum, while imports of maize declined as a proportion of total imports between 1961 and 1965; by 1968 there were surpluses of 50 000 tons of maize which had to be exported at a loss, and a stock of paddy equivalent to two years' sales.[15]

At least part of the reason for these increases should now be obvious: it was associated with the continuation of the capitalist expansion which started in the years before independence. This left room for plantations and settlers (reassured by British support for the peaceful transition to African rule, and by the promises of Nyerere) as well as African capitalists. The latter were certainly emergent: every study of peasant farming in the 1960s found that the larger farmers contributed a disporportionate share of marketed production.[16]

The best-known case is that of Ismani, studied by the Feldmans in 1970–1 and by Awiti in 1971–2, where forest land was quickly opened up for maize growing in the early 1950s after a mill had been opened in Iringa. Ploughing was frequently mechanized, while weeding and harvesting were done manually by seasonally-hired labourers. Most of these labourers migrated from Njombe, a highland area about 100 miles away, where the agricultural seasons were different, so that it was possible to cultivate in Njombe and to work as a migrant labourer in Ismani (this is not to say that Njombe prospered as a result of exporting labour: wages were too low for that, and the agricultural potential of the highlands has not been realized to this day). There were also smaller maize farmers in Ismani. However, Awiti estimated that more than a quarter of the marketed maize was produced by just two farms, which cultivated 600 hectares between them, that another quarter was produced by nine farmers cultivating between 40 and 140 hectares and that another 17 per cent was produced by nineteen farmers growing between 16 and 40 hectares. At the lower end, 155 farmers with less than 2½ hectares produced only 5 per cent of the marketed maize.[17]

In the 1960s the Ismani area provided a large proportion of the marketed surplus of maize in the whole country, without which it would have been necessary to import food to feed the towns. By 1970 the land was being overworked, and yields had fallen from around 40 bags per hectare to around 10 bags (Awiti 1972a: 58). Production was subsequently disrupted by the attempt to impose socialist production in 1970 and 1971, and has yet to recover.

The Mbulu story, documented by Raikes (1971: 79–102), is similar, yet with interesting differences in detail.[18] Wheat was first grown in the 1930s by poverty-stricken South African farmers who had trekked all the way from South Africa. During the Second World War these farmers increased their production, with government guarantees, and there was also a government mechanized wheat scheme in the area. The first Africans farming the crop were noted at the end of the war. At first they used oxen, but they soon began hiring tractors and combine harvesters from settlers; later they managed to purchase their own, second-hand, and eventually they purchased new tractors and combine harvesters. During the years of the Mbulu Development Scheme (1948–53) large areas of forest were cleared, in order to remove tsetse, and became available for wheat growing. The expansion of African (as distinct from European) cultivation was facilitated by the Meru Land Case, which made it politically impossible to allocate more land to whites, and so both the colonial and the independence administrations encouraged the African farmers, treating them as one of the 'focal points'. The expansion got under way in 1950s, continued in the 1960s (wheat production trebled between 1960 and 1966, most of the increase coming from Mbulu) and 1970s. By 1972/3 wheat production, largely from this area, and from another area of African large-scale production in near-by Hanang, was over 50 000 tons, more than three times that of 1962, and there were at least a hundred African-owned tractors in the area.

Tractors were also used successfully in north-eastern Sukumaland, especially in Maswa District. Indeed many farmers who hired out tractors for wheat cultivation in Mbulu subsequently took them across the Serengeti plains and hired them out to plough land for cotton in Maswa. The Maswa operators were boosted by the failure of the co-operative tractor schemes of 1964 and 1966—for the tractors imported were eventually sold off cheaply and were purchased by these private operators. But they could not have kept them running without the co-operation of two tractor multinationals (Ford and Massey-Ferguson) who, with quiet government encouragement, and the unofficial understanding that they would keep their near-monopoly of tractor imports, set up a number of tractor servicing stations where spare parts were stocked and operators, could, if they wished, repair their own tractors under expert supervision.

The African tobacco growers who were originally established on land cleared for the Groundnuts Scheme in Urambo have already been mentioned. They became a powerful group of medium–large-scale tobacco farmers, borrowing large sums of money to finance fertilizer purchases, hired labour, and even firewood collection, which was eventually to become a technical constraint as the forest boundaries were pushed further and further back.

Finally some less well known examples: the division of the best rice land on the fertile northern shore of Lake Nyasa was most unequal: out of an area of 50 acres, twenty households (10 per cent of the total) held 22 acres (45 per cent of the total) while 34 per cent of the farmers did not hold any of this good land (van Velsen 1973: 162). The allocation of land for tea growing in the West Usambaras was also unequal. Much of the coffee produced by African farmers in Kilimanjaro came from the bigger producers—often related to chiefly families, for example in Rombo District. Cashewnut growing up and down the coast was unequally distributed, with big farmers owning several thousand trees; so was ownership of fishing vessels and nets both at the coast and on Lake Tanganyika.

The kulaks did not, however, provide all the increased agricultural production; there is also evidence that in the 1950s and 1960s there were large increases in the acreages which smaller farmers devoted to cash crops. For example, coffee spread very quickly on Mount Kilimanjaro, until almost all the grazing land on the higher slopes was planted with the crop. There was an increase in yield, but the estimated area increased at least twice and probably three times between 1950 and 1970 (Saylor 1973, Tables 14.5 and 14.6, p. 274). A similar process took place on Mount Rungwe, south of Mbeya, where large grazing areas were planted to coffee and, later, tea. In Sukumaland the area under cotton increased, from about 142 000 acres in 1945 to 582 000 acres in 1960 (Fuggles-Couchman 1964: 22), and almost certainly continued to expand up till 1967. Cashewnut planting in the coastal and southern area multiplied several times, so giving a great boost to production when the trees became mature ten years later, and propelling cashewnuts into fourth place in Tanganyika's exports in 1972. In the central parts of the country there were increased plantings of maize and paddy.

The evidence suggests that those increases were made with only slight improvements in technique. They did not involve much use of fertilizer or insecticide, or follow many of the extension recommendations. When tractor hire services, or ox-ploughs, were available, the kulaks made use of them, and they used newly developed seeds, in particular new varieties of cotton from Ukiriguru research station (one of the few successful agricultural research projects of the period) and maize. They were not averse to technical change, but simply unwilling to risk capital on unproven innovations: they changed to planting on ridges when they realized that this lessened soil erosion and made better use of rainfall, but were unwilling to adopt tie-ridging because it took too much labour in vital months and reduced yields in good years (De Wilde and others 1967: Vol. 2, 429–30). Their caution was understandable: in one of many examples the extension service forced farmers on Ukerewe island to use fertilizer (and so run into debt to the co-operatives) until, faced with continuing resistance, researchers discovered that the soil had become acid, rendering the chemical action of the recommended fertilizer ineffective. Mistakes like this, repeated in different ways over the country, made farmers very cautious about adopting any form of risky technology.

So why did the area under cultivation by small farmers increase? Since technical changes had only a small impact, it can only have been because farmers chose to work harder. It is difficult to find conclusive support for this view, except by process of elimination.[19] Prices rose at the beginning of the period, and consumer goods became more readily available as the road network and motor transport improved. Peasants wore more attractive clothes, and began to purchase radios, bicycles, or metal roofs for their houses. Cash was also needed for school fees, though (with the exception of Mount Kilimanjaro and some other coffee-growing areas) this still affected mainly the richer farmers. But, above all, the production increases can be associated with the rise and triumph of the nationalist movement. Suddenly, in the last half of the 1950s, Africans began to gain new faith in what they could achieve. The co-operatives were not very democratic, but they were run by Africans. Nyerere and his colleagues toured the country talking of the time when Africans would rule, and within a few years it became clear that this was not far away. When it arrived everybody expected immediate prosperity, a future for every child. Nyerere realized that he had to counter these hopes for instant prosperity. And so his slogan for the early years was *Uhuru na Kazi*, 'Freedom and Work'; he taught that prosperity was not immediate, that it had to be worked for. It was hard work, rather than any fact of economics or agricultural science, that enabled agricultural production to continue rising so splendidly for the first five years of independence. The paradox was not just that most of the government policies failed, and were eventually to return as a burden (through taxation) on the producers. It was that the increases were largely achieved with exactly the type of capitalist production relations that Nyerere so much disliked, but which were, by 1967, too firmly entrenched to be easily overturned by any change in government policy.

18 INDUSTRY BEFORE THE ARUSHA DECLARATION

It was assumed that foreign private capital would easily flow into Tanzania if favourable conditions... were created.

RWEYEMAMU (1973: 39)

Before the Second World War very little manufacturing took place in Tanzania, other than the first-stage processing of such crops as sisal, cotton, or tea, which was essential if they were to be exported. Even the post-war development plans made little provision for investment in manufacturing; the government-inspired triple investment of the 1950s in meat canning, paint mixing, and tin-can manufacture discussed in Chapter 9 was really no more than a device to establish another form of agricultural export, that of canned meat.

But suddenly, about three years before independence, the private sector started investing in manufacturing for the local market. Within six years, nine textile factories had opened, plus another brewery, factories producing corrugated-iron sheets, aluminium cooking utensils, shoes, and cigarettes, three sisal-spinning factories, another sugar estate and factory, and at least twelve factories that made chemical, plastic, or rubber products from imported ingredients. By 1963 seven building contractors had facilities to make pre-cast concrete articles, a reflection of the building boom that was taking place and of the type of technology increasingly used in large construction projects.[1] By 1965 a cement factory, a glass-bottle factory, and an oil refinery were under construction.

Why did this investment not occur earlier? It was not because the market was too small, for Rweyemamu has shown that the local markets for most of these products, as determined by imports, were big enough to justify factories being built several years before they were actually built. He also identified the role

played by protection: virtually all these factories operated behind protective tariffs, which meant that consumers purchasing
an imported product had to pay high duties, whereas the imported inputs for the local factories were allowed in duty free.
Some of these duties were imposed to raise revenue, or as
general protection in advance of specific industrial proposals; for
example duties on various textile products were imposed in
1954, 1957, and 1961; others were specifically imposed by the
government of the day to enable particular factories to open,
such as the duty on cigarettes of 100 shillings per kg which enabled the British-American Tobacco Company (then the East
African Tobacco Company) to open its factory in 1962; the 70
cents a square yard duty on imported blankets which was given
to Blanket Manufacturers Ltd. the following year; or the 37½
per cent (later 50 per cent) duty imposed on imported transistor
radios in 1965. It would, however, be unwise to claim that this
protection caused the industrialization, for presumably other industrialists who wanted to invest could have persuaded the colonial government to grant them protection (Rweyemamu
1973: 122 f.).

Two other aspects, however, do provide an explanation of
why industrialization was so slow to start, and then so rapid.
The first is the role of the Asian community, and the second the
relation of Tanganyika to the much more advanced industrial
economy in neighbouring Kenya.

Martha Honey has pointed out that a large proportion of the
factories opened in this period involved the Asian community.
The capital was raised in a variety of ways: some, such as that
of the Karimjee family, who owned sisal estates, was raised
directly in agriculture. Some was raised through trade, either
produce export or the import of consumer goods. This surplus
was channelled into industry by communal investment banks,
such as Investment Promotion Services, set up by the Aga
Khan. The capital for many of the most expensive investments
was moved from other parts of East Africa.

In the late 1950s and early 1960s the Aga Khan encouraged
his followers to invest in industry in order to protect their future
in the country. Their traditional trading activities were
threatened by the co-operative movement, which was taking
over produce buying, and clearly wished to take over importing
and wholesaling, and, if possible, retailing as well. In fact, importing and wholesaling were not nationalized till 1970 and serious inroads into the retail trade were not made till the mid-

1970s. But the instinct was right; for trade was essentially insecure for the Asians, whereas, once they became involved in
manufacturing, they either had to be tolerated or compensated
if they were taken over.

The Asians moved money out of Kenya and Uganda because
for a time it seemed as if both of these countries were unstable.
There was a civil war (Mau Mau) in Kenya, with the prospect of
an independent white-settler state to follow. Uganda was uneasi-
ly divided between the Baganda and the rest. In any case the
rich Asian families recognized that nationalism would be a force
to reckon with in the future: they could not rely on the survival
of an East African Common Market, and so decided to spread
their risks. The Madhvani family, whose money came from thirty sugar plantations in south-eastern Uganda, and who had
already invested in sugar and biscuits in Uganda and Kenya,
beer brewing in both countries, and glass bottles and pottery in
Kenya, now proceeded to set up all these enterprises in Tanganyika as well. In 1957 this family was joined by marriage to
one of the most dynamic Tanganyikan Asian business families,
that of the Chandes, who had built up the grain-milling and oil-
crushing interests of Chande Industries. The Chandaria family
set up an aluminium factory in Tanganyika that mirrored its factory in Kenya, and was soon to produce a wide range of metal
products. The first two textile factories in Dar es Salaam were
built with capital brought in from Kenya (Honey 1974: 64–9).

By the time that the Asian community started investing in
manufacturing in Tanzania, there had been thirty years of industrial investment in Kenya. In 1963, the year of Kenyan independence, the manufacturing sector contributed £29 million to
the Kenyan economy, more than three times the contribution of
manufacturing to the Tanzanian GDP (Seidman 1972: 45–6).
However, 70 per cent of this came from just thirteen plants,
most of which were involved in last-stage assembly and/or processing. Of the materials used, on average 42.5 per cent were
imported; but the figure was as high as 95 per cent in textiles,
paper and paper products, and rubber, 90 per cent in paints and
metal products, and 85 per cent in footwear. One hundred per
cent of the parts used in motor vehicle repair were imported
(Seidman 1972: 22–5).

Five types of investor were involved. We have already mentioned the Asian families, such as the Chandarias and the
Madhvanis. But the initiative to get government backing for industrialization had come from the settlers, either as individuals

or as co-operatives such as Kenya Co-operative Creameries (making dairy products) or the Kenya Farmers' Association which became involved in agricultural processing and milling. Then there were the European trading companies which played major roles in importing and exporting during the colonial period: Smith-Mackenzie, the largest, which merged with one of its main competitors, Dalgety, in 1965, the whole subsequently being taken over by a syndicate of its African directors in 1975; Baumans; Mitchell Cotts, whose interests included world control of the market for pyrethrum; Wigglesworth, heavily involved in the sisal industry; and there were others, including subsidiaries of Unilever (the United Africa Company) and Lonrho. It was in fact through these trading companies that the multinationals, the fourth type of investor, frequently became involved.[2] Finally there were individual business men, nearly all immigrants who had been able to bring a little capital and a little expertise with them from some other country; many of them, from the Mediterranean, the Middle East, or South-East Asia, floated around the world after the Second World War, and a few came to rest in East Africa.

Several of the biggest companies involved settlers, trading companies, and multinationals working together. Thus in the 1960s the Chairman of East African Breweries, Sir Michael Blundell, was a leading settler and politician who was also a director of Ind Coope, one of Britain's biggest brewers, and a percentage of the shares were held by Courage, Barclay and Simmonds, another British brewing group. East African Industries, which produced soap and detergents, margarine, and toothpaste, among other products, became a subsidiary of Unilever, which already had many trading links with East Africa. The firms who invested in paint 'manufacture' (i.e. mixing) also involved trading companies, who could minimize their transport costs if the paint was mixed locally. Ralli Brothers Ltd. was an English firm involved in sisal and tea plantations, which rapidly diversified, taking over the Motor Mart and Exchange Group, one of the biggest importers of motor vehicles and other machinery, and then itself being taken over by Lonrho, which purchased widely from 1966 onwards, until ten years later it was probably the largest multinational firm (by value of assets) in Kenya. Its purchases included the Standard newspaper group (which published the Dar es Salaam *Standard* before its nationalization), a range of bus companies which included Dar es Salaam Motor Transport, various motor vehicle assembling and distributing companies, and agricultural plantations.[3]

The last two cases exemplify what happened in Tanzania before and after independence: many Kenyan companies started or purchased subsidiaries in Tanzania. East African Breweries built a new brewery in Dar es Salaam. Unga Limited, started by Lord Delamere and taken over by the Kenya Farmers' Association, opened modern grain mills in Dar es Salaam and Iringa. The Bamburi Portland Cement Company, with a plant in Mombasa, then owned by the Associated Portland Cement Manufacturers Ltd. (a British firm, the largest producer of cement in the world), and Cementia AG Zurich, a Swiss company, built the cement factory outside Dar es Salaam. British-American Tobacco, which opened a cigarette factory in Dar es Salaam in 1962, and the Bata shoe company, another multinational which opened a factory in Dar es Salaam in the 1960s, already had factories in East Africa. Most of the small Tanzanian operations of the 1950s and early 1960s were started by Kenyan trading companies, either for servicing their products, or for last-stage assembly, with the objective of continuing to control the Tanganyikan market even if the East African Common Market ceased to exist.

Thus the investment boom of 1955–65 was possible because Asians started investing in manufacturing, and because a number of companies established in Kenya (both Asian and multinational) decided to set up branches in Tanganyika. But there were also a few investments from newcomers. By far the largest was the oil refinery built in Dar es Salaam by ENI, the Italian state-owned petrol company. The project was agreed in principle in 1961, the agreement signed in 1963, and building work was carried out at speed between February 1965 and June 1966. The cost was 100 million shillings, of which 35 million were shares, half of which were purchased by the Tanzanian government in 1969. At 600 000 tons per annum designed capacity, the refinery was tiny by world standards (and small compared with the 2 000 000-ton refinery at Mombasa), but ENI was itself small in world terms, and did not have its own sources of crude oil; in order to expand it opened small refineries in a number of third-world countries, which mainly (as in this case) refined crude oil imported and owned by other oil companies such as Exxon and BP. This particular refinery ran at more than full capacity almost as soon as it opened, for Lonrho's pipeline from Beira in Mozambique through Malawi and Rhodesia to Zambia was closed following the Rhodesian UDI in 1965, and it became the main source of petroleum for Zambia as well as Tanzania.[4] Italian interests set up another company, half owned by Fiat and half by the Zambian and Tanzanian governments, which ran a lorry fleet to move the petrol to Zambia along the 'hell run'— then an earth road for most of its length. Yet another state-owned Italian firm designed and very quickly built a thousand-mile oil pipeline to Zambia, removing the need to transport most of the oil by road. But Zambia's copper exports were still coming out by road to Dar es Salaam; the Chinese were building a railway, but for the meantime the road was realigned and tarmacked; Italian contractors built long stretches of it, and would probably have built it all if the US government had not insisted (as a condition for World Bank finance) that nearly half the length be financed by USAID, so that only American contractors could tender. By 1976 Italian firms had enlarged the pipeline, expanded the refinery to 750 000 tons capacity, built a mooring buoy so that 100 000-ton tankers could discharge oil for the refinery, another refinery in Zambia, and a completely new pipeline.

Finally the government had a commitment to the processing of agricultural crops before export, which led it to support semi-mechanized shelling of cashewnuts and the manufacture of instant coffee, even though these were profitable only if the government supplied the inputs at prices below what could have been earned by exporting them unprocessed.

Thus from 1955 to 1965 Tanganyika was experiencing a process of import substitution, typical of industrialization in peripheral capitalist countries in everything except its late start. It was possible because the government gave tariff protection when it was asked for it, guaranteed that compensation would be paid for assets nationalized (the Foreign Investment Protection Act of 1963, reprinted in Smith (ed.) 1966: 285–94), and went out of its way to provide land and other services to potential investors. The conditions without which the multinationals in particular would not invest were such as to give them monopoly or near monopoly power in the local market. This affected the scale of their investments: they were often able to use machinery that embodied labour-saving technology, which required a relatively large guaranteed market if it was to justify its high capital cost; thus while value added in manufacturing rose from 109 million shillings in 1960 to 271 million in 1966, employment in manufacturing rose more slowly, from 20 000 in 1958 to 30 000 in 1966. Sometimes even with the protection the market was not big enough to justify the latest technology. There were then three alternatives: to use out-dated technology, often most easily purchased in the form of second-hand machines; to devise a technology specifically for small-scale operation, as did the giant Netherlands multinational, Philips, before investing in small assembly plants such as its factory in Arusha;[5] or to depend on the extra profit provided by the protective tariff, and to operate with over-capacity, at least until the market expanded. In any case profit could probably be made, and taken out quite openly (Table 18.1); it was later, when the long-run commitment to Tanzania of many of the multinational companies with whom it dealt was unclear, that resort had to be made to transfer pricing in order to take profits out of the country.[6]

TABLE 18.1
Gross profits outflows and net inflows of private capital 1961–1968

Year	Profit outflows (Million shillings)	Capital inflow (Million shillings)
1961	71.2	50
1962	73	58
1963	123	155
1964	93	79
1965	110	−6
1966	114	138
1967	159	−66
1968	114	76
Total	857.2	484

Source: J. Rweyemamu, 'The political economy of foreign investments in the underdeveloped countries', *African Review*, 1. 1(1971), 115.

Factories started in this way were only by accident linked to each other, or to other parts of the economy. The case of Madhvani, who began in sugar, then moved to beer, and then to glass bottles, was exceptional. The typical industry of the period, for instance the Mount Carmel Rubber Company, imported its raw materials, and sold most of its products locally. Cotton is one of the country's major agricultural products, but none of this cotton was spun locally till 1966. Before that date all Tanzania's raw cotton was exported, while its textile and garment industries depended on imported cotton, rayon or cloth. The way in which industries were started, involving processing

for export or import substitution based on imported raw materials or components, certainly gave little scope for intermediate
goods production, and virtually none for the production of
capital goods. Production of machines, or even of intermediate
products like steel or chemicals, would have required planning,
exporting, organized technical training, and more self-confidence
than could be found even in the First Five-Year Plan.

19 THE ARUSHA DECLARATION

> The Arusha Declaration marked a turning point in Tanzanian politics. The ideology of the country was made explicit by it; also the introduction of 'leadership qualifications', and the measures for public ownership, began a new series of deliberately socialist policy objectives.
>
> President Nyerere (1968: 231)[1]

Before the Arusha Declaration Tanzania was an ex-colony much like other ex-colonies in Africa. After the Declaration, rightly or wrongly, it was frequently listed alongside Cuba, North Korea, and North Vietnam as one of the few socialist countries in the underdeveloped world. While such comparisons were obviously premature—as Nyerere himself pointed out—the Arusha Declaration was undeniably a step in the direction of socialism. Although it was amended by the National Executive Committee of TANU, which discussed and approved it a week before its publication on 5 February 1967, the draft was written by President Nyerere, and the ideas and the strategy were largely his.

The Declaration began boldly: 'the policy of TANU is to build a socialist state', and then quoted the 'principles of socialism' from the TANU constitution. The first seven of these covered individual human rights, including freedom of expression, but the last two defined the role of the state:

That in order to ensure economic justice the state must have effective control over the principal means of production;

That it is the responsibility of the state to intervene actively in the economic life of the nation so as to ensure the well-being of all citizens, and so as to prevent the exploitation of one person by another or one group by another, and so as to prevent the accumulation of wealth to an extent which is inconsistent with the existence of a classless society.[2]

The Declaration then proceeded to define socialism as
(a) 'absence of exploitation', interpreted to mean that society
does not have 'an upper class of people who live on the work
of others';
(b) 'the major means of production and exchange are under
the control of the peasants and workers';
(c) 'the existence of democracy'; and
(d) a belief in socialism: 'socialism is a belief in a particular
system of living, and it is difficult for leaders to promote its
growth if they do not themselves accept it'.[3]
These suggest a lack of faith in democracy; for, if democracy is
effective and there is mass support for socialism, leaders who do
not believe in socialism will not be elected. 'Socialism', as defined here, could be an intellectual position promoted by a few
leaders who claim to act on behalf of the workers and peasants,
and control the major means of production. However, in 1967
there was indeed little mass commitment to any form of socialism, so perhaps control of the major means of production and
exchange by the nationalist state was the *only* road to socialism
at that time.[4] These issues are taken up again in the final chapter
of this book.

The third part of the Arusha Declaration, by far the longest
section, is an analysis of Tanzania's economic position, headed
'The Policy of Self-Reliance'.[5] It points to the inability of the
government to provide all the social services that are requested
of it, the dangers of reliance on foreign aid (whether loans or
grants), and the need to emphasize the role of agriculture and
rural development and to de-emphasize that of industry and
urban development, on the grounds that the majority of the
population live, and will continue to live, in the rural areas. The
only basis for 'development' is hard work by the people.

After a short section which clarifies the statement that anyone
who 'does not appear to accept the faith, the objects, and the
rules and regulations of the Party . . . should not be accepted as
a member', the Declaration concludes with the 'Arusha Resolution', passed by the National Executive Committee on 29 January 1967, five years and almost two months after independence.
It includes clauses that commit the Party to the economic policies described above, and it calls on the government to implement them; but its core is undoubtedly five 'leadership
conditions':[6]

1. Every TANU and Government leader must be either a peasant or a

worker, and should in no way be associated with the practices of capitalism or feudalism.
2. No TANU or Government leader should hold shares in any company.
3. No TANU or Government leader should hold directorships in any privately owned enterprise.
4. No TANU or Government leader should receive two or more salaries.
5. No TANU or Government leader should own houses which he rents to others.

A 'leader' was defined as any of the following:

Members of the TANU National Executive Committee; Ministers; Members of Parliament; senior officials of Organisations affiliated to TANU; senior officials of parastatal organizations; all those appointed or elected under any clause of the TANU Constitution; councillors; and civil servants in the high and middle cadres. (In this context 'leader' means a man or a man and his wife; a woman, or a woman and her husband).[7]

The Arusha Declaration was published on 5 February. The next day Nyerere announced that all the commercial banks in the country would be nationalized. Within the next week eight firms involved in grain milling (seven Asian-owned, one a branch of a large Nairobi company) were also nationalized, as were the six largest foreign-owned import-export houses. All insurance business was confined to the state-owned National Insurance Corporation, and the government announced that it would buy controlling interests in seven subsidiaries of multinational corporations: two brewery companies, British-American Tobacco, Bata Shoe Company, Tanganyika Metal Box, Tanganyika Extract (a subsidiary of Mitchell Cotts involved in the refining and export of pyrethrum), and Tanganyika Portland Cement. It also promised to take a controlling interest in the sisal industry, although exactly how this was to be done had not been worked out. In all these cases existing commitments would be honoured and the government would pay 'full and fair compensation for the assets acquired'.[8]

Another presidential paper, *Education for Self-Reliance*, was published just over a month later.[9] It was an attempt to reform the educational system so that it would provide useful training for the mass of the population and not just the few who would proceed to secondary education or university. In September, after another six months, a new rural policy of *ujamaa vijijini* ('socialism in villages') was propounded in yet another presidential paper, *Socialism and Rural Development*.[10] These papers, which were elaborations of ideas propounded in the economic sections of the Arusha Declaration, are discussed in more detail in the chapters which follow.

In nationalizing the banks and milling companies, the state took 100 per cent of the assets, while in the case of the manufacturing companies it asked for majority control. Barclays and the Standard Bank responded by removing their expatriate staff, but the newly created National Bank of Commerce survived its critical first three months, and eventually compensation terms were agreed for the assets taken over (Loxley 1973: 106–7). All the industrial companies except Bata shoe agreed to sell 51 per cent of their shares to the government; they probably welcomed the legitimacy conferred by a close association with the government, especially when they were offered management contracts to go on running their old companies, and were more than content to convert their equity holdings into loans to be paid back with interest at 8 or 9 per cent.[11] Sisal estate compensation took longer to negotiate, but since most of the estates were heavily in debt to the (now nationalized) banks, their net value was small, and there was not much to pay. In all, the 1967 nationalizations probably did not involve more than £20 million in compensation.[12]

Long before these negotiations were complete the government was nationalizing again. It took up its option to purchase 50 per cent of the shares in the oil refinery, and in early 1970 the President announced that by the end of that year all importing and exporting would be handled by the state. In 1971 anyone who owned buildings worth 100 000 shillings or more (other than the house he or she lived in) found them taken by the government, with compensation paid on a sliding scale which reduced to zero if the property was more than ten years old (on the grounds that property built for rental would have paid for itself within ten years).[13] Many other nationalizations and share purchases took place on a smaller or less publicized scale, including the takeover of butchers' shops in Dar es Salaam and other main towns in 1974. The main distributors of petrol (Esso, Shell, Agip, and Caltex) offered to sell a controlling interest in their local companies to the government (offers which must have been unsolicited, since the government decided to purchase shares in only two of the four—Agip and Shell; the others proceeded to slowly run down their Tanzanian operations). In 1976 the government actually nationalized the co-operative unions, replacing them by government corporations.[14] In less than ten years from the Arusha Declaration, the state had taken a controlling interest in virtually all productive institutions that could easily be nationalized. The effects of this are analysed in the chapters which follow.

Here it remains to consider the timing of Declaration, just over five years after independence, and the reasons for its acceptance. The Arusha Declaration can be seen as a reaction to a series of crises, which Nyerere used to introduce policies that fitted his own philosophy; some of these policies were popular, while others could only be forced through with the use of his tactical skill and feeling for timing.[15] As described in Chapter 16, by 1966 there had been a breakdown in relations with Tanzania's three most important foreign donors. Thus a policy of self-reliance, in the Arusha Declaration sense of minimizing the reliance on foreign government capital, was inevitable anyway. The first five-year plan had also seen a lower inflow of private investment from overseas than anticipated and most of what was built by the private sector was capital intensive and brought little employment; therefore, a policy which minimized the role of industrial investment also seemed more or less inevitable, at least for a period. There had also been the failure of the agricultural settlement schemes (discussed in Chapter 17), largely because, when presented with government-financed social services, the settlers had not produced; a policy which stressed that the only way to build the nation was by hard work was a logical reaction to this. And since most of the people lived in the rural areas, and the problems of rapid urban growth and unemployment were becoming more and more apparent, it was sensible to emphasize the need for investment in the rural areas. Moreover, as Pratt points out, 'the peasants had benefited very little, if at all, from the economic growth that had taken place since Independence so that widespread disillusion and discouragement seemed almost inevitable' (Pratt 1976: 227). This type of reasoning explains the need for the 'policy of self-reliance' of Part 3 of the Declaration.

But Nyerere was also faced with a deeper non-economic challenge, which appeared as a crisis in education. With so many administrative and professional positions to be filled, education, especially secondary or university-level education, was a passport to a well-paid job, the more so as salary levels reflected

European salaries while peasants' and workers' incomes certainly did not. Teachers and parents realized this and stressed the skills and examinations needed for entry to the higher educational levels. Those that passed through the system regarded themselves as privileged, with a right to salaries and power. In 1966 there were difficulties in the new University of Dar es Salaam where the second entry into the Faculty of Arts and Social Science, and the first into the Faculty of Science, were about to graduate. The immediate cause was the introduction of a new scheme of 'national service' under which those who left secondary schools and universities would undergo five months of military training following by 18 months in which they would work at their jobs but receive only 40 per cent of their salaries (tax free). In October 400 students marched to State House in their academic gowns with an ultimatum which ended: 'Therefore, your Excellency, unless the terms of reference and the attitude of our leaders towards students change, we shall not accept National Service in spirit. Let our bodies go, but our souls will remain outside the scheme, and the battle between the political élite and the educated élite will perpetually continue.' They carried placards protesting against the scheme (which they identified with Kawawa), one of which even proclaimed that 'Colonialism was Better.'[16]

Nyerere was furious. His impromptu speech, starting slowly and gradually working up to a crescendo of fierce anger, was recorded by a journalist who had followed the demonstration:

... I've accepted your ultimatum. And I can assure you I'm going to force nobody. You are right, your bodies would be there, your spirit wouldn't be there. You are right. I take nobody into the National Service whose spirit is not in it. Nobody. Absolutely nobody. (hesitant applause)

It's not a prison camp you know. I'm not going to get anybody there who thinks it is a prison camp, no one! But nevertheless it will remain compulsory for everybody who is going to enter government service. So make your choice . . .

You are right when you talk about salaries. Our salaries are too high. You want me to cut them? (some applause) . . . Do you want me to start with my salary? Yes, I'll slash mine. (cries of 'No'.) I'll slash the damned salaries in this country. Mine I slash by twenty per cent as from this hour . . .

Do you know what my salary is? Five thousand damned shillings a month. Five thousand damned shillings in a poor country. The poor man who gets two hundred shillings a month—do you know how long it's going to take him to earn my damned salary? Twenty-five years!

It's going to take the poor man in this country, who earns two hundred shillings a month, twenty-five years to earn what I earn in a year.

The damned salaries! These are the salaries which build this kind of attitude in the educated people, all of them. Me and you. We belong to a class of exploiters. I belong to your class. Where I think three hundred and eighty pounds a year [the minimum wage that would be paid in the National Service] is a prison camp, is forced labour. We belong to this damned exploiting class on top. Is this what the country fought for? Is this what we worked for? In order to maintain a class of exploiters on top?

. . . Forced labour! Go, go in the classroom, go and don't teach. This we shall count as National Service for three hundred and eighty pounds a year. You are right, salaries are too high. Everybody in this country is demanding a pound of flesh. Everybody except the poor peasant. How can he demand it? He doesn't know the language. Even in his own language he can't speak of forced labour. *What kind of country are we building?*

I have accepted what you said. And I am going to revise salaries permanently. And as for you, I am asking you to go home . . . (Edgett Smith 1973: 27–30).

The students applauded as the police moved in. Many did not realize that Nyerere had expelled them from the University.

This then was the context of the 'leadership conditions' of the Arusha Declaration three months later: the fact that ministers and civil servants were abusing their government allowances, beginning to take directorships of private companies in addition to their government posts, or starting to own houses for rental, was simply another part of the same story.

But Nyerere was also under attack from the left for his gradualist policies, as he had been since 1961. Admittedly he had neutralized the TANU Youth Leaguers, trade unionists, and army officers who wanted faster africanization and a take-over of the sisal estates. But there was still opposition internally from the 'populist' wing of the Party, including many of the politicians who had fought for independence, led by Oscar Kambona, and from a few socialist intellectuals, notably Abdulrahman Babu, the Zanzibari politician who had become a minister in 1964 and who wrote frequently in the Party newspaper, *The Nationalist*, demanding more aggressive socialist and nationalist policies.[17]

The intellectual *coup* of the Arusha Declaration, without which it would not have been passed by the Party National Executive Committee, was that it combined a huge concession on this front (i.e. the nationalizations) with a whole series of limita-

tions on the freedom of state employees to benefit personally
from their positions (the leadership conditions).

Even so, the opposition to the loss of privileges was considerable, and in the end two relaxations were made, allowing parents to deposit wealth in trusts for the benefit of their children,
and farmers to employ seasonal, but not permanent, agricultural
labour (Pratt 1976: 239). But when the Arusha Declaration
package was taken as a whole, it was impossible to oppose it.
Kambona tried to claim that the whole thing was not serious;
the nationalizations proved him wrong, and he soon fled the
country and campaigned ineffectively against Nyerere from outside.

What probably neither Nyerere nor Kambona anticipated was
that the Declaration would be wildly popular all over the country. Everywhere Nyerere was the hero, and the villains were the
politicians and civil servants who had been growing fat at the
expense of the masses ('blood-suckers', 'ticks', and 'parasites',
were three words used to describe them). Spontaneously, people
started marching to register their support. A young man died on
the 400-hundred-mile march from Arusha to Dar es Salaam and
overnight was made a national hero. By September marching
columns from all over the country were converging on Dar es
Salaam. In early October the President joined in, and marched
138 miles in eight days from his home village of Butiama to
Mwanza on Lake Victoria, where a TANU conference was held.
The arrival in Mwanza was described by *The Nationalist*:

Heralded by peasants' war cries, strains of brass-band tunes, and a din
of women's ululation, the President, beaming with revolutionary confidence, steered the Presidential column into the streets of the summit
town hedged with crowds of cheering masses... *Mwalimu's* brisk
march into the town stunned the masses who on seeing him in sound
health were driven wild with admiration and excitement to the borders
of near frenzy. The entire town was gripped with the revolutionary fer-
vour of the Spirit of Arusha.[22] (quoted by Edgett Smith 1973: 180).

Scenes like this had not been seen since independence itself.

By means of this carefully balanced package Nyerere ensured
that his personal position could hardly be questioned. He had
gained time in which to promote new policies in rural development, education, and in industry. It remained to see whether
they would be effective, and how they would affect the balance
of power in Tanzania.

PART VI: HARSH REALITIES

20 PRODUCTION AND INCOME DISTRIBUTION

> Over the last ten years we have done quite well in spreading basic social services to more and more people in the rural areas. More remains to be done; but we shall only be able to do it if we produce more wealth. And we have not been doing very well on that front.
>
> NYERERE (1977)[1]

For an evaluation of the performance of an economy, the conventional starting-points are the growth of its gross domestic product, and the behaviour of its balance of payments. The first is a measure of how much the economy is capable of producing for consumption or export, while the second begins with the balance of trade (the value of exports, less the value of imports) and shows how any deficit in that balance is financed.

There are, however, difficulties with measures such as these, based on adding up money values of goods and services. One difficulty is that an increase in the production of goods says nothing about the use of those goods—any increase may go to a small group of the rich, while the mass of the people get worse off.[2] This possibility is examined in the next section of this chapter, on income distribution.

A second difficulty is that gross domestic product, as conventionally measured, includes services as well as goods. Thus an increase in educational services, health provision, or even public administration, is counted in the measure as the cost of the wages or salaries paid to workers in those services. Now clearly such services are beneficial, in that people are better off with more of them than less. The difficulty is that a better health service, or a more efficient police force, is 'indirectly productive' —in the sense that it *may* enable others (workers, peasants, or companies) to produce more. But whether production increases or not, those who provide the services spend most of their incomes on what is produced directly, and thereby reduce the quantities of goods left for the rest of the production. If the increase in expenditure on government services is faster than the increase in production, then a strain is placed both on taxation and on the balance of payments (since some of the goods purchased by those who provide the services are imported, or have an import content). For this reason it is desirable to evaluate the performance of an economy not just on the basis of gross domestic product, but also to examine gross material product, a measure which includes the productive sectors but excludes services. Subsequently, in the following chapter, the main social services are examined one by one.

A third difficulty with aggregate measures is that they are affected by price changes over time. If prices rise, the value of GDP will rise even if the physical quantities of goods produced stay the same. The common practice, which we shall follow, is to measure everything as if prices had been frozen in some year (say 1966), a procedure which slightly understates growth rates.

The statistics provide evidence of a crisis in production, especially when the 1970s are compared with the 1960s: for example, the rate of inflation averaged only 2.1 per cent per annum between 1961 and 1971, but 22.5 per cent per annum between 1971 and 1977. The balance of trade, shown in Table 20.1, also showed a sharp deterioration, which started before the oil price rises, and owed more to declining export tonnages and unprecedented imports of food than it did to increased imports of capital goods.

The trade deficits reduced the country's foreign reserves almost to zero towards the end of 1975. As can be seen from Table 20.2, the economy was rescued by foreign exchange earned from services (mostly insurance and shipping, the former a consequence of the 1967 nationalizations) but above all by grants, loans, and special facilities arranged with the assistance of the International Monetary Fund and the World Bank. This strange phenomenon, that a country which was nationalizing property and officially committed to socialism became a large-scale recipient of Western 'aid', is considered in Chapter 24.

TABLE 20.1
Balance of Trade (Tanzania Mainland) 1965–1977
(Millions of shillings)

Year	Exports	Imports	Trade balance
1965	1400	1335	65
1966	1878	1691	187
1967	1760	1625	135
1968	1657	1834	−177
1969	1640	1659	− 19
1970	1713	2232	−519
1971	1777	2678	−901
1972	2025	2806	−781
1973	2302	3410	−1108
1974	2719	5137	−2417
1975	2434	5424	−2990
1976*	4108	5355	−1247
1977*	4482	6160	−1712

* Including Zanzibar.
Sources: IBRD (1977: Table 3.1) and Bank of Tanzania, *Economic and Operations Report*, June 1978, Table 20.

TABLE 20.2
Finance of trade deficits (Tanzanian mainland) 1970–1977
(Millions of shillings)

Year	Trade deficit	Income from services (net)	Transfers, grants, loans and SDRs (net)	Reductions in reserves	Unexplained residual
1970	519	226	603	114	−425
1971	901	209	1131	34	−473
1972	781	256	838	−390	76
1973	1108	130	944	−215	248
1974	2417	152	1632	606	28
1975	2990	451	2126	68	345
1976*	1247	466	1006	−156	−69
1977*	1712	602	2036	−992	66

* Includes Zanzibar.
Sources: IBRD and Bank of Tanzania.

The crisis is also apparent, though less obvious, in the figures for gross material product (Table 20.3). According to official figures GMP rose at above 4 per cent per annum in the 1960s and just below that figure in the 1970s, with manufacturing the most dynamic sector, especially in the 1960s. Mining was in decline, but the performance in agriculture appears highly respectable, rising above 4 per cent per annum in the 1970s. However, closer scrutiny reveals that apparently almost all this increase in the 1970s came from subsistence agriculture, rising at 6.5 per cent per annum, while monetary agriculture rose at only 1.6 per cent per annum, well below the population growth rate of 3 per cent. If we ignore the subsistence element, monetary gross material product grew at only 2.0 per cent during the 1970s. The rapid growth rate in the official figures for the subsistence sectors seems extremely improbable, since the years 1973–5 involved huge imports of food, much of which was distributed as famine relief in rural areas.[3] Since the figures for subsistence agriculture are compiled by adding together impressionistic estimates of production made by agricultural officers when they visit rural areas, a kind interpretation of the figures is that these officers were reluctant to admit that there was a crisis in subsistence production. The monetary figures, based on marketing authority

TABLE 20.3
Gross material product at constant (1966) prices 1965–1977

| | 1965 | 1968 | 1971 | 1974 | 1977* | Percentage growth rates per annum | |
						1965–71	1971–7
Subsistence agriculture	1381	1660	1664	1799	2420	3.1	6.5
Monetized agriculture	1194	1417	1502	1516	1656	3.9	1.6
Agriculture (total)	2575	3077	3166	3315	4076	3.5	4.3
Mining and quarrying	163	136	152	88	83	−1.2	−10.6
Manufacturing and Handicrafts	446	611	784	903	1013	9.8	4.4
Total GMP	3184	3824	4102	4306	5172	4.3	3.9
Monetary GMP	1803	2164	2438	2507	2752	5.2	2.0

* Provisional.
Sources: *Economic Survey 1977/8*, Table 3.

returns, are more reliable, and probably give a realistic interpretation of production trends in the rural areas.

In order to move from gross material product to gross domestic
product, the service sectors are added (see Table 20.4).[4] In the
last half of the 1960s the fastest-growing services were transport,
construction, electricity, and water supply, all growing at more
than 10 per cent per annum in real terms. In the 1970s the fastest-growing sector was public administration, including defence, public order, education, and health, growing at 11.2
per cent per year. Rapid growth was also shown by electricity and water supply, and in total the services were sufficient
to lift the growth rate of GDP to 4.8 per cent per annum in the
1970s—a convincing figure until one realizes that it depends first
on the suspiciously high figure for subsistence production, and
then on extremely rapid growth rates in government-provided
services.

Production figures support these conclusions: for example, the
figures for the main export crops in Table 20.5 show declines in

TABLE 20.4

*Gross domestic produce at factor cost at constant (1966) prices
1965–1977*

(Millions of shillings)

	1965	1968	1971	1974	1977*	Trend growth rates (percentage per annum) 1965–71	1971–7
Gross material product	3184	3824	4102	4306	5172	4.3	3.9
Electricity and water supply	53	72	96	127	150	10.4	−7.7
Transport, storage, and communications	400	618	814	958	1085	12.5	−4.9
Construction	198	309	380	413	374	11.5	−1.0
Trade and tourism	710	912	972	1068	1143	5.4	−2.7
Finance and property†	570	629	685	789	859	3.1	−3.8
Public administration and other services	658	764	952	1359	1804	6.3	11.2
Gross domestic product at factor cost	5773	7128	8001	9020	10 587	5.6	−4.8

* Provisional
†Less imputed bank charges.
Source: Economic Survey 1977/8, Table 3.

production for cotton and sisal, extremely slow growth for coffee and cashewnuts, and respectable growth from small beginnings for tea and tobacco, a completely different story from that
between 1960 and 1968 shown in Table 17.1, when the main
small-holder export crops were growing at 9 per cent per annum
or faster. The coffee figure is the hardest to understand in that
the coffee-growing areas were not affected by the villagization
programmes of 1973–5, and in 1976–7 the world coffee price
rose so rapidly that from a price point of view the country hardly suffered from the rise in oil prices in those years.[5]

TABLE 20.5
Production of major export crops 1966–1978
(tonnes)

	Average 1966/7 and 1967/8	Average 1971/2 and 1972/3	Average 1976/7 and 1977/8	Percentage growth rate per annum 1966/7 to 1977/8
Cotton	74 971	71 276	65 199	−4.1
Coffee	46 058	48 715	50 691	1.0
Sisal*	222 589	168 977	105 009	−7.5
Tea*	6 979	11 582	16 551	9.0
Cashewnuts	78 650	121 750	82 404	0.5
Pyrethrum	5 558	3 962	2 926	−6.3
Tobacco	—	13 577	19 350	7.3

* based on calendar years. For other crops figures refer to crop seasons.
Source: Bank of Tanzania, *Economic Bulletins*, Table 28.

The industrial production figures (Table 20.6) show the extent
of the creation of new industries in the 1970s, but also the limits
to the rapid growth. The table includes most of the large-scale
industries in the country (regrettably cashewnut processing,
cooking-oil production and glass bottle manufacture are not
included); note the absence of any reference to engineering,
machine production, or motor vehicles. Metal-working consisted
of rolled steel for the construction industry, iron sheets for
roofs, and aluminium for cooking utensils. The textile industry
had grown rapidly up to 1975, but then stagnated. Cement production was greatest in 1973, that of petroleum in 1972, fertilizer in 1975, and cigarettes in 1974. Sustained growth had been
shown by iron sheets, aluminium, ropes, wheat flour, batteries,
shoes, and rolled steel. Pyrethrum and canned-meat production
were in decline.

TABLE 20.6

Production in selected industries, 1966–1978

Commodity	Unit	1966	1967	1968	1969	1970	1971	1972	1973	1974	1975	1976	1977	1978
Textiles	'000 sq. metres	14 315	14 497	28 871	46 260	58 412	67 008	74 136	80 763	86 399	87 435	82 716	77 232	83 456
Beer	'000 litres	15 816	23 275[+]	31 185[+]	33 140[+]	38 601[+]	53 915[+]	64 823[+]	62 234	63 659	64 264	69 511	75 129	85 764
Cigarettes	millions	2 049	2 044	2 137	2 336	2 599	2 923	3 285	2 890	4 649	3 511	3 625	4 064	4 359
Cement	tonnes	—	146 910	156 338	167 632	176 826	179 313	236 956	314 000	296 000	266 000	244 339	246 500	272 000
Petroleum	tonnes	463 143	642 150	637 393	626 403	684 151	716 524	763 083	731 000	753 000	669 000	746 423	610 586	590 000
Iron sheets	tonnes	11 987	13 265	13 261	13 516	17 484	21 869	20 800	20 800	26 000	25 617	25 943	27 506	30 183
Enamelware	'000 pieces	5 306	3 841	4 881	5 608	5 436	5 561	4 267	4 150	1 378	2 657	2 183	2 838	2 331
Blankets	'000 sq. metres	3 444	3 584	3 577	3 644	4 154	4 077	4 583	5 476	2 686	4 309	3 676	3 514	2 706
Fishnets	tonnes	109	108	127	148	303	286	229	524	463	210	248	528	n.a.
Aluminium	tonnes	2 666	1 524	2 073	2 323	2 701	3 427	3 602	3 332	3 660	3 247	3 446	4 005	4 048
Sisal ropes	tonnes	10 332	15 126	16 718	18 724	20 404	23 138	22 575	25 354	29 496	25 492	42 377	36 535	31 423
Pyrethrum extract	tonnes	203	291	190	177	110	177	204	156	148	189	138	128	62
Wheat flour	tonnes	40 351	41 820	42 916	42 075	43 119	50 002	47 459	51 979	34 194	35 485	72 690	80 975	87 940
Canned meat	tonnes	9 310	9 673	6 824	6 988	7 980	8 362	4 878	1 401	4 740	2 193	1 650	580	764
Batteries	'000 pieces	—	—	5 543	11 278	15 026	24 012	36 552	45 049	48 001	50 301	57 870	64 684	70 914
Shoes	'000 pairs	—	—	1 490	2 200	2 100	1 600	2 457	2 320	2 800	2 700	3 689	6 331	6 383
Rolled steel	tonnes	—	—	—	—	—	—	—	4 776	8 591	9 298	10 500	11 912	16 423
Chibuku	'000 litres	—	—	—	—	—	—	—	7 092	6 203	9 612	10 365	13 580	15 226
Fertilizer	tonnes	—	—	—	—	—	—	—	32 594	58 778	59 327	42 146	36 886	44 443
Konyagi	cases	—	—	—	—	—	—	—	56 127	42 500	52 200	52 966	60 333	50 233

+ Beer and Chibuku.

Source: Bank of Tanzania. *Economic Bulletin*, March and December 1978, Table 27.

Import substitution took place, as shown in Table 20.7, in the sense that the proportion of imports spent on consumer goods declined while the expenditure on machinery, intermediate goods, and spare parts rose. An increasing proportion of an increasing sum was spent on machinery, reflecting the greatly increased investment budget. However, as is typically the case with this type of import substitution, many of the new factories involved only the last stage of manufacture or assembly of imported inputs, and were consequently intensive in their use of foreign exchange. In a survey of 39 plants in 1974 and 1975 Wangwe (1977: 69) found that 38 per cent were using less than half their available capacity, while nearly 80 per cent were affected by foreign exchange shortages, and of these 60 per cent imported 80 per cent or more of their material inputs. There were other reasons for the excess capacity: transport problems (20 per cent of the sample), shortages of credit (26 per cent), machine breakdowns (25 per cent), water shortages or cuts (20 per cent), power cuts (55 per cent), while in 45 per cent lack of demand for the products caused underutilization of capacity. There was a decline in labour productivity in manufacturing of approximately 3 per cent per annum between 1969 and 1974.[6] This was despite the new investment in the sector, most of it underwritten by the government. The World Bank calculated that whereas in 1968 an extra unit of output in manufacturing was associated with 3.6 units of investment, by 1973 the figure was 6.6 units; this implies a disastrous fall in the productivity of capital, although this can be partly explained by the falling capacity utilization in existing factories (IBRD 1977: 62).

TABLE 20.7
Percentage composition of imports 1967 and 1977

	1967	1977*
Total imports (millions of shillings)	1625	6200
of which (%):		
Consumer goods+	36	19
Building and construction materials	14	5
Other intermediate goods and spare parts	27	40
Transport equipment	8	11
Other machinery	15	25

* Provisional
+ Includes a portion of passenger cars.
Source: *Economic Survey 1977–8, Table 9.*

Central government income (excluding parastatal receipts but including most parastatal investment financed through the government budget) rose to over 30 per cent of the gross domestic product in 1973/4 (Table 20.8), but declined to 25 per cent by 1976/7, in a period of rapid inflation. Income tax receipts rose five times in ten years (owing to higher tax rates, especially on higher incomes, and the inflation which brought more salary earners into the higher brackets). Indirect taxes rose nearly as fast, largely due to the imposition of a highly successful sales tax and high excise duties on a number of non-essential products (including cigarettes, soft bottled drinks, alcoholic drinks, and petrol). These figures go far to disproving the view that a poor country such as Tanzania cannot raise a large proportion of its income in taxation. Since the sales tax was waived on some necessities (such as wheat and maize flour, and salt), and not collected on many local sales of agricultural produce, and there were high rates of import duty on imported consumer goods, the over-all effect of the tax system was progressive, in the sense that rich people paid a higher proportion of their incomes in tax than poor people (Huang 1976). Table 20.8 also shows the sixteenfold increase in financing from abroad between 1967/8 and 1976/7, nearly all of which was made available for 'projects' in the development budget. Without these inflows, the balance of payments deficits of the early 1970s could not have been sustained.

TABLE 20.8
Sources of government income 1967/8 1973/4 and 1976/7
(millions of shillings)

	1967/8	1973/4	1976/7*
Income taxes	264	697	1 377
Indirect taxes	589	1 911	3 394
Income from property	108	154	187
Foreign borrowing and			
aid—grants	3	214	626
—loans	81	467	777
Internal borrowing	194	723	−69
Others	171	261	244
Total	1 409	4 427	6 536
GDP at market prices	7 609	14 498	26 095
Government income as % of GDP	18.5%	30.5%	25.0%

* Provisional.
Source: *Economic Surveys*, Table 17.

Most of this government income went towards paying for government recurrent expenditure, and in particular for the salaries and maintenance costs of government staff and institutions, concentrated in the social services (Table 20.9). Only small proportions were available for investment, and these declined following the 1974/5 drought years when government expenditure (and foreign exchange) was diverted to importing food.

Nevertheless, both capital formation and gross savings exceeded 20 per cent of the gross domestic product in the early 1970s (IBRD 1977: 38–9). Much was financed from abroad, including the Tazara railway project, various highway projects and hydroelectric schemes, and investment in manufacturing and agriculture. The over-all picture is one of government taking increasing control of the economy, putting great emphasis on provision of social services and on increasing the rate of investment through use of foreign capital transfers and high rates of domes-

TABLE 20.9

Allocation of central government expenditure

| | 1967/8 | | 1976/7* | |
	millions of shillings	per cent	millions of shillings	per cent
Agriculture	143.7	10.2	705.7	10.8
Industry	16.8	1.2	444.4	6.8
General administration	269.5	19.1	803.9	12.3
Public order and safety	116.7	8.3	351.7	5.4
Defence	88.2	6.3	910.0	13.9
Education	194.0	13.8	1003.1	15.3
Health and social security	86.3	6.1	525.1	8.0
Housing	41.7	3.0	22.6	0.3
Water and electricity	69.8	5.0	545.4	8.3
Transport and communication	154.0	10.9	446.1	6.8
Other services	32.5	2.3	235.4	3.6
Pensions	48.0	3.4	82.0	1.3
Purchases of financial assets	14.7	1.0	72.5	1.1
Debt service	133.2	9.5	388.8	5.9
Total	1409.1	100	6536.7	100

* Provisional.
Sources: Economic Surveys, Table 18.

tic taxation, but being frustrated by failures in agricultural production and by low productivity in manufacturing.

PERSONAL INCOMES

One of the aims of the Arusha Declaration was to make income
distribution more equal, by cutting or holding down wages and
salaries, while emphasizing agricultural programmes in order to
increase incomes in the rural areas. It is convenient to examine
first the urban wage sector, then the rural areas, and finally the
situation of top income earners.

A factor which all classes had to learn to live with in the
1970s was inflation. Before 1972 this never exceeded 8 per cent
in any year; but in 1973 the index of retail prices for minimum
wage earners in Dar es Salaam rose 11 per cent, and in 1974 it
rose almost 75 per cent, largely owing to substantial increases in
food prices in November that year. The minimum wage was
raised substantially in 1973, and again along with the price rises
in 1974, but it was not raised again until 1980. The result was

TABLE 20.10
Standard of living of minimum wage earners in Dar es Salaam
1965–1978

Year	Minimum wage (shillings per month)	Minimum wage Index (1969 = 100)	Retail price index (1969 = 100)	Standard of living index 1969 = 100
1965	150	88	89	99
1966	150	88	89	99
1967	150	88	95	93
1968	150	88	99	89
1969	170	100	100	100
1970	170	100	104	96
1971	170	100	107	93
1972	240	141	119	119
1973	240	141	129	109
1974	340	200	169	118
1975	380	224	249	90
1976	380	224	307	73
1977	380	224	358	80
1978	380	224	419	53

Notes: retail price indexes are for minimum wage earners in Dar es Salaam; minimum
wages are as at the end of the years concerned.
Sources: compiled from data on employment, annual wage bills, and retail prices in *Economic Surveys* and Bank of Tanzania, Economic Bulletins.

that both minimum wage earners and those receiving average wages in manufacturing were better off in 1973 and 1974 than they had been before, but by 1978 anyone unlucky enough to have been left at the minimum wage was getting only just over half the real income he would have enjoyed ten years earlier (Table 20.10).

Between 1969 and 1975 the urban labour force grew at more than 9 per cent per annum (Table 20.11). Regular wage employment grew at 5.4 per cent, and there was a somewhat faster growth in the employment of casual labour, but the majority of those who moved to the towns either remained unemployed or joined the 'informal sector' of low-income self-employed, whose numbers increased from about 27 000 to about 78 000 in six years. Dr Collier, on whose work this paragraph is based, pointed out that in this period 'really serious poverty became a problem for the first time. The proportion of households living on less than 40 shillings a month at 1969 prices (83 shillings in 1975) rose from under one per cent to nearly ten per cent as a consequence of the increased number of households deriving income solely from the free entry (informal) sector, combined with the drastic fall in real incomes in that sector' (Collier 1977: 16.).

TABLE 20.11
Urban employment and unemployment 1969 and 1975

	1969	1975	Average growth rate per annum %
Total urban labour force	219 600	375 400	9.2
of which:			
Regular wage employment	153 200	210 500	5.4
Casual employment	17 100	27 700	8.4
Low-income self-employment	26 900	78 000	19.4
Unemployed	22 400	59 200	17.6
Unemployed as a percentage of the labour force	10.2	15.8	

Source: IBRD (1977: 16), based on Collier (1977).

Any analysis of the position in the rural areas is complicated by the problems of obtaining accurate data on agricultural production. However, a recent study by Frank Ellis, summarized in Table 20.12, found that between 1969/70 and 1978/9 the rise in

prices paid by rural consumers for what they purchased from
outside the rural areas exceeded by more than 25 per cent the
rises in the prices they received for their crops. Purchasing power in the rural areas fell to only 73 per cent of its 1969 value by
1974, large falls in the income from export crops being partially
compensated by increases in income from food crops. The position would look slightly less bleak from the farmers' point of
view if both the income from unofficial (and hence unrecorded)
sales was included and that from cassava, sorghum, millet, and
various beans, production of which increased at the end of the
1970s.

TABLE 20.12
Standard of living of rural producers 1969/70–1978/9
(indices 1969/70 = 100)

Year	(1) Index of producers' prices[a]	(2) Price index of goods purchased in rural areas[b]	(3) Farmers' Terms of Trade Index[c]	(4) Index of quantity marketed[d]	(5) Standard of living index[e]
1969/70	100.0	100.0	100.0	100.0	100.0
1970/71	101.1	104.2	97.0	114.8	111.4
1971/72	104.4	110.4	94.6	110.8	104.8
1972/73	110.8	126.6	87.5	114.2	99.9
1973/74	116.3	152.9	76.1	104.3	79.4
1974/75	131.2	203.5	64.5	101.7	65.6
1975/76	198.8	213.2	93.2	91.0	84.8
1976/77	259.4	236.4	109.7	93.4	102.5
1977/78	225.5	264.0	85.4	98.4	84.0
1978/79	219.1	293.9	74.5	97.7	72.8

Notes:
[a] Based on nine export crops and seven 'domestic' crops.
[b] Index adapted from the National Consumer Price Index.
[c] Figures from column (1) divided by those from column (2).
[d] The total income from the sixteen crops, divided by the indices in column (1).
[e] The total income from the sixteen crops, divided by the indices in column (2); no allowance is made for population growth, non-official crop sales, or income from other crops
or livestock.
Source: Ellis (1980: Appendix C).

The earlier study by Collier (1977: 20) calculated per capita
income in rich regions (Tanga, Kilimanjaro, and Arusha), poor
regions (Kigoma, Mtwara, Lindi, Mwanza, Ruvuma, Coast and
Dodoma), and middle-income regions (the rest). There were interesting differences. The cash income of smallholders in the

rich regions hardly fell between 1969 and 1975, but middle-income regions lost nearly 20 per cent of their cash income, while the poor regions lost nearly half.

The top income earners in the country were affected by the government wage policy. Upper income earners suffered from inflation, increases in income tax, and indirect taxes to the extent that they consumed beer, smoked cigarettes, or tried to run private motor vehicles. The ratio between the top salary in the civil service and the bottom narrowed from about 20:1 after tax in 1967 to 9:1 in 1976 (Nyerere 1977: 51), while Collier estimated that the real pre-tax incomes of 'capitalist entrepreneurs' declined by 47 per cent between 1969 and 1975 (Collier 1977: Table 15, p. 20). The leadership conditions of the Arusha Declaration prevented civil servants and parastatal managers from owning property for rental or shares in businesses, although these conditions were relaxed (at least unofficially) after the food crisis of 1975. Senior civil servants and managers also benefited from the increased availability of fringe benefits (such as subsidized housing and company cars) and by promotion to higher salary scales.

It is not easy to compare the cost of living in the country with the cost of living in the town. An urban worker might have to pay for bus fares to and from work, for rent, for higher prices of some goods (although the variety of goods available would be greater), and he would have to accept that in the town his wife would not find it easy to get either work or productive land to cultivate. In 1966, after five years in which wages had risen much faster than smallholder incomes, the average earnings of those in wage employment were approximately three times the gross domestic product per family arising from small-scale agriculture.[7] By 1975 one of the poorest groups in Tanzania were those in 'low-income self-employment' in the towns, who earned slightly less than the average smallholders in poor regions, who themselves earned only a third of the average incomes of regular wage earners in towns. Average smallholders in middle-income regions earned less than half the earnings of regular urban wage earners, while average smallholders in rich areas earned about two-thirds of the urban earnings—and in real terms were often as well off as urban workers. The World Bank (IBRD 1977: 11–24) concluded that the effect of the Arusha Declaration measures had been to prevent income distribution becoming more unequal, but that fundamental improvements had not been made.

To summarize a complex situation: rural producers, urban workers, and upper income earners were all worse off at the end of the 1970s than they had been at the beginning. It is possible that rural producers took a somewhat smaller decline in their living standards than urban workers, though the statistics on which such a statement is based are unreliable. Perhaps the situation may be highlighted by a comparison (Table 20.13) of the results of two nutrition surveys, one in a poor area of Dar es Salaam (Manzese) and the other in a poor rural area only about twenty miles away (Bunju village):

TABLE 20.13
Malnutrition among children in and outside Dar es Salaam

	Manzese, Dar es Salaam	Bunju, Coast Region	Average of eight rural areas
Date of survey	June 1976	July 1975	1975–7
Number of children examined	609	165	6519
Protein/energy malnutrition	2.5%	62%	31%
Severe protein/energy malnutrition	0.3%	8.5%	5.2%

Source: Tanzania Food and Nutrition Centre (1978: Table 29.2).

ZANZIBAR

The figures and discussion in this chapter hitherto refer to Mainland Tanzania; it is appropriate to turn now to Zanzibar and Pemba, though any discussion must be sketchy owing to the lack of data.[8]

Vice-President Karume was assassinated in April 1972, but until then he had ruled effectively as Head of State, for the terms of the union left Zanzibar responsible for its internal affairs, and even on some of the matters that were nominally the concern of the United Republic, such as immigration and the custody of foreign exchange reserves, Karume was unwilling to cede control.

Much can be deduced about the economic situation of the islands from Table 20.14, because, apart from small quantities of copra and cinnamon, cloves were the only export.[9] The fluctuations in production, with a good year usually followed by a poor one, can be clearly seen in the left-hand column of the table. In the 1950s and early 1960s the Clove Growers' Association purchased the crop and stored it if the price fell too low, with the result, also clear in the table, that production in a given year did not generally correspond to exports. From 1961 to 1968 the price of cloves was stable at a little more than 5000 shillings per tonne. But in 1969 it leapt to 20 000 shillings, a price maintained till 1974, and in 1975 there was another sudden rise to approximately 40 000 shillings per tonne.[10] As a result, from 1969 the Zanzibar authorities reaped a windfall rise in income. It is quite understandable that they were reluctant to share it with the much poorer Mainland.

TABLE 20.14
Zanzibar: production and export of cloves 1960–1978

Year	Production[a] (tonnes)	Exports[b] (tonnes)	Value of exports[c] (£ UK)
1960	6 500	n.a.	n.a.
1961	15 200	8 535	2 414 000
1962	5 900	7 749	2 080 000
1963	20 000	11 395	3 052 000
1964	3 900	8 159	2 191 000
1965	15 600	8 575	2 297 000
1966	1 500	13 727	3 687 000
1967	14 200	17 700	n.a.
1968	15 000	11 716	3 478 000
1969	n.a.	7 341	8 869 000
1970	5 100	4 769	6 370 000
1971	3 600	9 034	10 327 000
1972	n.a.	11 578	13 468 000
1973	n.a.	10 791	13 564 000
1974	n.a.	3 665	5 262 000
1975	n.a.	7 515	19 567 000
1976	n.a.	7 242	16 812 000
1977	n.a.	5 900	16 944 000
1978	n.a.	1 500	4 000 000[d]

Notes: [a] Figures refer to crop year: e.g. 1960 to 1960/1 crop year. *Source*: Adamson and Robbins 1975: Table 1.
[b] *Sources*: 1961–72 Adamson and Robbins, Table 2; 1972–7 calculated from Bank of Tanzania, *Economic Bulletin*, Dec. 1978, Table 22, and *Economic Survey* 1977/8, Table 15c.
[c] *Sources*: 1961–72 Adamson and Robbins, Table 2; 1973–7 Bank of Tanzania *Economic Bulletins*, Table 22 adjusted by exchange rates from Bank of Tanzania, *Economic and Operations Reports*.
[d] Based on the export value for cloves of 59.4m shillings in Bank of Tanzania, *Economic Bulletin*, Dec. 1978, Table 22(a), and a price of approximately 40 000 shillings per tonne.

Returns to the clove pickers were kept down, and (at least up to 1972) so were imports, to such an extent that there were shortages of food. At least £30 million was banked in the London branch of the Moscow Norodny Bank instead of being made available to the Bank of Tanzania as it should have been under the terms of the union with the Mainland. Foreign capital in the early years came from East Germany (at least 36 million shillings) and was used for the construction of a large hospital and many blocks of flats.[11] Loans from China were used to build a number of import substituting factories. State rice farms were opened up, and attempts were made to counteract two serious diseases that were affecting the clove trees, but there seemed to be little awareness of the fact that sooner or later the clove boom would end and a more secure economic base would be needed. There was certainly not much co-operation with the Mainland in economic planning: several of the new factories duplicated factories on the Mainland.

Politically the two countries became closer after Karume's death. Nyerere was asked to give a preference between the two obvious contenders for the succession, Thabit Kombo and Aboud Jumbe; he chose the latter, an ex-schoolmaster who already had experience in the union cabinet (he had been Minister for Health). Jumbe toured widely on the Mainland, and gained a reputation as a sincere and honourable man. In April 1977 the two political parties—the Tanganyika African National Union on the Mainland, and the Afro-Shirazi Party on the islands—joined to form the Chama cha Mapinduzi (CCM), the Party of the Revolution. This long-awaited merger coincided with the end of the clove boom. It also committed Zanzibar politicians and civil servants to the leadership conditions of the Arusha Declaration. In July 1980 there was talk of a possible *coup* on the island, and arrests were made.

Zanzibar and Pemba's population of about half a million was only 3 per cent of the total Tanzania population, and below the average for a Tanzanian region, although its clove income made it potentially richer than most Tanzanian regions. In 1980 the islands and the Mainland were still almost totally separated economically, although they were coming closer politically. For most purposes it was still correct to treat them as separate countries.

21 SOCIAL CLASS AND SOCIAL SERVICES

> Both coercive/repressive and ideological apparatuses
> are relied upon to increase social control over the
> peasant labour force.
>
> MBILINYI (1979: 225)

Statistics of income distribution, or economic growth, give little indication as to what it is like actually to live in a country. This chapter is an attempt to redress the balance by looking at what Tanzanians do with their leisure time, at the role of religion and the family, at the position of women, and at the main social services—health, housing, education, water supply, transport, and law and order—which government policy emphasized in the 1970s. Much of the discussion will presuppose an idea of social class—in the sense that some Tanzanians were better off than others—while leaving most of the questions about how class differences are created and maintained to Chapter 25.

On average, rural families were worse off than their urban counterparts, although the numbers of urban poor greatly increased in the 1970s (Collier 1977: 16). In the rural areas those who were particularly badly off included the sick or disabled, and old men or women who had never accumulated much for their old age (or had lost what they had) and had no younger relatives to support them. Even in areas where land was still available on demand, young men found it extremely difficult to survive the early years in which they were clearing new land and waiting for tree crops to become established, or until they had accumulated sufficient cattle to marry, thereby gaining the extra labour of wife and children. In areas where all the land had been taken, poverty could mean landlessness; for example Mount Kilimanjaro, the most prosperous area in the country, contained families with few rights to land, living in the traditional straw huts, and dependent on insecure work from the families living in the big, modern house nearby. Owing partly to this group, and partly to the low food value of the staple food (bananas), malnutrition statistics for Moshi District were worse than for many less prosperous parts of the country (Swantz and others 1975).

Young educated people—male or female—had the best chance of escaping rural poverty and obtaining work in the towns. Sabot found that a high proportion of those seeking employment in urban areas were primary-school leavers, while Bernstein found coastal villages almost entirely denuded of young people.[1] The villagizations of 1973–5, discussed in Chapter 22, had the unfortunate side-effect of encouraging this migration; on the one hand much valuable capital investment, in the form of established tree crops, permanent houses, or even grazing land, was lost; while on the other 1974 and 1975 were such bad years that in some places there seemed little point in starting to cultivate in new places.

There were also Tanzanians who were better off than the average in both urban and rural areas. An obvious group were the civil servants, whose numbers expanded at about 11 per cent per annum during the 1970s.[2] The entry qualifications for many training schemes (such as those for agricultural extension workers, teachers, and many types of technician) were upgraded, so that the normal entry requirement was Form IV of secondary school. This affected technical jobs in factories, as well as the civil service, and as a result the demand for Form IV leavers was seriously underestimated in the Second Five-Year Plan.[3]

In the urban areas there were some fairly successful African business men, though they had to compete with the established Asian family businesses, and with a government policy which favoured government or parastatal enterprises and was often suspicious of the African private sector.[4] In the rural areas, the absolute numbers of those cultivating large land areas with hired labour and machinery, involved in trading, or running buses or lorries, were a small proportion of the total.[5] They were, however, important in the productive process in many areas, and, even where they were less important, tended to maintain tactical alliances with the increasing numbers of government and party officials in the rural areas.

The industrialization of the 1950s and 1960s (Chapter 23) produced for the first time a settled working class in Dar es Salaam. It was predominantly coastal, Swahili speaking, and Muslim, whereas the managerial cadres (nicknamed the 'nizers' or 'Africanizers', i.e. those who 'africanized' jobs previously held by

Europeans) were mainly from up-country, spoke English as well
as they spoke Swahili, and were Christian. The result was workers and workers' leaders who could use the national language
better than their bosses. Since most managers were poorly
trained in manual skills, and did not stay long in one post, they
depended on the experienced workers to keep the machines
running. It is not surprising that the managers, as a class, were
insecure when confronted by articulate workers and their
elected leaders (von Freyhold 1977b: 15–18).

It is difficult to assess the role of religion.[6] Nominally, nearly
one-third of the population described itself as Muslim, yet
there were few large mosques (other than for the Asians, the
largest group of which, the Ismailis, were Shia Muslims), and
work did not stop for prayers, even on Fridays. However, most
Party and village leaders in the coastal areas, including Dar es
Salaam, and in many other towns, were Muslim, in contrast to
the cabinet and civil service, where Christians predominated.
    There were fewer Christians than Muslims, and they were di-
vided between Roman Catholics (the largest group), Lutherans,
Anglicans, and several smaller denominations. In contrast to the
situation in Kenya, Malawi, and elsewhere in Africa, African independent churches were not large in terms of numbers of adhe-
rents (Iliffe 1979: 361–3). The Christian missions themselves
had varied greatly, even within one denomination, and Christian
influence was strongest in certain rural areas where missions had
been successful. In the towns the churches provided meeting-
places and emotional and ideological support for the educated
and for newly arrived migrants from 'Christian' areas.
    Despite the pressures of migration and poverty, the family re-
mained a strong institution. In town or country, a man would
aim to live in a house big enough for his wife and children and a
number of other relatives. Weddings were big occasions. The
custom of bride-price, whereby a man paid the father of his
bride a large sum (traditionally in cattle, or other animals, but
today usually measured in money) before he could marry, which
would be returned if the bride misbehaved, went some way towards preserving the stability of marriage, although it gave a lot
of freedom to the men. Women were often neglected or exploited, and it was becoming more common for them to follow
the Caribbean pattern and reject marriage in favour of the
independence to earn money and bring up children as they
liked.[7]

In the rural areas women did more than their share of the work in agriculture, water-carrying, and cooking. In some parts of the country men were responsible for the cash crops, and women for food, though the women would certainly have to work long hours in the fields at times of the year critical for cash crop cultivation (such as cotton- or coffee- picking). They married young, and bore many children—it was a common sight to see women working with children on their backs.[8] Contraception was cautiously supported by the government, despite Muslim and Catholic suspicions.[9] A USAID project provided training and drugs, but did not recognize an unmarried woman's right to contraceptives, which were (officially) only available to married women. Schoolgirls who became pregnant were expelled, but (inconsistently) college students who became pregnant were allowed to return once they had given birth. A progressive piece of legislation allowed women three months' maternity leave, and enabled most educated married women to keep their salaried jobs. But promotion prospects for women in the civil service or the professions were not good. *Umoja wa Wanawake wa Tanzania* (UWT), the Party organization for women, was involved in social occasions, but was often unsympathetic to demands for women's liberation outside the framework of the conventional family.[10]

The draft of the 1971 Marriage Act was sent to Party branches for comment before the Act was finalized, and the result was a fairly liberal piece of legislation, with Christian influence.[11] Polygyny was provided for, but only in non-Christian marriages, and if the first wife agreed. Women were allowed to own and retain property. Divorce could be obtained if it could be shown that a marriage had broken down for three years. The main weaknesses of the Act proved to lie in what followed divorce. Since property stayed with the spouse who had earned it, unless the court directed otherwise, many wives were left dependent on unreliable maintenance payments from their ex-husbands to support themselves and any children they were bringing up. The Act provided that children should normally stay with their mothers until they were seven years old, but that then the custody would be reviewed, taking into account the wishes of the children and the customs of the area concerned. In practice this meant that fathers could usually reclaim their children when they were seven, a harrowing experience for women who lost their children after sacrificing and struggling to bring them through the difficult early years.

The main relaxation was talking and drinking, especially for men (women, with food to prepare, water to collect, and children to look after, following a hard day's work in the fields, did not have much time to relax). There were 'clubs' where local beer was brewed even in areas where the population was highly dispersed. Two games of skill—draughts and *bao*[12]—were widely played. The national sport was football, but the rivalry between the main teams in Dar es Salaam was conducted as much off the field as on it, and the national team did not win even an East African trophy in the 1970s. A few outstanding athletes were discovered, including the long distance runners Filbert Bayi and Soloman Nyambui, but not the stream of world-class long distance runners produced by Kenya during the 1970s.

Tribal dances, revived after independence, continued both in rural areas and in the suburbs of towns such as Dar es Salaam. The traditions of dance and mime were drawn upon in a few films, and President Nyerere translated two Shakespeare plays (*Julius Caesar* and *The Merchant of Venice*) into Swahili. But dramatic performances were not part of life for most Tanzanians. Television was not introduced, except in Zanzibar, on the (very logical) grounds that it could not reach the majority of villages, and so would benefit a minority; instead resources were used to improve the radio service. The nearest thing to a national literary culture was a tradition of Swahili poetry built on by the nationalist poet Shabaan Robert who began writing in the 1930s (he was an active member of the African Association) and died in 1962 (Iliffe 1979: 37, 379–80; Whiteley 1969). Swahili poems were published in the newspapers almost every day. The most original artistic creations were carvings, and later oil paintings, of the Makonde tribe from northern Mozambique and southern Tanzania whose exaggerations of human and animal forms stand comparison with fashionable sculpture in the West, though government and party pressure eventually ensured that fewer sexually explicit carvings were available for sale to tourists.

The written word was most widely disseminated in newspapers—*The Daily News* in English, *Uhuru* in Swahili, government newspapers such as *Ukulima wa Kisasa* (Modern Farming), which usually appeared monthly, and a number of small independent papers. *The Daily News* printed 30 000 copies, far more than any Swahili paper. On occasion it was willing to follow the liberal terms of reference given to its predecessor *The Standard* when it was nationalized in 1970,[13] and to attack abuses of power or confusions of policy, although there were strict limits beyond which it would not venture. Its correspondence column provided a safety valve which enabled English-speaking Tanzanians to express some of their feelings about what was going on in the country.

Some novels and plays were published, in English and Swahili, but no major novelist or dramatist emerged, which was surprising given the ambiguities and conflicts which could have been explored in political novels or on the stage.[14] Overall, 'culture' was treated ambiguously. The state felt that it ought to use plays and films to further its nationalist ideology; part of that ideology was that the people should be allowed to criticize the state if need be; yet if the criticism was too severe it became a threat to the state itself. Hence the strict controls on the press, and the strong censorship law for dramatic performances.

The picture which emerges is one in which life was seldom easy, for rich or poor. There was inflation, financial insecurity, the risk of ill health, the need to get children into school. The government invested heavily in the social services, especially health, education, and water supply, yet at the end of the 1970s all these services faced fundamental problems. It is to these, and the ways in which they affected different classes of people, that we now turn.

HEALTH

Like most tropical countries, Tanzania has not yet conquered its endemic debilitating (in some cases killing) diseases: malaria, bilharzia, tuberculosis, polio, measles, whooping cough, hookworm, and other gastric infections including typhoid and (recently) cholera. All these are made much worse by malnutrition, which, for example, makes measles a killing disease among children—responsible for one-third of all hospital deaths caused by disease in 1975. About one-third of all Tanzanian children suffer a degree of malnutrition during childhood. Surveys suggest that at any given time more than half have malaria, and about 20 per cent hookworm. Many mothers carrying children are severely anaemic.[15]

The government has to face the fact that there are many sick people, and will be for a long time, and thus a continuing demand for hospital beds in which they can be treated. The colonial medical service provided a fairly high standard of curative medicine for 'Grade A' patients, i.e. expatriates and senior civil servants, and a minimal service for the rest. In the rural

areas most of the hospitals were run by Christian missions, with
evangelistic overtones. Fees were charged for both out-patient
and in-patient treatment. Not until 1972 was it recognized that it
would be cost-effective to give priority to preventive medicine
—that more lives would be saved if the limited resources available were directed to preventing people from catching the illness-
es in the first place, rather than trying to cure those who were
sick.[16] But by then curative medicine (i.e. hospitals) consumed
87 per cent of the Ministry of Health's recurrent expenditure
(Table 21.1); and there was strong pressure to maintain the
growth of these services.

TABLE 21.1
Estimates of recurrent expenditure on curative and preventive
medicine 1970–1972
(shillings million)

	1970/1	1971/2
Curative services	81.3	91.3
Preventive services	13.5	13.7
Curative as percentage of total	86	87

Source: adapted from Segall 1972: 162.

Three consultant hospitals had been built, in Dar es Salaam,
Mwanza, and Moshi. Muhimbili Hospital (opened in 1956 as
Princess Margaret Hospital) was expanded with Swiss and West
German aid to become the medical faculty of the university, as
well as the only government hospital in Dar es Salaam (with a
maternity wing at Ocean Road, in the buildings of the old German hospital); the capital cost of about 90 million shillings for
the Moshi and Mwanza hospitals had been provided by the
West German government, but channelled through missionary
organizations, Catholic for Mwanza and Protestant for Moshi.
The overwhelming majority of the patients treated in these hospitals came from only a few miles away. Muhimbili hospital
alone, covering perhaps 5 per cent of the population, received
16 per cent of the curative vote in 1970/1, and no less than 41
per cent of the money for drugs and equipment—and then over-
spent this allocation by more than 100 per cent (Segall
1972: 152).
    The policy change in 1972 meant that no more large hospitals
were built,[17] but many more dispensaries and health centres. By

the end of 1975 there were 160 health centres, with medical assistants in charge, and nearly 1800 dispensaries, distributed so that 90 per cent of the population was within 10 kilometres of some health facility. Training programmes, including several at mission hospitals, had been greatly expanded for medical assistants (a three-year training from Form IV of secondary school) and rural medical aids (three years of training for primary-school leavers), and for various types of community nurse.

There were, however, formidable vested interests operating against the change of policy. Many doctors who had been trained as consultants resisted the argument that the money could have saved many more lives if spent on preventive medicine, and demanded facilities not unlike those they would expect in the West. Expenditure on drugs rose at 33 per cent per annum, until by 1975/6 it consumed 22 per cent of the total recurrent expenditure on health, nearly 80 per cent of the drugs being used in hospitals. The drug cost per in-patient was about 12 shillings per patient in a district or regional hospital, 24 shillings per patient in the Kilimanjaro Christian Medical Centre (the large German-financed hospital in Moshi), and almost 75 shillings in Muhimbili, on average, but 108 shillings for a Grade A patient with 47 shillings for other patients. The study that produced these figures found widespread prescribing of expensive drugs when much cheaper drugs could have been as effective; this in turn was linked to a huge promotional activity by the drug companies. There were 147 drug company representatives in the country, compared with only 600 doctors; in Britain the ratio is approximately one representative to 30 doctors, in Tanzania it was one to 4. Most of these representatives were medical assistants attracted away from the medical service by higher salaries and commissions on sales offered by the drug companies. They were backed up by free samples, literature, and gifts of drugs to hospital pharmacies. In just one of several examples of drugs with potentially dangerous side-effects being prescribed for common symptoms, anabolic steroids were recommended for 'malnutrition and weight loss, to stimulate appetite, and for excessive fatiguability in school children'. In 1976 aminopyrine and dipyrone were widely prescribed as alternatives to aspirin; it is likely that they killed 630 of the 117 000 or so people who took them—with a high fever occurring eight or ten days after the drug was taken and therefore not obviously associated with it. In the United States these drugs can only be used as a last resort for patients with terminal illness; in Tanza-

nia they were described as having 'a wide margin of safety', and could be freely purchased in chemists' shops (Yudkin
1978).

Aggressive salesmanship was also used to promote the sale of
baby foods, and large quantities were imported in the mid-1970s
(Table 21.2). Unless the feeding bottles and the water used to
dilute the baby-milk powder are sterilized, they will spread sto-
mach infections. If a mother bottle-feeds her baby, and then
cannot afford to buy a new tin of milk powders, and instead
uses more water and less feed than recommended, she can easily starve her baby. The dangers are so great that baby-milk
powder has rightly been called 'the baby killer';[18] it should only
be used if there is an assured supply of powder and no other
way of feeding the baby.

TABLE 21.2
Imports of baby foods (1973–6)

Type	1973	1974	1975	1976
Cerelac	34.7	128.6	110.5	179.3
Lactogen	168.8	896.5	608.0	844.6
Nan	126.0	115.9	49.8	206.6
SMA	7.6	53.7	29.3	41.8
S-26	4.8	29.5	8.2	17.2
Mama	—	30.0	36.0	9.6
Similac	6.0	13.2	9.4	24.2
Oster milk	5.6	6.6	3.2	37.8
Nespray	281.9	632.1	73.2	161.6
Total	635.4	1906.1	927.6	1523.7

Source: Tanzania Food and Nutrition Centre (1978: Table 20.8).

Both the drug scandal and the import of baby-milk were well-
publicized, but the ministries concerned were unwilling to confront the interests involved. A strictly controlled import of drugs
would have interfered with doctors' freedom to prescribe; while
the parastatals which imported the drugs and baby food had interests in selling them. Some doctors resigned from Muhimbili
hospital to set up private clinics where they could treat rich patients (and parastatal employees) for a fee. This made it difficult
to maintain standards in government hospitals. The government
threatened to end private practice altogether, but did not do so
until July 1980; at the time of writing it was unclear what effect
this would have.

The theory of health care for the masses was correct and convincing. Some steps had been taken to put it into practice. But little account had been taken of the interests that were working against it: doctors, drug salesmen, importers, and behind them the multinationals. Neither the analysis, nor the practice, was willing to stand up to these, even though the country could have saved both money and lives by (for example) rationalizing its purchases of drugs.

HOUSING

In the rural areas of Tanzania most people lived in houses built to local designs using local materials. A person wishing to build a house would do much of the work himself, probably employing a local specialist for the roof, and recruiting labour for the mud walls by brewing local beer. Although many of these traditional designs are cool and airy (others are not), the tendency has been for those who could afford 'better' houses to build in mud brick (in place of mud daubed on to a timber frame) or with blocks made from cement and mud, to line the floor with cement, and to complete the roof with corrugated iron. In the urban areas, according to the 1967 census, more than a third of the houses were 'permanent' in this sense; in the rural areas the proportion was less, with most villages possessing only a few such houses, inhabited by government staff or villagers who in the past had some connection with the towns, or who hired labour in order to cultivate bigger than average farms (Mascarenhas 1973: 98–118; Mascarenhas and Mascarenhas 1976).

The possession of consumer goods was minimal. In a survey of households carried out in 1969, and almost certainly biased upwards, Ian Livingstone found an extremely limited possession of consumer items, and used this to justify much greater planning emphasis on small-scale production of basic consumer items (Table 21.3).

In colonial days Dar es Salaam was racially zoned. The areas around the government offices and the seaside suburb of Oyster Bay were reserved for Europeans (and their house-servants living in one-roomed 'quarters'). The central 'commercial' and shopping area, and the suburbs of Kisutu and Seaview were for Asians, and in the central area housing associations and private landlords built tenements with ground-floor shops for renting, giving this area (and others like it in up-country towns) a flavour of the Indian subcontinent. An open space divided the Asian

TABLE 21.3
Household possessions 1969

	No.	per cent	No.	per cent	No.	per cent
Tables	0	10	1–2	66	3 or more	24
Chairs	0	28	1–4	38	5 or more	34
Stools	0	20	1–4	66	5 or more	14
Bedframes	0	16	1–4	66	5 or more	18
Cupboards	0	31	1–2	64	3 or more	6
Large mats	0	34	1–2	45	3 or more	21
Small mats	0	43	1–3	42	4 or more	14
Containers	0	1	1–5	56	6 or more	43
Pots and pans	0	0	1–4	18	5 or more	82
Plates, cups, etc.	1–9	29	10–39	59	40 or more	12
Doors in house	1	27	2–4	46	5 or more	27
Window frames	0 or 1	22	2–5	57	6 or more	21

Source: Livingstone (1970: Tables 1–14).

and African areas, and, as the city grew, African suburbs sprang up further and further out along the main roads. In these areas housing was 'traditional'—usually adaptations of the six-roomed 'Swahili' house with a central corridor, in which the rooms could be let out individually or jointly (Sutton 1970: 7–18).

Outside the old European areas and parts of the Asian suburbs, conditions were not luxurious (Table 21.4). In 1967 in Dar es Salaam 27 per cent of households had electricity, 31 per cent had piped water inside the house and another 35 per cent had it outside, 66 per cent had just one room, and another 17 per cent had two rooms (30 per cent of all households in Dar es Salaam had just one member, while another 21 per cent had two). The over-all room occupancy averaged nearly two people per room.

Even before independence, there were some government housing schemes (mostly one-roomed quarters) for key workers, but the main government housing was for expatriates in Oyster Bay. After independence these houses were reserved for expatriates and Tanzanians in the top grades of the civil service, and positions of similar rank in parastatals. Since the numbers in these ranks (expatriate or Tanzanian) increased, there was a constant pressure on this type of housing, even though the resulting life-style physically distanced the administrators from the masses.

The government did attempt to improve conditions in the African suburbs, but the resources were never sufficient to make more than a small impact. In the 1960s the National Housing

TABLE 21.4
Urban housing conditions 1967
(percentage)

	Dar es Salaam	All urban areas
Type of housing: permanent	35	34
semi-permanent	57	54
Size of household: 1 person	30	25
2 persons	21	18
3–6 persons	40	42
7 or more	10	14
Proportion of households with:		
1 room	66	46
2 rooms	17	24
3 rooms	9	14
4 or more rooms	8	16
Households with electricity	27	19
Households with water: inside	31	34
outside	35	36
Rent in shillings per household per month:		
0–9	0.3	5
10–29	54	57
30–199	39	32
200 or more	6	6

Source: Mascarenhas (1973: 98f.).

Corporation 'slum clearance' schemes enabled houseowners in Magomeni to have their property replaced by an improved type of Swahili house, which they could subsequently rent for a very moderate sum.[19] This was financed by West German aid, and the houses were built with direct labour; later on, new estates were built in Kinondoni and elsewhere very cheaply, with unit costs around 8000 shillings to 15 000 shillings in the late 1960s. But, as in Zanzibar, there was pressure to build flats, for aesthetic reasons more than for the convenience of living in them; however, the cheapest flats that could be built in the early 1970s cost more than 25 000 shillings per unit, and were too small for large families. They were built by contractors—which meant less bother for the NHC management, and offered possibilities for corruption.

But Dar es Salaam grew much faster than the NHC built

houses or flats, so there was no reduction in overcrowding, although there was an improvement in quality, with most of the *makuti* (coconut palm) roofs being replaced with corrugated iron. In the Second Five-Year Plan 'site and service schemes' were proposed, in which the NHC provided a site, with road access, drainage, and water; but the early attempts actually provided much more than this (a bathroom and kitchen unit) and cost almost as much as the cheapest NHC house[20], and it was not till the mid-1970s that a World Bank project began to make economic sense of the idea. Meanwhile Dar es Salaam grew from 270 000 in 1967 to probably about 700 000 ten years later; unemployment also rose, from the low figure for an African capital of 10 per cent in 1969 to 16 per cent in 1975 (IBRD 1977: 16). The most noticeable feature of its housing was the variety: palaces in Oyster Bay or at the University, and shacks in the squatter areas of Manzese or Kinondoni, where a house could be built for as little as 3000 shillings in the early 1970s, and a room subsequently let for 25 or 30 shillings a month. The 'Grade A' housing was rented by expatriates or senior officials for 12½ per cent of their salaries, about half the economic rent which would have been required to give a return on the capital. This did not give them much incentive to move; yet when the Tanzania Housing Bank (a nationalized building society) offered mortgage loans with interest at 10 per cent, many Tanzanian officials took the opportunity to have houses built, as much as anything as a hedge against inflation.

In short, housing was a sector in which government intervention was ineffective. Mascarenhas (1973: 118) concluded: 'the picture one gets is that the people in the households are crowded and the quality of amenities available to them range from poor to appalling.' In the rural areas villagization destroyed many of the most substantial permanent houses. Nyerere had promised 'operation nyumba' (houses) to change this situation, but the results were yet to be seen.

EDUCATION

Nyerere's 1967 paper *Education for Self-Reliance* was enthusiastically received by liberal educationalists all over the world; its aim of a 'practical' education as an end in itself, rather than an élitist education designed to prepare a lucky few for a higher level of education, seemed to meet the needs of most ex-colonial countries in the 1960s. It was in fact part of the process of deflating the hopes of the masses after independence; parents who made the sacrifices to see their children through primary school had at least expected them to get wage employment, and most children who passed through secondary school could expect further training, technical or academic, and high salaries. But in the 1967 paper it was made clear that this could no longer be so: many primary-school leavers were to finish up as peasant farmers, not very different from their parents.

This 'practical' education had various aspects. Children were to be decision-makers on school farms, or other 'self-reliance activities', and in various aspects of the running of their schools. The school entry age was to be raised, in order that primary-school leavers could be old enough for adult work. Examinations would be downgraded. School students would learn co-operative work, and where possible participate in village decision-making. The objective was to change society by changing education; it failed to recognize that in any society the educational system is likely to reflect the entrenched class interests.[21]

Even though fees were abolished for primary and secondary education, the rich were able to ensure that most of their children had places in secondary school. Even the fact that there were books in their houses, and people who could read and write, gave these children an advantage. If a child failed the primary leaving examination, rich parents could often enable him or her to sit again, either by agreement with the local headmaster, or in some other part of the country. If that failed, there were private schools where fees were charged. The number of places in the bottom forms of private secondary schools rose from 500 in 1965 to 5000, or 37 per cent of the total, ten years later (Table 21.5), and the headmasters of state schools often accepted children who wished to transfer from private schools into the state system after a year or two, regardless of earlier examination results (Mbilinyi 1979: 224).

Teaching methods and the administration of schools remained authoritarian, while large classes and shortages of equipment made it difficult to teach other than by rote learning. In Mbilinyi's words (1979: 222):

Teachers are as alienated as their students. They teach curricula which they do not design; and teach for examinations which they do not set. Teachers and their Heads carry out directives from above, in a pattern of work relationship not unlike that between teacher and student. Genuine teacher complaints about over-stocked, irrelevant syllabi are ignored or else teachers are criticized as being incompetent. Lack of

TABLE 21.5
Numbers in school 1965–1975

		1965	1970	1975
Primary standard I	— Government	149 000	173 000	433 000
	— Private	23 000	6 000*	33 000
	Total	172 000	179 000	466 000
Primary standard VII	— Government	34 000	66 000	138 000
	— Private	1 000	1 000	1 000
	Total	35 000	67 000 ·	139 000
Secondary form 1	— Government	5 900	7 400	8 600
	— Private	500	3 000	5 100
	Total	6 400	10 400	13 700
Secondary form 4	— Government	4 500	6 700	8 200
	— Private	—	2 000	2 500
	Total	4 500	8 700	10 700
Secondary form 6	— Government	600	1 400	1 900
	— Private	—	—	200
	Total	600	1 400	2 100

* 1971.
Source: Ministry of National Education.

feedback from the classrooms to the curriculum developers not only frustrates teachers, but it also removes the chance for creative curriculum development through practice.

The greatest educational achievements were in raising the numbers trained. In the first ten years of independence the priority was secondary and further education: the number of secondary-school places grew from about 12 000 in 1961 to over 40 000 by 1971[22] and the University of Dar es Salaam was built and expanded to cater for 3000 students. Primary education only kept pace with population growth, so that as late as 1970 only 48 per cent of the children of primary school age attended school.[23] However, in the 1969 Second Five-Year Plan a target for universal primary education (UPE) was set for 1989, and in 1974 this target was brought drastically forward to 1977. The result was crash programmes for the training of teachers by correspondence and in colleges, and the use of unemployed school-leavers as volunteer teachers, as well as students from the higher forms of the schools. In 1976 almost 670 000 children entered school, compared with 190 000 in 1967 (Nyerere 1977: 49).[24] By 1977 probably 80 per cent of the children of school age were in school, a remarkable achievement that would not have been possible without the villagization. The expansion was not without difficulties: shortages of materials and books were leading to two types of primary school, those started before the expansion and those started during it, while the full cost implications had not yet been realized, since the expansion still had to work itself up through the schools; moreover initially many teachers had begun working for very low pay in the expectation that eventually they would be accepted on crash training programmes and receive government salaries. The ratio between the numbers leaving primary school and those going on to a government secondary school had become so low (about 1:16 in 1975) that peasants were saying that secondary-school places were for the children of teachers only.

Great progress was also made in adult literacy: in five years over 5 million people registered in literacy classes, 3.8 million of whom preserved for long enough to sit a national test (Nyerere 1977: 49). Much of the material with which they learnt to read was designed to acquaint them with useful information on agriculture or health.[25]

The story of the University is told in Appendix 1 to this chapter. It is of special interest because university graduates were recruited into the higher levels of the administration and parastatal management, and so played a key role in the economy.

WATER SUPPLY

Clean water is not easy to obtain in most parts of Tanzania. Rainfall is low and concentrated into a few months of the year, and often just a few days in those months. Rivers are few and far between. Deforestation of mountain areas has increased the frequency and the intensity of flash floods, while lessening the number of permanent streams.[26]

In 1970 the government accepted a master plan for water supply by which every Tanzanian would be within easy reach of a clean water supply within twenty years. The capital cost was estimated then at 100 shillings per person per year for twenty years—no small sum for a country with a GDP of only 700 shillings per person per year. The plan was based largely on deep boreholes, and pipeline distribution systems from major rivers or reservoirs in the mountains, often over hundreds of miles.[27] It depended, at least initially, on Swedish aid. The first agreement was signed in 1966. The aid was untied, and allowed specific schemes to be designed after the agreement was signed, and funded subject only to the signature of a Swedish engineer in the water department's office in Dar es Salaam. Gerhard Tschannerl showed how these arrangements allowed technical considerations to overrule the wishes of the villagers for whom the schemes were designed. The 'experts' would not listen when villagers suggested an improved alignment, of no extra length or cost, for a proposed pipeline; they were reluctant to employ self-help labour (on the grounds that it was unreliable) until directed to do so by the government; they were more interested in the construction of new projects than in the maintenance of existing ones, and made few efforts to train villagers to maintain what they had built; and they insisted on doing things *for* the villagers:

In the limited context of the programme of providing water supplies, the dominant ideology is that of the 'experts'. They emphasise the importance of physical structure, detailed engineering plans, rigid adherence to procedures and job responsibilities, and the efficiency of their organisation. They control the entire process of the creation of a scheme from planning to maintenance. The role of the peasants, if they are involved at all, is limited to some technical consultation (but the decision is made by the experts) and a contribution of unskilled labour under the experts' supervision. (Tschannerl 1973: 103.)

TRANSPORT

Colonial policy was not to build roads where there were already railway lines: as late as the early 1960s, for example, the wet-season road route from Dar es Salaam to Mwanza was via Mbeya! Two railways ran inland from the coast, from Dar es Salaam to Kigoma and Mwanza, and from Tanga to Moshi and Arusha. The two lines were not directly linked until after independence. But improvement of road and rail connections took more government money than any other sector in both the first and second five-year plans. By the end of 1973 there were tarmac roads from Dar es Salaam north to Moshi, Arusha, and the Kenyan border, south almost as far as the Rufiji river ferries, and south-west to the Zambian border.[28] Construction by the Chinese of the TAZARA railway to Zambia was proceeding far ahead of schedule, in one of the most exciting development projects on the whole continent—described in detail in Appendix 2 to this chapter.

Buses ran on almost all roads, including some very minor ones. Many were owned by small operators, Asian, Arab, or African. Some were run by co-operatives. The largest single operator, the Dar es Salaam Motor Transport Company, ran the city bus service in Dar es Salaam and a variety of long-distance routes, and was owned by United Transport, a company acquired by Lonrho in the 1960s. It was nationalized in 1970 and divided into two, one company for Dar es Salaam and the other for the up-country routes. Both found great difficulty in retaining good mechanics and keeping their buses on the road. The situation in Dar es Salaam, which had never been good, soon became critical; as the city expanded so did the need for efficient transport, and the city service became so unreliable that companies and even offices purchased their own buses to get their workers to work. *Usafiri Dar es Salaam* (The company responsible for the city service) was tempted into a short-cut solution; it purchased 80 Ikarus buses from Hungary, ready-built with soft springs, large glass windows and microphones for the driver to speak to the passengers. Some of the buses were articulated, better suited to the boulevards of Budapest than to the narrow streets of Dar es Salaam. They were a step backwards from self-reliance; previously only chassis were imported, and the coachwork built locally.[29]

The story of road haulage was similar. A government corporation was set up with a fleet of Scania trucks from Sweden. Inexperienced management and vehicles largely untried in Tanzanian conditions again failed to keep much of the fleet on the road. Since the private sector was not allowed to import many vehicles, government and co-operatives experienced increasing difficulty in moving crops from the villages—cotton and cashewnuts were particularly affected.

The importation of private cars was restricted by high import duties imposed in 1970/1, and from 1974 onwards virtually no foreign exchange was made available for the purchase of vehicles by private individuals. This was combined with an order requiring all vehicles registered for less than four years to be sold to a new parastatal, the State Motor Corporation, which then sold most of them to other parastatals. Private individuals could buy only old vehicles, at extremely high prices, and this, plus shortages of spare parts, high taxes on petrol, and a prohibition of any driving without a special permit from 2.00 p.m. on Sun-

days to 6.00 a.m. on Monday mornings, made possession of a
car expensive and often frustrating. The policy was logical, but it
could only have succeeded if accompanied by the creation of an
efficient public transport system.

So, to generalize, while the infrastructure—roads, railways,
bridges, ferries—improved, there were many problems over its
maintenance and operation. For both rural and urban passengers travel by road decreased in comfort and reliability in the
1970s, and increased in cost.

LAW AND ORDER

African colonies were governed under authoritarian legal codes,
with a good deal of arbitrary power exercised by officials. In
Tanzania, as elsewhere, independence did not mean much
change. The penal code (which defined the main criminal
offences) remained virtually as before, although the sentences
for property offences were greatly increased. The power to
make by-laws under the Native Authorities Ordinance was retained by District Councils, and Regional and Area Commissioners continued to use arbitrary powers from time to time.
The 1962 Preventive Detention Act, which provided that anyone
could be detained at the President's wish, and which is often
criticized as an example of repressive post-independence legislation, replaced a very similar colonial ordinance (R. Martin
1974: 8–9; Williams 1979: 13–14).

The law is an instrument in the hands of the state. In the long
run it reflects the realities of power, in that those who hold
power can change the law; if they cannot, for example owing to
fear of repercussions abroad or inability to enforce an unpopular
measure at home, this indicates the limitations of their power.
Social democracies have a tradition of 'equality before the law',
which requires that law is written down, approved by democratic institutions, and then administered by an 'independent'
judiciary. In principle a poor man has the same rights as a rich
man (without this it would be harder to persuade the poor man
to accept the legitimacy of the state). Yet in practice the rich
have many advantages; they can employ expensive lawyers and
take their cases to appeal, and much of their power is itself enshrined and supported by the law. Even so, in times of
emergency, such as war, much of this liberal tradition is suppressed and the state rules by decree.

The Tanzanian judiciary inherited such a liberal tradition, continued by Chief Justice Georges, a Trinidadian who stayed till 1972,

and judgements in the High Court were usually clear and fair. In lower courts the situation was never so satisfactory. The lowest were presided over by primary court magistrates, who interpreted the 'customary' (or tribal) and Muslim law which before 1962 had been administered by the chiefs. Although attempts were made to write this law down, much was left to the judgement of the magistrates, and it is hardly surprising that the rich frequently got the better of the arguments (e.g. in land disputes) (van Velsen 1973: 172–3 and *passim*).

Above them district magistrates had taken over the judicial powers of the colonial administrative officers, and heard cases under the penal code. This part of the system deteriorated from about 1970 onwards. Petty corruption became so widespread in the police that the easiest way to defend a case was to bribe an officer to 'lose' the case file. This led to repeated adjournments, waste of witnesses' time, and even more inequality. It became hardly worth while prosecuting for burglary or assault, unless the unfortunate offender was nearly destitute.

The authority of the legal system was further undermined by the unwillingness of the politicians to enshrine what they were doing in law. For example, from 1967 to 1975 there was no legal basis for land holdings by ujamaa villages. Individuals whose land was cultivated by villages could in principle have sued for compensation (which would have been paid had the land been acquired for a state farm or government project), but the courts refused to hear such cases. Those whose homes were destroyed during the 1973–5 villagization could also have claimed for compensation, as the government belatedly admitted. There was no legal basis for the enforced closure of privately-owned shops by the simple expedient of depriving them of supplies from the state-owned wholesalers, or for enforcing workers in Dar es Salaam to carry identity cards to prove that they were employed, without which they risked 'repatriation' to their home areas. The local courts were used to enforce government campaigns—parents were fined for not letting their daughters attend school (tradition would surely have supported the parents), farmers for not working on communal farms, for not cultivating minimum acreages of crops, and for refusing to use fertilizer. These measures might have been progressive in themselves; but their basis in law was often obscure or non-existent (Williams 1979: 3–13).

Preventive detention was widely used. Some five hundred trade-unionists and soldiers were detained after the 1964 mutiny, although most were quickly released. In 1967 no less than 4000 people were detained as suspected cattle thieves, and by the end of the 1970s the Act 'was used on a wide scale to detain, for example, suspected cattle thieves, smugglers, hoarders, or corrupt persons against whom there is not sufficient evidence to obtain a conviction in court or even following an acquittal by a court' (Williams 1979: 13). Many arrested under the Preventive Detention Act or the 1969 Resettlement of Offenders Act were held in 'resettlement centres' (effectively minimum security prisons) for indefinite periods, and released during presidential amnesties on public holidays (for example 4436 prisoners were released on Union Day, 25 April 1980). In many such cases the correct procedures for detention were not followed (the Preventive Detention Act required a warrant personally signed by the President for each individual case). Yet the courts would not order the release of people who had been illegally detained. Even if they had, it might have had little effect, for Williams (1979: 8–10) gives several examples of court orders being ignored (e.g. for the return of property confiscated by the police).

In Zanzibar the process went even farther. The colonial law was abandoned (as a reactionary institution, dedicated to the maintenance of property) and replaced with a system of 'people's courts' where justice was dispensed by members of the Afro-Shirazi Party. Almost anything was possible; some of the Zanzibari politicians enjoyed an exotic life-style (there was no question of their accepting the conditions of the Arusha Declaration) and in 1970 gained international notoriety when four of them took Iranian girls, of the Ithnashari sect, as additional wives, without their parents' consent. The marriages were carried out by another member of the Revolutionary Council and justified as an attempt to bring about racial integration on the island. They were publicized in the Mainland newspapers, and condemned internationally as well as by UWT, the TANU womens' organization on the Mainland (Edgett Smith 1973: 133).

More serious cases either never came to court (people disappeared without trace, including two well-known politicians, Othman Sheriff and Kassim Hanga, who were handed over to the Zanzibar authorities by Nyerere in 1969) or else were tried under a unique system in which the prosecuting counsel was also the defence counsel. This was the procedure used in the treason trial which followed the 1972 assassination of Vice-President

Karume. More than a thousand suspects were detained, and more than a year after the assassination eighty-one of them were charged, the evidence consisting almost entirely of confessions extracted under torture. Abdulrahman Babu, who had been relieved of his position as Minister of Planning in Dar es Salaam a few months previously, and seventeen others were tried *in absentia*, Nyerere refusing to allow them to be moved from the Mainland where they were detained. Nearly all were found guilty, but allowed to appeal, and the publicity given to the appeal in October and November 1976 did much to discredit both the evidence and the Zanzibar legal process. Babu was kept in detention until April 1978, when he was released and allowed to leave the country.[30]

LIFE IN TANZANIA

The 1970s were not easy years. The honeymoon of independence was over and much of the cost of mistakes in the 1960s was counted in the 1970s. The real incomes of most Tanzanians declined, as did some of the most important services, such as transport, and at the end of the decade the war in Uganda meant shortages of food and consumer goods. Where the government claimed success, in literacy, primary education, water supply, and (to some extent) preventive medicine, it was in the provision of services that could be organized bureaucratically. Where, as in secondary education, curative medicine, or housing, there were entrenched interests, the policies were less successful. The country became much more conscious of authority, and this added to the insecurity of life. People became more careful about what they said in public places, while peasants did the minimum needed to keep on the right side of the authorities. The social order stressed innovation imposed from above, and people waited for changes to come; they had little incentive to innovate for themselves.

—APPENDIX 1. THE UNIVERSITY OF DAR ES SALAAM

The annual per capita income in Tanganyika is £19
6s. The cost of keeping a student at this College will
be about £1000 per year.

PRESIDENT NYERERE, opening the new university
campus, 21 August 1964[1]

Eight weeks before independence, in October 1961, Julius
Nyerere, then Prime Minister, opened the University College,
Dar es Salaam. It was started in a hurry, and opened in premis-
es in Lumumba Street that had been built to become the headquarters of TANU (subsequently they housed the Institute for
Adult Education). There were just fourteen students, and one
Faculty, the first Law faculty in East Africa, thus continuing the
arrangement whereby the university colleges in East Africa specialized in different fields (Morrison 1976: 116).

In 1964 the university moved to its present site on a hill about
six miles from the city centre, and the Faculty of Arts and Social Science enrolled its first ninety-four students. Other faculties
followed: science in 1965, medicine (incorporating the Dar es
Salaam Medical School founded in 1963) in 1968, agriculture (at
Morogoro, 120 miles from Dar es Salaam) in 1969, and engineering in 1973. The majority of the students reading science,
and many of those reading arts, were destined to become
teachers, and read for degrees which included education and
two teaching subjects, awarded after three years of study. There
were also research institutes—an Economic Research Bureau, a
Bureau of Resource Assessment and Land Use Planning (an applied geography bureau), an Institute of Education, and for a
time an Institute of Public Administration (Van der Laar
1969: 233).

From 1963 to 1970 the college was part of the University of
East Africa, but on 1 July 1970 this divided into three indepen-

dent universities, one in each country. President Nyerere, previously Chancellor of the University of East Africa, became Chancellor of the new University of Dar es Salaam, and Pius Msekwa, previously Secretary-General of TANU, became Vice-Chancellor. More than 2000 students were then in residence, and some 500 had graduated from the university college. By 1977, when Msekwa was replaced by Ibrahim Kaduma, previously Minister for Foreign Affairs, there were more than 3000 students in residence and 5000 had graduated.

The university was always an élite institution. Its accommodation was lavishly designed and largely built with grants from American, British, and Scandinavian sources. The choice of a site outside the city centre distanced the institution from the masses. The students lived on the site in individual study bedrooms in tower blocks—although, with increasing numbers, some of the rooms were shared. Their food and allowances, and the books in the library and the equipment in the labs, were superior to those in other educational institutions. The élitism was intensified by the speeches of politicians who stressed the urgent need for the trained manpower that only the university was supplying (Saul 1968: 279).

Having absorbed all this, the students thought that they were indispensable. They disliked the decision of the government to direct (for five years) the employment of any student with a government bursary. They resented the attempt to make all students spend two years in the National Service after graduation, partly because this involved a loss of salary, but also because it meant living and working alongside graduates from other educational institutions, and those with no education at all. The élitism and arrogance were caught in the slogans on the placards which they carried when, dressed in their red academic gowns, they marched to State House in October 1966: 'NATIONAL SERVICE TO HELL'; 'KAWAWA MUST QUIT' (another reference to the National Service, of which Kawawa was in charge); 'REMEMBER INDONESIA' (emphasizing the power of students to bring down a government); and above all 'TERMS HARSH—COLONIALISM WAS BETTER'. Nyerere's reaction to the demonstration was to send down 80 per cent of the students in the Faculties of Law and Arts and Social Science (including most of the first intake into the latter faculty who were by then in their third year), alongside smaller numbers of science and medical students; they were only allowed to return after a full year in disgrace (Morrison 1976: 237–48;

Edgett Smith 1973: 27–30; Pratt 1976: 233–5).[2] By then the
Arusha Declaration had been followed by *Education for Self Reliance* and *Socialism and Rural Development*. Student leaders
were less openly careerist, and student publications took positions to the left of the government. This was particularly true of
Cheche ('the Spark', in Swahili), the magazine of the University
Students African Revolutionary Front. Many of the students
who wrote for *Cheche* were involved in a critical research project on tourism in Tanzania, papers from which were published
in *The Standard* and later collected together as a book (Shivji
(ed.) 1973). In 1970 *Cheche* published Shivji's long essay 'Tanzania: the Silent Class Struggle' (which included a critical reas-
sessment of the Arusha Declaration) and was immediately
banned.[3] But another journal, *Maji Maji* with similar format,
produced by many of the same individuals, but under the auspices of the University branch of the TANU Youth League,
came out in its place, and eight years later was still publishing
some of the most interesting theoretical and empirical analyses
of the Tanzanian state.

From the start the university attracted staff interested in
socialism, especially in the Faculty of Arts and Social Sciences.
The historian Walter Rodney, from Guyana, was probably the
most well known.[4] In political science, John Saul and Lionel
Cliffe formed a powerful team. Economics professors at Dar es
Salaam all had, or gained, international reputations. Many expatriate staff were liberals, attracted to Tanzania by Nyerere's
rhetoric, who expected to see the fruits of socialist policies,
whether in government planning, education, or merely in the
way history or politics was studied and used. Their work could
be seen in the numbers of papers published by the research
bureaux in the early years, and in the establishment of a 'Dar es
Salaam view of history', with its slogan of 'putting the African
back into African history' popularized by the first professor of
history, Terrance Ranger (Ranger 1969), and carried through in
the collection of articles *A History of Tanzania* edited by two
Tanzanian lecturers in the Department (I. Kimambo and A.
Temu) and published in 1969.[5]

The students were influenced by the Black Power ideas of
Stokely Carmichael (who visited the campus in 1967) and Franz
Fanon (popularized through the teaching of Walter Rodney).
They sabotaged Ray Day in 1968, campaigned against imperial-
ist irrelevancy in the law syllabus and in favour of FRELIMO
and the National Liberation Front in Vietnam in 1969, and

against tourism policy in 1970. In July 1971 the President of the Dar es Salaam University Students' Organization was sent down, accused of disrespect in an open letter to the Vice-Chancellor. This was the culmination of a breakdown in relations which followed the appointment of the new Vice-Chancellor in November 1970. The students felt that they were not sufficiently consulted in the formulation of the constitution for the independent university, and wanted representation on various committees. They boycotted classes for five days, and then for a whole year refused to have anything to do with any university organizations (including all sporting fixtures. They even boycotted the university bar—an impressive piece of passive resistance). Normal relations were not resumed until November 1972 (Saul 1970a: 289–291; Morrison 1976: 287 and footnote 129, p. 304).

The same period also witnessed a crisis that affected the leftist staff in the Faculty of Arts and Social Sciences. From as early as 1967 a group of nine lecturers had argued that the traditional Western division of social science into economics, political science, sociology, geography, etc., was irrelevant in an underdeveloped country building socialism, where most of the problems (e.g. of rural development) were *interdisciplinary* in nature. Instead they wanted social science teaching that involved an interdisciplinary common core taking up perhaps half the teaching time, coupled with a number of interdisciplinary career-oriented specializations in rural planning, industrial planning, resource assessment, public administration, or whatever. This concept of interdisciplinary teaching did not require traditional university departments: the power was to be held by those elected to co-ordinate the various career streams, who might come from any of the disciplines involved.[6]

Between 1967 and 1972 these proposals gradually passed through the planning machinery of the university. A paper by Manfred Bienefeld (Bienefeld 1970) defined, in terms of man-power planning, the numbers required in each specialization. And the left had small majorities on most of the relevant committees, including the Faculty Board of Arts and Social Science, so that it seemed likely that the proposals would be accepted. But by 1972 a new generation of Tanzanian professors and heads of departments was taking over. They were mainly American trained, and more conservative than their predecessors. They did not welcome a proposal to remove them from their secure positions as heads of traditional departments. And so at the last possible opportunity they moved to sabotage the proposals that had been carefully worked on for more than five years. A *coup* was organized in the history department (which probably had most to lose from the proposed reorganization) and was successful because Walter Rodney changed sides, splitting the leftist majority. A watered-down version of the reorganization was accepted, which included a limited amount of 'common core' teaching. It included career streams, but they were placed firmly under the control of the traditional departments. The expatriate left felt betrayed, and its spokesmen either departed quietly or found that their contracts were not renewed. But Rodney had recognized an important principle: never again would expatriates challenge Tanzanians over major policy issues in the university. In that sense history was indeed on his side.

The years from 1972 to 1976 were years of comparative peace. The faculty reorganization worked smoothly, and the university produced graduates who could be absorbed by the government bureaucracy. The Faculty of Engineering was begun with German assistance, and emphasized workshop skills as well as scientific knowledge. The Musoma Resolutions of TANU in 1974 insisted that students should have at least two years' experience of work, and a positive recommendation from their local TANU branch, before admittance. The immediate effect was to admit those who had earlier missed the chance to study at university; in Arts and Social Science it produced serious students, although it was found necessary to relax the requirements in order to admit sufficient women, and to fill the places in science and engineering.

But as the government increasingly came to depend on capital from abroad, so the centre of gravity of the university moved to the left. There was less co-operation between the research institutes and the government, the latter preferring to use foreign consultants. Many university staff and students were openly critical of management agreements with multinational corporations, the increasing use of foreign aid, and, above all, of the way in which the villagization was carried out. Many of the staff lecturing in the common interdisciplinary course in the Arts and Social Science Faculty, and in similar courses in other faculties run by the Department (later the Institute) of Development Studies, followed Issa Shivji and interpreted events in terms of a 'bureaucratic bourgeoisie' which had hijacked the Tanzanian state (Shivji 1972 and 1975).

The clamp-down began in 1977, following the appointment of a new Vice-Chancellor, Ibrahim Kaduma. His predecessor, Pius

Msekwa, had mellowed after his confrontation with the students in 1970/1, and took a fairly tolerant view of the debates on the campus. He recognized that student radicalism died the nearer most students came to salaried employment, and was himself (like the President) prepared to admit that mistakes had been made in the past. Kaduma was less subtle. He had risen in the civil service to be Principal Secretary at the Treasury, but had then been moved to head the Institute of Development Studies at the university, which he clearly wished to turn into a Party 'ideological institute'. He was authoritarian in approach and disliked the free-ranging debates about government and party policy which were a feature both of teaching and of public meetings on the campus. He served as Minister of Foreign Affairs for eighteen months before returning to the university as Vice-Chancellor in February 1977.

In April 1977, during the long vacation, five left-inclined senior Tanzanian academic staff were suddenly 'retired in the public interest' without warning and then offered employment elsewhere in the civil service. They included the Dean of Arts and Social Science (the historian Arnold Temu), the heads of the departments of economics and management, and two other lecturers. Temu had recently been re-elected Dean, with an overwhelming majority, and petitions in his support were soon circulating, along with letters to *The Daily News*, and the retirements were even raised by four MPs in the National Assembly.

Kaduma was also in conflict with the students. After two groups of students were expelled in October and November, the students held protest meetings (which Kaduma claimed were illegal) and boycotted classes for two days. They also refused to elect student officers, preferring a more flexible 'caretaker committee' of twelve students. Then, on 27 February 1978, *The Daily News* announced that ministers, senior party officials, and members of parliament would get substantial salary rises—as much as 40 per cent in many cases. This seemed to be a clear contradiction of the Arusha Declaration, and so on 5 March about 1500 students (including some from the nearby Water and Lands institutes) protested by marching from the campus towards the city centre six miles away. The students had marched in the past, but never before had they openly demonstrated against a decision that had just been made by the Party. The demonstration was broken up by the police in the working-class suburb of Manzese; some students were injured but many of the rest re-formed nearer town and headed for the office of the Eng-

lish-language newspaper *The Daily News*, where they hoped to
hand in a manifesto. Instead they were rounded up by armed
police and taken away in buses. After some days, and without
any legal procedures, more than 400—including many who were
in the middle of their final examinations at the time—were
taken by the police to their home areas. After some months all
but forty were allowed to return—the 40 comprised 21 who
were alleged to have organized the demonstration and 19 who
had given false information (usually false names and addresses)
to the police.[7]

The students were treated to a good deal of abuse in the
press. They were accused of having opposed ujamaa village
managers (there was no evidence of this) and of having marched
instead of accepting an invitation to talk things over with President Nyerere (the evidence suggests that this invitation was received when it was already too late to stop the march). The
march itself was peaceful, and the students received enthusiastic
support from crowds along their route; the disruption of it was
violent, with several students seriously injured.

The contrast between the marches of 1966 and 1978 was
almost total. In 1966 the students marched to maintain their privileges; in 1978 they joined exploited workers and peasants to
protest about a bureaucracy which was granting itself privileges
contrary to the Arusha Declaration. The reaction shows that
they were perceived as a real threat.

Since then, till at least the end of 1980, there was an uneasy
truce on the campus. Some expatriate contracts were not renewed, and there was a reluctance to speak out on sensitive
issues. On the other hand the President made it clear that he
did not see the university as merely an ideological institute, and
Vice-Chancellor Kaduma was removed to a ministerial post early in 1980, and replaced by Nicholas Kuhanga, previously Minister of Education. It was, however, clear, as perhaps it should
have been long before, that the university could never be a
socialist institution. Its economic function was, and would continue to be, to train a privileged class of technicians, managers,
and administrators. Those who argued for socialism would be
tolerated only so long as they did not expose the weaknesses of
the state.

APPENDIX 2. THE GREAT UHURU RAILWAY

The 'Great Uhuru Railway' runs from Dar es Salaam to Kapiri Mposhi, where it joins the Zambian railway system. It is 1869 kilometres, or 1162 miles, long—roughly the distance from London to the southern tip of Italy. By 1975, four years after construction began, trains were running the whole length of the line. A total of 75 000 men (25 000 Chinese and 50 000 Tanzanians and Zambians) worked on the project. More than 300 000 tons of rails, 300 000 tons of cement, and virtually all the equipment, locomotives, and rolling-stock were imported from China. The cost of 4610 million Tanzanian shillings (approximately 450 million US dollars) was entirely financed by an interest-free loan from China, with eight years of grace and repayment over thirty years. When there was an escalation of cost the Chinese increased the loan, on the same terms, by 450 million shillings. Even so, for the twenty-two years during which repayments will be made, the cost will be only 11.5 million shillings each year for Tanzania and Zambia—and repayment can be made either in goods or in convertible currency.

A railway from the coast to the south-west had been considered since German times, in order to open up iron and coal deposits near Lake Tanganyika. A section of it would also have formed part of Cecil Rhodes's dream of a Cape-to-Cairo railway, but the project was shelved during the depression of the 1930s, and again shortly after the Second World War, because of its cost. It was only when Tanganyika became independent in 1961, and it was clear that Zambia would also soon be independent, that the idea was revived. 'Tiny' Rowland, of Lonrho, produced a feasibility study in 1963, and (at Zambian initiative) so did the World Bank. The latter, published in 1964, was sceptical, maintaining that the traffic could be moved more cheaply by road. Yet, when Rhodesia proclaimed UDI in November

1965, it was clear that Zambia needed a new outlet to the coast, and road transport along the 'hell run' to Dar es Salaam soon proved costly as well as dangerous (Hall and Peyman 1976: 58–64):

There is evidence that Nyerere discussed the project with the Chinese as early as 1963, and that the Chinese became seriously interested following Nyerere's visit to Peking in 1965. Kaunda would have preferred Western finance, and diplomats and politicians in London persuaded the British and Canadian governments to pay for yet another study. This was completed in 1966, and came out in support of the railway, but by then it was clear that the Chinese terms were more favourable than anything that would be offered by the West; and so the Chinese offer was accepted following a successful visit to China by Kaunda in June 1967 (Hall and Peyman 1976: 51, 72, 78–101).

The Chinese valued the railway as a demonstration both of their technological advancement and of their solidarity with the newly independent nations of Africa. They were therefore concerned that they should not be accused of exploitation: hence the interest-free loan, and their willingness to finance the local costs. This was done through a commodity credit—instead of providing convertible currency, the Chinese allowed the Tanzanians and Zambians to import consumer goods, and the local currency gained from their sale was used to pay the local costs of the railway. Tanzanian and Zambian buyers received priority and favourable prices at the annual Canton fairs, and the effect was to fill the shops with Chinese consumer goods—which Tanzanian and Zambian importing agencies did not even have to pay for immediately, since they were counted against the loan for the railway.

The construction was incredibly quick for a project of this size and complexity. Detailed ground surveys of the route were carried out in 1968 and 1969; construction proper began in 1970 and within a year more than 500 kilometres of line had been built, and a start made on the 160-kilometre Mlimba–Makumbako section where the railway climbs into the Southern Highlands. This section involved by far the heaviest engineering work, including most of the nineteen tunnels on the line and much of the 80 million cubic metres of earth-moving. Yet by April 1974 not only had this section been completed, but the railway had reached the Zambian border, a thousand kilometres from Dar es Salaam. Within five years of starting, trial trains were running the whole length of the line, which was already making a contribution to Zambia's trading problems. The railway was officially opened for passenger and freight traffic in October 1975.

The labour force fluctuated around a figure of about 30 000 men. Although earth-moving was by machine and lorry, and track-laying (about 6 kilometres a day) by machine, labour-intensive methods were also used, for example to protect cuttings and embankments from erosion. Cement sleepers and concrete rings to make pillars for the bridges (of which there are more than 300) were manufactured centrally. Stations and repair shops were built on a magnificent scale. Gardens, mainly growing vegetables for the labour force, sprang up along the line. The logistics of the operation—getting all the equipment to the right place at the right time—showed an immaculate attention to detail. Very few construction projects in Africa proceed ahead of schedule, especially if that schedule allows only five years to build more than 1800 kilometres of railway.

Operation of the line proved less successful than its construction. Although Dar es Salaam harbour was expanded, it remained inefficient, and Zambian goods piled up as they had before the line was built. There were not enough wagons; the planners had assumed an efficient turn-round but instead wagons disappeared on the Zambian side, where they were used for storage on the copper belt. Inside Zambia, the railway was unpopular with business men, who found it cheaper and more convenient to reopen the rail routes to the south, and some key bridges were blown up during the later stages of the civil war in Zimbabwe. In 1979 there was a strike of railway workers in Zambia while in Tanzania severe flooding put the line out of action for several months. In September 1980 the Chinese agreed to supply spare parts, technicians and materials to repair the locomotives and the track ('Chinese help for broken down trains'—*The Times*, 3 Sept. 1980).

The aim of using the railway to open up the mineral deposits in the south was enshrined in the Tanzanian Third Five-Year Plan. The Chinese agreed to build connecting links to the coal and iron ore deposits, and several donors were willing to build the steel works. One day the south-west would be the industrial heartland of Tanzania, and the country would have the capacity to produce basic materials such as steel (for rails and bridges) and cement, instead of importing them, as was necessary for this railway to be built quickly.

The Uhuru railway is a monument to the determination of Presidents Kaunda and Nyerere, and to the Chinese, Zambian, and Tanzanian workers who built it. The problems of maintaining it, operating it successfully, and, above all, of building industrialization around it, remain for the future.

22 UJAMAA AND VILLAGIZATION

> A Catholic leader at Kihinda village, John Nkerere,
> has been jailed six months by a District Magistrate,
> Ndugu P. Mayunga, for inciting villagers not to use
> fertilizers on their farms. He told people that taking
> fertilizers was adding to their burden of debts to the
> Government. The magistrate said that the accused's
> campaign was contrary to the Government's cam-
> paign on intensified farming.
> (*The Daily News*, 24 March 1979, quoted in Williams
> 1979: 3)

The Swahili world *ujamaa* was first used in a political context by
President Nyerere in his 1962 pamphlet *Ujamaa—the Basis of
African Socialism*. He was searching for a word to describe his
particular interpretation of socialism. He rejected *jamii* and
ujima, since both had been used to translate the English 'com-
munism', and instead chose the abstract noun that comes
directly from the word for the extended family; he himself translated *ujamaa* as 'familyhood'.[1]

In the 1962 pamphlet socialism is described as 'an attitude of
mind', a matter for the individual and his conscience. A mil-
lionaire can be a socialist provided that he 'values his wealth
only because it can be used in the service of fellow men'. 'The
basic difference between a socialist society and a capitalist society does not lie in their methods of producing wealth, but in the
way that wealth is distributed.' Socialism is a matter of distribution, not of what is produced, or of how the production is organized. It was not a matter of class conflict, for Nyerere denied
that there were classes in African society; instead he argued that
the attitude-of-mind which he identified with socialism was concerned with moral obligations, and in particular that the rich
should work for the greater national good; in this way he recon-
ciled his socialism with the nationalism that brought him to power (Nyerere 1962a: 162f.).

The main argument of the pamphlet is contained in the following paragraphs:

When I say that in traditional African society everybody was a worker, I do not use the word 'worker' simply as opposed to 'employer' but also as opposed to 'loiterer' or 'idler'. One of the most socialistic achievements of our society was the sense of security it gave to its members, and the universal hospitality on which they could rely. But it is too often forgotten, nowadays, that the basis of this great socialistic achievement was this: that it was taken for granted that every member of society—barring only the children and the infirm—contributed his fair share of effort towards the production of its wealth. (p. 165)

The other use of the word 'worker', in its specialized sense of 'employee' as opposed to 'employer', reflects a capitalist attitude of mind which was introduced into Africa with the coming of colonialism and is totally foreign to our own way of thinking. In the old days the African had never aspired to the possession of personal wealth for the purpose of dominating any of his fellows. He had never had labourers or 'factory hands' to do his work for him. But then came the foreign capitalists. They were wealthy. They were powerful. And the African naturally started wanting to be wealthy too. There is nothing wrong in our wanting to be wealthy; nor is it a bad thing for us to want to acquire the power which wealth brings with it. But it most certainly is wrong if we want the wealth and the power so that we can dominate somebody else. Unfortunately there are some of us who have already learnt to covet wealth for that purpose, and who would like to use the methods which the capitalist uses in acquiring it. That is to say, some of us would like to use, or exploit, our brothers for the purpose of building up our own personal power and prestige. This is completely foreign to us, and it is incompatible with the socialist society we want to build here.

Our first step, therefore, must be to re-educate ourselves; to regain our former attitude of mind. (p. 166)

The foundation, and the objective, of African socialism is the extended family. The true African socialist does not look on one class of men as his brethren and another as his natural enemies. He does not form an alliance with the 'brethren' for the extermination of the 'non-brethren'. He rather regards all men as his brethren—as members of his ever extending family.

'Ujamaa', then, or 'familyhood', describes our socialism. It is opposed to capitalism, which seeks to build a happy society on the basis of the exploitation of man by man; and it is equally opposed to doctrinaire socialism which seeks to build its happy society on a philosophy of inevitable conflict between man and man. (p. 170)

These extracts are typical of Nyrere's writing of this period. The blame for moral decline is put on colonialism: an ideal pre-colonial society is contrasted with the contradictions of colonial capitalism. But the historical analysis is inaccurate: it is not true that 'in the old days the African... never had labourers'—unless one takes very idealized views of chiefs like Chabruma or Kimweri—and it seems far-fetched to assert that Mirambo or Nyungu ya Mawe did not accumulate wealth for its own sake. Finally, in these extracts, the definition of socialism is negative: its essential feature is the absence of various unpleasant features of 'capitalism' and 'doctrinaire socialism'.

Nyerere conceded that his ideas were not yet the basis of any mass movement. Nationalist politics had arisen along with the creation of individualistic attitudes in the co-operatives and trade unions as well as in agricultural production and education. Most of the few who called themselves socialists had been trained in the Soviet Union or other East European countries on trade-union scholarships, and for them socialism was 'democratic centralism'—a strong workers' party controlling the state, consulting workers' committees at factory and farm level on production matters. Nyerere's own position was closer to that of the British Labour Party, or of the Fabians with whom he had been associated in Edinburgh,[2] or even of 'Christian Socialism'; but these were political creeds to which few in Tanganyika (other than some expatriates) had been exposed.

A different strand in Nyerere's thinking about the rural areas had been prominent well before 1962. This was 'villagization', or the idea that a good life was possible for those who lived in villages, but not for those who lived on small family farms dispersed over wide areas. Nyerere's speech on becoming President in December 1962 is a mature version of the argument:

If we want to develop, we have no choice but to bring both our way of living and our way of farming up to date. The hand-hoe will not bring us the things we need today. ... We have got to begin using the plough and the tractor instead. But our people do not have enough money, and nor has the Government, to provide each family with a tractor. So what we must do is to try and make it possible for groups of farmers to get together and share the cost and the use of a tractor between them. But we cannot even do this if our people are going to continue living scattered over a wide area, far apart from each other... The first and absolutely essential thing to do, therefore, if we want to be able to start using tractors for cultivation, is to begin living in proper villages... unless we do so we shall not be able to provide ourselves with the things we need to develop our land and to raise our standard of living. We shall not be able to use tractors; we shall not be able to build hospitals, or have clean drinking water, it will be quite impossible to start village industries. (Nyerere 1962b: 183–4)

Three (related) assumptions implicit in this extract go far to explain what was to happen later. One is the absolute commitment to modernization theory (see Chapter 10)—agricultural progress is only possible with tractors; there is no stress on the consequences if tractors break down, or on the cost if they have to be imported. The second is the obverse of this: the dismissal of existing forms of agriculture, apparently without consideration of how well adapted they were to the difficult ecological conditions in most parts of the country; they had after all led to a rate of growth of agricultural production in the 1950s that made Tanganyika the envy of many other underdeveloped countries. Finally, this position implied a very positive role for the government, as the only body that could provide the hospitals, the drinking water, and probably also the tractors and village industries on which the argument depends.

In response to speeches in this style, 'spontaneous settlement schemes' sprang up all over the country. Cliffe and Cunningham estimate that about a thousand were started between 1960 and 1963.[3] About half the total were the initiative of the TANU Youth League, with the aim of settling young people on the land. Many grew sisal, and the settlers were ex-sisal workers who had expected that they would take over the plantations after independence, but who were told instead to go and produce on their own. Some involved groups of unemployed from the towns, with little experience of farming. Almost all had difficulty getting good land and food for the period while they waited for their first harvest. Those who planted sisal could not expect a cash income for at least three years.

Most of the schemes did not last that long. The conditions were difficult. At Mbambara 150 former sisal labourers slept in four communal houses, eating the food purchased with the earnings of ten of their number who worked as labourers on a nearby estate, while the rest planted maize between the rows of their growing sisal crop. They had joined expecting to get rich, but this hope was dashed when the price of sisal fell between 1964 and 1965 (Wisner et al. 1975: 380). Villages that survived, like Mbambara and the villages of the Ruvuma Development Association discussed at the end of this chapter, were held

together by the socialist commitment and example of exceptional leaders, and became highly politicized. Most of the rest gave
up, and the government concluded that what was needed was
more planning, more advice from its 'experts', and more capital
investment. This was the main justification for the capital-
intensive village settlement schemes of the 1964–9 First Five-
Year Plan, whose failures were discussed in Chapter 17.

The village settlement policy was formally abandoned in
April 1966 (Kawawa 1966: 9) leaving the government without a
consistent rural policy. Kawawa suggested improving 'traditional' agriculture through the co-operative movement. Paul Bomani
suggested that 'the creation of a need and desire on the part of
our farmers to acquire a variety of consumer goods should . . . be
the strategy of rural development'. (Bomani 1966: 24). Nyerere
realized that both these suggestions were covers for a continuation and intensification of capitalist farming, but it was not till
September 1967, after the Arusha Declaration, that an alternative policy, formulated in his paper *Socialism and Rural Development*, was accepted by the Party.

In this paper the idea of ujamaa is married to the earlier idea
of villagization in the concept of an ujamaa village. This would
be a small group of politically committed farmers who worked
together on a communal farm, using their savings to purchase
equipment that would benefit the group. Nyerere did not promise
instant wealth; just as in the 1962 paper, his first concern was
that the new policy should reverse the trend towards class differentiation that was associated with the emerging African capitalism:

The essential thing is that the community would be farming as a group
and living as a group . . . The return from the produce of the farm, and
from all other activities of the community, would be shared according
to the work done and to the needs of the members, with a small
amount being paid in taxes and another amount (which is determined
by the members themselves) invested in their own future. There would
be no need to exclude private property in houses or even in cattle . . .
Such living and working in communities could transform our lives
in Tanzania. We would not automatically become wealthy, although we
could all become a little richer than we are now. But most important of
all, any increase in the amount of wealth we produce under this system
would be 'ours'; it would not belong just to one or two individuals, but
to all those whose work had produced it. At the same time we should
have strengthened our traditional equality and our traditional security.
For in a village community a man who is genuinely sick during the har-

vest would not be left to starve for the rest of the year, nor would the man whose wife is ill find the children uncared for—as he might do if he farms on his own . . .

Group work of this kind, too, would almost certainly allow for greater production and greater services in the community, with a consequent benefit to all members. It would be possible to acquire some modern tools if the members were willing to invest in them; some degree of specialization would be possible, with one member being, for example, a carpenter who makes the tables, chairs, doors and other things needed by the community, and works on the land only during times of greatest pressure, like the harvest. Another member could be responsible for building work, another for running a nursery where the children could be cared for and fed while most of the mothers are in the fields, and so on. By such division of labour arranged by the members according to their own needs, the villagers could make their whole lives more fruitful and pleasant. (Nyerere 1967d: 352–3)

Socialism and Rural Development is a dream of an ideal world; and even though it takes up thirty pages in Nyerere's collected essays, it does not proceed beyond the level of generalities. Force is not to be used in starting villages, and the responsibility for this is left entirely to committed individuals. It is not made clear whether those who have large holdings, or have to move away from permanent crops or houses, should be compensated when they pool their land or move away from it. Only a few of the problems of dividing village income are discussed, and little guidance is given as to what happens to those who work poorly, or give prior attention to private work, or on whether or how villagers can be expelled from a village; these were all to prove difficult practical problems, especially in villages with large labour forces. The paper proposes a step-by-step process of converting a traditional village into an ujamaa village, without showing why the richer villagers, who would have most to lose by this, should agree to more than the first step. It failed to provide a clear role for either the departments of central government or for the regional government and party bureaucracies.[4]

It is therefore understandable that initially the process of starting ujamaa villages was slow. By the end of 1968 just 180 were recognized by the government (Ellman 1971: 319)[5]. In early 1969 two changes were made in order to speed up the process. The first, in Presidential Circular No. 1 of 1969, ordered government departments to give priority in their spending plans to the villages; this meant that they could promise groups of

TABLE 22.1
Registered ujamaa villages 1969–1974

Region	1969 No. of Villages	1970 No.	1970 Population	1971 No.	1971 Population	1972 No.	1972 Population	March 1973 No.	March 1973 Population	January 1974 No.	January 1974 Population
Mtwara/Lindi	412	750	243 700	1320	574 688	1714	616 323	1692	635 181	1391	753 014
Dodoma	40	75	26 400	245	239 366	299	400 330	336	378 915	354	504 952
Iringa	60	350	11 600	651	216 200	630	207 502	659	243 527	619	244 709
Mara	19	174	84 700	376	127 371	376	127 371	271	108 068	111	233 632
Coast/D'Salaam	46	56	48 300	121	93 503	185	111 636	188	115 382	263	171 786
Singida	12	16	6 800	201	51 230	263	59 420	263	59 420	317	141 542
Kigoma	14	34	6 700	132	27 200	129	114 391	129	114 391	123	111 477
Mbeya/Rukwa	22	91	32 900	493	64 390	713	98 571	715	103 677	655	111 039
Tanga	37	37	7 700	132	35 907	245	77 858	245	77 957	255	67 557
Ruvuma	26	120	9 000	205	29 433	205	29 433	242	42 385	180	62 736
Mwanza	10	28	4 600	127	18 641	211	32 099	284	49 846	153	40 864
Tabora	41	52	16 700	81	18 408	148	25 115	174	29 295	156	28 730
Morogoro	16	19	6 000	113	10 513	116	23 951	118	19 732	96	25 509
Arusha	20	25	3 200	59	14 018	92	19 818	95	20 112	110	25 356
Shinyanga	6	98	12 600	150	12 265	113	15 292	108	12 052	134	18 425
West Lake	21	22	5 600	46	9 491	83	16 747	85	13 280	77	15 966
Kilimanjaro	7	9	2 700	11	2 616	24	5 009	24	4 934	14	3 176
Total	809	1956	531 200	4484	1 545 240	5556	1 980 862	5628	2 028 164	5008	2 560 470

Source: Economic Survey 1973–4, Tables 33 and 35.

peasants that if they registered as villages they would have a much greater chance of getting a water supply, or a school, or some land in a forest reserve, or whatever they wanted. Secondly, at about the same time, the President allowed a limited use of compulsion in the Rufiji valley, where peasants who lived on the flood plain were persuaded to move to 'planned villages' on the banks (Turok 1971: 397–401). Earlier, in Handeni and West Lake, party officials who had used force to start ujamaa villages had been punished; in the Rufiji the government claimed that force was not used; many houses had been destroyed by an unusually large flood, and the people needed famine relief food: the only way that they could get it was by agreeing to move. It had been intended that the Rufiji villages should have communal farms, but the villagers refused to work them; instead the government accepted 'block-farms'—small plots side by side, together forming large fields, but with each plot the responsibility of an individual. This was to be the pattern of the future, and from 1973 onwards they were called 'planned villages' or 'development villages', and distinguished from 'ujamaa villages' where working together and not just living together was the key feature. But initially all were referred to as ujamaa villages, so that the statistics are highly confusing. For what they are worth, the official number of registered villages (including those with little or no communal agriculture) rose to 809 at the end of 1969; a year later there were 1956; by the end of 1971 there were 4484, and by February 1977, ten years after the Arusha Declaration, there were 7684 villages involving 13 million people (*Economic Survey 1973/4*: 52; Nyerere 1977: 41).

Thus in the years from 1969 to 1972 there were three distinct types of village: first, the early villages, many pre-dating 1967, which were small, highly politicized, and committed to communal work; second, villages which started to get aid or other concessions from the government and which were in essence corrupt from the beginning, with only minimal commitment to communal work; and third, much larger villages with little or no commitment to communal work started in government or party 'operations'. We shall consider each of these in more detail.

The politicized villages were usually small—thirty or forty families was typical. They tried to put into practice the 1967 paper, but an even clearer description of what they were trying to do can be found in a paper called *Freedom and Development* which Nyerere wrote in 1968 when he discovered a constant tendency on the part of his officials to use force to start villages:

Ujamaa villages are intended to be socialist organizations created by the people, and governed by those who live and work in them. They cannot be created from outside, nor governed from outside. No one can be forced into an ujamaa village, and no official—at any level—can go and tell the members of an ujamaa village what they should do together, and what they should continue to do as individual farmers. No official of the Government or Party can go to an ujamaa village and tell the members what they must grow. No non-member of the village can go and tell the members to use a tractor, or not to use a tractor. For if these things happen—that is, if an outsider gives such instructions and enforces them—then it will no longer be an ujamaa village!

An ujamaa village is a voluntary association of people who decide of their own free will to live together and work together for their common good. They, and no one else, will decide how much of their land they will cultivate together from the beginning, and how much they will cultivate individually. They, and no one else, will decide how to use the money they earn jointly—whether to buy an ox-plough, install water, or do something else. They, and no one else, will make all the decisions about their working and living arrangements.

It is important that these things should be thoroughly understood. It is also important that the people should not be persuaded to start an ujamaa village by promises of the things which will be given to them if they do so . . .

The fact that people cannot be forced into ujamaa villages, nor told how to run them, does not mean that Government and TANU have just to sit back and hope that people will be inspired to create them on their own. To get ujamaa villages established, and to help them to succeed, education and 'leadership are required. These are the things which TANU has to provide. It is our job to explain what an ujamaa village is, and to keep explaining it until the people understand. But the decision to start must be made by the people themselves—and it must be made by each individual. For if a group of 20 people discuss the idea and only 7 decide to go ahead, then that ujamaa village will consist of 7 people at the beginning. If 15 decide to start, then it will begin with 15 members—others will join as they are ready. There is no other way forward, because by joining a man has committed himself to a particular kind of life, and five who come in unwillingly can destroy the efforts of the 15 who want to work out a new pattern for themselves. (Nyerere 1968c: 67–8)

The best-known examples of ujamaa villages founded in this tradition are those of the Ruvuma Development Association, described in an appendix to this chapter, and Mbambara Village in Tanga Region, the subject of Wisner, Kassami, and Nuwagaba's study in 1971. Mbambara village, only forty miles from

Tanga, was founded in 1963 by sisal-plantation workers, under the auspices of the TANU Youth League. By the end of 1964 numbers were declining, and a new leader, Bernardo Kilonzo, was elected from among the villagers. Kilonzo was to be an inspiration to the villagers, and indeed to all who met him, until in 1971, after six years, he broke down under the strain of running the village, and fled to Kenya taking a small sum of the village's money with him.[6] By the end of 1965 the villages had planted 139 acres of sisal (still less than 1 acre per adult member), were largely self-sufficient in food, had started to build a dam for fishing, and to hold literacy classes. It was not till 1967 that the first sisal was cut, producing the first cash income, just 180 shillings per member. In 1968 the income was only 150 shillings—not much for a year's work. In 1969 it was 250 shillings, and the village was given a lorry by President Nyerere, but in 1970 there was drought, and the village (like most villages in Tanga Region) depended on government famine relief. By 1972 the level of political consciousness (documented by a film crew that spent several months in the village—see Cliffe *et al.* (eds.) 1975: 392–5) was profound—the villagers had discovered the benefits of working together, the difficulties of leadership, and the need for villagers rather than officials to take decisions and responsibility (they had been misled over and over again by government officials and 'experts', both locally and in Tanga); but economically the villagers of Mbambara were still among the poorest in the country, and their choice of sisal as a cash crop meant very little prospect of changing this situation.

The second type of ujamaa village was founded in the hope of getting investment or some other concession from the government. Fieldwork, for example, in different parts of Tanga region by Michaela von Freyhold in 1971 and John Sender in 1973 found few successful villages, but a whole range of unorthodox reasons for the foundation of villages: five out of seven villages studied by Sender in the mountainous Lushoto District were started to get possession of areas of land previously owned by settlers or demarcated as forest reserve; in the lowland areas von Freyhold found that villages were registered as means of getting government services, capital investment, or famine relief; but there was also a village that received so much attention and aid from government staff that the researcher described it as a 'staff people's village', and a village which prided itself on its progressive reputation, and became an ujamaa village because this was the progressive thing to do at the time. Not one of these villages made a success of communal work over a number of years.[7]

Von Freyhold described what she called a bargaining process between these villages and the government. Government and party officials at regional and district level were under pressure to report a reasonable number of ujamaa villages in their areas (the authorities in one District were so concerned to impress the President on the day he was visiting that they used prisoners from the local gaol and claimed that these were villagers—Ingle 1972: 253–4). Villagers were prepared to move their homes, if this was necessary, and to do sufficient communal work to be registered as an ujamaa village, in return for something they wanted—a water supply, famine relief, or whatever. In 1970 the resulting 'contract' was even written down—in 'five-year plans' that were prepared for most registered villages in the country by teams of civil servants, and which specified on the one hand what the government and credit agencies would provide, and on the other what the villages would grow. The production targets were usually totally unrealistic ('no village ever tried to meet the unrealistic labour targets'—von Freyhold 1979: 48). The villages made token efforts for a year or two, usually clearing less than 1 acre of communal land per adult member, and doing so in such a way as not to interfere with the agricultural activity on their private farms. Since planting was often late, weeding neglected, and the fields not properly protected from birds, pigs, and monkeys, the yields were very low, and the resulting income seldom exceeded 100 shillings per household per year. This was one reason why government officials generally discouraged distribution of the proceeds to village members; instead they tried to persuade the villagers to invest it in communal assets for the village. The result was to remove virtually every possible sanction for those who failed to turn up or worked half-heartedly. The disillusion was increased by what happened to the hard-earned incomes. The most popular investment (described by Sender for Mayo village, but common all over the country) was purchase of the stock of a co-operative shop; if, as at Mayo, this went bankrupt, owing to theft by the shopkeeper or village committee, the villagers wondered for what (or whom) they were working (Sender 1974: 33). The incentive for communal work ended altogether when they realized that once a plan for a water supply, school, or dispensary had been approved by the relevant government department, the project was not cancelled even if communal work declined or ceased. By the end of 1970 the government had recognized quite a large number of villages, but there were few examples of successful communal work. Communal production was never sufficient for the government to produce figures, but it could not have been more than 1 or 2 per cent of total production.

A paradoxical result of villages started to get concessions from the government was that often they were either started by rich peasants or the villagers elected rich peasants to lead them, on the grounds that such people would be the most experienced in negotiating with the government. This was the case in most of the villages studied by von Freyhold and Sender; for example:

At Mgwashi Ujamaa Village the chairman had been a chief in colonial times. Two of his sons are Government employees with rather high salaries, and his children are the most educated in the village. The village secretary was a tax collector, or local court clerk in the colonial period . . . One of the committee members is certainly among the richest people in the area; he runs a duka [shop], hires labour to work his shambas [farms], and used to be employed as a Village Executive Officer. (Sender 1974: 22)

In such situations the opportunities for petty fraud by the leaders were considerable, and there was plenty of evidence that it occurred. For example:

At Mlesa Ujamaa Village the lack of an adequately worked out distribution system almost broke up the entire village in 1972 . . . In general very few members of the village know anything about village income and expenditures. An ujamaa maize shamba was harvested in 1972 but no-one in the village could tell the researchers what the yield was. The chairman was making withdrawals from the village funds without obtaining the consent of the financial committee. Despite earnings of approximately 700/- from tea so far, no bank account has been opened, and no cash income from the tea distributed to those who produced it. Again it is not clear how this income could be equitably distributed since some attenders at ujamaa work arrive very much later than others and all finish at the same time, with no differences being recorded in the secretary's logs. (While a piece-work system operates for some tasks, it does not for others, such as tea plucking.)

As at Kihitu and Mlesa, at Mgwashi too the amount of income received from communal activities was unknown to the vast majority of members. (Sender 1974: 30–1)

It was in this context that government and party officials created a third type of 'ujamaa' village by compelling all the farmers in selected areas to live in villages. The first implementation of this policy was in the Rufiji river delta, 100 miles south of Dar es Salaam, where the farmers were among the richest in the country, making good use of the natural irrigation and fertilizer (silt) brought down by the Rufiji flood waters. Their main crop was rice, and in order to guard this from birds many of them lived on their farms, in houses raised on stilts to withstand the flood water. They planted cotton as the waters receded, and in years of severe flooding (when the rice crop was destroyed by the water) this and fishing gave them their greatest income. This effective use of the Rufiji flood waters has been compared with that of the Nile in Egypt, and it provided food surpluses for export to Zanzibar long before the coming of colonial rule. In years of severe flood there was, however, a period between the planting and the harvesting of the cotton when the people were without food. Under British rule the government provided famine relief in these periods, only to find a few months later that the farmers were exceedingly well off. This continued after independence. The situation demanded a system of taxation in good years to finance the provision of food in bad years; but the government decided to end the necessity for famine relief by moving the people out of the delta altogether (Kjekshus 1977: 31–2; Iliffe 1979: 71; Sandberg 1974; Yoshida 1972).

In 1968 less famine relief was given than usual, and in 1969 the government took the opportunity of unseasonal floods to persuade the people to move. Village sites on higher ground were laid out by surveyors from the regional office. Houses were built by the National Service. Water supplies were provided by the government. The only way to get famine relief was to agree to move. It was hoped initially that cultivation would continue in the flood plain; but many of the new villages were too far from the old farms, or on the wrong side of the river. The government also hoped that communal cultivation would be carried out, and arranged for fields in the flood plain to be ploughed by tractor. The farmers, however, refused to harvest the resulting crop of rice, apparently fearing that if they did so the government would take the crop, and they would effectively be turned into agricultural labourers (Angwazi and Ndulu: 1973). The over-all result was that large areas of the flood plain were abandoned to elephant from the neighbouring Selous Game Reserve, while the farmers found themselves cultivating cassava and cashewnuts on the much poorer soils that were not flooded by the river, the income from which was about half what they had had before.[8] Yet from the government point of view 'Operation Rufiji' was a success. The people had moved, and party and government officials, including Vice-President Kawawa and Songambele, the Coast Regional Commissioner who conceived the move, but also the low-level functionaries who chose village sites, felt that something had been achieved, in sharp contrast to the other two forms of ujamaa which made them feel entirely ineffective.

The principle was quickly extended to Dodoma Region, another area in which the government frequently found itself giving out famine relief. In 1970 three 'Presidential Planning Teams' approved village sites and prepared plans for them. At that stage movement into these new villages was voluntary; but in 1971 the greater part of the population moved into these villages—because in this way they could receive famine relief food. Nyerere himself lived in Chamwino village, some twenty miles from Dodoma town, where he met Olaf Palme, Prime Minister of Sweden, in September. Chamwino was soon equipped with electric power (which even Kondoa, a District capital, did not have), a large community centre and 'state lodge' built by the National Service, and a few very splendid houses alongside many ordinary ones (Hill 1975: 243—4).

Presidential Planning Teams were also sent to Kigoma, Mtwara, Mara, Tabora, Sumbawanga, and West Lake, to work out sites and plans for villages. The teams were staffed by young Tanzanian professionals, and led by members of the TANU Central Committee. They worked fast—one Dodoma team allowed only two days per village. Some of the specialists in the teams clashed with the more experienced officers in the regional headquarters; and one Regional Commissioner, Dr Klerruu, disowned the presidential team and instead used his own staff for village planning. By the end of 1970 his region, Mtwara, claimed 750 villages out of less than two thousand in the whole country.[9] Klerruu was transferred to Iringa Region, where the number of villages suddenly increased, to 650 by the end of 1971. But on Christmas Day 1971 Klerruu was shot dead by an African large-scale maize farmer in Ismani, not far from Iringa. Klerruu was a Chagga (from the most individualistic area in the country, Mount Kilimanjaro); he also possessed a Ph.D. in political science, an unusual qualification for a politician, and was probably the most able organizer in the party, and certainly the most effective in creating ujamaa villages. It is a measure of his commitment that he was out campaigning on Christmas Day, trying to persuade the Ismani labourers to group themselves in villages and take over the land farmed by the large-scale African maize farmers (Awiti 1972b).

Klerruu's death made politicians even more reluctant to confront large-scale farmers, especially when there was a decline in production from Ismani. The 1972 TANU statement on agricultural policy, *Siasa ni Kilimo* ('Politics is Agriculture')[10] advocated technical means of increasing production—the use of oxen, early planting and spacing, use of manure and fertilizer—and was notable for not stressing communal work as a means of increasing production, or saying anything about confronting capitalist farmers.

In 1972 one region (Kigoma) and one district (Chunya) were 'villagized'. At President Nyerere's personal request, the Agricultural Development Service (a World Bank planning team based in Nairobi, and largely staffed by expatriates who had worked on the Kenyan 'million-acre schemes') was asked to take an interest in the planning of Kigoma, and it eventually produced a $10 million plan which directed investment into 135 selected villages out of 192 in the region (*The Daily News*, 5 and 6 November 1974). This plan was to provide the model for other foreign regional planning teams who were invited for all the other regions in 1975. The Chunya villagization was remarkable for the small number of villages (only eight for 15 535 people, or 3000 families) into which the population was concentrated (*The Daily News*, 6 May 1972); for the older peasants this must have brought back memories of similar concentrations forty years earlier, justified then as measures to prevent the spread of sleeping sickness (Kjekshus 1977: 168–76).

In September 1973 the TANU Biennial Conference resolved that by the end of 1976 the whole rural population should live in villages. As early as November 1973 Nyerere himself was quoted as saying that 'To live in villages is an order' (*The Daily News*, 7 November 1973) and by the end of 1975 almost everyone had moved. The exceptions were those living in urban areas, villages with populations of 200 or so families, and some highland areas including the Uluguru mountains and the well-established coffee areas of Mount Kilimanjaro and Meru, West Lake, and the slopes of Mount Rungwe in the south-west. At the end of 1976 thirteen million people were reported to be living in villages—a village being defined as a site acceptable to

the party with adequate agricultural land and at least 250 families (Nyerere 1977: 41).

This was a huge administrative exercise. Apart from countries
at war, or socialist countries where the objective was collecti-
vization of agriculture rather than merely villagization, it is hard
to think of anything comparable. It raises at least five very fundamental questions:

1. Was it voluntary? If not, how were the logistics planned
   and implemented largely without bloodshed?
2. Why was it carried out between 1973 and 1975 rather than
   earlier or later?
3. What did the government expect to achieve from it? What
   were the expected benefits of villagization?
4. What were the costs?
5. What happened to the earlier ideas of ujamaa—involving
   voluntary co-operative agriculture—which Nyerere promoted
   in 1967 and 1968?

The rest of this chapter is an attempt to provide answers to
these questions.

The move was most definitely not voluntary in the sense that
those who did not wish to move could have stayed where they
were. Quotations from different parts of the country show how
it carried out.

From Morogoro region:

The year 1974 will be remembered in Tanzania as the year of villagisation. There was not much variation between the regions in the methods
used to move the peasants. In many villages physical coercion was used
resulting in hardships to the peasants and some destruction of property...

No 'elaborate' preparations were taken in moving the peasants at Bigwa. Army lorries were used in moving the peasants who were caught
by surprise, although they were aware that the government had decided
to implement the villagisation programme as was happening elsewhere
within the region. The peasants were ... bundled into the lorries and
dumped at Misongeni, for most of them hardly a mile from their
homes. The place was overgrown with thorny bushes and the quality of
land was unquestionably below that of Bigwa and was inadequate for
both residential and farming purposes. (Lwoga 1978: 12, 13)

From Iringa:

Many people objected not so much to the move as to the way it was

done. 'We were treated like animals' some said. Government representatives (militia, Tanu Youth League members, government and party employees) simply told people they must move to a particular place
by a given date. While available transport was mobilised to help move
people this was often inadequate and people were therefore forced to
move themselves . . . To assure that people remained in the new villages, former houses were usually made uninhabitable by ripping out
doors and windows and knocking holes in the mud walls or by setting
fire to the thatch roofs. In some cases grain stored in or near the house
also caught fire and the family's food supply was destroyed. . . .

In the short run the problems created by *Operation Sogeza* [Opera-
tion Push] outweighed any benefits it might have bestowed. (De Vries
and Fortmann 1977: 130, 131)

From Mara:

[Operation Mara] started in October 1973, only two weeks after the
10th bi-annual conference of TANU ended its deliberations with Resolutions 14 and 15 calling for rapid villagisation in the whole country
before 1976 . . .

The officials decided that people should move immediately and so
the Police, Army, National Service and Militiamen were mobilised to
move the people. People were ill-treated, harassed, punished in the
name of TANU, under socialism, and those who questioned it were
told 'this is Nyerere's order', usually followed with a hysterical rebuke
'wewe ni mpinzani mkubwa wa TANU na Rais' ['you are a big trouble-
maker of TANU and the President']. This . . . makes TANU alienated
from the peasants whom it vowed to save from colonialism and
neocolonial bondage; peasants start seeing a different TANU. This is
because of a few inefficient and irresponsible officials who have misrep-
resented and stage-managed the TANU policy to the peasants, the
allies of socialist reconstruction in this country. (Matango 1975: 17)

From Maasailand:

'Operation *Imparnati*' [permanent settlements] was launched in
September 1974 in and around Monduli . . . Beyond the drawing board
stage, the implementation of the operation was not a mass transformation campaign. It was precisely an 'Operation'—a programme implemented by the government and ruling party officials . . . When I suggested to the TANU District Secretary that the party should investigate
the circumstances of the harassment [a team had been burning down
houses and kraals] . . . his reply was that such proceedings would un-
necessarily delay the implementation of the operation. (Parkipuny
1976: 154–5)

These quotations are from research reports by university lecturers—and similar reports are available for several other areas, providing over-whelming evidence that the methods used were more or less uniform over the country (e.g. McHenry 1979; Boesen, Madsen, and Moody 1977; von Freyhold 1979). But one last quotation, from a report written without regret, and covering a large area of Sukumaland, is by a senior civil servant who was himself involved in the move in Shinyanga District:

In some instances houses were burnt down when it was realized that some people, after having been moved, returned to their former homes again after a few days. But this method was rarely used and in all cases officials concerned made sure that goods and food were removed from the houses prior to their being put on fire. Many more people moved on their own without waiting for Government assistance. There are two good reasons why this happened in Shinyanga District. First, there was news from neighbouring Geita and Maswa districts, that people's houses were being put on fire indiscriminately, sometimes with food and goods inside them. So the people decided not to wait for Government help lest a similar catastrophe happened to them as well. Second, good leadership; for example, in the Tinde Ward . . . everybody had moved on his own and had started building by the time the 'moving squad' arrived . . . The TANU chairman in this area . . . is an excellent leader, notable in the district. (J. V. Mwapachu 1976: 119)

The 'operations' were organized by the Regional Commissioners (or Regional Party Secretaries) assisted by the experienced civil servants who had been sent to the regions and districts in the 1972 'decentralization', discussed in more detail below. They could call for assistance on the army, the national service, but above all on the militia, the 'home-guard' organization of armed volunteers created in 1971 and strongest in the towns where it included many skilled and semi-skilled government employees and unemployed youth.[11] For transport they could use army and government vehicles. For detailed knowledge of the rural areas the fact that there were by then salaried party officials in every division and ward made the whole thing possible, these were frequently the people who showed the officials and the militia where to go.

Government spokesmen have consistently claimed that the people were consulted over the choice of sites. The following two quotations from a study of the Coast Region[12] suggest that this claim was (to say the least) oversimplified, and are fully consistent with reports from other regions:

Such an operation is initiated by the Regional TANU Secretary (until recently called Regional Commissioner) and Regional TANU Executive Committee, discussed and defined by the team of regional officers and the Regional Development Committee and passed for detailed suggestions and implementation to the Districts. The plans are passed on and discussed in the Ward Development Committees and presented in village meetings.

A number of village leaders are members of the Ward Committees and the Ward Councillors represent the people in the District Committees, in addition to the TANU chairmen. The village meetings tend to be occasions for informing people of decisions taken or policies pursued and questions about them may be answered. Committee decisions are often taken after a discussion in the Committee, not giving the people's representatives an opportunity to consult their constituencies. As long as village representatives agree to decisions it can be said that people have been consulted . . .

So who was consulted when the village sites were chosen?

Some are of the opinion that the people made the decisions. The people are of the opinion that the sites were chosen for them. In cases where the people's decisions are referred to, they had been made by a few well-to-do representatives of the people. For example, representatives from a village like Mohoro made decisions for the whole area, deciding that the Mohoro population did not need to move whilst they advocated the moving of the delta population.

Contacts with a few village leaders do not guarantee that the opinions of the people have been obtained. When moving of the people is done hurriedly so that insufficient time is given for planning, choosing the site, finding out the wishes of the people, finding out the knowledge that the people have accumulated about the patterns of cultivation, crops grown and their whole habitat and life pattern, then one can expect faulty decisions to be made.

The second of our five questions was why 1973 was chosen as the date to begin villagization over the whole country. It is not easy at this stage to do more than suggest reasons. Firstly, by the end of 1972 the bankruptcy of many villages founded to get concessions out of the government was very obvious, and communal work was not making a significant contribution to production. Secondly, the politicized type of socialist production unit was clearly not going to be accepted by many farmers, and was regarded with suspicion or dislike by most politicians, and particularly by members of the Central Committee of TANU. But, thirdly, the option of going back to peasant farming —emph-

asizing price policy rather than bureaucratic organization—
would have meant accepting that the previous five years' work
had been misdirected. Finally, the idea of villagization (without
ujamaa) was popular, with most urban-based professional politicians and at least acceptable to the civil servants who had been
'decentralized' to the regions: it gave them a defined job to do,
a sense of their own importance, and a chance to exert their influence on the peasants who otherwise were so reluctant to do
what they proposed:

The new approach was much more in line with bureaucratic thinking
and with what a bureaucracy can do effectively: enforced movement of
the peasants into new 'modern' settlements, i.e. settlements with the
houses placed close together, in straight lines, along the roads, and with
the fields outside the nucleated village, organised in blockfarms, each
block containing the villagers' individual plots, but with only one type
of crop, and readily accessible for control by the agricultural extension
officer and eventual cultivation by government tractors. (Boesen 1976: 13)

The 'decentralization' of July 1972 could equally well have
been called a 'centralization'; for it meant the end of local government, which was replaced in each region and district by an
arm of the central civil service, under the Prime Minister's
Office (Nyerere 1972). The word 'decentralization' refers not to
power, but to staff: many senior officials were 'decentralized',
i.e. physically transferred from the technical ministries to the
departments of the Prime Minister's Office that were set up to
administer the regions and districts. A similar reorganization of
the Party strengthened the salaried officials at the expense of
those who were elected (such as Members of Parliament) so
that, for the first time, there was a strong, well-paid party
bureaucracy at regional, district, divisional, and ward level.[13]
For example, the Party official responsible for about 2000
households earned the salary of a primary school headmaster,
and was far more influential than the (elected) chairman of any
of the villages in his area. Moreover, he was appointed by the
District officials, and his career depended on maintaining good
relations with regional and district officials. He was not
appointed by the villagers, nor was he particularly dependent on
them; he might well come from a quite different area, or a tribe
which by tradition felt superior to them. But Ward and Divisional Secretaries were 'consulted' before village sites were
chosen, and usually made the detailed arrangements for moving
people on the ground.

It was also clear to the decentralized civil servants that their future depended on the smooth creation of villages. The first year of the decentralization (July 1972 to June 1973) was spent transferring and training staff, and creating new accounting systems and methods of working. By the second half of 1973 they were in a position to act. The training courses and manuals of the McKinsey corporation,[14] the management consultants who assisted the government in every stage of the decentralization, had led these people to believe that they had special responsibilities for 'management', and villagization was the one thing they could do which the previous administrators had not done. One of the decentralized civil servants explained why the move was undertaken in 1973 in these terms:

The answer is linked to the TANU and Government decision in June 1972 to overhaul the Governmental administrative structure. In particular, the regional administration was to move from its original law and order and revenue collection function into a more development-based management function with the people thoroughly involved at the grass-roots level in planning and implementation of development projects . . . . Therefore, one year after the decentralisation programme was effected, TANU and Government saw the need to reinforce the participatory development institution by creating a firmly established, participating institution—planned villages. (J. V. Mwapachu 1976: 116)

As we have seen, the way in which villages were created hardly encouraged grass-roots participation, because there were such obvious shows of government force, and so little time for discussion or real planning. In the same paragraph Mwapachu shows his belief in modernization theory, the ideology of the bureaucracy and, indeed, of villagization: 'For we must remember that the problems of the rural peasantry have been based fundamentally on their traditional outlook and unwillingness to accept change.' (p. 117.) It is hard to see how those who think like this could really value the contribution that peasants could make towards planning their own future. But Mwapachu is probably right to link decentralization and villagization. Certainly villagization (unlike ujamaa) was accepted as desirable by nearly all government staff, and gave them something that they could be proud of at a time when economically the country was not doing very well. By allowing villagization Nyerere maintained the unity and loyalty of his ruling class.

This may also be the deeper answer to the third of our five questions, what did Nyerere, and the TANU leadership, expect to achieve by villagization. None of the other arguments put forward are entirely convincing, either singly or together. *The Daily News* and most of the bureaucrats claimed that villagization would make it easier (or possible) to provide services—schools, water supplies, dispensaries, famine relief, or agricultural extension—just as Nyerere had argued since before independence.[15] There is no doubt that villagization has made it easier to provide these services, and we have seen that some Tanzania's most spectacular achievements of the 1970s were in the fields of literacy and primary education; but there are still difficulties with the argument. In particular, since government has to *provide* most of these services, through its staff and recurrent expenditure, was it not embarrassing itself by creating demands for social services which it must have realized could not be satisfied without greatly increased production? Moreover, there were some areas, such as the Sukuma heartland, where people were moved even though the population density was so high that most of the services could have been built within two or three miles of the majority of holdings. Together, these arguments suggest that provision of services was not the only consideration behind the move.

It was also claimed, by Nyerere and leader writers, especially from 1975 onwards when there were very large imports of food, that the object of the villagization was to increase agricultural production. Frances Hill has claimed that this was the object from as early as 1971.[16] But neither she, nor Nyerere, explained precisely *how* villagization in itself would increase production. It did not imply communal work, at least initially, so there could be few benefits from economies of scale.[17] In the short run it would inevitably disrupt production, while in the long run Tanzanian farmers had already shown that if new technology was clearly profitable they could take it up even if they were living dispersed on their farms.

Or was the idea to increase agricultural production through coercion? It certainly allowed for easier supervision of junior staff by their superiors in the District offices (an overriding requirement for village sites was that they be on or near all-weather roads). Was it the intention to enforce minimum acreage rules, or other rules governing crop and agricultural husbandry? Such rules were reintroduced in many places in 1974 and 1975. Or was the idea (as Leonard confidently predicted) to use forced communal work to extract a surplus from the rural areas, which would be used to finance investment either in the villages themselves, or in heavy industry in the towns? (Leonard 1976: 17–18). Such a view is completely contrary to Mwapachu's position (p. 124) and to the 1975 Ujamaa Viillages Act, under which Village Councils were set up to allow the villagers to make decisions affecting their own lives. It would also have been contrary to the colonial experience, in which peasants had shown how effectively they could resist such coercion.

It is not easy to explain precisely what Nyerere and the Party expected to achieve from villagization. Looking at events as they were reported and justified, one would conclude that during the actual villagization (1974–5) the main arguments centred on the provision of social services, and that it was recognized that this would require road transport. Thus villages were located around existing social services, such as schools, dispensaries, water points, or trading settlements, and almost always on or very near roads. The size and layout of the new villages were based on the economics of providing social services, and not on production; but at this stage it was believed, as an article of faith, that increased production would follow villagization.

Once the villages had been established (1976 onwards), faith was no longer sufficient. Communal work was not seriously considered (it had failed in the past, in government eyes, and was relegated to a second—advanced—stage of registration in the 1975 Ujamaa Villages Act[18]). The main hope lay in the packages of improved seeds and fertilizers which characterized the large agricultural World Bank projects of the 1970s, and which were, on the face of things, consistent with villagization, since they implied rather intensive cultivation of small areas by large numbers of individual farmers.

But what if the farmers refused to cultivate the World Bank crops, or to use the new inputs? We have seen that, from the farmers' point of view this might often be justifiable (the World Bank/USAID 'National Maize Project' went so far as to provide credit for inputs on maize growing in Dodoma and some other low rainfall regions; the mistake was admitted after a few years of failure, and more attention devoted to sorghum and other draught-resistant crops). Yet the bureaucracy was not prepared to allow freedom of choice, and so it started to reintroduce minimum acreage regulations and other by-laws (such as compulsory weeding under cashewnut trees, or the growing of cassava) designed to benefit the farmers, who were fined or imprisoned if they did not obey them. As the quotation which heads the chapter shows, they even imprisoned a church leader who warned that taking loans for fertilizer might put the farmers in debt. Villagization had shown the officials that force could be used without immediate dire consequences; now they followed up by using force in an attempt to increase agricultural production.

From the agricultural, or ecological, point of view there are in fact several arguments for relatively *dispersed* living, especially where livestock are kept. In the words of a distinguished professor of agriculture:

It is unsatisfactory for several reasons, such as transport of manure and feeding-stuffs, to kraal the cattle away from the holding. It is equally unsatisfactory for the animals to be penned on the holding at night if the farmer is not there. They may be attacked by wild animals as well as thieves; they may break out in the night; they may need attention in parturition and other emergencies; and the farmer will not be there to let them out in the morning, so that grazing is curtailed. If mixed farming is to be introduced to communities hitherto living in villages, some of them at least will have to move into scattered homesteads. (Masefield 1955: 66.)

Professor Masefield points out that in parts of England where livestock are important 'a much greater proportion of the farmers live in isolated homesteads' (p. 67). But he also concedes that in parts of Africa, such as West Africa, where the people live in villages, there is greater specialization and much more advanced craft skills are to be found.

Even with crop agriculture, dispersed settlement enables the family to live on or very near its fields, and so to keep watch for attacks on the crops by birds or animals; when fields are far from the houses, peasants frequently build temporary shelters from which they can watch, and sleep, at night. Living in villages minimizes the walking to schools, dispensaries, shops, buses, and services generally, while maximizing the distance from living quarters to the fields. If the village is large, and the fields distant, the walking time to the fields may be considerable; in parts of Mwanza Region, the new villages had to be divided to reduce the distances to the fields; while in Mtwara and Tanga regions villagization led to the loss of many developed plantations of cashewnut trees. In one village in Njombe District, if each person had received the target of 4 acres of land, some would have had to walk 8 miles to their fields. There is also the danger of soil exhaustion on land near the villages. With increasing population, maintenance of soil fertility would eventually have become a problem anyway, but the villagization suddenly made it an immediate one.[19] On many African soils, with low humus content, it is certainly not straightforward to replenish the soils simply by applying chemical fertilizer; permanent cropping is possible, but needs a lot of labour, and may only prove economic if organic matter is added to the soil as well as chemicals; precisely what has to be done in every particular situation can only be discovered by a patient process of trial and error, best carried out over many cropping seasons. Finally, dispersed settlement keeps down game populations; John Ford was the first to suggest that concentrating population in villages in an attempt to suppress sleeping sickness could lead to more game animals carrying the disease, and more (rather than less) danger to man and cattle. Mrs Swantz has already hinted at a similar possibility following villagization on the edges of the Ruvu valley.[20]

Inevitably there were also short-term problems, some of which affected just the villagers while others affected the country as well. Over 90 per cent of a sample of villagers questioned in Njombe District, Iringa Region (De Vries and Fortmann 1979), reported that they had had some problems in moving. Nearly 60 per cent had problems building houses, intensified because the move took place during the dry season when it was difficult to get sufficient water to make mud, while the nights were unpleasantly cold for sleeping out. When the rains started, the villagers were then faced with a choice between building houses and preparing land; by November most of the land would normally be planted, but in November 1974 the researchers found that in 60 per cent of the villages studied 'very little or nothing had been done to prepare the land'. Of those interviewed 31 per cent reported problems with 'lost, stolen or damaged property'—apparently mainly theft of food by other villagers or the militia; 32 per cent reported difficulties with animals, either in getting water for them or finding somewhere to keep them at night. Although only 4 per cent mentioned it as a problem, villagization also increased the risk of disease: pneumonia through sleeping outside on cold nights, and intestinal diseases which spread rapidly in villages when not everyone used latrines. In the years that followed villagization there were unprecedented epidemics of typhoid and cholera.[21] One could also add as a cost the value of the good houses that were destroyed; for although the government subsequently mounted a drive for better housing, the money for new corrugated iron, and often cement, still had to be found.

While there is some doubt over the supposed benefits of villagization, there is little difficulty in itemizing the costs. They divide into two broad groups: those associated with living in villages *per se*, and short-term costs of the move itself. From the government's point of view there were two types of cost: the direct cost of staff and vehicles involved in carrying out the move, and the cost of the crops that were not planted, thereby causing reduced exports and greatly increased food imports during the years of the villagization. Neither is easy to calculate. The loss of crops was disguised to the world by the claim that Tanzania was caught up in the 'great Sahelian drought' of 1973–5. Rainfall figures do not bear this out: they show a drought in 1973–4 but sufficient rain for a reasonable harvest in several parts of the country in 1974–5 (Lofchie 1978).[22] But what is not in dispute is that marketed production of almost all crops fell, leading to a deficit of over a million tons of cereals spread over the four years 1974–7 (Table 22.2). This deficit was made up with imports costing about 2000 million shillings and exhausting the Bank of Tanzania's holdings of foreign exchange during 1975, but also with food aid: more than 200 000 tons, most of it promised at the 1975 World Bank Consultative Meeting for Tanzania, including 70 000 tons from the United States (Table 22.3). The cotton crop also declined, from 77 000 tons in 1972/3 to 42 500 in 1975/6. Cashewnut production fell by a third. These declines were associated with the villagization, although other factors (such as a low price for cashewnuts) were also involved (Ellis 1979a). The total costs of the villagization, including the

TABLE 22.2
Net Cereal Imports 1974–1977
('000 tons)

	1974	1975	1976	1977
Maize[a]	254.7	231.4	72	0
Rice[b]	71.2	64.0	8.8	15
Wheat[a]	102.7	157.5	3	30
Sorghum/Millet	−0.2	4.8	0	n.a.
Total	428.4	457.7	83.8	45.0

Notes a The figures for maize and wheat include imports of maize and wheat flour, converted to their equivalents in grain.
       b Milled rice.
Source: Tanzania Food and Nutrition Centre (1978: Table 20.3).

TABLE 22.3
*Food Aid Received by National Milling Corporation, September
1974—June 1977*

Date	Product	Amount (tons)	Donor country
1974 Sept.	Maize	1 000	Yugoslavia
1975 Feb.	Wheat-flour	1 000	North Korea
Mar.	Wheat	22 800	Canada
May	Wheat	15 000	Sweden
June	Wheat-flour	7 720	Finland
July	Wheat	19 000	Canada
July	Wheat	10 000	Australia
Sept.	Rice	20 000	USA
		95 520	
1976 Jan.	Maize	19 800	EEC
Feb.	Maize	1 500	Belgium
Feb.	Maize	5 600	W. Germany
Aug.	Maize	5 000	UK
Sept.	Maize	2 000	EEC
Sept.	Maize	34 000	USA
		67 900	
1977 Jan.	Wheat	23 600	Canada
Jan.	Maize	6 000*	W. Germany
Feb.	Wheat	6 000	Australia
June	Rice	17 000	USA
		52 600	

* This was spoilt when it arrived.
Note: Durations other than those from the USA were on a grant basis.
Source: National Milling Corporation.

value of property destroyed, the direct costs of the 'operations', and the value of crops that were not planted or harvested, were evidently very great indeed.

Anyone who has read this far must, like the writer, conclude that these costs were not calculated before the decision to go ahead was taken, and that the very real problems facing Tanzanian rural producers were scarcely taken into account. Villagization cannot be said to have failed—although it changed the face of Tanzania—for the achievements in the field of social services also have to be taken into account, as we saw in Chapter 21.

But the acid test is production over time; if food and cash crop production do not increase faster than population growth, it will be hard to provide the promised social services, or to invest in industries.

One last question remains: what happened to the idealism of 1967 and 1968, to the few ujamaa villages that *were* started with a faith in socialism and hard communal work? The clearest answer can be found in the story of an association of villages in Ruvuma Region, told in detail in an appendix to this chapter. The Ruvuma Development Association was the model for much of Nyerere's writing in the 1960s. Most of what was recommended in *Education for Self-Reliance* had been pioneered in the primary school at Litowa, and the description of small villages of politicized farmers given in *Freedom and Development* could apply to most of the RDA's 17 villages, with an average of about thirty farmers in each. Yet in September 1969 it was declared a prohibited organization. Its abolition was announced to the nation with the newspaper headline 'TANU to run all ujamaa villages', and was to be followed by restatements, including several in the 1971 *Mwongozo*, that 'The Party is Supreme'. But the RDA story, along with the Mount Carmel case (Chapter 23), shows that 'the Party' in this slogan did not mean a grass-roots organization of workers and peasants: it meant the party officials and professional politicians. Only a bureaucracy distanced from peasant life could have forced through measures as draconian as villagization, and with so little productive effect.

APPENDIX: THE RUVUMA DEVELOPMENT ASSOCIATION[1]

On 7 November 1960, before independence, fifteen TANU Youth League members from Peramiho, near Songea crossed the river Luhira and started a TYL settlement scheme at Litowa 26 miles from Songea, the headquarters of Songea District in the south-west corner of Tanzania. They built themselves a shelter, a temporary foot-bridge over the river, and planted three or four acres of maize. Within three months all had left: they were frightened by lions, baboons spoilt their crops, and they had no food to live on while waiting for their first harvest.

A few months later another start was made, with the encouragement of the local agricultural extension worker. One of the few who returned was Ntimbanjayo Millinga, the original leader, who, after the initial disappointment, had been accepted for a nine-month course in politics and economics at TANU's new ideological institute, Kivukoni College in Dar es Salaam. The course started in July 1961, not long after the village was refounded. At Kivukoni Millinga met Ralph Ibbott, who was in Dar es Salaam on holiday from Nyafaru, a 2000-acre agricultural enterprise involving the Tangwena people of (Southern) Rhodesia. Millinga invited him to visit Litowa, and eventually, in April 1963, Ibbott and his family took up residence there.

During 1962 and 1963 'spontaneous settlement schemes' were started in many parts of the country in response to the President's calls. Hinjuson, the first Area Commissioner in Songea, encouraged Millinga and Ibbott to visit several of these groups. Ibbott felt strongly that villagers themselves (and not experts, advisers, or other outsiders) should make the decisions that concerned their lives, and accept the responsibility for them. To facilitate this, Hinjuson made possible the registration of the Ruvuma Development Association under the Societies Ordinance. The constitution included a management committee, with

the Regional Commissioner as Chairman and regional party officials, civil servants, and representatives from each village in
the Association as members. At the first meeting, in September
1963, Millinga was elected Secretary while Ibbott was recognized as 'Adviser'.

The RDA grew slowly, mainly by welcoming, and giving discipline and coherence to, existing villages or groups of settlers.
Large numbers of villagers were not involved: at no time did
any single village have more than forty families, except for Litowa which at the end had about sixty including various staff and
the teachers in the primary school. Several prospective villages
were either refused registration or had their registration delayed
for several months until their commitment to working together
became clearer. Slow, steady, progress was made. While traditional villages stagnated, and the settlement schemes of the Village Settlement Agency (where those who joined had been
promised that in a few years they would be rich enough to own
motor cars) collapsed, the RDA villages became self-sufficient in
food, improved their health and nutrition, built a school and
water supplies, and started village industries. Slowly other villages asked to join.

A new constitution was approved in principle by President
Nyerere, who visited Litowa for the first time in August 1965. It
turned the Association into a co-operative body, owned and
controlled by its members, the villages. The details were discussed in lengthy meetings in the constituent villages, after which
changes were made. The central feature of the new constitution
was the meeting, held three months, of representatives from
each village; it became the body ultimately responsible for decision-making and financial control in the Association. Also explicitly incorporated in the constitution was the 'Social and Economic Revolutionary Army' (SERA): This was

a group of understanding people from within those projects with which
the Association is connected . . . who are most able to quickly increase
their understanding of the development of African Socialism and who
are prepared to give up their membership of any group so as to be free
to visit developing village projects with which the Association is working to give advice and help forward development of the lives of the
people. This Social and Economic Revolutionary Army, hereafter called SERA, will be soldiers of peaceful economic development helping
to bring about the Social and Economic Revolution necessary to enable
people to lift themselves from the clutches of the enemies of ignorance,
poverty and disease.

The Social and Economic Revolutionary Army was thus a group of politicized cadres who were also practical experts in various fields, and who could be moved around from village to village. They were able to explain socialist policies, to gather information, and to strengthen any village which had special problems. Yet they were not outsiders: it was recognized from the start that SERA members had to come from the villages of the Association, and it was soon found desirable that they should, as far as possible, be associated with their home villages.

The RDA operated within this framework from 1965 until its sudden end in September 1969. The number of villages slowly increased. In 1967 there were seventeen, although some were very small indeed, and by that time at least two of the original villages were no longer fully committed to the ideals of the Association. The villages were spread out over a vast area: one was 200 miles east of Songea, another, on the shore of Lake Nyasa, was over 100 miles to the west. Matetereka was a similar distance to the north. The total number of families involved was, at its greatest, no more than 400—a tiny fraction of the rural population of Ruvuma Region.

Initially the villages concentrated on securing their food supply. This was more important than a cash income, or even the building of permanent houses or water supplies. One of Ibbott's earliest contributions had been to arrange a small grant to assist in covering the food requirements of the small group of settlers who returned to Litowa in 1961. But by the second harvest Litowa was self-sufficient in food, and the other villages quickly became self-sufficient. The policy was from the start to develop a communal plot, but also to allow individuals plots—usually in the first instance 1 acre per family. As a village gained in self-confidence the communal plot was increased in size, while the individuals plots were slowly reduced. In two of the most advanced villages, Litowa and Liweta, by 1968 more than enough food was produced from the communal plots to feed the villagers, and surpluses were available for sale.

The local co-operative society was the only legal purchaser of maize in the Region. Yet it frequently lacked either the funds or the transport or storage facilities to buy all the crops. Moreover, when purchasing maize it paid 18 shillings for a 90 kg bag, and when selling maize flour it sold it for 60 shillings for a bag of the same size. The only maize mill in Songea capable of regularly supplying maize on contract to such institutions as boarding-schools and the prison was owned by an expatriate, and as early as 1962 an official of the Co-operative Development Division suggested that the RDA should buy it. The purchase was made in 1966, using 90 000 shillings provided for the purpose by President Nyerere himself. This meant that the villages in the Association had a guaranteed outlet for their maize, and could earn money by selling flour, or by milling the maize brought to the mill by other people living in or around Songea.

The cash crop approved by the government for the Region was fire-cured tobacco. Litowa grew several acres of this crop in the 1961/2 and 1963/4 seasons, and quickly discovered that it required a lot of labour for very little reward. The price was about a third that of flue-cured tobacco grown in other parts of the country. With the exception of a few areas of virgin soil, the crop required fertilizer, which was expensive; but then if there was too much rain, leaf spot disease greatly reduced the price. Total production was declining, and the processing factory in Songea was inefficient and losing money. The RDA villagers did not like the crop, though they continued to grow a limited acreage. When Peter Barongo, the Regional Commissioner between December 1965 and April 1968, introduced a by-law which made it compulsory for each family in the Region to cultivate one acre of the crop, most of the peasants in the region resented beinng forced to grow it, but those in the RDA had an organization through which they could articulate their discontent: this was to be one of the main focuses of their conflict with the government.

In the initial years the villagers were very poor. The first permanent (i.e. burnt-brick) buildings at Litowa were not built until 1966, and dwelling-houses on permanent sites not until 1967—and they were still of solid mud or unbaked mud-block construction. The first permanent buildings at Liweta and Matetereka were crop stores, started in 1968.

In 1965 a water supply was installed at Litowa. The money for the pipes and water-driven pump came from the British charity, Oxfam, but the tank for the water, the dam to feed the pump, and the installation, were built by the villagers themselves. Three years later the government built a water supply for Liweta village: it had three times the capacity of the Litowa supply for a much smaller population (the Litowa scheme had to supply the water for 300 children in the school), but it was planned and built by the government, and the villagers did not enjoy the same sense of achievement as at Litowa. Similarly, at Matetereka the government built a grain store. But at Liweta the government provided money only for the roof, so that the villagers were left to plan the building, decide how many baked bricks it required, bake the bricks, and build the building. The resulting building was more appropriate to the climate of the area than the one at Matetereka. Again the value of the villagers doing things for themselves was demonstrated.

In the six years from 1963 to 1969 only seven children died at Litowa. This was despite the fact that the school for the whole Association was started there in 1964, and by 1968 contained more than 300 pupils. Since it has been estimated that in Ruvuma Region nearly 40 per cent of babies died before they were five years old,[2] this was a most impressive performance. It was achieved without great cost. The first innovation, starting in 1963, was for two of the women to come in early from the fields to cook an evening meal for all the children; in this way all were assured of a basic meal, prepared before they were too tired to eat it. The principle was soon extended to the midday meal as well.

The second innovation was for one of the villagers to be sent for three months to the local hospital, to observe what went on and to learn as much as he could. On his return he opened a small dispensary. The population at Litowa was too small for the government to provide a salaried worker. This villager was not paid a salary for his work, but his dispensary was soon attracting peasants from several miles around. One by one the other villages selected a member, sent him to the local hospital for training, and opened similar small dispensaries. Later the RDA recruited two Swiss volunteer nurses. Not long after they left, a trained Rural Medical Aid offered his services, and surrendered his government salary to become a member of Litowa village; but this was only two months before the end.

The question of education concerned the villagers at Litowa from the beginning. A few of the first group of settlers already had children in school, and a decision was made to pay their school fees out of Association funds. But in the discussions which preceded this decision much wider issues were raised:

Very early on the question came up as to what was the purpose of sending children to school when experience showed that if one did so they left the village and went to the towns. The members felt that they would be wasting their time starting on village development, which was a very long-term business, if because of schooling their children then left the work that their parents had started. In fact it was very obvious that much of the success in the long term depended on people's skill in bringing up their children to follow on after them.

So it was decided to create a form of education that would prepare the children for life in the villages of the Association. Early
in 1964 a start was made, with two villagers with some primary
education gathering some of the children around them for
elementary lessons in reading, writing, and arithmetic. By the
time the school was registered in 1965 there were three classes,
and it had been decided that the school at Litowa should be a
boarding-school, to which would be sent all the children from
the villages in the Association. In the same year President Nyerere visited Litowa and gave his approval to the idea that the
school should develop in an experimental way, creating its own
syllabuses and integrating its educational work into the life of
the villages.

    Much was achieved during the next three years. In an article
written in May 1968, Suleiman Toroka, the headmaster from
early in 1967, described the school (Toroka 1968: 268). Much of
the time was spent on 'projects'—most were agricultural, but
there were also projects involving the production of wool from
sheep, and work with very young children, and there were plans
for a range of projects concerned with keeping livestock. Toroka was clear on the requirements for a successful project: it had
to be profitable in itself, it should not be too big, it should be
related directly to the life and work of the people, and it should
not be optional. The integration of the school into the community was shown in a number of ways: children regularly worked
on the village communal farms, while villagers, when required,
assisted on the school plots; the children and their parents worked together on building projects, including roads, bridges, and
houses as well as the school buildings themselves; during school
holidays the children were sent in groups to the various villages
of the Association, to assist in work, but also to see some of the
problems for themselves and to discover 'that often the best
leaders do not come from the educated élite'. The school succeeded in combining academic and political education:

The main object in all the lower primary standards is to help the children accustom themselves to think and work together. The content of
the lectures is similar throughout the standards: i.e. the teaching and
telling of stories, songs, and plays of the revolutionary spirit, and of the
idea of good and bad in terms of Ujamaa behaviour.

    Finally, in perhaps the most remarkable of all its innovations,
in 1969 the villagers and the pupils planned the vocations of the

first generation of primary-school leavers. Thirty-six children had reached the end of Standard VII, which meant that no village could expect more than two or three of these school-leavers: so there were many more jobs requiring skills available than there were school-leavers to fill them. They were asked to fill in a form indicating what they would like to do when they left school. Only two (both from nearby non-ujamaa villages) chose to try and proceed to a secondary school. Some of the students had already been prepared for careers through practical work in the school, for example in wool preparation, agriculture, carpentry, or nursing. The students' choices were then discussed by the village leaders, careers were selected, and suitable training programmes (involving where necessary time spent outside the villages) were prepared. Unfortunately the end of the Association in September 1969 prevented this plan being carried further.

It was one of Ibbott's original insights that, even in the rural setting, industry could not be separated from agriculture. The purchase of the grain mill in Songea was a first step towards putting this philosophy with operation. The expatriate who owned the grain mill also owned a sawmill in Songea town, and this was purchased in 1967 with money raised abroad, mainly from the Swiss charity *Fonds für Entwicklung und Partnerschaft in Africa*. It was the only medium-scale sawmill in the vicinity, and therefore the only reliable source of supply of sawn timber for government development projects. As owners the villagers were able to retain the profit from their labour spent in identifying and felling suitable trees—profit which would not otherwise be shared with the workers and peasants on whom the operation depended.

Wool processing—washing, carding, spinning, dyeing, knitting, and weaving—was conceived as a cottage industry. The original idea was to knit warm clothes. The earlier stages of the processing were added when it was discovered that fleeces could be obtained from Kenya. When the Kitulo wheat/sheep scheme in neighbouring Mbeya region started shearing its woolly sheep, a cheaper source of raw material became available. Finally in 1967 Matetereka, one of the villages in the Association and situated on a plateau ecologically similar to Kitulo, started to keep sheep. In the whole operation, only the dyes were imported, but research was put in hand to make dyes from roots or other locally available materials. The soap industry was another small-scale venture based on local raw materials—in this case pig-fat

available from the mission farm at Peramiho. Later the fat from
pigs killed in the village was used. Experiments were undertaken to find a suitable recipe and technique: for the villagers it
was important not just that soap was made but that they made it
themselves.

In order to ensure the transfer of skills, the Association did
not hesitate to employ outsiders; in practice this often meant expatriates—there were usually seven or eight working in the
Assocation at any given time. The villages also received many
donations from outside the country, and a remarkable line of
visitors including the President (twice), the Second Vice-
President (Kawawa), at least six other ministers, two ambassadors, the representatives of most of the agencies who gave
money, and others who were interested in the development of a
socialist community in the most remote and cut off part of the
country. So what happened at Litowa, and in the other villages
of the Association, was from the start something that was
known about nationally.

The RDA attracted opposition almost as soon as it became
firmly established, from about 1963. The earliest opposition was
from officials in the government's village settlement schemes
who felt that the RDA villages would attract their potential settlers. There was also opposition from Party leaders in Songea
town, who feared the democracy of the villages and the school,
and the self-confidence of the villagers and school students who
argued publicly against some of their policies (the compulsory
growing of tobacco in particular). These fears were aggravated
when the RDA achieved economic power by purchasing two of
the three local industries, the grain mill and the sawmill. The
grain mill threatened the co-operative movement by paying
higher prices and giving the villagers another outlet for their
grain, while the sawmill was the only supplier of timber for government projects. But this local opposition was overcome, not
least because the Association was supported in Dar es Salaam:
it was following policies very close to those of Nyerere's 1967
and 1968 papers, and Nyerere himself took a personal interest
in the villages, authorizing the school to experiment and giving
money to purchase the grain mill.

Given this support, the decision to disband the Association
could only be taken at the national level. In 1969 the Central
Committee of TANU was reformed, to include a majority of
members elected by regional party branches. Thus professional
politicians from the regions suddenly achieved power at the cen-

tre of the Party. In July 1969 the new Committee met in Hand-eni to discuss ujamaa for a whole month, and decided that its members, in groups of three, would spend five weeks living in some of the most advanced ujamaa villages in the country, in-cluding four of the RDA villages. These visits confirmed their worst fears: the RDA was an autonomous organization receiving funds and personnel from abroad, and promoting a form of socialism which did not depend on a strong central party. If RDA organizations became the norm nationally, the profession-al politicians would be in a much weaker position. Moreover, by mid-1969 another model was available, much more attractive to them: good reports were coming in from the Rufiji valley, the first large-scale movement of all the people in an area into plan-ned villages. This was organized by party officials (rather than by any grass-roots organization of the peasants) and gave the of-ficials an obvious sense of achievement. It was soon to become the policy nationally, and it was entirely incompatible with the existence of groups of independent, politicized peasants, such as those of the RDA villages, which would be small, voluntary, and might well oppose central direction. On 24 September 1969 the Central Committee met in Dar es Salaam, under President Nyerere's chairmanship, and 21 out of its 24 members voted in favour of disbanding the RDA.

There was little or no planning as to how this decision would be implemented. On 25 September the Minister for Rural De-velopment and Regional Administration flew by government plane to Songea, with members of the Central Committee, to announce the decision to the people. This assets of the Associa-tion were confiscated—the grain mill, the sawmill, the mecha-nical workshop, vehicles, and equipment. The police were sent to take away any Association property in the villages. The ex-patriate staff left quietly within a few days. The villagers got on with their work as best they could. Within a week the teaching staff in the school had been transferred to posts throughout the country—to Mara, Kigoma, Mbeya, Dodoma, and Singida re-gions. The model for *Freedom and Development* and *Education for Self-Reliance* had been destroyed.

23 PARASTATALS AND WORKERS

> Tanzania has seen and shall continue to witness the
> creation of public business institutions as centres of
> initiative and dynamism in our economic activities.
> C.D. Msuya, Minister of Finance (1974)[1]

The years after the Arusha Declaration certainly saw a 'proliferation of public institutions in Tanzania'. Parastatals, or government corporations, were set up in almost every sector: industry, agriculture, banking, finance, trade, transport, and housing;
there were even a few in education, health services, and public
administration. In 1967 there were 64 parastatals; by 1974 there
were 139 and the number was still increasing (Nyerere
1977: 38).

A parastatal is distinguished from a civil service department
by its accountancy. In government departments, estimates of the
expenditure allowed on different activities, and the amount of
revenue expected, are voted for a year at a time in the annual
budget. The procedures and record keeping are designed to prevent corruption and to ensure that money is spent for the purposes for which it is voted, rather than to assess how well it is
spent. Parastatals, on the other hand, like private companies,
produce profit and loss accounts, which show the profit and return on capital in a financial year. The government is a shareholder, often the sole shareholder, although there may be other
partners; [2] as such it is entitled to appoint Directors, who sit on
a Board of Directors which meets from time to time to approve
the policy of the parastatal. But many Board members are busy
men, with other concerns, and in practice parastatals which report profits can normally expect considerable freedom in how
they spend money, whom they employ, and what prices they
set. When, however, they fail to perform well financially, when
scandals publicize abuses of their freedom to buy or sell, or
when their wage or price policies have implications for the coun-

try as a whole, governments may take a closer interest in their affairs.

In Tanzania, parastatals have a long history. The German East Africa Company, which administered the colony between 1885 and 1891, could be described as a parastatal, set up by the German government to avoid the necessity of direct government involvement in administration. Under British rule railways and harbours, posts and telecommunications, and East African Airways were run by corporations on an East African basis. Electricity generation, originally privately owned, passed into public ownership in the 1950s, and was expected to be profitable. Water supply, on the other hand, was regarded as a public service and remained a government department, even in cities like Dar es Salaam where many individuals had private connections to their houses. Marketing Boards were parastatals created to take the marketing of peasant production out of the hands of Asian traders, and to cream off surpluses. These surpluses were invested on the London market, where they earned low rates of interest; other parastatals that wanted investment funds could borrow on the same London market, at considerably higher rates of interest (Loxley 1973: 102–4).

The colonial government also acquired shareholdings in a few parastatals directly concerned with production, including the Tanganyika Agricultural Corporation (created to make money on the land cleared for the Groundnuts Scheme), 81 per cent of the shares in the Nyanza Salt Mine, 51 per cent of Williamson's Diamonds (accepted by the government as part payment of death duties), and 51 per cent of Tanganyika (Meat) Packers. In the two latter cases, however, it was scarcely involved in management, which was left in the hands of the private-sector partners, De Beers and Liebigs.

Even before independence TANU was determined to be involved in profit-making enterprises; the Mwananchi Development Corporation, owned by the Party, was set up for this purpose, and invested in the National Printing Company (which printed the Party newspapers *Uhuru* and *The Nationalist*) and the Mwananchi Engineering and Construction Company (MECCO) among other ventures. At the same time the cooperative unions were purchasing or building cotton ginneries, edible oil-mills, hotels, transport companies, farms, and other small businesses. In 1964 the National Union of Tanganyika Workers Act allowed NUTA, from that date the only legal trade union, to collect workers' contributions from their employers, but it also required that 60 per cent of this income be invested in social or economic enterprises; so the Workers' Development Corporation was created and was soon involved in 'a mixture of small sound and sick enterprises' (Msuya 1974: 3).

The idea of a holding company to manage government shareholdings was suggested for African countries generally by Lord Hailey in 1952, and for Tanganyika specifically in the report of the 1960 World Bank mission. But it was not till 1962 that the Tanganyika Development Corporation was created, with an initial capital of £500 000. There was no clear idea of how it would operate: according to Coe (1964: 26–31), the initial capital was entirely invested in the Tanganyika Development Finance Corporation, one of two foreign-controlled investment banks which lent money to the private sector.[3] Early in 1965 the National Development Corporation took over the assets of the Tanganyika Development Company, the Tanganyika Agricultural Corporation, and the various government shareholdings. The government shareholdings gave NDC an income approaching 20 million shillings a year, and it quickly diversified its interests, investing in agriculture, manufacturing, trade and tourism.

After the Arusha Declaration of February 1967 it became clear that the parastatal sector was to play three roles: it was, first and foremost, to limit the transfers of profit out of the country; it was to invest in productive sectors, especially manufacturing, but also agriculture and tourism; and it was to strengthen the productive infrastructure, especially in transport, construction, and power generation. We shall consider each of these in turn.

In order to limit tranfers of profit out of the country, it was necessary to control a wide range of financial institutions, as well as the import and export trade. This was achieved in a single-minded way, unique in Africa at the time (Loxley 1972; 1973). The colonial monetary system was effective in ensuring that most of the surplus gained in the colony was transferrred to Britain. For most of its life the East African Currency Board issued local currency only if an equivalent amount of foreign exchange was deposited in London. This meant that an expansion of the domestic market, or a greater use of money in transactions, would not be accompanied by more coin and notes in circulation unless exports also rose; it also implied that funds that could have been available for long-term investment were instead locked up in London. Insurance companies, building societies, and the commercial banks were all branches of foreign organizations which invested their deposits in London or Nairobi. The pension funds of government staff were invested in government stock on the London market. It is hardly surprising that the 1960 World Bank mission concluded that 90 per cent of the investment funds for the period 1960–6 would have to come from abroad.

Although the currency board system was beginning to change before independence, it had no power to prevent the capital outflow which followed the 1960 (Kenya) Lancaster House conference. It was not till 1965 that exchange control was imposed on transactions with countries outside East Africa; it was extended to include transfers within East Africa in 1967, but this was suspended during the negotiations which led to the creation of the East African Community a few months later, and not reimposed till 1971. Meanwhile a Central Bank, the Bank of Tanzania, was created in 1966; it issued currency, performed the function of banker to government (which meant that it could lend to the government), policed the exchange controls, and (somewhat later) operated a strict system for licensing imports. Nationalization of commercial banking took place in stages. In 1962 a Co-operative Bank started lending large sums of money to the co-operative unions to finance their purchases of crops— highly profitable business previously handled by the commercial banks. In 1965 the government purchased a 60 per cent holding in a small commercial bank, and renamed it the Tanzania Bank of Commerce. Then in the days after the Arusha Declaration, the government announced the nationalization of all commercial banks and the creation of the National Bank of Commerce to replace them. This was taken as an unfriendly act by Barclays Bank DCO and the Standard Bank, who immediately withdrew their European staff (nearly 60) and froze 40 million shillings of investments outside the country, expecting that the new bank would collapse. If this was indeed the calculation, it was misjudged. With the aid of staff who were left (including several non-citizen Asians who were promoted to branch managers), economists from the university, and twelve expatriates, including a number of volunteers from Scandinavia, the new bank survived its first three months. By the end of the year its credit procedures were operating smoothly, and foreign exchange transactions were resumed. By cutting overhead costs, and restricting the numbers of branches where previously two or more had competed, costs were reduced, and the new bank was soon making large sums of money available to the government and to other parastatals. Eventually Barclays and the Standard recognized that it was there to stay, and negotiated compensation terms.

The National Insurance Corporation was set up as a small agency in 1963; in 1967 it was suddenly made responsible for all the insurance business in the country. Since the other insurance companies were merely branches of Nairobi companies, there was virtually no insurance expertise in the country, and yet considerable sums of money were involved, especially for life insurance. The NIC did not gain a reputation for efficiency, but it too quickly made large sums available to the government.

There were other new institutions. The National Provident Fund was set up in 1965 as a 'compulsory savings scheme for both employers and employees' (Loxley 1973: 105). It soon became the single most important purchaser of government bonds. The building society which had effectively gone bankrupt with the departure of expatriates in 1960 was reconstituted with the help of the Commonwealth Development Corporation in 1967, and eventually became a government-owned Housing Bank, lending on a mortgage basis for house-building or purchase, and mobilizing savings by offering interest on deposit accounts.

It was recognized from an early stage that financial control would not be complete unless foreign trade was also controlled. The purchasing of cotton and coffee from co-operative unions was largely under the control of marketing boards even before independence, and after independence cashewnut purchase was also confined to a marketing board. Sisal was brought under government control after 1967 when the government nationalized 60 per cent of the sector. Another plantation crop, tea, was largely left alone. The attempts to control the import and distribution of consumer goods were not so successful. In 1967 eight of the largest foreign-owned import–export houses were nationalized and merged with a co-operative trading company (INTRATA) to form the State Trading Corporation (STC). Then in early 1970 the President announced that all importing and exporting would be confined to national organizations by the end of that year. The story of what followed is told in an appendix to this chapter. There was considerable disruption and shortages, and yet STC, which eventually split into 23 separate parastatals, did enable the state to take control of importing, and in particular to divert purchases away from Kenyan producers and to ensure that the Chinese commodity credit associated with the Tanzania–Zambia railway was used.

The second broad role of the newly created public institutions was to channel investment into productive activities. To achieve this three types of institution were created: investment banks, parastatals that were holding companies for productive enterprises, and parastatals directly involved in production. There were three investment banks: the Tanzania Rural Development Bank, which inherited the staff and some of the commitments of earlier rural credit agencies and was responsible for lending to the rural sector, especially for small-scale rural production; the Tanzania Investment Bank, for larger investments in any sector, but particularly in manufacturing; and the Tanganyika Development Finance Company, an investment bank lending in the main to medium-scale industrial ventures in the private sector. All three proved suitable vehicles for the receipt and channelling of foreign funds into Tanzania. The Rural Development Bank inherited a close relationship with the World Bank, and was used in the 1970s to allocate and monitor the credit components of a series of World Bank projects intended to stimulate agriculture.[4] It also received funds from Sweden, the United States, and some other bilateral donors. The Tanzania Investment Bank negotiated lines of credit with the Canadian, Swedish, and other governments, and with the World Bank; several of these would have found it difficult to transfer funds to industries owned by the Tanzanian government, but were willing and able to transfer them to an investment bank which could on-lend to both parastatal and privately owned projects. The Tanganyika Development Finance Company was itself a joint venture between the National Development Corporation (NDC) and Government investment agencies from three European countries—Britain, France, and Germany.[5] Its capital was added to several times, and provided a reliable source of investment funds for the Asian- and expatriate-owned private-sector companies which were not otherwise encouraged by government policy after the Arusha Declaration.

The second type of parastatal involved in productive investment was the holding company. The model for these was NDC, created at the beginning of 1965, and at the time intended to be the sole national agency of government investment in business (Msuya 1974: 3). In 1966 it received a cabinet instruction to adjust its investment policy so as to ensure that major investments were under national control (Pratt 1976: 230; Svendsen 1968). It was thus logical that NDC should take over the government shareholdings in the six subsidiaries of multinational corporations purchased at that time. These together with its holdings in Williamson's Diamonds and Tanganyika Packers gave it a net income of about 20 million shillings annually. It commissioned architects and consultants to produce feasibility studies in a wide range of sectors, built an extravagant headquarters in Dar es Salaam, and hired the McKinsey management consultancy to give it an appropriate management structure. Its general manager, George Kahama, cultivated the image of Tiny Roland, the creator of a successful and expanding multinational holding company.[6] Cabinet ministers and civil servants soon felt that it was too powerful, so in 1969 it was divided into four; NDC retained responsibility for mining and industrial investments, but agricultural projects, tourism, and construction were placed under newly created holding companies. Subsequently there was further division, with new companies for mining, textile production, livestock, forestry, and fisheries.

The subsidiaries of these holding companies were the parastatals directly involved in production. They can be divided into those which existed before the Arusha Declaration and those founded after it; since the managerial resources of the holding companies were limited, it was perhaps inevitable that most of the new enterprises were created by means of turnkey projects (i.e. a foreign partner was responsible for all aspects of the investment) and managed by foreigners employed under management agreements.[7]

The third and last role of parastatals was that traditionally associated with government corporations, the provision of infrastructural or other services. Railways, Harbours, Posts and Telecommunications, and East African Airways continued as parastatals under the East African Community until its break-up in 1977, when control passed to the three national governments. The Tanzania–Zambia Railway Authority, responsible for the new railway to Zambia, was just one of several transport parastatals established in the 1970s.

In 1976 the co-operative unions were replaced by Crop Authorities—parastatals which combined the functions of marketing boards with involvement in extension, crop processing, and transport. The new authorities took over the cotton ginneries, processing factories, and the transport operations of the co-operative unions. Hotels, farms, petrol stations, and other small investments were handed over to District Development Corporations, set up in most of the sixty or so Districts from 1971 onwards, and expected to make money in small-scale production or trade. The parastatal form seemed so convenient to administrators frustrated by government regulations (e.g. about salaries and accounting procedures) that even educational establishments such as the University of Dar es Salaam, some foreign-aided integrated projects (for instance the Kibaha Educational Centre and the Lushoto Integrated Development Project), and Muhimbili Hospital in Dar es Salaam, were allowed to become parastatals.

Table 23.1 shows the rapid increase in the value of parastatal assets between 1964 and 1971, and their distribution. Of the assets owned by parastatals in 1971, 17 per cent had been own-

TABLE 23.1
Growth of parastatal assets 1964–1971
(millions of shillings)

Sector	Value of assets in 1964	Investments[1] in existing parastatals 1964–71	Nationalizations 1964–71	New companies 1964–71	Value of assets in 1971
Manufacturing	25	211	324	549	1109
Mining	241	70	—	—	311
Construction	25	137	—	—	162
Electricity	231	294	—	—	525
Transport	—	80	—	288	368
Tourism	15	13	1	128	157
Commerce	13	142	347	12	514
Agriculture	56	60	120	14	250
Finance	4	67	96	16	183
Total	610	1074	888	1007	3579
Per cent of total in 1971	17	30	25	28	100

Source: Clark (1978: 109).

TABLE 23.2
Regular wage employment 1969 and 1974

	1969	1974
Parastatals	42 522	90 220
Private sector	107 614	101 132
Public services	75 444	171 289

Source: Bureau of Statistics (cited by Collier 1977: Table 3).

ed by them in 1964, 25 per cent was obtained by nationalization, 28 per cent was investment in completely new ventures, while 30 per cent was in parastatals in which the government already had a shareholding in 1964, the largest single amount going to the electricity supply company. Table 23.2 shows regular wage employment doubling between 1969 and 1974; yet employment in the private sector was almost stagnant and the increase came from the public service and parastatal sectors.

The expansion of the numbers of parastatals, and of their responsibilities, meant an explosion in managerial positions. Many able Tanzanians were attracted away from the civil service and into parastatals which could offer higher salaries, more attractive fringe benefits, and more satisfying jobs. And yet, as we have seen in Chapter 20, the performance of the parastatals gave cause for concern, from 1967 onwards. They seemed to exercise little control over the resources available to them, or over their expatriate managements. This concern is supported both by studies of the parastatal sector as a whole and by studies of individual parastatals.

Edmund Clark found that in 1971 parastatal firms in manufacturing were more capital intensive than private-sector firms, and yet each employee in a parastatal firm contributed less to production than his opposite number in the private sector. Clark also found differences between parastatal firms established before the Arusha Declaration and those established between 1967 and 1971: the post-Arusha firms were more capital intensive (both within each sector and because of the sectors chosen), very much more intensive in their use of imports (74 per cent of their inputs were imported, compared with 30 per cent for the older firms), and each unit of labour contributed only half as much to production as in the older firms (Clark 1978: 117, 135–6; see also Chapter 20).

Similar findings were reported by Barker, Bhagavan, Mitchke-Collande, and Wield, who in 1975 studied twenty-eight factories, including several of the largest parastatal firms. They too found significant differences between firms started between 1961 and 1967 and those started between 1967 and 1975 (most of the latter being parastatals). In 1973 the older firms generated domestic savings valued at 32 per cent of their capital stock, while the newer firms saved less than 4 per cent. Nearly 80 per cent of the value added in the older firms was retained within the country, but only 50 per cent of the value added in the more recent firms. 'The conclusion is that the post-Arusha period is characterised by industrial investments which are efficient vehicles only for transferring surplus outside the national economy' (Barker *et al.* 1976: Chapter IV, p. 3). This is odd at first sight —since one would not expect parastatal firms to be taking surplus outside Tanzania. It is, however, supported by another study (Van Hall 1979) which identified transfer pricing in at least ten parastatal companies. Either the Tanzanian managers knew what was going on and were party to it, or, more probably, they were so distant from the actual decisions about buying and selling that they were ignorant that it was happening.

In many instances, the low productivity of capital and/or labour can be documented directly. Clark claims that the automated bakery built in Dar es Salaam was more capital intensive than the oil refinery (Clark 1978: 143, fn. 10). The problems that faced the Tanga fertilizer factory, the country's most expensive investment in manufacturing, have been well documented. The plant, a turnkey project, was small and inefficient by world standards. It used only imported inputs (a total of 167 000 tonnes of imported raw materials per annum to make 105 000 tonnes of various fertilizers), and was built with an expensive supplier's credit which had to be paid back in German marks. After it opened, a series of problems kept production down to 50 per cent of its designed capacity (Coulson 1977a).

Cement production at Wazo Hill outside Dar es Salaam declined from a peak in 1973, but there was an increase of 40 per cent in the number of workers employed there. Investment in new pans for producing salt from the brine springs at Uvinza had to be largely abandoned; the new pans were built on the top of a hill in the unproven (and mistaken) belief that this would spend up the evaporation process. A cashewnut shelling plant in Mtwara had to be abandoned because the process would not work. A factory to make bags at Moshi was to use kenaf grown on a nearby irrigation project, but only a few agricultural trials had been carried out. The Italian 'partner' sold bag-making machinery that did not work well, and far more kenaf seed, of an unsatisfactory variety, than could possibly have been planted in one year. After some years, kenaf growing was abandoned, and the irrigation farm turned over to sugarcane. A bicycle manufacturing plant not only polluted streams in the surrounding residential area, but manufactured bicycles that were twice the price of equivalent imported models.

A final illustration from the many that could be considered is provided by the nationalized textile mills. As noted earlier, the

first textile weaving factory opened in 1959 using imported
yarns. The first factory spinning local cotton opened in 1966. In
the late 1960s the government built two large-scale integrated
spinning and weaving mills, based on the local cotton crop. The
Friendship Mill, built by the Chinese in Dar es Salaam, opened
in 1968; the Mwanza Textile mill, opened in 1969, was designed
by Sodefra, a French company who also took a minority share
in the equity. Some relevant comparisons are shown in Table
23.3. 'Friendship'—with the largest factory work-force in East
Africa—is a triumph for appropriate technology. Using two and
a half times as much labour per tonne as Mwatex, and only 40
per cent of the capital, it still managed to produce at lower cost.
Mwatex, a 'modern' plant, had most of the faults of partnership
ventures undertaken with Western multinationals. Yet in 1975,
when the government decided to expand textile production, it
chose a 30 per cent expansion at Friendship, a 100 per cent expansion at Mwatex, and a complete new copy of Mwatex, to be
built in Musoma. It is true that it was advised by the World
Bank, who lent most of the money; but it was also (separately)
advised that the specifications could have been written so that
machinery comparable to the Chinese machinery in the
Friendship Mill, but manufactured in India or Brazil, could have
been purchased with World Bank money.

TABLE 23.3
Friendship and Mwanza textile mills

Capital Cost up to 1969 (millions of shillings)	61.5	106.5
Production of woven fabrics in 1975 (millions of linear metres)	24.0	22.5
Number of employees in 1975	5057	2486
Profit in 1975 (millions of shillings)	2.8	2.3
Cost of carded cotton in 1973 (shillings per tonne)	2512	2910
Labour hours per tonne of carded cotton in 1973	247	98

Sources: NDC; TEXCO; *The Daily News*, 17 July 1976; Williams (1975).

Such misallocations are sufficient to explain the decline in the
performance of the manufacturing sector in the 1970s discussed
in Chapter 20. This is not to say that ministers and civil servants
were unaware of what was going on, but rather that they tended

to intervene after major investment decisions had been taken, when it was expensive to change them; moreover they had no answer to the fundamental problem posed by parastatals: in the last resort, all they could do was to sack the management and replace it with another which might be no better; there was no way in which they could operate the companies themselves. They therefore devised procedures to limit the freedom of parastatal managements and to ensure that they acted in accordance with government objectives, but in so doing they got close to undermining the ideal of commercial freedom with which parastatals were set up in the first place.

The first government attempt to limit the power of the parastatals was the 1969 division of NDC into four. Since the profit-making subsidiaries all stayed with NDC, this did not restrict that parastatal's freedom, until in 1973 a separate mining parastatal took away Williamson's Diamonds and the cement factory, two of the most profitable NDC subsidiaries. The agricultural, tourism, and construction parastatals created in 1969 were, however, all inherently unprofitable, and therefore much more accountable to the government.[8]

The next initiative, following a 20 per cent expansion of the money supply in 1970, and a balance of payments crisis, was exchange control and import control. There was, however, little restriction on imports classified as 'capital goods', however undesirable and costly they might be.[9] Moreover, it was difficult for the government to deny the import licences needed to keep factories operating, however import-dependent they were. At about the same time a 'credit plan' was introduced in order to limit lending, and a 'standing committee on management agreements' was set up, with legal representation, to examine management agreements before they were signed. A 'price commission' was created, which required documentary evidence to show that costs had risen before it would approve price rises. Last, but not least, the General Superintendence Company, a Swiss firm, was employed to give a valuation of all imports into Tanzania before they left their ports of departure, in an attempt to prevent transfer pricing. Four hundred contracts—including many in the parastatal sector—were suspended within three months of it being employed. In theory this set of controls should have controlled most of the abuses. But taken together they involved a mass of paperwork, discouraged initiative (e.g. to export), and made it difficult for managements to take quick decisions.[10]

WORKERS AND MANAGEMENT

The introduction of one other form of control was attempted, and is worth considering in some detail because of its significance for an understanding of where power lay in the Tanzanian state; this was control of managerial abuses by the workers. The formation of trade unions has been described in Chapters 12 and 13, and their restriction in the years 1962–4 was discussed in Chapter 16. In October 1969 the President announced the formation of Workers' Councils, with management and worker representation, which would 'bring the workers close to the management of industries and promote better industrial relations while giving the workers more say in formulating policies'.[11] Workers' Committees already existed, with trade union (i.e. National Union of Tanganyika Workers) representation, created in 1964 as part of a new code for disciplining or sacking workers. There were also TANU branches in many factories, whose functions were never clearly defined, but which were supposedly concerned with the ideological commitment of their members and the country (Mapolu (ed.) 1975: 203–6).

The new Workers' Councils were slow to meet, and proved to be dominated by the management representatives, who, in so far as they were prepared to accept the Councils at all, did so in the hope that they would serve as a means of raising productivity. This slow action was to be overtaken by the sudden approval by the Party, in February 1971, of the *TANU Guidelines*, or *Mwongozo*[12] in which key clauses were as follows:

The responsibility of the party is to lead the masses, and their various institutions, in the effort to safeguard national independence and to advance the liberation of the African. The duty of a socialist party is to guide all activities of the masses. The Government, parastatals, national organizations, etc., are instruments for implementing the Party's policies. Our short history of independence reveals problems that may arise when a Party does not guide its instruments. The time has now come for the Party to take the reins and lead all the people's activities.

(Clause 11)

There must be a deliberate effort to build equality between the leaders and those they lead. For a Tanzanian leader it must be forbidden to be arrogant, extravagant, contemptuous and oppressive. The Tanzanian leader has to be a person who respects people, scorns ostentation and who is not a tyrant. He should epitomise heroism, bravery, and be a champion of justice and equality.

Similarly, the Party has the responsibility to fight the vindictiveness of some of its agents. Such actions do not promote Socialism but drive a wedge between the Party and the Government on the one side and the people on the other.

(from Clause 15)

If development is to benefit the people, the people must participate in considering, planning and implementing their development plans.

The duty of our Party is not to urge the people to implement plans which have been decided upon by a few experts and leaders. The duty of our Party is to ensure that the leaders and experts implement the plans that have been agreed upon by the people themselves. When the people's decision requires information which is only available to the leaders and the experts, it will be the duty of leaders and experts to make such information available to the people. But it is not correct for leaders and experts to usurp the people's right to decide on an issue just because they have the expertise.

(from Clause 28)

The conduct and activities of the parastatals must be looked into to ensure that they help further our policy of socialism and self-reliance. The activities of the parastatals should be a source of satisfaction and not discontent. The Party must ensure that the parastatals do not spend money extravagantly on items which do not contribute to the development of the national economy as a whole.

(Clause 33)

The *Mwongozo* was prepared and approved by a Party Conference called in the wake of the *coup* in Uganda, when Idi Amin toppled Milton Obote. A few months before, the Portuguese had invaded Sekou Toure's Guiné. These events demonstrated two dangers facing the Tanzanian state: subversion within, and invasion by white armies from outside. Yet the Portuguese had been driven out of Guiné. The lesson drawn from Uganda and Guiné was, therefore, that even with external support, a fully prepared revolutionary state could only be overthrown if there was internal conspiracy and dissatisfaction.

Most of the *Mwongozo* was concerned with security and defence, but paragraphs which dealt with the role of the Party, the failures of many leaders 'in their work and in day-to-day life', and argued that the time had come for 'the Party to supervise the conduct and the bearing of the leaders' were used against 'arrogant and oppressive managers', and enabled it to become —briefly—a workers' charter. There were several strikes, many of which took the managements concerned by surprise. Thirty-one were reported in the newspapers in the period from the promulgation of the *Mwongozo* (February 1971) to September 1973. Under the 1962 and 1967 Acts, these were illegal unless sanctioned by the NUTA General Council. Moreover, they were not, at least on the surface, about pay:

> These strikes ... were directed mainly against the commandism and abuses of the managers and bureaucrats. The promulgation of *Mwongozo* in 1971 with a penchant clause on commandism armed the workers with a potent weapon with which to deal with the bureaucracy. For the first time in history, we had in Tanzania numerous strikes not concerned at all with wages and other remunerations. The age of docility and humbleness at the oppression and humiliation of the petty bourgeoisie had passed for the Tanzanian workers. (Mapolu 1973: 32).

Mapolu puts the end of this 'first phase of the workers' movement' as August 1972, when the government crushed a strike at the Sungura Textile Mill outside Dar es Salaam by dismissing thirty-one workers. Other employers began mass dismissals, and it was clear that they could count on government support to suppress 'illegal' strikes. So the tactics changed:

> From then on the tactic of strikes generally faded; in its place the lockout technique came to the fore. Instead of striking because of the commandist or abusive practices of a boss, the workers would simply lock out the boss in question until their grievances were solved satisfactorily ... At times the workers have made it a point to step up production during that period just to ward off any accusation that they are causing damage to the 'national economy' ...
> Increasingly, the lock-outs stemmed from managers misusing public funds, squandering resources, failing to uphold national policies and so forth. The clauses in *Mwongozo* referred to often became no longer solely clause 15, which deals with commandism, but clause 33 which says, in part, 'the Party must ensure that the parastatals do not spend money extravagantly on items which do not contribute to the development of the national economy as a whole'. (Mapolu 1973: 33.)

The climax came between May and July 1973, when the 900 workers at the British-American Tobacco factory in Dar es Salaam (in which the government had taken 51 per cent of the shares in 1967) locked out their personnel manager. The case was argued before the Permanent Labour Tribunal in July 1973. The officer was accused of wasting company resources, and of favouring his own tribesmen in his recruitment policies. He was defended by the (British) General Manager of the company, but the case went against him, and he was dismissed. The accusations highlighted the differences in life-style and eating habits between a member of the management and the workers—and the way in which a company like BAT made possible parties, trips, expensive meals, and other extravagance. The workers were threatening the new bourgeoisie in the parastatal sector created by the Arusha Declaration (Shivji 1976: 140–2).

In the public sector, the tactics involved locking out salaried staff—usually general managers or personnel officers. In the private sector, owners were locked out as well, so that the private ownership of means of production was threatened. Three private company takeovers received widespread publicity. The first, Rubber Industries Ltd., was owned by a group of Asians, with financial support from IPS (the Aga Khan's investment bank). The second, Night Watch Security Company, was owned by an Asian who had already left the country. The third, Mount Carmel Rubber Factory Ltd. was to break the workers' movement (Mapolu 1973: 37–40; Mihyo 1975: 72–84). The company had been started by an Iranian business man and engineer in 1952. By 1965 the Tanganyika Development Finance Company had invested 460 000 shillings in it—more than half its value at that time—and as late as 1973 the expatriate General Manager of TDFL was Chairman of the Mount Carmel Board.

Mount Carmel was a profitable company, and an innovative one, producing rubber spare parts for motor vehicles, roller printer sheets for the textile industry, and the rubber solution used in retreading car tyres. Working conditions were harsh, and of the seventy workers about thirty were employed on a day-to-day basis, and paid less than the minimum wage for Dar es Salaam. A Workers' Committee should have been started in 1964; but no steps were taken till January 1971, when some NUTA officials visited the factory. They seemed more interested in getting a list of all the workers' names (so that the employer could be instructed to deduct union dues from their wages) than in meeting the workers, but at least a Committee was started. It achieved little. A collective agreement drafted by NUTA officials was lost before it could be signed by either workers or management. In February 1972 the workers threatened to strike if the agreement was not signed. The Ministry of Labour failed to sanction the strike, or to take any steps to discuss the grievances.

After another year's delay, in March 1973, the workers next door, at Rubber Industries Ltd., took over their factory, and on

17 June 1973 the Mount Carmel workers followed suit. The Commissioner of Labour visited the factory, but was refused admission because he came with the employer. On 19 June he returned with the Dar es Salaam Regional Commissioner; the workers told him that they would accept any leadership other than that of their Iranian owner. Meanwhile the production manager of Aluminium Africa (probably the largest manufacturing firm still in private hands, owned by the Chandaria group) had been locked out, and the workers at the Hotel Afrique (also Asian owned) were preparing to take over the hotel. The government position suddenly changed. Whereas on 6 June the Regional Commissioner had 'hailed the workers for their revolutionary action in fighting against exploiters in the country',[13] on 20 June:

An official from the Ministry [of Labour] accompanied by a number of policemen called at the factory in Chang'ombe and issued to all the workers what he called a Government Order. He said that those workers who were not ready to work under Mr. Yadzani [the owner] should stay apart from those who accepted his leadership. All workers who refused to accept their employer's leadership were ordered to enter parked vehicles. Sixty-two were driven away to the Central Police Station leaving the industry with only fifteen workers... At the Central Police Station the held workers said that although they did not know their fate they still stood by their refusal to work under Mr. Yadzani, whom they described as an exploiter and an oppressor. 'We are members of TANU and it would be a sin for us to work under this man, whose character contradicts TANU policies'. (*The Daily News*, 21 June 1973).

The government issued a statement that 'it could no longer tolerate such unruly action on the part of the workers'. The fact that two firms had been taken over 'did not mean and shall not mean that TANU and the government have now permitted anew the workers to invade industries or that it should now be the method of nationalizing industries'. After a few days in the cells, the workers were 'repatriated' to their 'home areas'. The government newspaper *The Daily News* had on 9 June carried a piece by its influential columnist Chenge wa Chenge which included the followiing encouragement:

Workers have been seizing capitalist property and converting it into people's property. How good! How revolutionary! There is no need to justify the seizure of capitalist property by workers. The issue is as clear as day. In any case the time for justifying our actions to exploiters has long passed . . . Capitalists in Tanzania and elsewhere in Africa must tremble at what is taking place. They must gnaw their teeth and groan . . .

By 22 June it was justifying the government action in arresting the workers which 'in the final analysis was for the benefit of the workers themselves'. On 26 June the Dar es Salaam Regional Commissioner who had received such contradictory publicity was transferred to Dodoma, where he now had a powerful incentive to make a success of his new job of organizing the population into villages (see Chapter 22).

Why was the about-turn so sudden? In the final instance it was probably the behind-the-scenes activity of TDFL—whose four shareholders were government-supported development corporations in Britain, West Germany, the Netherlands, and Tanzania itself. TDFL had been an investor in most of the medium-sized import substitution industries that had sprung up since independence. A dispute with TDFL meant taking on the capitalist world, especially once it became clear that to allow the Mount Carmel workers to take over would lead to workers' control of many other factories. The government, and the interests entrenched in the parastatals created since 1967, were not prepared to allow socialism to develop in this way.

In the months which followed, elected workers' leaders who stood up to management were dismissed. It became necessary to have official Party approval before any mass action could be taken, whether or not it would affect production. Shop-floor initiative was crushed, and the control of factories remained firmly with management. Workers would not control their factories, and they would have little or no power over the Tanzanian state.

APPENDIX 1. THE STATE TRADING CORPORATION 1967–1972[1]

In 1961 the government commissioned a study of wholesale and retail trade from the Economist Intelligence Unit (Hawkins 1965). It concluded that overall the margins obtained by traders were not high, and that, considering the difficulties of distances, small markets, and seasonal fluctuations, the average costs of distribution were remarkably low.

The study also pointed out that prices rose rapidly as soon as there were shortages of goods, that bargaining in shops meant that the consumer constantly felt cheated, and that short weight was widespread. In the Southern Region a cartel of wholesalers limited competition, while credit was often used to bind farmers to particular traders.

By 1961 the role of the Asian or Arab trader as buyers of agricultural produce was threatened by the co-operative movement, although in the southern and central parts the co-operatives were still in their infancy. During the next few years the co-operatives in these areas were expanded with government support, and the Consumer Supply Association of Tanganyika (COSATA), a consumer co-operative association, began opening co-operative shops. In 1963 a European import/export house was taken over and renamed INTRATA, and it was hoped that it would work closely with COSATA. But by 1965 both COSATA and INTRATA were in debt, the former mainly through failure to control sales on credit, especially to people in high places, and the latter mainly through overstocking. It was decided to restrict retailing to a few carefully managed shops, while INTRATA's debts were paid off by making it the only legal importer of *khanga* and *kitenge* (the printed cloth worn by Tanzanian women) on which it was given a 12 per cent commission in the price structure.

In 1967, following the Arusha Declaration, eight of the biggest foreign-owned import/export houses were nationalized and combined with what was left of INTRATA to form the State Trading Corporation (STC). Many small Asian importers remained, and manufacturing companies often ordered their requirements directly, so that STC was responsible for only a fraction of total imports. Moreover the companies taken over retained their existing clients, agencies, and specializations, so that there was only the beginning of an attempt to rationalize the process of importing. However, in 1969 the complete take-over of wholesaling, importing, and exporting was included as policy in the Second Five-Year Plan.[2] Expatriate advisers had pointed out the manpower required for this task, and the difficulties in other countries, such as Ghana, which had tried to socialize all trade; the plan, therefore, was for STC to increase its range of imports by gradually 'confining' new categories to STC (making it the only legal importer of those items).

In February 1970, however, President Nyerere suddenly announced that all importing, wholesaling, and exporting would be socialized by the end of the year. STC was not expected to do this entirely alone, since NDC subsidiaries and other parastatals would import their own input requirements, as well as finished products in the product areas in which they were involved (e.g. the Tanzania Fertilizer Company, an NDC subsidiary, was to become responsible for all imports of fertilizer into the country, including types of fertilizer which it did not produce itself). Nevertheless, the main task of importing small quantities of a wide range of processed foodstuffs, household items, consumer durables, drugs, building supplies, and industrial and agricultural inputs was left with STC. Some 65 000 different items were involved, and a turnover of about 600 million shillings a year, about a third of the country's imports by value (Resnick 1976: 76). The decision was taken for three reasons. First, because the method of confining groups of items to STC was not working well; in particular, it was disrupted by importers who managed to import large stocks of the goods concerned just before they were confined to STC. Secondly, it had become clear that it was not possible to prevent capital flight while importing remained in the hands of many small importers who could over-invoice imported items. The third and most pressing reason was that the arrangement agreed upon for the Chinese loan for the TAZARA railway required Tanzania to purchase approximately 250 million shillings of goods from China in each of the five years that it took to build the railway. It would have been difficult to redirect trade to China to this extent if it had not been controlled centrally by a nationalized corporation.[3]

In the months which followed there were more shortages of consumer goods than at any time since the years immediately after the Second World War, and the performance of STC caused more complaint than any other nationalization, or indeed than any other political move since independence. What happened makes a classic study of bureaucratic reaction to events. In February 1970 an Implementation Committee was set up, consisting of four senior Principal Secretaries and the Heads of the State Trading Corporation, the National Development Corporation, and the National Bank of Commerce. One of its first moves was to invite McKinsey's, the firm of management consultants who at the time were preparing management systems for NDC, to do the same for STC.[4] The McKinsey consultancy was not completed till July, and in the meantime the Implementation Committee had a series of complex problems to solve. No one knew the size of the Tanzanian market in more detail than the broad categories of the Annual Trade reports. In particular, there was little information about the markets in northern Tanzania and the Lake Victoria areas, which had been supplied mainly through Mombasa. There was a possibility that the whole Asian community would shut its doors, causing nearly all business in the country to grind to a halt—a fear increased by the nationalization of buildings in 1971.

It seemed more important to keep people's confidence than to risk shortages. So, without much knowledge of quantities, STC started buying, and if there was any doubt it over-ordered. Its overdraft at the National Bank of Commerce rose quickly to 100 million shillings, and then to over 150 million by November 1970, and to over 200 million shillings by May 1971. There was a corresponding drain of foreign exchange, but this was not detected in the statistics of the Bank of Tanzania until October 1970. In November a credit squeeze was started, but the overdraft continued to rise. Eventually, in the budget of May 1971, an overdraft ceiling of 160 million shillings was imposed. The attempt to keep within this figure caused the shortages, as bills were not paid, goods were ordered in smaller and smaller quantities, and many essential items for industry were purchased after long delays, so that local production as well as importing was affected.

A stock check supervised by the auditing firm Cooper Brothers in July 1971 established that there was a high proportion of what was generously called 'slow-moving stock'. It also revealed failures of accounting in the organization which made control or management almost impossible, and enabled staff to steal money or goods. The financial controller, chief accountant, and credit controller were all dismissed in January 1972.

The corporation was bureaucratic and centralized. Every individual had been issued with instructions detailing exactly what he should do, but, for example, it took eighteen administrative steps for a branch office to add a salesman to its payroll (Resnick 1976: 78). There were also some vital omissions. No guidance was given as to what to do if the government imposed a credit squeeze, and, even more surprisingly, there was no procedure for introducing new goods to customers—a serious omission when many new items started arriving from China. The McKinsey system separated importing from selling: eighteen specialist 'product divisions' imported the goods, but the Sales Division, with its up-country branches, was separate from these. Procedures were laid down to determine the quantity of each item that should be ordered, and the stock level at which the item should be reordered. McKinseys did not prepare any manuals for accounting, so the success or otherwise of a branch was to be judged by whether goods were in stock. There was no means of telling whether a particular item was selling at a profit or a loss. If the system failed to work (and it was hardly ever possible to use it as designed) there was no way of allocating the blame.

The first problem was to select the items to order from the bewildering variety of brands and makes available. An identical item was often found with different descriptions, or was being ordered separately under different product numbers by different parts of the system. STC was ordering 65 000 different products, but it never managed to make out a satisfactory list of all these items. The next problem was where to put goods when they arrived. Many of the old importers had used small stores, or space in their shops. The McKinsey system was designed to work with just four or five huge stores. Instead, STC found itself with about forty stores, many very small, in different parts of Dar es Salaam. Moreover, when goods were ordered from China, a whole year's supply often turned up at once, and had to be stored. Soon no one knew precisely what was in many of the stores. By the time the position was at least broadly known (July 1971), the overdraft was being cut, and orders from product divisions were being cut or refused in head office on an arbitrary basis.

The accounting system hurriedly improvised in 1970 provided little information. Branch and product division accounts were produced late or not at all, and Cooper Brothers refused to certify the 1970 accounts as correct. Without accounts, financial ceilings could not be used to control the overdraft, and there was no incentive for branches or divisions to control stock levels, vehicles, or the use of staff. The resort to direct bureaucratic intervention was inevitable. All orders for goods had to be approved in head office, for a time by one man who was arbitrarily cutting orders in order to reduce the overdraft. The management hoped that their problems would be solved by their computer. In 1971 they ordered a bigger computer with the intention of computerizing stock control, ordering, and the accounts; almost at the same time the staff responsible for the computer, writing in the 1971/2 corporate plan, made it clear that a computer could not begin these tasks until many other aspects of pricing and ordering policy had been settled. They never were, and the computer was eventually recognized as an expensive white elephant.

The obvious solution was decentralization, as was recognized by early 1972 and implemented between then and early 1973. Six specialized importing companies were created, together with seventeen wholesaling companies (one for each region), with STC remaining as a holding compnay for these twenty-three subsidiaries. Paradoxically, this was almost the same solution that was evolving before the McKinsey plans were implemented in 1970, as the various companies taken over were gradually specializing in particular product areas. Instead, three million shillings were spent on a foreign management consultancy which delayed rationalization by two years and, more than any other single cause, was responsible for the shortages.

Even with all the problems described, STC had its successes. It managed the importation of the Chinese goods. It reduced the prices of whole ranges of goods, such as pharmaceutical products. And on many individual items it was able to use its monopoly position in the Tanzanian market to strike hard bargains with overseas suppliers. The decentralization did not solve all problems. But it did make the results of corruption and fraud visible locally. Thus after the very shaky start described here, the Tanzanian state succeeded in taking control of importing. Without this any form of planned industrialization would be impossible.

APPENDIX 2. THE MWANANCHI ENGINEERING AND CONSTRUCTION COMPANY (MECCO)[1]

In 1963 the Mwananchi Development Corporation (the economic arm of the National Union of Tanganyika Workers) purchased a minority share in a building company started and run by a Mr Tara Singh Dogra, an Asian who had been in the building business since the 1920s. In 1966 the assets of the Mwananchi Development Corporation were transferred to NDC, and not long afterwards NDC purchased Mr Singh's shares, to become sole owner of the company. In February 1967 40 per cent of the shares were sold for two million shillings to a Dutch company, the Overseas Construction Company (OCC), a member of the Nederhorst group. An agreement was signed under which OCC would provide management for the company: expatriate staff would be recruited by OCC and paid salaries comparable to those they would have received as employees of OCC; in return OCC would be guaranteed an income of 100 000 shillings per year together with a management fee of 1 per cent of the turnover of the company. The agreement also required the company to train craftsmen and technicians at all levels in the industry, to keep its accounts up to date, and to set up financial control systems on its building sites.

Two and a half years later (November 1969) the company was making losses. The accounting system was confused, and each site manager was using his own method of controlling costs. There was no training programme, but there were twenty expatriate staff in the company, and the management was trying to bring in more (they had advertised for a foreman carpenter in Holland); meanwhile the best local staff were leaving. This situation might have continued for some time without government intervention, since NDC was often willing to use profits from profitable companies to cover losses on companies such as

MECCO. But in August 1969 NDC was split up, and MECCO became an independent parastatal under the Ministry of Lands, Housing and Urban Development, with no other organization in a position to reduce its rapidly growing overdraft at the National Bank of Commerce.

Economy measures were taken in November that year. The General Manager and nine other expatriates were transferred out of the company, and five others brought in (thereby reducing the expatriate team by five). Steps were taken to establish some kind of cost control. The (more or less non-existent) training programme was officially 'suspended' in the interest of economy. But the government concern continued, not least because while MECCO was losing money, OCC was benefiting. In addition to the 1 per cent of turnover, 100 000 shillings, and payment of expatriate salaries, there was evidence that goods were being imported from Holland that could have been purchased more cheaply elsewhere. There was one particular contract—a factory building for General Tyre (an NDC subsidiary in partnership with General Tyre of America)—where MECCO had not been the lowest tenderer. The Americans asked OCC (not MECCO) to redesign the project, and arranged to pay it directly in Holland. OCC subcontracted the contruction work to MECCO, but there was no control over the price paid to MECCO, and it looked very much as if OCC was using MECCO as a means of winning contracts and taking money out of the country. It was not, however, easy for the government to remove OCC. An attempt to persuade it to leave voluntarily failed. The company was technically bankrupt; but when the National Bank of Commerce threatened to foreclose if the overdraft was not repaid within a certain time, OCC appealed to the Dutch ambassador and put pressure on Tanzanian leaders and officials, arguing that other foreign companies would not be safe if the Tanzanian government acted like this. The Bank withdrew its deadline, and pressed instead for an auditor to be appointed and for an individual nominated by the Bank to report on the operation of the company. OCC accepted these terms.

In October 1970 the workers of MECCO petitioned NUTA. They claimed that the management was not sympathetic to the aspirations of the country, brought allegations of racial discrimination, and argued that worker/management relationships had reached a critical state. Their particular grievance was that the company continued to depend on casual labour and was not training a permanent labour force. In November the government threatened to purchase the OCC shareholding, in the interests of securing greater control over the economy, and on 12 December it announced that it had agreed to purchase the shares for the same price at which they had been sold to OCC, and that the management agreement would be terminated at the end of the year. The announcement stressed that the termination had been mutually agreed, and that no compensation would be paid to OCC. Nevertheless, by paying the company two million shillings for shares by then virtually worthless, the government paid it to leave.

With hindsight, it is clear what happened. The initial justification for bringing in outside management was to enable the company to compete for complex building and engineering contracts, hitherto taken by foreign contractors. OCC, like the government negotiators, probably thought that it would be easy to make profits. But in any case its equity investment was relatively small, it was well protected in the management contract (based on turnover rather than profit), and it may well have perceived other potential benefits from a partnership involving the Tanzanian government. But by the end of 1969 it was clear that it was easy to make losses in the Tanzanian market. There were a limited number of contracts, a number of well-established firms, and the rate of profit was insufficient to absorb MECCO's overhead costs swollen with the expatriate salaries (MECCO's overheads were approximately 13 per cent of its turnover, compared with about 5 per cent for the Asian firms). The government Central Tender Board was not prepared to allocate work to MECCO if another contractor would carry it out more cheaply. After November 1969, OCC replaced its general manager and cut the overheads, but by then it had lost the confidence of the government. When the company realized this it concentrated even more on protecting its interests in Holland: it maximized turnover (taking on large contracts even when it expected to lose money on them); it over-invoiced (a tower crane was purchased in Europe for much above its cost price); and it sought means of transferring money from MECCO to OCC (on a project involving the construction of new berths in Dar es Salaam harbour, where OCC was the main contractor, MECCO accepted rates for earth-moving which were so low that they did not even cover the running costs of the machinery).

The Operations Division of NDC and the Tanzanian members of the Board of Directors were slow to act, but there was no

way in which they could have controlled a management that was
unable to run the company profitably and yet was willing to go
to considerable lengths to cover its tracks. When bankruptcy
was suggested, a wide range of individuals supported OCC; they
included the lawyer who had drafted the original agreement, the
Board of NDC, various government officials, bankers and economists who pleaded that if too much publicity was given to this
case Tanzania's reputation would be spoilt so that it would be
difficult to attract other foreign firms, and the OCC management was backed by the Dutch ambassador. Their opposition in-
hibited the government, and prevented it taking the most force-
ful line of action, which would have been to bankrupt the company (while allowing the receiver to keep an organization intact
to complete the work in progress). The treatment of OCC
would have become an example of what might happen to other
firms who attempted to manipulate management agreements to
their own advantage. But instead the government announcement
terminating the agreement indicated an intention to sign another
agreement with another agent, and shortly afterwards OCC was
allowed to be part of a consortium of Western firms which was
awarded the 234 million shilling contract for the Kidatu hydroelectric project.

It took more than two years for MECCO to complete the
loss-making projects that had been tendered for by the Dutch
before they left. By then the overdraft was no smaller, and the
vehicle fleet was in urgent need of replacement. A shortage of
working capital was restricting rapid progress on some projects
and contributing to labour problems. And yet progress was
being made: the Dutch team had been replaced by an individual
who was sympathetic, hardworking, and who knew the local
scene; training of Tanzanians was proceeding, and work on
some of the biggest projects (for example the 30 million shilling
National Insurance Corporation building) was directed entirely
by Tanzanians; a cost control system was in operation; and the
labour situation was under discussion. Without the complication
of foreign management, it had become possible to consider the
problems of setting up a nationalized construction company, and
the contribution that could realistically be expected from one.

24 DEVELOPMENT STRATEGY AND FOREIGN RELATIONS

> How can we depend on foreign governments and companies for a major part of our development without giving those governments and companies a great part of our freedom to act as we please? The truth is that we cannot.
>
> The Arusha Declaration (1967)[1]

The slogan of the Arusha Declaration was 'socialism and self-reliance'. 'Socialism' meant national control of the economy, democracy, and the absence of classes. 'Self-reliance' could have a number of meanings. In the Declaration itself the primary meaning was willingness to exist without foreign aid, a policy necessary at the time because of the alienation of three of the country's most important aid donors.[2] But it could also mean a strategy of internally based growth, or a minimization of trade;[3] or self-reliance in manpower, a refusal to employ foreigners; or self-reliance at decentralized levels, with each parastatal or village making do with local techniques and materials and minimizing dependence on central government;[4] an extension of this interpreted self-reliance as rural development (in contrast to urban development or industrialization) on the grounds that it was only in rural areas that the majority of the population could be self-reliant; finally, it could mean non-alignment—no reliance on any one Great Power and the refusal to accept that the national boundaries lay within any nation's sphere of influence.

These interpretations were used at various times, but none was pursued consistently. Tanzania became a major recipient of foreign aid, and continued to export the traditional agricultural products, and to use expatriate manpower. Its parastatals and villages did not become independent of central government—if anything they relied on it more than in the past. It did not direct all its investment to rural areas, or follow an internally oriented development strategy, and by the mid-1970s Western (especially US) influence was considerable. These paradoxes are examined in the paragraphs which follow.

The Second Five-Year Plan was published in mid-1969. It had been researched and written during the previous eighteen months by an expatriate team headed by Brian van Arkadie, assisted by inter-ministry working parties and working closely with the Principal Secretary in the Ministry of Economic Affairs and Development Planning, C. D. Msuya.[5] Self-reliance was interpreted as rural development, and provided the main emphasis of the policy sections of the Plan. The draft was discussed at a special meeting of the TANU National Conference in May 1969, following which references to ujamaa were inserted into the document wherever possible.[6] It was argued that everyone should make at least a small step towards ujamaa during the plan period—the so-called 'frontal approach', contrasted with a 'selective approach' which would have concentrated resources on a few villages.[7] But for this to be feasible, ujamaa had to be interpreted very broadly, so that even the creation of a village shop, or an extension of co-operative marketing, were acceptable steps. Considerable investment sums were also allocated to a capital-intensive and import-intensive programme of state farms, to infrastructure (transport, power, and water supply), and to manufacturing (though it was recognized that the industrial policy was only partially thought through; the Plan mentioned a list of no fewer than 385 industrial projects, but only forty were included in the list of projects for funding).[8]

The financial projections were more ambitious than those of the first plan, and assumed a much greater mobilization of local resources, made possible by taxation changes but also by the success of the 1967 nationalizations. The target growth rate was to be 6.5 per cent per annum in real terms, compared with the target of 6.7 per cent in the first plan, and the actual realization of about 5 per cent.[9]

The planners had not, however, anticipated the commitment in early 1970 to confine trade to national organizations, which, in combination with the ambitious investment programme of the new plan, provoked by the end of that year a rapid rise in borrowing from the banks, a balance of payments crisis, and the beginning of price inflation.[10] But neither had the planners anticipated the amount of foreign capital that would become avail-

able—by 1980 it put Tanzania into the top two or three countries in Africa south of the Sahara in terms of receipts of non-
military foreign 'aid' per capita. China had already offered an
untied loan in 1966 and signed the agreement to build the railway in 1967. The US built a tarmac road along almost the
same route, sharing the cost with the World Bank. The Scandinavian countries (Sweden in particular), West Germany, the
Netherlands, Canada, and at least fifteen other countries
financed Plan projects, mainly in the rural areas, on a grant or
loan basis (Table 24.1). The World Bank, which had invested in
rural credit in 1966, in the 1970s became involved in expensive
projects to promote first the main export crops, then livestock,
and subsequently even a few food crops, as well as 'integrated
rural development projects' providing a range of services in specified districts. It also invested in power generation, urban water
supply, and eventually, in the third plan period, in manufacturing industry (Table 24.2). USAID took a particular interest in
key agricultural projects (Table 24.3).

The greater part of this money was spent either by government departments or by the parastatals; a proportion was channelled through parastatal banks to the private industrial sector,
or to small or medium scale African farmers. The policies described in the previous chapters, including villagization, would
not have been possible without these impressive capital inflows.
The terms were not onerous: in 1975 the loans outstanding had
an average interest rate of less than two per cent, an average
original life of more than 35 years, and an average grace period
of nearly ten years[11]. Thus although Tanzania's indebtedness
rose from less than $150 million in 1967 to more than $750 million in 1975, the total of interest plus repayments of medium
and long term loans was in 1975 still less than 5 per cent of export earnings.[12]

The Arusha Declaration had warned that 'loans and grants
will endanger our independence'; however it did not say that
overseas finance would be refused, and the policy was quickly
clarified to mean that Tanzania would not 'bend its political,
economic or social policies in the hope of getting overseas aid as
a result'.[13] The paradox was that self-reliance in this sense was
attractive to many countries, or at least gave them the justification they needed to give 'aid' to a country they wished to support. Why they should wish to do so is considered at the end of
this chapter.

TABLE 24.1

Commitments of external public loans and grants by sources, 1967–1975
('000s of US dollars)

	Commitments								
	1967	1968	1969	1970	1971	1972	1973	1974	1975
A. Type of Creditor									
Suppliers' Credits	—	14 894	10 140	3 086	—	—	—	—	—
Private Bank Credits	15 451	2 400	1 384	—	—	4 200	—	—	—
Public Issued Bonds	—	—	—	—	833	—	—	—	—
Other Private Debt	6 228	2 973	16 860	5 194	—	—	—	—	—
Loans from International Organizations:	5 200	4 300	27 500	39 000	9 800	14 057	24 389	133 300	47 100
African Development Bank	—	—	—	—	—	3 257	1 789	7 100	7 100
Arab Fund for Econ. and Social Dev.	—	—	—	—	—	—	—	—	—
IBRD	5 200	4 300	7 000	30 000	—	—	—	65 000	30 000
IDA	—	—	20 500	9 000	9 800	10 800	22 600	61 200	10 000
Loans from Governments	17 794	20 404	48 762	232 530	25 393	47 117	82 757	127 136	91 269
Bulgaria	—	—	—	—	—	3 000	3 000	—	—
Canada	416	—	925	2 675	2 079	7 419	57 606	—	4 327
China, People's Republic of	—	799	1 999	200 811	—	1 876	—	76 458	—
Czechoslovakia	5 677	—	—	—	5 398	—	—	—	5 428
Denmark	—	—	—	—	—	5 285	—	15 612	17 442
Finland	—	38	—	—	3 731	—	—	2 662	7 611
Germany, Fed. Rep. of	—	—	—	—	—	6 595	14 534	17 091	8 148
India	—	—	—	—	—	—	—	—	—
Israel	—	67	—	—	—	—	—	—	—
Italy	—	—	10 000	—	—	10 860	—	—	—
Japan	—	5 600	—	—	—	—	—	—	—
Kuwait	—	—	—	—	1 028	—	—	—	15 517
Netherlands	—	—	—	—	6 457	5 296	3 955	14 154	7 927
Sweden	6 572	—	17 977	18 944	—	—	—	—	4 829
United Kingdom	196	—	—	—	—	751	—	—	—

United States	1 600	13 900	—	10 100	6 700	4 900	2 600	—	20 040
USSR	3 333	—	16 665	—	—	—	—	—	—
Zambia	—	—	1 196	—	—	—	—	1 159	—
Multiple Lenders	—	—	—	—	—	1 135	1 062	—	—
Loans—Total	*44 673*	*44 971*	*104 646*	*279 810*	*36 026*	*65 374*	*107 146*	*260 436*	*138 369*
B. *Source of Grants*									
Multilateral Agencies	*2 990*	*2 990*	*3 050*	*5 110*	*4 490*	*3 300*	*4 480*	*6 600*	*10 130*
UN Development Programme	2 990	2 990	3 050	3 030	—	—	—	2 980	3 740
UN Regular Programme	—	—	—	400	200	180	140	520	410
UN Children's Fund	—	—	—	190	320	280	450	470	790
UN FAO World Food	—	—	—	1 360	410	2 210	3 400	340	1 460
UN High Commission on Refugees	—	—	—	100	2 780	630	490	2 290	3 480
Other United Nations	—	—	—	30	780	—	—	—	250
European Development Fund	—	—	—	—	—	—	—	—	—
Governments	*28 180*	*17 770*	*18 010*	*37 350*	*25 200*	*23 560*	*19 820*	*55 010*	*89 870*
Australia	120	90	100	80	80	80	100	150	790
Austria	20	30	10	20	30	10	20	—	—
Belgium	—	10	20	—	20	10	10	10	40
Canada	1 430	1 790	1 670	3 910	3 480	2 340	1 460	3 490	6 130
Denmark	730	760	850	4 080	2 680	1 480	1 280	5 520	8 840
Finland	—	—	—	—	—	—	—	—	5 800
Germany, Federal Republic of	5 150	3 220	3 620	5 620	3 620	4 180	3 540	7 790	10 550
Italy	30	30	30	100	—	450	30	370	60
Japan	20	180	250	730	710	670	330	1 020	1 880
Netherlands	—	—	—	2 560	900	1 130	—	3 360	5 120
New Zealand	—	—	—	—	—	—	—	—	30
Norway	410	410	440	3 480	2 910	1 390	750	6 890	10 760
Sweden	1 630	1 760	1 560	9 110	3 180	2 110	2 990	17 540	29 500
Switzerland	20	60	220	210	170	410	180	470	310
United Kingdom	7 620	2 430	4 240	3 450	3 420	4 300	4 130	3 400	3 060
United States	11 000	7 000	5 000	4 000	4 000	5 000	5 000	5 000	7 000
Grants—Total	*31 170*	*20 760*	*21 060*	*42 460*	*29 690*	*26 860*	*24 300*	*61 610*	*100 000*

Source: IBRD.

TABLE 24.2
World Bank lending programme in Tanzania up to June 1978
(US $ million)

	Fiscal year	IDA	IBRD
Agriculture			
Agricultural credit	1966	5.0	
Livestock development (beef)	1969, 1973	19.8	
Tobacco (including processing)	1971, 1977, 1978	31.0	
Smallholder tea	1971	10.8	
Geita cotton	1974	17.5	
Cashewnut processing	1974, 1978	23.0	21.0
Kilombero sugar	1975	9.0	9.0
Integrated regional development projects	1975, 1977, 1978	40.2	
National maize project	1976	18.0	
Dairy development	1976	10.0	
Fisheries	1977	9.0	
Forestry	1977		7.0
Education	1964, 1969, 1971, 1973, 1976	34.2	
Infrastructure			
Highways	1967, 1969, 1971, 1975	48.2	8.0
Hydroelectric power	1967, 1970, 1974, 1977		70.2
Morogoro water supply	1977		15.0
Low-cost housing	1975, 1978	20.5	
Trucking	1978	15.0	
Industry			
Tanzania Investment Bank	1974, 1976, 1978	6.0	30.0
Textiles	1975, 1978	25.0	35.0
Morogoro Industrial Complex	1977	11.5	11.5
Programme Assistance (untied)	1975, 1977	15.0	30.0
Technical Assistance	1976	6.0	
Subtotal		374.7	236.7
One-third share of loans to East African Community for railways, harbours, & telecommunications	1965–73		81.3
Total		374.7	318.0

Source: IBRD.

FOREIGN POLICY

Tanzanian foreign policy was built on two principles: non-alignment and the liberation of southern Africa.[14] Nyerere argued that by involving many governments in the financing of

TABLE 24.3
USAID projects under implementation 1977

Agriculture	Years	US contribution ('000 000s of US dollars)	
Agricultural research	1972–	4.4	Concentrated on breeding of new maize varieties.
Seed multiplication	1970–80	4.2	Multiplies and distributes improved seeds, mainly maize and oil-seeds.
Masai livestock and range management	1970–80	3.6	One of the few projects in Tanzania for pastoralists.
Livestock marketing and development	1974–	4.4	Support for the parastatals concerned.
Sterility methods for tsetse control	1972–	3.0	Control of tsetse by the release of sterile males.
Dairy production (heifers)	1975–	1.5	Importation of calves from the USA.
Agricultural marketing	1971–9	2.3	Staff support for the National Milling Corporation.
Agricultural credit	1974–	3.8	Loans and staff for the Tanzania Rural Development Bank.
Arusha drought	1976–8	2.9	
Agricultural manpower development	1973–	3.4	Training in the USA.
Education African manpower development	1977–	0.1	Training in the USA.
Vocational primary schools	1976–82	0.1	Pilot project for a new type of primary education.
Non-formal education	1976–	0.2	Adult education.
Family planning Maternal and child-health aids	1973–82	6.4	This project supports the programme of 'child spacing'.

Source: USAID.

development projects he could maintain the principle of non-alignment. Where possible he played one off against another. The Chinese were building a railway to Zambia; partly to counter the propaganda value of this the Americans (and the World Bank) were persuaded to build the road; Nyerere tried to involve the Soviet Union in a hydroelectricity and cement project near Tukuyu, not far from the new road and railway.

Within Africa, liberation was the priority, and Tanzania gave moral and material support (including training camps, head offices, and rights of movement through the country) to liberation movements from South Africa, Zimbabwe, Mozambique, Angola, and Namibia. Tanzania's support for FRELIMO enabled that movement to open a front in northern Mozambique in 1964; five years later the FRELIMO President, Eduardo Mondlane, was killed by a letter bomb, almost certainly sent from the Portuguese, at his beach house outside Dar es Salaam.[15] In Angola, Tanzania consistently supported MPLA, the movement which did the most fighting, and which eventually controlled much of the land area of the country. Tanzania also supported the South-West Africa People's Organization (SWAPO), the most active Namibian liberation movement. In Zimbabwe it supported both ZANU and ZAPU, while using its influence to persuade the two to come together, as they did to some extent during the war as the Patriotic Front, although the two armies remained separate, the ZANU branch being based in Zambia and working closely with President Kaunda, while ZAPU fought from Mozambique with support from President Machel. Tanzania also supported both the African National Congress and the Pan-African Congress of South Africa. Tanzanian policy, fairly consistently maintained, was to support whichever movements were willing to fight and so showed most chance of taking control of their respective countries.[16]

The policy on liberation affected Tanzania's relations with other African countries. Her greatest contempt was reserved for those who traded or received assistance from South Africa. The tendency in the Organization for African Unity was not to intervene in any way in the internal policies of other countries. Suspicion of Tanzania, especially in West Africa, was reinforced by Tanzanian support for 'Biafra' in the Nigerian civil war of 1967–70, which was apparently dictated mainly by concern about the way in which the multinational oil companies and the British government were supporting Nigeria.[17] When 'Biafra' lost, Tanzania had gained nothing but had aroused the disapproval of every country in Africa with tribes that might consider secession.

Tanzania also opposed Idi Amin from the moment he seized power in Uganda, and this was one cause of the collapse of the East African Community in 1976, but a more fundamental cause was the long-term conflict of interest between Tanzania and Kenya. Before 1967 there had been a common market covering Kenya, Tanzania, and Uganda, a common external tariff, and 'common services' run from Nairobi—the Railways and Harbours, Posts and Telecommunications, Customs and Excise, and East African Airways. The difficulty was always that Kenya, the most advanced industrially, and well-placed across the main communications to Uganda and northern Tanzania, had most to gain from a common market because of its existing industries, was the natural centre for few industries to serve the whole East African market, and gained many advantages by hosting the headquarters of the common services. The attempt in 1964 to allocate some proposed new industries between the three countries succeeded in bringing a number of factories to Tanzania, but broke down in that other multinationals making the same products (aluminium sheets, car tyres, and radios) invested in Kenya so that the Tanzanian factories were unable to supply the whole East African market.

The 1967 *Treaty for East African Cooperation* was, however, a serious attempt to redress the balance. It allowed for 'transfer taxes' to be imposed on the Kenyan borders with Tanzania and Uganda for a limited number of years, in order to protect infant industries in those countries. It also moved the headquarters of the Posts and Telecommunications to Uganda, the Harbours to Dar es Salaam, and the headquarters of the Community, including the tax collection services, to Arusha in northern Tanzania.[18] The Tanzanians were proud of what they negotiated in 1967, and especially the proposed transfer of the Community headquarters to Arusha, which should have given a welcome stimulus to industry and trade in the north. The Kenyans tended to play down the transfer taxes, since these were for a minimum of only eight years on any particular product. For them the loss of the Community and other headquarters was the price to pay for the retention of an East African common market in the long run.

But in early 1970 Nyerere announced that by the end of that year all importing into Tanzania would be managed by parastatals, and at about the same time the Chinese began building the railway to Zambia. The terms of the loan were such that the

TABLE 24.4
Mainland Tanzania's trade with Kenya and Uganda 1962, 1967, 1972, 1977
(million shillings)

Principal commodities	1962	1967	1972	1977*
Exports				
Meat and meat preparations	1.6	2.3	1.3	—
Cereal and cereal preparations	5.0	2.8	3.3	—
Dairy products and margarine	3.4	0.6	1.0	—
Beans, peas, and other legumes	5.7	6.4	8.5	—
Other food products	8.9	7.2	11.8	2.9
Tobacco, unmanufactured	1.3	5.7	15.8	2.7
Vegetable oils	8.1	8.4	1.3	—
Chemicals	0.8	2.6	3.6	1.6
Cotton piece-goods	1.6	1.5	20.2	0.2
Clothing	0.2	1.3	2.7	2.3
Footwear	3.8	2.1	0.3	—
Aluminium circles	—	5.4	10.6	2.8
Other manufactured goods	11.8	11.9	23.8	12.9
Other commodities	12.6	24.8	28.8	5.1
Total	64.8	83.0	133.1	30.5
Imports				
Meat and meat preparations	7.7	4.6	2.6	—
Cereal and cereal preparations	23.4	20.6	14.4	9.1
Dairy products**	7.3	15.7	39.5	2.4
Other food products	27.4	22.6	30.7	5.6
Beer	12.6	5.6	6.6	—
Petroleum products	0.2	35.1	31.1	6.2
Chemicals***	9.0	21.1	43.7	13.5
Cement	11.3	10.9	9.6	1.4
Cotton piece-goods	18.4	16.9	0.5	—
Clothing	14.4	3.0	5.0	0.2
Footwear	10.3	6.5	7.6	—
Soap	11.7	5.8	12.2	0.1
Other manufactured goods	35.3	68.9	79.9	39.8
Other commodities	52.8	42.7	48.1	99.1
Total	241.8	280.1	331.5	177.4

*   Provisional figures.
**   Milk, eggs, margarine, and shortening.
***   Excluding soaps.
—   Nil or insignificant
Source: *Economic Survey* 1977–8, Tables 11 and 12.

local costs of the railway—about half the total cost—were paid by importing and selling Chinese consumer goods, and using the money realized for the local costs. So from 1970 onwards the officials of the STC had large sums of money to spend each year at the Canton Fair, in China. The Chinese were careful not to overcharge for these goods—which were frequently rather cheap when they appeared in the Tanzanian shops. But much of what was purchased in China—detergents, sugar, textiles, china, and many metal or plastic consumer items and tinned goods—would otherwise have been purchased from Kenya. When the STC did purchase from Kenya—and imports by no means ceased—it demanded highly competitive prices. The Kenyans felt cheated out of their markets in Tanzania and, having failed in a legal challenge to the STC, they resorted to obstruction, first by delaying transfers of staff to Arusha, then by not returning railway wagons that had taken loads into Kenya, and finally by refusing to let the three big ferries on Lake Victoria leave Kenyan ports. It was not easy for the Tanzanians to reply to this, but in 1975 Nyerere forbade the lorries of KENATCO, a road transport company in which the Kenyatta family had a stake, to use Tanzanian roads, and in 1976 he closed the Tanzania–Kenyan border, immobilizing fifty or so Kenyan safari vehicles that were in Tanzania at the time. The border was still closed at the end of 1980, more than four years later, by which time the East African Community had been formally wound up.

Relations were complicated by the *coup* in Uganda in January 1971. Nyerere supported Milton Obote, the deposed President, who was given refuge in Tanzania. In September 1972 both he and the Second Vice-President of Tanzania, Rashidi Kawawa, were implicated in a poorly conceived plan by Ugandan exiles to commandeer an East African Airways plane from Dar es Salaam airport and fly it full of armed men to Entebbe. The plane got no further than Kilimanjaro International Airport, where it landed heavily on its undercarriage, and was found in the morning deserted and immobilized; at the same time a force of about a thousand Ugandan exiles invaded across the Kagera river and attempted to capture the principal towns in south-west Uganda, Masaka and Mbarara. They were transported in Tanzanian National Service lorries and issued with Tanzanian army rations. Their plans were naïvely optimistic in every respect; they met resistance from troops loyal to Amin and when their limited ammunition ran out fled back to Tanzania as best they could, within twenty-four hours of invading. Nyerere was blatantly implicated, and Tanzania suffered a humiliating diplomatic defeat, and was fortunate that President Barre of Somalia assisted in negotiating a truce (the Mogadishu Agreement) which laid down a demilitarized zone 10 kilometres on either side of the border. But this agreement also required Tanzania to give up propaganda hostile to Amin, and weakened Nyerere's position at the 1974 meeting of the Organization of African Unity in Mogadishu, where it was agreed that Kampala should be the venue for the 1975 meeting, and the host, President Amin, OAU President for the year.[19]

In Uganda the murders of intellectuals, soldiers, and many others continued. In late 1978, Ugandan forces invaded and annexed a small land area in north-west Tanzania. The Tanzanian army succeeded in driving them out, and then advanced to take Masaka and Mbarara. This time the plans were thought out. The army was disciplined, and the population of southern Uganda welcomed the invaders. There was little to prevent them moving on, until in April 1979 they were able to take Kampala and force Amin to flee the country. Their military tactics, involving marching on foot with small amounts of artillery support, and living as far as possible off the land (a cross between guerrilla action and a conventional invasion) added a new chapter to military theory. Their biggest problem was that there was no political organization to take over from the Tanzanian army. A conference of Ugandan exiles was hastily convened in Moshi, in northern Tanzania, a few days before Kampala fell. Yusufu Lule, an elderly ex-Vice-Chancellor of Makerere University and a Muganda, was elected interim leader, but soon upset the non-Buganda exiles. Sixty-eight days after his installation as President he was replaced by Godfrey Binaisa, a lawyer who ruled for nearly a year of continuing lawlessness, until in May 1980 he was replaced by a military leadership headed by Paul Muwanga, who immediately allowed Milton Obote, the man replaced by Amin in 1971, to return from exile. A general election in December 1980 returned Obote to power, although there were allegations of corruption, and the Buganda areas voted solidly against him. It was not long before the Uganda Patriotic Movement, a left-wing faction based in the Buganda areas, was claiming responsibility for acts of sabotage (Southall 1980).

The Tanzanians were very disappointed at the lack of stability. They had driven Amin out, at a cost to Tanzania of perhaps $500 million, but received little thanks for it from African neighbours such as Kenya and Sudan or from the international community, despite an appeal to their major Western donors. From early 1980 Tanzania was in the grip of unprecedented shortages of wheat flour, rice, diesel, and many other crucial imported items.[20]

THE THIRD FIVE-YEAR PLAN

The Second Five-Year Plan had been intended to run from July 1969 to June 1974. The Third Plan would thus have started in the middle of villagization and in the middle of an economic crisis. At the last possible moment the Plan was postponed, and it did not come into operation till July 1976, while the revised document was not published till 1978.[21] Even then, there was a danger that the growth rates would appear unrealistic; the target for the economy was 6 per cent per annum growth in real terms, compared with the target of 6.5 per cent in the second plan, and the actual realization of no more than 4.6 per cent. Even this would only be feasible if there was heavy investment, almost half of which was expected to be financed outside the country.[22]

The Plan stressed the need to increase food production and to consolidate the villagization. A great deal of thought had been given to the industrial strategy, a modified version of a basic industries strategy, following the ideas of the Caribbean economist Clive Y. Thomas, whose book *Dependence and Transformation* was written in Tanzania in 1972 and 1973; similar thinking can be found in Justinian Rweyemanu's *Underdevelopment and Industrialisation in Tanzania*,[23] and Rweyemanu had a significant influence on the formulation of the Plan, first as a member of the Planning Commission and later as an adviser in State House.

A basic industry strategy, as defined in Thomas's theoretical book, means industrializing around the production of a few key intermediate products, produced where possible from local raw materials.[24] Given these intermediate products (steel, some other metals, sulphuric and nitric acid, the alkalis, PVC and plastics, cement, paper, rubber, leather, textiles, and a few others), most consumer goods can, it is argued, be produced from local resources without the need for substantial additional imported components. Thomas summarized his strategy in terms of two 'iron laws'—first the structure of production must be made similar to that of demand, i.e. the economy should produce its own requirements, gain foreign exchange by exporting surplus production of those same goods, rather than, as in a colonial economy, producing export products to satisfy someone else's needs and importing all intermediate and capital goods as well as many consumer items. Second, the structure of production should reflect the needs of the masses; it is not just a matter of producing a wide range of semi-luxury items for a minority who can pay for them, with the poor getting worse off, as, for example, in India or Brazil; instead the strategy requires a distribution of income, and a structure of production and employment, in which the poor not only produce the goods and services they need but also have the purchasing power to buy them.

There are many difficulties in implementing this strategy in Tanzania. One is that competitive production on a world basis may require a size of plant greater than the Tanzanian demand for a product in the foreseeable future (for example, Tanzania could not use seven million tons of steel per annum, the size of a single efficient plant in Japan, for many years to come. Thomas argues that the extra costs of below optimal scale production are not great and that a country such as Tanzania should pay them in order to save the foreign exchange involved in importing the basic products.) The strategy is evidently expensive (at least during a 15–20 year 'period of transition'); it is intensive in its use of engineers and requires access to modern technology. If these resources are imported from outside (e.g. from multinational corporations) they have to be paid for, and the contracts involved are precisely the type that created such difficulties for Tanzania in the 1970s (Chapter 23).[25] If the technology is to be imported and paid for without capital from abroad, there is then a need for a foreign exchange surplus (presumably from agriculture or minerals such as copper or oil), effective technical education, and a transfer of resources through taxation or the price mechanism from the agricultural and service sectors to industry. In Tanzania's case agriculture would have to carry a treble burden, earning the foreign exchange, feeding the country, and providing employment and purchasing power for the masses. A real danger would be insufficient food production, since the strategy would grind to a halt if hard-earned reserves of foreign exchange had to be used to import food instead of machines.[26]

The Third Five-Year Plan did not deal directly with these difficulties. It was prepared at a time when the productivity of both labour and investment was low and declining, and to make sense of any industrial strategy it was necessary to assume that these would improve in future.[27] Moreover, certain investment decisions taken during the second plan period would be implemented during the third, including a trebling of sugar production between 1975 and 1981 and a decision to process as much as possible of the country's agricultural produce before export. The World Bank provided much of the money, but also (inconsistently) advised against these investments, pointing out that the world market for sugar was notoriously unstable, while those for cotton textiles, leather shoes, sisal twine, and shelled cashewnuts were likely to be as unremunerative as those for the unprocessed products; but by then the decisions had already been taken.[28] Finally, some projects were included for their revenue-raising potential, even though they were non-basic luxury products, such as beer, cigarettes, and polyester textiles ('Takron' and 'crimplene'). The inclusion of these projects meant that the basic industry strategy of the Third Plan was by no means pure, but it did include proposals to press ahead with iron, steel, and coal production in the medium term, chemical production from the Songo Songo gas field at an unspecified date,[29] and engineering immediately. In industries where it was economically feasible, it suggested small-scale or labour-intensive techniques, although the pressures—from parastatals as well as multinationals—in favour of large-scale production in 'modern' plants had usually proved irresistible in the past. In agriculture the main increases were expected to come from intensification of labour and the use of inputs such as seeds and fertilizer without a large share of investment. In short, while this plan avoided some of the dangers of the second five-year plan (which sailed perilously close to implying that a sustained rise in living standards was possible from rural development alone without industrialization), it did not show how the huge problems of mobilizing a food and foreign exchange surplus and then of successfully implementing a basic industry strategy would be solved in the short term.

FOREIGN 'AID'

In practice the development effort had become intimately tied up with the diplomatic effort to mobilize capital abroad. The remainder of this chapter is devoted to a consideration of some of the causes of the sudden increase in 'aid' to a country in which the government had nationalized the banks and various other companies, and shown that it was determined to intervene in virtually every sector.

A prerequisite was considerable negotiating and diplomatic skill on the part of Nyerere, his Ministers of Foreign Affairs and

Finance, and their officials. They succeeded in playing one
donor off against another: for example the Americans increased
their aid at least partly to prevent the country becoming a communist satellite. Later fifteen different donors were invited to
prepare plans for the regions (Table 24.5), and those who prepared the plans came under considerable pressure to finance
them. Another successful move was the creation of banks—
notably the Tanzania Rural Development Bank, lending mainly
to co-operatives and villages, and the Tanzania Investment Bank
lending to industrial and other parastatals. It was not normal
practice for foreign governments to give low-interest loans to
local private companies, or to individual African farmers, but it
was possible for them to open lines of credit to these banks, and
the banks could then lend the money either to parastatals or to
the private sector.

TABLE 24.5
Aid Donors involved in Regional Planning 1975/7

Donor	Regions
Canada	Coast; Dar es Salaam; Dodoma
Denmark	West Lake
European Economic Community	Iringa*
FAO (UNDP)	Iringa
Finland	Lindi; Mtwara
Germany (Federal Republic)	Tanga
India	Singida
IBRD (World Bank)	Kigoma; Mara; Mwanza*; Shinyanga*; Tabora*
Japan	Kilimanjaro
Netherlands	Morogoro; Shinyanga
Norway	Mbeya
Sweden	Arusha; Mwanza; Tabora
United Kingdom	Lindi*; Mtwara*
USA	Arusha
Yugoslavia	Ruvuma

* Donor invited to rewrite or finance plans prepared by another agency.
Source: adapted from Mushi (1978: 94) with additional information.

Nyerere also managed to appeal to the liberal ideals of many
individuals and some political parties in the West. Up to 1974
few questioned that what Tanzania was attempting was in the
interests of the masses: emphasis on rural development, education, a more equal income distribution, national ownership of
property, and a strong stand against racial discrimination.
Moreover, corruption was less apparent than in several other

African countries. Western governments did not wish to be seen offering all their aid to avowedly right-wing regimes: 'socialist' Tanzania was a useful corrective. It gave a moral justification to politicians in Sweden, West Germany, and Britain who were criticized for trading and investing in South Africa. The World Bank needed to legitimize itself by lending to some 'socialist' states, and with the exception of the nationalization measures, most of Macnamara's recommendations about rural development, education, and income distribution in successive annual reports of the World Bank were already official policy in Tanzania. The position were reinforced by Western academics, of a left-liberal inclination, who published books like *One Party Democracy* (edited by Lionel Cliffe, 1967), *Socialism in Tanzania* (edited by Lionel Cliffe and John Saul, 1972–3), *The Critical Phase in Tanzania—Nyerere and the Emergence of a Socialist Strategy* (Cranford Pratt, 1976), and uncritical biographies of Nyerere based on expositions of his political thought.[30] .

Another reason for giving aid to Tanzania was its increased strategic and diplomatic importance as the countries of Southern Africa liberated themselves from white rule. Nyerere became the natural leader, strategist, and, at times, moderating influence, of the 'front-line' states. As Britain and the US manoeuvred behind the scenes to talk (or force) Ian Smith into a negotiated compromise settlement, influencing Nyerere, to say nothing of maintaining stability in Tanzania, became a political objective. Increased corruption and political instability in Kenya and Zaire (the largest recipients of Western military support in the area), Idi Amin in power in Uganda, and left-wing governments in Mozambique, Ethiopia, and Somalia, made stability and Western influence in Tanzania appear even more important.

It may well be that such diplomatic considerations are sufficient to explain the support which Tanzania received. It was support particularly from the Americans and the Scandinavians (Table 24.1); British aid was not resumed till 1974, and then only slowly, and in 1972 the British attempted to veto a World Bank loan for small-scale tea growing, on the grounds that the Tanzanian government was paying inadequate compensation to British subjects (almost entirely Tanzanian Asians) who had had property nationalized in 1971; the Bank staff sent a deputation to Tanzania which prepared a report sympathetic to Tanzania; and the Americans refused to support the British, so that the loan went ahead. Later, in April 1975, the Bank arranged a special meeting to deal with the food and foreign exchange crisis, the documentation for which was largely prepared by the Bank; substantial quantities of food aid, and hard currency with which to purchase food, were pledged.

But there is another way of looking at the rapid increase in US and World Bank aid, first suggested by Gerhard Tschannerl.[31] This is that by 1970 US leaders such as Macnamara realized that in many underdeveloped countries the operations of free enterprise alone could bring neither reliable markets nor a rise in living standards for the poor; it was therefore necessary for post-colonial states to play a role. Tanzania became a kind of laboratory or testing ground for various forms of state involvement. It had a political philosophy that could justify intervention to support the greater good of the masses, and a state that was willing to intervene. It was prepared to create new institutions. The Bank used its influence to legitimize lending to Tanzania; it put money into the development of agriculture—food crops to feed the cities, and export crops for capitalist world markets; it produced a series of reports on the Tanzanian economy, more detailed and far-reaching than in any Tanzanian government publications; it inevitably became involved in villagization, giving its support because villagization simplified the administration of the agricultural projects (such as the tobacco programme). At the same time the Bank warned against communal work and against the extravagance of moving the capital from Dar es Salaam to Dodoma;[32] both were de-emphasized. Some Bank officials even concluded that there was an intellectual case for a basic industry strategy, even though they did not much care for it personally and it would involve state underwriting of large-scale investments in heavy industries.

But whatever the explanation, and it would be a rash analyst who thought that a single theory would explain the behaviour of all the governments involved, the fact remains that the power taken by the state from 1967 onwards was reinforced by these inflows of capital. 'Aid' agreements are negotiated by civil servants of one country with their counterparts in another. A department largely financed from overseas, such as the Water Development Division, became free of most of the checks imposed on government spending through shortages of finance and manpower. To a remarkable extent the interests of Tanzanian bureaucrats in political stability and increased agricultural production coincided with those of the World Bank and the US. It is to the nature of this state, and Nyerere's role in it, that we turn in the last chapter of this book.

25 THE TANZANIAN STATE

Tanzania is not prepared to devalue its currency just because this is a traditional free market solution to everything and regardless of the merits of our position. It is not prepared to surrender its right to restrict imports by measures designed to ensure that we import quinine rather than cosmetics, or buses rather than cars for the elite.

My Government is not prepared to give up our national endeavour to provide primary education for every child, and basic medicines and water for all our people. Cuts may have to be made in our national expenditure, but we will decide whether they fall on public services or private expenditure. Nor are we prepared to deal with inflation and shortages by relying only on monetary policy regardless of its relative effect on the poorest and less poor.

Our price control may not be the most effective in the world, but we will not abandon price control; we will only strive to make it more efficient. And above all, we shall continue with our endeavours to build a socialist society.

PRESIDENT NYERERE (1980)[1]

In discussing contemporary Tanzania, relating the present to the past, I have avoided describing the country as socialist or non-socialist, or using the terms 'class' or 'the state' in any rigorous way.

'The state' is a term which covers all national institutions: the civil service, government corporations (parastatals), parliament, the Party, but also the army, the police, the security, and the judicial service. The state administers economic policy—tax and credit, financial institutions, foreign borrowing—but also economic and social infrastructure—education, health services, transport, communications, public administration. Instead of referring to the state in the abstract, it is often more illuminating to

use the term 'state power', and to ask who can use the power of
the state, and in whose interest it acts. If the state acts consistently to support one class in society, or if one class directly
controls state power, then we would call it a 'ruling class'; but it
may not always be possible to identify a single ruling class in
this way.

In the Tanzanian case it is easy to identify classes which do
not control the state. In particular it is not controlled in any
simple way by a capitalist bourgeoisie owning manufacturing industry. The most important industrial enterprises are owned
either by the state or by the state in partnership with foreign
companies. There are some local industrialists, of Asian and of
African origin, and a tendency in some sectors (such as construction) for Asians to sell out to Africans. By the end of the
1970s this local private sector was getting more favourable
treatment from the state, but no commentator would have dared
to suggest, by any stretch of the imagination, that it controlled
it.

In a similar way, no single class was associated either with
large-scale agricultural production or with trade. Plantation
companies had either been nationalized or had stayed in foreign
hands, and a few white settlers remained; where they had sold
out or abandoned their farms, the land either returned to bush
or was allocated to villages (and hence relatively small-scale production) or to parastatals, including District Development Corporations. Large-scale (tractor-owning) African farmers wield-
ed influence in some regions (notably Arusha) but had little
representation at the national level. Wholesale and import/ex-
port trade had at one time been dominated by foreign trading
companies and Asians, but it had been taken over by the state
before a class of wealthy African traders had formed.

It was also clear that the state was not controlled by workers
or by peasants. From 1962 the state acted against workers' organizations, restricting or imprisoning their leaders (1962 and
1964), limiting their freedom to negotiate better conditions for
their members and nominating union leaders (1967), and dismissing a large proportion of elected workers' leaders (1973 and
1974). It is true that between 1969 and 1973, and to some extent
subsequently, attempts were made to involve workers in industrial decision-making; but it is clear from the documents of the
period that this was an attempt, on government's part, to limit
some of the freedoms enjoyed by managers and owners, and
that most parastatal managements interpreted it at most as a

chance to improve industrial relations by co-opting workers.[2] As
soon as workers showed that they wished to go beyond consultation and 'participation', in the direction of control of enterprises, the state intervened against them and in support of the
owners and managers. The Mount Carmel case (Chapter 23)
was a watershed, because in the months which followed, experienced workers' leaders, in nearly all factories, lost their
jobs.

The watershed in the rural areas was earlier—the disbanding
of the Ruvuma Development Association in 1969, discussed in
Chapter 22 and its appendix. The RDA was a local organization
of politically inspired producers who were gaining economic
power at the local level, in particular by developing their own
marketing outlets for grain. It successfully organized communal
production and provided social services for its members, but its
strength lay in its ideology (closely followed by the President in
his 1967 and 1968 papers) which stressed democracy and self-
reliance in the sense of independence from central government.
The RDA was seen as a threat by regional politicians, and once
it was crushed they made sure that similar organizations of villages were not started elsewhere. Instead, 'villagization' was
planned in Regional and District offices, with the assistance of
salaried officials in the Divisions and Wards, and implemented
with the backing of the militia. There was no possibility that so
many peasants would have moved in such a short space of time
if they had been given a free choice. It is true that the Ujamaa
Villages Act of 1975 provided for 'village councils' on which vil-
large representatives would have had majority control. But all
the evidence suggests that these were dominated by the official
representatives, backed by the resources of government; and as
trained and salaried 'village managers' were posted to more and
more villages, to organize production, social services, and if
possible communal work, the state imposed itself even in very
remote areas.

Many of these points can be illustrated from a research project co-ordinated by S.S. Mushi which compared small-scale development projects in three districts before and after the 1972
'decentralization' reforms which were supposed to pass more
power to local organizations, but which in practice increased the
power of the officials (Mushi 1978: 85–93). Decisions taken at
village, or even District, level could be overturned by officials in
the regional office, or in the Prime Minister's office in Dodoma.
Projects had to be documented, which meant official involve-

ment. The result was that in 1974, after decentralization, two-thirds of the projects implemented in the three districts studied were proposed by officials, and only one-third by elected representatives. When individuals could be identified who had spoken in favour of particular projects, 60 per cent of those individuals were government civil servants, 16 per cent were paid party officials, and only 23 per cent were elected. In 14 per cent of the projects implemented the main beneficiaries were civil servants, and 20 per cent of the projects benefited a few (usually rich) individual farmers. Only 55 per cent of the projects were 'successful'; 21 per cent were 'unsuccessful' (e.g. a poultry project that cost more to run than it earned, or buildings erected and then abandoned), and 24 per cent were of mixed success (such as a water supply that failed during the dry season, or a road that stopped short of its destination because a bridge had not been built).

There have been times when it seemed that the richer peasants, or kulaks, had a disproportionate influence on government policy. They were certainly important in production, as shown in Chapter 17. They were also influential in the co-operative movement, which in a sense was their creation, and they took the lion's share of rural credit schemes. On the other hand their power was lessened by the 1967 ujamaa policies, the 1973–5 villagization (which included an element of land reform, and made it difficult for kulaks to farm large areas near villages), by the abolition of co-operative unions and their replacement by state corporations in 1976, and by the general preference in trading and transport operations (often associated with kulak farming) given to village, co-operative, or District Development Corporation activities.

This raises a somewhat broader possibility: it has often been suggested that the Tanzanian state is controlled by the petty bourgeoisie. This term originally referred to small shopkeepers, traders, transport operators, and the like, in an era when 'the state' as we know it now was less important. 'Clerks' were also included; they were not manual workers, nor part of a capital-owning bourgeoisie. But by an extension of this categorization, the whole of the civil service in a modern state is sometimes classified as part of the petty bourgeoisie—which can be highly confusing, since their interests are frequently different from those of shopkeepers and traders. It is preferable to consider the 'classical' petty bourgeoisie and the state employees separately.

The former overlap with the kulaks, and many of the same conclusions apply. Traders, for example the members of the Mwanza African Traders' Cooperative Society who chose Paul Bomani as their treasurer/accountant in 1947, had much to do with the establishment of the co-operative movement. On the other hand the co-operative ideology was directed *against* traders, and took business away from them. The ambiguity was kept within limits so long as most of the traders were Asians or Arabs, and the co-operatives provided suitable private rewards to those who were employed by them. This partly explains why the government was so slow to clamp down on well publicized abuses within the co-operatives (the alternative would have been a return largely to Asian private traders) and why eventually the co-operatives were replaced with national *parastatal* organizations (the crop authorities). The other citadels of traders and business men were the urban branches of the Party. Many urban business men had beeen involved in the nationalist movement, in the hope that a nationalist victory would widen their business opportunities; and to the extent that they gained priority in the allocation of trading licences, bus routes, and government contracts, this was realized. Many urban party branches were opposed to socialist measures, and supported authoritarian Regional and Area Commissioners. It is, nevertheless, hard to argue that a petty bourgeoisie of this type controlled the state, when so many limitations were put on private trade and business, when the ideology of the state was against it, and when the elected organs of the Party lost influence in relation to those who were centrally appointed.

As far as the petty bourgeoisie in the second sense—the government and party officials—is concerned, this is still not a homogeneous class. Many of the junior officials are workers—for example those employed in forestry or on state farms, or to maintain government vehicles. Those at the top of the civil service have executive power, but those in the middle are at the mercy of those at the top, and hold very little power; but how can a line be drawn between the middle and the top?

Issa Shivji's 'bureaucratic bourgeoisie' and Michaela von Freyhold's 'nizers' are both attempts to define a class of top administrators and managers: 'the ministers, principal secretaries, the general managers of the larger parastatals, the heads of the appointed party bureaucracy at the different levels, the heads of the repressive apparatus'.[3] This is still not well defined: what happens to the manager of a smaller parastatal? or the de-

puty general manager of a larger one? or a Vice-Chancellor of
the University of Dar es Salaam, who was a cabinet minister a
few weeks previously?

A ruling class must have a defined relation to the means of
production; it must have a means of reproducing itself (and the
means of production) over time; and it should possess a consciousness of its interests as a class, although there may be situations in which this interest is suppressed or confused. If a
'bureaucratic bourgeoisie' exists in contemporary Tanzania, and
if it is to fulfil these requirements, then it can only be defined
rather generally, as a coalition between the nationalist politicians of the independence movement and the university graduates. This recognizes both its origins in the nationalist struggle
and its ability to reproduce itself by getting most of its sons and
a number of its daughters into university, from where they are
'bonded' to work in government or parastatal service for at least
five years. It is not a class with a historic origin associated with
any form of accumulation. It *disposes of* (although it does not
own) a large part of the means of production, that part which is
controlled by the state. It has a consciousness of itself as 'the
educated', or 'leaders', in Tanzania. It gets close to meeting the
conditions required to define a ruling class.

A comparison has often been made between supposed
'bureaucratic bourgeoisies' in Tanzania and in the Soviet Union
or Yugoslavia. A more illuminating, if paradoxical, comparison
is with the United Kingdom[4] where there is a political party (the
Labour Party) created by the trade unions and some intellectuals, but committed to non-revolutionary change and with sufficient popular support to win power in parliamentary elections.
Its programme includes the provision of social services, a more
equal distribution of income and wealth through taxation and
other measures, and increased state ownership of industry
through nationalization and through holding companies such as
the National Enterprise Board. It holds an uneasy relation with
the multinational corporations, on the one hand fearing them (on
nationalist grounds) and hoping to control them by nationalization, but on the other envying them and wishing to get access to
their technology through joint ventures. The civil service, in
many ways more powerful than the political institutions, is committed to a process of slow change and 'modernization'. Even
when there are major contradictions (as in Northern Ireland) a
political consensus is maintained through the institution of parliamentary democracy, in which members of parliament are

elected from a wide political spectrum; but parliament is often little more than a talking shop, ratifying decisions already taken by civil servants or industrialists. The administrative class reproduces itself through education. Its children go mainly to fee-paying schools, and to the universities of Oxford and Cambridge, to which some of the most intelligent children of petty bourgeois families are also admitted (and a few of manual workers), most of whom, by the time they graduate, have become committed to the prevailing ruling-class ideology. Property is unequally distributed, but most administrators, managers, and other professionals own shares; despite this more than half the shares in the stock exchange are owned by pension funds and insurance companies. If one defines the ruling class to include owners of capital, then it includes a large body of professionals; on the other hand, this group is coherent, with an ideology promulgated by the newspapers and found in all the main political parties.

A comparison between Britain and Tanzania should not be taken far, because the industrial bourgeoisie is much weaker in Tanzania, and there is nothing comparable to the City of London, with its international links. Moreover, the professionals in Tanzania do not own property to the same extent as their counterparts in Britain. But they do have the same solidarity, and the same feeling of superiority towards other classes, and a large influence over the productive activities within the country. The most successful families have brothers, sisters, and cousins in professional or executive positions in a wide range of 'national' institutions, and in the private sector. Parliament does not function as a forum in which government policies can be debated, since, with few exceptions, Members of Parliament do not feel free to speak their minds publicly on matters of national policy. But the Party does play that role, although its important meetings are held behind closed doors. Like parliament in a social democracy, the Party in Tanzania feels that it should control the economic, as well as the political, life of the country ('The Party is supreme' is the much-used slogan[5]), although objectively most of the important decisions are taken in the civil service or parastatals. Moreover, the period when the Party asserted this claim (from about 1969 onwards) was also a period in which the power of *appointed* party officials was strengthened; the party headquarters was reorganized, and salaried officials were posted to divisions and wards, where they facilitated the 1973–5 villagization (Chapter 22). From about 1976 salaried 'village managers' were posted to villages, with more power than (elected) village chairmen, since they could influence party and government officials in the district and regional offices, and so bring government funds into the villages.

By the end of the 1970s, in almost every sector of life in Tanzania, power resided with officials. If there was a ruling class within the country, it could only be them; but there is an important alternative, that the ruling class lay outside the country. Michaela von Freyhold, for example, distinguishes between a 'ruling class', or 'metropolitan bourgeoisie'—the owners of capital in the centres of international capitalism—and a 'governing class', the local bureaucratic bourgeoisie, which carries out their wishes (von Freyhold 1977c: 76f.).

This is an extension of a·well-known formulation by Poulantzas, but in von Freyhold's hands it becomes an extreme form of dependency theory. It reduces all local classes to the status of puppets, denying the possibility of local initiative. Any accumulation of capital must be in accord with the wishes of the (external) ruling class, and for their profit, and thus (by definition) must increase dependence; it becomes underdevelopment rather than development. This may be accurate as a description of what happened in many countries, but it can never be a law of capitalist development, since it denies local classes a role in shaping their own destiny.[6]

The concept of 'class' used so far has been sociological (or descriptive) and largely static: it has related classes to the existing economic structure but not to the accumulation of capital. This issue is complicated in that a ruling class may have power, in the sense of control of property and labour, and hand that power to its children, but yet fail to use it to expand the productive forces. Moreover, it is clearly impossible to separate a discussion of accumulation in one country from considerations affecting competition and accumulation in the rest of the world.[7]

Olle and Schoeller (1977: 11f.) present data showing that the average productivity of labour varies considerably between capitalist countries, and that even US multinationals operating abroad are affected by the conditions in the different countries in which they operate. They also show the great variation in wages, and somewhat lower variation in labour costs per unit of production, between countries. A country with lower productivity can often only compete by paying lower wages, and this affects distribution and accumulation in such a country. No one would seriously question this type of analysis in a discussion of competition between (say) Britain and West Germany; Olle and Schoeller extend it to countries such as Brazil and Mexico and, by implication, to Tanzania and Kenya. It implies the existence of national capitals, with different labour costs and productivities, infrastructure, and raw materials, struggling to accumulate in the context of international world markets. The state is involved in lowering the costs of production in key areas of the economy (by providing education, health care, and other infrastructure, subsidizing innovation, lowering fuel or transport costs, and investing directly in productive corporations). The absolute levels of productivity and wages within a country are determined by the class struggles within that country, as well as the competitive conditions outside.

If we recognize a Tanzanian capital, associated with the nation state, then we can analyse its struggle to accumulate. We can note the efforts to cut the outflows of capital to companies overseas, and to Kenya; we can see the attempts to promote import substitution and the processing of agricultural products before export, as well as agricultural production; we can see the nationalist drive in the quotation which heads this chapter, and note the attempts to promote better standards of living for all people.

We can also note the severe restrictions on the process of accumulation: the almost total lack of intermediate and capital goods production enforcing a dependence on trade and foreign borrowing, especially if the country wishes to purchase machinery; the restrictions on returns to labour, in agriculture and industry, which derive from colonial policy; the dependence on a number of agricultural products which can only be exported profitably on world markets if they are produced with large quantities of low-wage labour; the poor infrastructure, especially in health and transport, which must be expanded at great cost before much production can take place outside the capital city; the limited research, even in agriculture; and the small numbers of Tanzanians with technical skills. We can also note that all these conditions were slightly less adverse in neighbouring Kenya. Together they made it hard to accumulate in Tanzania without the heavy involvement of the state. The public-sector involvement of the Arusha Declaration, and the nationalizations of the financial institutions, were probably essential if accumulation was to take place.

We can also note various aspects of the dynamics of the competitive system internationally, which particularly affected Tanzania. For example, world commodity markets operated so that
an improvement in the productivity of a commodity worldwide
was frequently followed by a drop in its price, making it even
harder to accumulate on the basis of exports of agricultural
primary products.[8] Something similar happened with manufactured products such as textiles: when many low-wage countries
began to export them, their world prices were forced down, so
that none of these countries gained much benefit. We can also
notice the desire to gain foreign exchange leading to a neglect of
food production in many countries, and so to food imports, and
a waste of foreign exchange, but also lower rural incomes and
narrow internal markets for manufactured goods. We can also
see a concern to reverse these tendencies leading to a temptation for governments to intervene in many areas of economic
life, and hence to a proliferation of bureaucracy.[9] Finally, we
can see increased concern among leaders in the advanced capitalist countries at the poverty in the less advanced countries, and
a (limited) willingness to move capital in (e.g. through foreign
'aid') to reduce the chance of revolutions but also to increase
the markets for their industrial products and machinery.[10]

These conditions can be related to our conclusions about the
Tanzanian ruling class. We have seen that it was not a class of
accumulators: it had little experience of industrial production
and marketing; it had no experience of large-scale agriculture,
and little faith in small-scale agriculture (indeed, most of its
leaders and their parents had sacrificed to get their children into
schools precisely in order to remove them from the necessity of
hard work for little reward on the land). When allocating resources, it did not think instinctively of investment and competition; rather it wanted 'the fruits of independence' in the form of
higher living standards, more consumer goods, and better social
services. These had been available to the colonialists; now they
should be made available to the mass of the population. It
blamed the poverty of the country and the lack of social services
on the colonial system—the transfer to surplus overseas (no
wonder dependency theory was so attractive). But when, after
independence, more of the surpluses were retained internally,
this did not produce an instantaneous transformation. That
would only have occurred if a large part of the surpluses and
been successfully invested in productive projects. The nationalists found it very difficult to accept that improvement of living

standards would only be possible *after* there was a strong local industrial base and a dynamic agriculture.

The leadership was authoritarian. Many of its number (including Nyerere himself) came from chiefly families, and inherited perceptions of their right to rule, to give orders. This sense of hierarchy was reinforced by secondary education in boarding-schools modelled on English public schools. Those who received orders were expected to carry them out even if they knew in their hearts that they would not bring the desired results. There was no tradition of leaders willingly subjecting themselves to self-criticism, or to criticism from their subordinates.[11]

In short, the Tanzanian ruling class was almost uniquely un-suited to bringing about economic transformation. It had learnt (mainly from the British) how to take over and operate the colonial institutions, and it was able to extend this and develop excellent relationships with a number of overseas governments willing to provide capital on concessionary terms. But its allocation of resources internally was always likely to be unplanned, and in the extremely difficult world competitive conditions of the 1960s and 1970s this would not allow it to make much progress towards developing a strong integrated economy.

How does Nyerere fit into this picture? It is certainly wrong to write a history of modern Tanzania as if he did not exist.[12] It is equally unhelpful to exaggerate his knowledge and power, or to write Tanzanian history as if he was the only person who made it.[13] Nyerere has been the leader of the Tanzanian mainland for twenty years, and of Zanzibar and Pemba for fifteen. This makes him one of the world's survivors, and Tanzania one of the most stable countries in Africa. They were not easy years; they involved both the deflation of the hopes raised by the independence struggle and economic failures. Nyerere survived not least because he possessed three talents, the combination of which is unusual in politicians: a perspective of where he wanted to go in the long term, a realism and feel for tactics in the short term, and an imagination and common touch in his speeches and writing which earned the respect even of those who did not agree with him.

Nyerere's long-term vision is one of Fabian socialism, in which the state owns most of the means of production, equalizes income, and provides a wide range of social services. Such a state would be controlled by elected representatives (such as MPs) with co-operative organizations at the local level in both production and distribution. Nyerere has no illusions that this vision has been reached in Tanzania; on the contrary, in his 1977 review of *The Arusha Declaration Ten Years After* his view of the achievements of the decade amounted to a claim only that some of the pre-conditioned for this kind of socialism had been established, and he confessed that he then thought it would take much longer to initiate than he had ten years earlier (Nyerere 1977: 43).

Nyerere would not have held power for so long if he had not also been a shrewd tactician. He made the most of situations as they arose: the Arusha Declaration package is a good example, or the sending-down of university students in 1966 when he subsequently admitted that he left them in disgrace for longer than necessary in order to make the maximum demonstration in the country as a whole. He sometimes acted very decisively, but often seemed to delay action, perhaps waiting for the right moment. He frequently compromised when he realized that he could not carry his close associates with him, and he usually dealt with those who opposed him, or transgressed in other ways, not by public disgrace but by quiet transfers from their posts; as President he had the power of patronage to appoint civil servants down to Assistant Director level, general managers of parastatals, judges, ambassadors, the deans of the university, and no doubt other posts; the danger was that those who said yes and mouthed slogans stayed in their posts rather too long, while others who had original contributions to make became unpopular and were removed. He also—deliberately or otherwise —produced new policies so frequently that it was difficult to judge whether the old ones were wrong, or merely taking time to settle down. One commentator elevated this to the level of a strategy of 'we must run while others walk' (Hyden 1975a), but, deliberate or not, it had the effect of making it difficult to criticize old policies, or new ones which obviously needed time to prove themselves one way or the other.

Thus not everything that Nyerere said or wrote survived for very long, or was accepted by many people, but most of the ideas which were adopted by the Tanzanian state derived from him. Ideology was internalized only if it was consistent with the interests, as they perceived them, of the bureaucracy. Examples where Nyerere's ideas were not internalized are the idea of small ujamaa villages free of government interference (1967 and 1968), pupil's involvement in decision-making in schools (1969), workers' participation in management (1969 and 1970), and power to elect village organizations (1972 and 1975). A particularly interesting example is the 1971 *Mwongozo* or TANU Guidelines which were not written by Nyerere, although he no doubt assisted in ensuring their acceptance by the Party. The *Mwongozo* was passed in a period of national self-searching which followed Idi Amin's *coup* in Uganda. Most of it was concerned with defence against attack from enemies outside, or within. Towards the end of the document there are clauses about the way of life that should be followed by leaders, and about the need to eliminate waste and corruption in the parastatals. These clauses were seized upon by the workers, and used to justify a series of industrial actions against managers who were arrogant towards workers or who misused parastatal property. Eventually the government intervened against the workers; it is a paradox of the *Mwongozo* that its longest-surviving consequences was not the clauses dealing with oppressive managers but the 'people's militia', intended as a sort of 'home guard' to protect the country against external aggression but actually used to enforce the 1973–5 villagization.

In Nyerere's ideology, the state is a unifying factor, the provider of good things for the masses, the bastion against capitalist domination from outside. This paternalism is fully consistent with Fabian thinking, and indeed with various versions of Leninism. But Nyerere has linked it with a view of the state similar to that found in papal encyclicals, which can be traced back to Aristotle and Thomas Aquinas, in which the state is expected to be just and fair to all people, distributing services and ensuring freedom and justice for the poor.[14] It is a small step from this to Nyerere's modernization theory, which rejects the past (as 'traditional') and inherited patterns of production (as destructive and backward, despite the evidence to the contrary). Ultimately this viewpoint is authoritarian and implies social engineering (or 'management' by the state apparatus) rather than democracy, although Nyerere himself does not take the logic that far, at least in his writing.

This view of the state illuminates much which otherwise appears contradictory in Tanzania. At the time of the Arusha Declaration, civil service and party leaders took cuts in their salaries, and accepted limitations on their freedom to accumulate—they were no longer allowed to own shares, private businesses, or property for rental. Subsequently their salaries were frozen and they accepted sharply progressive increases in income tax, so that top administrators became substantially worse off unless they could achieve regular promotions in their jobs. They accepted all this because they were persuaded that it was in their broader class interest (Von Freyhold 1977c: 87–9). The Arusha Declaration also meant a great increase in the power of officials, as new sectors of the economy were brought into state ownership. The tax increases were certainly not popular, but one part of the state apparatus (the Treasury) was committed to using every means open to it to raise revenue in order to finance the increases in state power in other sectors (agriculture and social services); even so, they could not avoid using deficit finance, and this was one of the causes of the price inflation which began in 1970. Nevertheless, the years after the Arusha Declaration witnessed a coherence of the bureaucracy in the face of adversity which would probably not have lasted as long as it did without the combination of egalitarianism and state ownership in the Arusha Declaration.[15]

Some observers have been unwise enough to claim that there is a 'progressive' group within the bureaucracy and party, of which the President is part. This is to misunderstand the position of the intellectual in a class society. It is normal for a few members of every class to have unorthodox ideas, or views that are not consistent with their class interests. Lecturers and students in universities are likely sources of ideas, but one should not associate intellectuals only with universities, or with 'educated' men and women. In this sense Nyerere is an intellectual, as are some members of the civil service and the party; they are tolerated, but only so long as they do not provide a threat to the interests of the ruling class, over a period of time.[16]

At the economic level, Nyerere's writing has sometimes obscured the issues. Talk of 'Tanzanian socialism', plus a denial that it can exist for many years to come, may serve as ideology to unite the country, but it does not provide a clear economic strategy. This is not to say that there was an easy alternative: the technical skills were absent, as was any clear articulation of what 'development' would mean. The result was a failure ruthlessly to pursue any single class interest (apart from the bureaucracy's interest in expanding the functions of the state). The worst results were in rural policy, a series of despairing dashes for freedom, with what seemed like short cuts actually leading further and further into the mud; similar ambiguities could be found in industrial policies, and in most other sectors, but their consequences were not so immediate as the food shortages and declines in the production of crops for export.

Can the future offer something better? On the basis of the performance of the 1970s, the answer is no. And yet there are elements in Tanzania's favour: the stability of the country, its openness to change and experimentation, the lack of entrenched interests (the power of the bureaucracy not withstanding), a slow recognition of the technical requirements for living standards to be raised.

The contradiction which has not been recognized is that of implementing a radical programme with a 'bureaucratic bourgeoisie'—the servants of the state (with an obvious interest in expanding its services) in the paradoxical position of controlling the state. If the ambiguities and compromises of the past are to be avoided, either a section of the bureaucracy will have to become a 'national bourgeoisie' and pursue a more ruthless capitalist accumulation,[17] or else the workers and the peasants will have to use Nyerere's ideology to take control of the state through democratic organizations, so that workers and peasants can produce for their own good, and innovate, experiment, and work for a better life in the long run.[18] By 1980 it was clear that Nyerere and the Tanzanian leadership would countenance neither alternative, and that the contradictions and stagnation of the 1970s were likely to continue.

NOTES

CHAPTER 1

[1] In. J. K. Nyerere, *Freedom and Socialism* (Oxford University Press, 1968), p. 235.
[2] *Education for Self-Reliance* and *Socialism and Rural Development* (1967), reprinted in *Freedom and Socialism*, pp. 267–90 and 337–66.
[3] J. K. Nyerere, *The Arusha Declaration Ten Years After* (1977), reprinted in A. C. Coulson (ed.), *African Socialism in Practice: the Tanzanian Experience* (Spokesman Books, 1979), pp. 43–71.
[4] In 1977 Nyerere reported that 13,065,000 people were living in 7684 villages (ibid., p. 65). But this exaggerates the numbers who moved, since those who lived in highland areas, some existing villages, or at the sites chosen for new villages did not have to move.

CHAPTER 2

[1] Morgan W. T. (ed.), *East Africa: Its Peoples and Resources* (Oxford University Press, Nairobi, 1968; 2nd edn. 1972), includes, among others, chapters on Peoples (by P. H. Gulliver), Physical Features (L. Berry), Soil (R. M. Scott), Climate (J. F. Griffiths), Natural Vegetation (C. G. Trapnell), Rangeland (J. R. Peberdy), and Agriculture and Land Tenure in Tanzania (A. Hammersley). See also W. Allan, *The African Husbandman* (Oliver and Boyd, 1965).
[2] In the sense of I. Wallerstein in *The Modern World-System: Capitalist Agriculture and the Origins of the European World-Economy in the Sixteenth Century* (Academic Press, 1974).
[3] This paragraph is based on A. Sheriff, 'The Rise of a Commercial Empire: an aspect of the economic history of Zanzibar 1770–1873' (unpublished Ph.D. thesis, London 1971).
[4] E. A. Brett, *Colonialism and Underdevelopment in East Africa* (Heinemann Educational Books, 1973), chapters 7 and 9.

CHAPTER 3

[1] For a brief discussion of the economic foundations of pre-colonial societies see J. Iliffe, *A Modern History of Tanganyika* (Cambridge University Press, 1979), pp. 13–17.
[2] For a sympathetic discussion of the economics of pastoralism see F. Kjaerby 'The Development of Agro-Pastoralism among the Barabaig in Hanang District', Research Paper No. 56, Bureau of Resource Assessment and Land Use Planning, University of Dar es Salaam, 1979.
[3] F. T. Masao, 'The Irrigation System in Uchagga: An Ethno-Historical Approach', *TNR* 75 (1974), 1–8. J. E. G. Sutton, 'Engaruka and its Waters', Seminar Paper, Department of History, University of Dar es Salaam, 20 Feb.

NOTES FOR PAGES 16–45

1973. Sutton dates the hey-day of Engaruka at 'somewhere betwen two and seven centuries ago'. The works were largely abandoned during the eighteenth century.

[4] Iliffe points out that 'early nineteenth century Tanganyika was not inhabited by discrete, compact and identifiable tribes' (op. cit. p. 8), and is reluctant to use the word 'tribe' to describe the military states formed by the warlords of the last half of the nineteenth century (pp. 52–66). These broke down during the German conquest so that, when the British attempt to establish 'indirect rule', frequently there was no well-defined tribal succession that they could use. Hence, in Iliffe's words, they 'created tribes' (pp. 318–25). See also J. D. Graham, 'Indirect Rule: the Establishment of "Chiefs" and "Tribes" in Cameron's Tanganyika', *Tanzania Notes and Records*, Nos. 77/8 (1976) pp. 1–9.

CHAPTER 4

[1] H. Neville Chittick, 'The East Coast, Madagascar and the Indian Ocean', in R. Oliver (ed.), *The Cambridge History of Africa*, Vol. 3 (Cambridge University Press, 1977), pp. 183–231, to which this and the following paragraphs are indebted.

[2] Sheriff's interpretation. The following paragraphs also draw heavily on his work.

CHAPTER 5

[1] The Maji Maji was not the end of armed resistance to the Germans; Marguerite Jellicoe ('The Turu Resistance Movement', *Tanzania Notes and Records* No. 70, 1969) describes a revolt in 1908 among the pastoral tribes around Singida.

[2] This position is associated with the work of John Ford (*The Role of the Trypanosomiases in Africa Ecology*, Oxford, 1971) and Helge Kjekshus (*Ecology Control and Economic Development in East African History*, Heinemann Educational Books, 1977). For a precise description of the mechanism by which the tsetse recolonized large areas see Kjaerby, op. cit., pp. 15–18.

CHAPTER 6

[1] Quoted by John Iliffe in *Tanganyika under German Rule* (Cambridge University Press, 1969), p. 91.

[2] This explanation and the following paragraph draw on a paper by D. Arnold ('External Factors and the Partition of East Africa', History Teachers' Conference, Morogoro, 1974, pp. 14–15 and 22 f.).

[3] Iliffe, *Tanganyika under German Rule*, pp. 57–63, 99–103, and *Agricultural Change in Modern Tanganyika* (East Africa Publishing House, 1971), pp. 12–27. The rest of this chapter draws heavily on these sources.

CHAPTER 7

[1] Sir Donald Cameron, 'Agriculture and Labour', 5 Aug. 1926, Tanzania National Archives 215/121/48, quoted in J. Iliffe, *Agricultural Change in modern Tanganyika*, p. 12.

[2] The Mandate is reproduced in full in V. Harlow and in E. Chilver (eds.), *History of East Africa, Vol. II* (Oxford University Press, 1965), pp. 690–5.

[3] The classic study of migrant labour in Tanzania was P. M. Gulliver, *Labour Migration in a Rural Economy*, East African Studies Paper No. 6 (East African Institute of Social Research, Kampala, 1955). See also J. Iliffe *Agricultural Change in Modern Tanganyika*, pp. 16–18.

[4] N. R. Fuggles-Couchman, 'Final Report on the Northern Provinces Wheat Scheme' (typescript, Rhodes House Library, Oxford, 1950), p. 1.

[5] For the Groundnuts Scheme see Overseas Food Corporation, *Annual Report and Statement of Accounts for the year ended 31 March 1955*, (HMSO, 1956); S. H. Frankel, 'The Kongwa Experiment: Lessons of the East African Groundnuts Scheme', in *The Economic Impact on Underdeveloped Countries* (Harvard University Press, 1953); and Alan Wood, *The Groundnut Affair* (Bodley Head, 1950).

CHAPTER 8

[1] A. G. Rwegoshora, 'The Bukoba Cooperative Union: A Success?', in G. Hyden (ed.), *Cooperatives in Tanzania* (Tanzania Publishing House, 1976), p. 75.

[2] The account of the KNPA is based mainly on Susan Rodgers, 'The Kilimanjaro Native Planters' Association: Administrative Responses to Chagga Initiatives in the 1920's', *Transafrican Journal of History* (Nairobi), Vol. IV, Nos. 1/2 (1974), pp. 94–114. See also J. Iliffe, 'The Age of Improvement and Differentiation' in I. Kimambo and J. Temu (eds.), *A History of Tanzania* (East African Publishing House, 1969), pp. 136–8, and Iliffe, *Agricultural Change in Modern Tanganyika*, p. 22.

[3] P. M. Redmond, 'The NMCMU and Tobacco Production in Songea', *Tanzania Notes and Records*, Nos. 79/80 (1976). Iliffe (*A Modern History . . .*, pp. 274–6) draws attention to other African crop-purchasing organizations of the early 1930s, but none of them appears to have been registered as a co-operative.

[4] Government of Tanganyika, *Report by His Majesty's Government . . . to the Council of the League of Nations on the Administration of Tanganyika Territory, 1937*, pp. 206–13.

[5] B. Bowles 'Colonial Control and Cooperatives in Tanganyika 1945–1952' (unpublished manuscript, 1979), p. 2. The argument which follows draws heavily on this paper.

[6] G. A. Maguire, *Towards Uhuru in Tanzania* (Cambridge University Press, 1969), pp. 83–99, on which the following paragraph is also based.

CHAPTER 9

[1] Governor MacMichael quoting a dispatch of 4 December. See Brett *Colonialism and Underdevelopment . . .*, 1973, p. 274.

[2] As described, for example, by W. Allan in *the African Husbandman* (Oliver and Boyd, 1965; reprinted by Greenwood Press,1977), which has sections explicitly on Tanzania on pp. 161–6, 171–5, 191–218; 302–7.

[3] The possible end-uses of raw materials available in Tanzania are discussed in G. Jones, *Technology and Self-Reliance in Tanzania* (forthcoming, Tanzania Publishing House).

[4] C. Leubuscher (*Tanganyika Territory: A Study of Economic Policy under Mandate* (Oxford University Press, 1944), pp. 103–4). The quotation is from the Bowring Committee report, reviewed in the *Report of the Kenya Tariff Committee, 1929*, p. 3.

[5] See Chapter 11.

[6] Tanganyika, Government of, *An Outline of Post-War Development Proposals* (1944) and *A Ten-Year Development and Welfare Plan for Tanganyika Territory* (1946). The main features of both can already be found in the *Report of the Central Development Committee* (1940).

[7] Brian Bowles points out the limitations of this process; much of the surplus

gained from agriculture in this period was invested in London, spent on high-priced British products when cheaper alternatives were available, or spent on consumer goods, especially food ('Export Crops and Underdevelopment 1929–1961', *Utafiti* (Dar es Salaam), Vol. 1, 1976, pp. 81–4).

[8] Tanganyika, Government of, *Annual Report of the Labour Department*, 1945 (p. 324) and 1955 (pp. 76–7).

CHAPTER 10

[1] John Iliffe described this as 'the age of improvement and differentiation' (the title of his article in Kimambo and Temu (eds.), *A History of Tanzania*).

[2] A slogan used by both Livingstone and Cardinal Lavingerie. See J. Cameron and W. A. Dodd, *Society, Schools and Progress in Tanzania* (Pergamon Press, 1970), p. 52.

[3] This and the next paragraph follow Roland Oliver *The Missionary Factor in East Africa*, 2nd Edition, (Longmans, 1965), pp. 50–65.

[4] Rivers-Smith writing to the Chief Secretary in 1925, quoted by Marjorie Mbilinyi, 'African Education in the British Colonial Period'. Revised (1975) version of a paper presented to the 1974 History Teachers' Conference, Morogoro, p. 7.

[5] The comparison between the *practice* of *Education for Self-Reliance* from 1967 on and the policies of the 1950s is even closer, as Mbilinyi has pointed out several times, e.g. in her paper 'Education for Rural Life or Education for Socialist Transformation?', East African Social Science Conference, Dar es Salaam, December 1973.

[6] Table 10.1.

[7] Judith Listowel gives evocative pictures of both Tabora Boys' and Tabora Girls' Schools in *The Making of Tanganyika* (Chatto and Windus, 1965), pp. 88–94.

[8] *The Annual Report of the Education Department*, 1924, included a report on 'Bukoba Central and District Schools' by W. B. Mumford (pp. 216–34). The quotation in the text is from p. 228. The attitude towards chiefs and educated Africans comes through clearly, e.g. referring to school prefects: 'Starting with the idea that most of the boys in the school would be Chiefs or Sultans in the future and that it would be advantageous to give them some training in "hearing cases in Court" and in government, a School Council was formed amongst the Chiefs. ... When observing these boys quietly pursuing their duties I feel that there is no doubt that the school holds great possibilities of influencing the future of the district. At present there seems little sign of the creation of the conceited clerical type or young political agitator.' (p. 231.)

[9] Cameron and Dodd, *Society, Schools and Progress . . .*, pp. 61, 72; Listowel *The Making of Tanganyika*, p. 114; *Report by his Majesty's Government . . . to the Council of the League of Nations on the Administration of Tanganyika Territory for the year 1934* (HMSO, 1935), Appendix V, p. 159.

[10] Nyerere today is more guarded than he was in 1962 when he said, 'If we want to develop, we have no choice but to bring both our way of living and our way of farming up to date. The hand-hoe will not bring us the things we need today' ('President's inaugural Address' in *Freedom and Unity*, p. 183). But most educated Tanzanians would accept this view unhesitatingly, and it appears frequently in the newspapers (e.g. *The Daily News* editorial of 22 Oct. 1975). At best it is a half-truth, ignoring the contribution of the hoe to production of tea, coffee, vegetables, etc. At worst it implies an attitude of mind in which fertilizers and tractors (rather than people who have to be motivated to work hard and intelligently) are seen as the keys to increased agricultural productivity.

CHAPTER 11

[1] Article 2 of the Covenant with the League of Nations, reproduced in V. Harlow and E. Chilver (eds.), *History of East Africa*, Vol. II (Oxford University Press, 1965), pp. 690–5.

[2] 'Indirect rule' is identified with Lord Lugard and his rule in Nigeria 1898–1906 and 1912–19, although its roots can be traced back to British administration in India in the eighteenth century. Lugard's philosophy was propagated through his book *The Dual Mandate in British Tropical Africa* Wm. Blackwood and Sons, 1921; 4th edition 1929; 5th edition, Frank Cass and Co., 1965).

[3] W. Morris-Hale, 'British Administration in Tanganyika from 1920 to 1945' (Ph.D. thesis, University of Geneva, 1969), p. 284, quoted by M. Mbilinyi in her revised (1975) paper for the 1974 History Teachers' Conference at Morogoro entitled 'African Education in the British Colonial Period', p. 18.

[4] Quoted by Morris-Hale (ibid, p. 265), in Mbilinyi op. cit., p. 5.

CHAPTER 12

[1] Lord Hailey, *Native Administration and Political Development in British Tropical Africa* (HMSO 1942), pp. 253 and 10.

[2] This argument, as much else in this chapter, derives from Iliffe, *A Modern History*... p. 381f.

[3] John Iliffe, 'The Spokesman: Martin Kayamba', in Iliffe (ed.), *Modern Tanzanians: A Volume of Biographies* (East African Publishing House, 1973), pp. 66–94, on which this and the following three paragraphs are based.

[4] Martin Kayamba, *African Problems*, Africa's Own Library, No. 18 (Lutterworth Press, 1948).

[5] This account summarizes Iliffe in 'The Age of Improvement...' (1969) pp. 147–9.

[6] This and the following four paragraphs are based on Iliffe 'A History of the Dockworkers of Dar es Salaam', *Tanzania Notes and Records*, No. 71 (1970), pp. 119–48.

[7] This point of view was also expressed very strongly by the *East African Royal Commission 1935–5* (HMSO, 1955).

[8] Iliffe 'A History of the Dockworkers...', p. 138–47; W. H. Friedland (*Vuta Kamba: The Development of Trade Unions in Tanganyika,* Hoover Institution Publication 84, Stanford Institution Press, 1969, p. 195) describes a 'trade union entrepreneur' who in 1960 resigned a well-paid civil service post to become a union official. His 'salary' was the promise of 25 shillings a month from each of eight friends.

[9] For an argument to the effect that the three East African states after their independence depended on merchant capital (and hence the exploitation of the peasantry) see A. C. Coulson, 'Contradictions of Merchant Capital in East Africa' (East African Social Science Conference, Nairobi, 1975). Compare C. Leys, *Underdevelopment in Kenya* (Heinemann Educational Books, 1975), pp. 154–9, and Gavin Kitching *Class and Economic Change in Kenya: The Making of an African Petite-Bourgeoisie*(Yale University Press, 1980), pp. 413f.

CHAPTER 13

[1] J. K. Nyerere, Introduction to *Freedom and Unity* (1966); p. 1.

[2] United Nations Trusteeship Council, Visiting Missions to Trust Territories in East Africa, *Report on Tanganyika together with Related Documents*, 1948, 1952, 1955, 1958, 1960. For the ineffectiveness of the Permanent Mandates Commission see Chapter 9 and 11 above.

[3] Sources for the Meru Land Case are Listowel, *The Making of Tanganyika*,

pp. 209–17; K. Japhet and E. Seaton, *The Meru Land Case* (East African Publishing House, 1967); A. Nelson, *The Freeman of Meru* (Oxford University Press, 1967), pp. 13–88.

⁴ See Note 3.

⁵ Quoted in Iliffe 'The Age of Improvement...', p. 153.

⁶ In August 1948 the African Association expelled its Zanzibar branch for passing confidental information to the colonial authorities and renamed itself the Tanganyika Africa Association (TAA). It retained this name until 1954, when it was reformed as the party, TANU.

⁷ There is no adequate biography of Nyerere; but see W. Edgett Smith, *Nyerere of Tanzania* (Gollancz, 1973), J. C. Hatch, *Two African Statesmen: Kaunda of Zambia and Nyerere of Tanzania* (Secker and Warburg, 1976), W. R. Duggan and J. R. Civille, *Tanzania and Nyerere: A Study of Ujamaa and Nationhood* (Orbis Books, 1976), and Listowel, *The Making of Tanganyika*.

⁸ Government of Tanganyika, *Annual Report on Cooperative Development*, 1959, p. 4.

⁹ For Rashidi Kawawa's early career see Listowel, *The Making of Tanganyika*, pp. 234–6.

¹⁰ Including a National Union of Dockworkers and two 'general' unions for workers who did not fit into craft unions.

CHAPTER 14

¹ R. C. Pratt, *The Critical Phase in Tanzania 1945–1968: Nyerere and the Emergence of a Socialist Strategy* (Cambridge University Press, 1976), p. 58. This chapter is indebted to Pratt, especially his Chapter 3 (pp. 43–59), and to Listowel *The Making of Tanganyika*, pp. 334–90.

² See Chapters 8 and 11.

³ International Bank for Reconstruction and Development (World Bank), *The Economic Development of Tanganyika* (Johns Hopkins University Press, 1961).

⁴ Arthur D. Little, Inc., *Tanganyika Industrial Development*, (Government Printer, Dar es Salaam, 1961). Extracts from this and from most of the other reports quoted below may be found in Hadley E. Smith (ed.), *Readings on Economic Development and Administration in Tanzania* (Oxford University Press, 1966).

⁵ The implementation of these policies in considered in Chapter 17.

⁶ Government of Tanganyika, *Development Plan for Tanganyika 1961/2 to 1963/4* (Government Printer, 1961).

⁷ The report was reprinted as H. C. G. Hawkins, *A Survey of Wholesale and Retail Trade in Tanganyika* (Praegar, 1965).

⁸ *Report of the Tanganyika Salaries Commission, 1961* (Chairman A. L. Adu); J. L. Thurston, 'Human Resources and Manpower Planning in Tanganyika' (mimeo, Ministry of Finance, 1960; J. D. Kingsley and J. L. Thurston, 'Some Problems associated with Localisation of the Tanganyikan Civil Service' (mimeo, Ministry of Finance, 1961); see Pratt, *op. cit.* pp. 105–8.

⁹ *East Africa: Report of the Economic and Fiscal Commission* ('The Raisman Commission'), (HMSO, 1961).

CHAPTER 15

¹ The first schools were for freed slaves. There was a small French (Catholic) school in 1862. Kiungani School, which eventually took pupils from Universities Mission to Central Africa primary schools all over East Africa, opened in 1869 (N. R. Bennett *A History of the Arab State of Zanzibar* (Methuen 1978), pp. 83–4, 113–5).

² E. Batson, *The Social Survey of Zanzibar* (Department of Social Studies, University of Capetown, n.d. (1949?), 21 volumes). The survey had been planned before the strike; see M. Lofchie *Zanzibar: Background to Revolution* (Princeton, 1965), pp. 85–93.

³ Lofchie, Chapter VI. The term 'Shirazi' refers to the original inhabitants of the islands, who claimed to have come, at some point in the past, from Shiraz Iran. From the start, therefore, the ASU was an uneasy alliance between mainland Africans on Zanzibar and Shirazis (including many clove growers) on Pemba.

⁴ B. Bowles 'The Political Economy of Zanzibar' (History Teachers' Conference, Morogoro, 1976), pp. 24–5. See also footnote 3.

⁵ Okello's story is told in his autobiography, *Revolution in Zanzibar* (East African Publishing House, 1967) written with support from John Nottingham.

⁶ See also Chapter 16.

CHAPTER 16

¹ From the speech 'Dissolving the Independence Parliament', 8 June 1965, reprinted in *Freedom and Socialism*, p. 48.

² From the editorial note introducing the resignation speech in *Freedom and Unity*, p. 157.

³ He also worked on the draft of *Democracy and the Party System*, published in January 1963.

⁴ The offices of Provincial Commissioner and District Commissioner were also abolished. The new Regional and Area Commissioners took over some of their powers, but overall more power was now held at Ministry headquarters in Dar es Salaam.

⁵ This change did not receive much publicity at the time, but in 1971 Nyerere described it as 'land nationalization' and claimed that 'By this Act of Parliament, and without any fanfare, Tanganyika achieved a basic socialist objective which more aggressive socialist parties elsewhere in the world had almost given up advocating because of its difficulty' (*Ten Years After Independence*, reprinted in *Freedom and Development*, p. 273).

⁶ Nyerere *Democracy and the Party System* (1963), reprinted in *Freedom and Unity*, pp. 195–203 (see especially p. 202). See also L. Cliffe (ed.) *One Party Democracy* (East African Publishing House, 1967), and Pratt *The Critical Phase*, p. 207.

⁷ Tordoff *Government and Politics in Tanzania* (East African Publishing House, 1967), pp. 147–8, 156–8. At least half of the unions' funds were to be spent on social services or productive investments.

⁸ Relations with Britain were further clouded by the stipulation imposed as part of the independence settlement, that Tanzania should be responsible for payment of pensions to British officers who served the colonial government before independence (Cmnd. 1813 of August 1962). When diplomatic relations were broken, Tanzania also stopped paying the pensions; the matter was not resolved till 1976 (Cmnd. 6949, ratified in October 1977), and it was only then that relations were normalized.

CHAPTER 17

¹ Reprinted in J. K. Nyerere *Freedom and Socialism* (1968), p. 342.

² The 1960 Lancaster House Conference, concerned with the future of Kenya, affected the morale of settlers in other parts of East Africa as well. This figure is based on estimates in J. Loxley, 'Structural Change in the Monetary

System of Tanzania' in L. Cliffe and J. Saul (eds.), *Socialism in Tanzania*, vol. 2, 1973, p. 104.

[3] From the speech 'National Property' reprinted in *Freedom and Unity* (1966), pp. 55–6.

[4] Figures from the Tanganyika Sisal Marketing Board monthly labour returns quoted by J. Rweyemamu in his paper 'Some Aspects of the Turner Report' (Paper 69.20, Economic Research Bureau, University of Dar es Salaam, 1969) p. 1, where he shows that the decline in over-all Tanzanian wage employment in the 1960s was associated more with this fall in sisal prices than with the wage rises of 1962 and 1964.

[5] Tanganyika, Government of, *The Tanganyika Five Year Plan for Social and Economic Development, July 1964–June 1969*, Vol. 1, pp. ix and 14.

[6] International Bank for Reconstruction and Development *The Economic Development of Tanganyika*, pp. 5–6; *Tanganyika Five Year Plan*, Vol. 1, pp. 14–15.

[7] *Tanganyika Five Year Plan*, vol. 1, pp. 14–15, 21, 91.

[8] They were also utopian in that they did not allow for the fact that prosperity would require integrated industrial and agricultural change.

[9] United Republic of Tanzania, *Report of the Presidential Special Committee of Enquiry into Cooperative Movement and Marketing Board* (Government Printer, Dar es Salaam, 1966), p. 5.

[10] Ibid, pp. 10, 11.

[11] S. Migot-Adholla, 'The Politics of a Growers' Cooperative Organisation' in L. Cliffe *et al.* (eds.), *Rural Cooperation in Tanzania* (Tanzania Publishing House, 1975), *passim*. The Kilimanjaro, Nyanza (Victoria Federation), and Bukoba unions were more organized than the others, and acted as a focus for local investment. They were, nevertheless, still involved in questionable practices, as Migot-Adholla makes clear.

[12] *Tanganyika Five Year Plan* Vol. 1 (1964), p. 19; *Tanzania Second Five Year Plan*, Vol. 1 (1969), pp. 38–9; *Tanzania Third Five Year Plan*, Vol. 1, p. 21.

[13] In the report of an election speech *The Daily News* (Dar es Salaam), 21 Oct. 1975.

[14] Its functions were transferred to a new Ministry of Local Government and Rural Development; a separate department continued till Decentralization in 1972.

[15] Tanzania, United Republic of, *Background to the Budget: An Economic Survey 1967/8*, 1967, p. 64; I. Livingstone, 'Production, Price and Marketing Policy for Staple Foodstuffs in Tanzania', Paper 70.1, Economic Research Bureau, University of Dar es Salaam, 1970, p. 10.

[16] The evidence is summarized by J. Sender 'Some Preliminary Notes on the Political Economy of Rural Development in Tanzania', Paper 74.5, Economic Research Bureau, University of Dar es Salaam, 1974, pp. 2–17.

[17] A. Awiti, 'Ismani and the Rise of Capitalism', in Cliffe *et al.*, (eds.), *Rural Cooperation in Tanzania* (Tanzania Publishing House, 1975), pp. 51–78 and Table V (with figures in acres converted to hectares on the basis of one hectare to 2½ acres); R. Feldman, 'Custom and Capitalism: A Study of Land Tenure in Ismani', Paper 71.14, Economic Research Bureau, University of Dar es Salaam, 1971. All the farmers involved were African.

[18] For a similar story in the near-by Hanang area, see F. Kjaerby 'The Development of Agro-pastoralism...', pp. 31–3.

[19] K. Malima's econometric analysis ('The Determinants of Cotton Supply', in K. S. Kim, R. Mabele, and M. Schultheis (eds.), *Papers on the Political Econ-*

340 NOTES FOR PAGES 168-178

omy of Tanzania, Heinemann Educational Books, 1979) failed to find any strong correlations.

CHAPTER 18

[1] *Annual Report of the Labour Department for 1963*, Appendix II, Table 7, p. 52.

[2] For details see N. Swainson, *The Development of Corporate Capitalism in Kenya 1918-1977* (Heinemann Educational Books, 1980); R. Kaplinsky (ed.), *Readings on the Multinational Corporation in Kenya* (Oxford University Press, 1978); C. Leys, *Underdevelopment in Kenya* (Heinemann Educational Books, 1972) and 'Capital Accumulation, Class Formation and Dependency', in *The Socialist Register 1978* (Merlin Press, 1978), pp. 241-66.

[3] Swainson, op. cit., pp. 273-84; A. Seidman, *Comparative Development Strategies in East Africa* (East African Publishing House, 1972), pp. 33-6, 49-52. C. Barker and D. Wield ('Notes on International Firms in Tanzania', *Utafiti*, Vol. 3 No. 2, 1977, pp. 316-41) give the ownership of 234 Tanzanian companies and include a chart (Appendix 1) showing the interrelationships between 23 Tanzanian companies owned by Lonrho in about 1974. Lonrho's assets in Tanzania were nationalized in 1978.

[4] 'Tiper Refinery', *Jenga* (Dar es Salaam), No. 8 (1971) pp. 23-7.

[5] J. C. Ramaer, 'The Choice of Appropriate Technology in a Multinational Corporation: A Case Study of Messrs. Philips, Eindhoven', in E. A. G. Robinson (ed.), *Appropriate Technology for Third World Development* (Macmillan, 1979), p. 245; C. Barker, M. Bhagavan, R. von Mitschke-Collande, and D. Wield, 'Industrial Production and Transfer of Technology in Tanzania: The Political Economy of Tanzanian Industrial Enterprises' (Mimeo, Institute of Development Studies, University of Dar es Salaam, 1976), Ch. III.1, p. 26.

[6] Barker *et al.*, Ch. IV, p. 3, See also Chapter 23 below.

CHAPTER 19

[1] From the note introducing the Declaration when it was republished in *Freedom and Development* (1968). The Declaration had earlier appeared as pamphlets in English and Swahili (Government Printer, 1967). Quotations here are from the 1968 edition.

[2] Ibid., pp. 231-2.

[3] Ibid., pp. 233-5.

[4] See Pratt, *op. cit.* p. 228. A commitment to democracy (or its absence) will, in the long term, determine the success of socialism. For if democracy is not enshrined, there is nothing to prevent a minority gaining control of the state and its institutions and using socialist slogans to impose its policies in the name of the workers and peasants. Socialists who truly serve the masses need not fear democracy, and can only benefit from having to explain their actions in comprehensible terms to the masses. Socialist parties in the Soviet Union and Eastern Europe, and socialist intellectuals in Western Europe committed to social engineering, have been equally reluctant to accept this logic, and have thereby made it possible for 'socialists' to gain power and subsequently not pursue the interests of the working classes.

[5] pp. 235-48.

[6] p. 249.

[7] p. 249.

[8] These points were clarified a week after the Arusha Declaration in an article 'Public Ownership in Tanzania', reprinted in *Freedom and Socialism*, pp. 251-6. See especially pp. 252-3.

[9] Reprinted in *Freedom and Socialism*, pp. 267–90.

[10] Ibid. pp. 337–66.

[11] In the 1960s the capitalist business community no longer saw governments as necessarily antagonistic, and accepted the necessity for various forms of government involvement. The ideologist of this convergence of interests was John Kenneth Galbraith (*The New Industrial State*, Penguin, 1967). The readiness to accept partnership with parastatals in underdeveloped countries was consistent with this philosophy.

[12] This figure is based on E. Clark, (*Socialist Development and Public Investment in Tanzania*, University of Toronto Press, 1978, Table 30, p. 107), but the figure is not unambiguous, as his footnote 3 makes clear.

[13] This nationalization cost approximately 250 million shillings (paid in local currency) and struck at the heart of the Asian commercial community, which had invested much of its profit in property. See Clark, op. cit., p. 107, and I. Shivji *Class Struggles in Tanzania*, (Heinemann Educational Books and Tanzania Publishing House, 1975), pp. 80–2.

[14] This was a bold step, since the co-operative unions had been one of the three pillars of the pre-independence nationalist movement, and retained popularity among some of the better-off farmers who profited from their dispensations of patronage (including educational scholarships). On the other hand, by 1976 all the co-operative unions were heavily in debt, and the marketing service they offered, on which every farmer depended, had deteriorated to unacceptable levels in most areas. It was clear, however, that the long-term success of this nationalization would depend on whether the parastatals that replaced the unions could improve these services.

[15] This interpretation is influenced by Pratt, op. cit. pp. 227–37.

[16] D. R. Morrison, *Education and Politics in Africa: The Tanzanian Case* (Hurst and Co, 1976), pp. 237–48; Edgett Smith, op. cit. p. 27. See further Chapter 21 below, Appendix 1 (on the University of Dar es Salaam).

[17] H. Bienen *Tanzania: Party Transformation and Economic Development* (Princeton University Press, 2nd edn., 1970, pp. 209–10). Babu's journalism ceased when he was arrested following the assassination of Vice-President Karume in 1972, but recommenced after his release in 1977.

CHAPTER 20

[1] Nyerere, *The Arusha Declaration Ten Years After*, reprinted in Coulson (ed.), *African Socialism in Practice* (1979), p. 32.

[2] This is the weakness of GDP as a measure stressed in much recent writing, for example, Dudley Seers, 'What Are We Trying Measure?', *Journal of Development Studies*, Vol. 8 No. 3 (1972). For an attempt to improve on it directly see G. Pyatt and A. Roe *et al.*, *Social Accounting for Development Planning* (Cambridge University Pres, 1977), Chapters 4–6.

[3] The implausibility of the official production figures has been pointed out by Frank Ellis ('Agricultural Pricing Policy in Tanzania 1970–1979: Implications for Agricultural Output, Rural Incomes, and Crop Marketing Costs' (Seminar on Development, Employment and Equity Issues, University of Dar es Salaam, 21–25 July 1980), p. 24.

[4] Strictly GMP should include those parts of the service sectors without which production could not occur. But official statistics, as in Tanzania, frequently do not distinguish between water and electricity provision to factories (part of GMP) and to private consumers (not part of GMP), or between transport associated with production and other types of transport. The figures for GMP in Tables 20.3 and 20.4 are therefore underestimates, but their growth rates should be approximately correct.

[5] The stagnation or decline in agricultural production continued to the end of the 1970s. See Ellis *op. cit.*, Appendix B, Table 1, and Chapter 22 of this book.

[6] *Annual Manpower Report to the President* (1974), Appendix 3, Table 2, p. 9.

[7] *Background to the Budget: An Economic Survey 1967–8*, pp. 16, 81, 85.

[8] But see *The Gross Domestic Product of the Protectorate of Zanzibar 1957–1961*, East African Statistical Department, 1963 (an extract is reprinted in H. Smith (ed.) *Readings on Economic Development and Administration in Tanzania*, Oxford University Press, 1966, pp. 66–79).

[9] The interpretation of this paragraph derives from A. D. Adamson and S. R. Robbins, *The Market for Cloves and Clove Products in the United Kingdom*, Publication G 93, Tropical Products Institute, London, 1975).

[10] *The Economic Survey 1977–8*, Table 15C, p. 28.

[11] *Background to the Budget: An Economic Survey 1967–8*, pp. 107–10, especially Tables 87 and 88.

CHAPTER 21

[1] R. H. Sabot, *Economic Development and Urban Migration: Tanzania 1900–1971* (Oxford University Press, 1979), Ch. IV; H. Bernstein—personal communication.

[2] This figure is derived from the rate of expansion of the GDP figure (at constant prices) for 'Public Administration and Other Services'.

[3] For a discussion of manpower planning in Tanzania see International Labour Office, *Towards Self-Reliance: Development, Employment and Equity Issues in Tanzania* (Jobs and Skills Programme for Africa, 1978) pp. 235–50.

[4] This suspicion lessened towards the end of the 1970s, and an increasing number of graduates left the public sector to join foreign-owned companies or to start their own businesses.

[5] As Professor Gottleib ('The Extent and Characterisation of Differentiation in Tanzanian Agricultural and Rural Society', *African Review*, Vol. III No. 2 (1973), pp. 241–62) pointed out, although his figures almost certainly underestimate the total.

[6] Traditional religion and the impact of the Muslim and Christian religions are treated at length in Iliffe *A Modern History* ... (1979).

[7] On the role of women and family see D.F. Bryceson and M. Mbilinyi 'The Changing Role of Tanzanian Women in Production: From Peasants to Proletarians' (Conference on Women and the Process of Development, University of Sussex, 1978). An earlier paper is M. Mbilinyi 'The "New Woman" and Traditional Norms in Tanzania', *Journal of Modern African Studies*, Vol. 10, 1972.

[8] The crude birth-rate in 1973 was 48 per thousand, and total fertility 6.6 (P. S. Maro and W. I. Mlay 'People, Population Distribution and Employment', *Tanzania and Notes and Records* No. 83, 1978, Table V, p. 4).

[9] 'Child-spacing clinics' were at first operated by the Family Planning Association of Tanzania (UMATI); in 1975 the Ministry of Health began a Maternal and Child Health Service in which family planning advice was an integral part.

[10] There were exceptions to this, and in particular UWT fought hard and successfully to ensure that the provisions for maternity leave were extended to unmarried women.

[11] *The Law of Marriage Act, 1971*, Act No. 5 of 1971.

[12] A game played with stones placed in four rows of holes. National *bao* championships were held intermittently.

[13] 'The new "Standard" will give general support to the policies of the Tanza-

nian Government, but . . . will be free to criticise any particular acts of individual Tanu or Government leaders, and to publicise any failures in the community, by whomever they are committed. It will be free to criticise the implementation of agreed policies, either on its own initiative or following upon complaints or suggestions from its readers.' President Nyerere, *The Standard*, 5 Feb. 1970, p. 1.

[14] Possible exceptions to this generalization are the plays of Abdullah Hussein (including *Kinjitekele*), the satirical novel *A People's Batchelor* by Austin Bukenya (East African Publishing House, 1972), and the short novel *The Wicked Walk* by W. E. Mkufya (Tanzanian Publishing House, 1977).

[15] The relevant statistics were compiled by the Tanzania Food and Nutrition Centre in their 'Data Report on the Food and Nutrition Situation in Tanzania 1972/3—1976/7', mimeo, March 1978.

[16] The point had been made forcibly some years earlier in a report by Professor Richard Titmuss and others, *The Health Services of Tanganyika: A Report to the Government* (Pitman Medical Publishing Co., 1964).

[17] Until in 1979 the British government agreed to build a fourth consultant hospital, in the south of the country.

[18] The slogan of the War on Want campaign that publicized these consequences of multinational promotional activity. See also *The New Internationalist* (Wallingford), No. 6(Aug. 1973). It should, however, be pointed out that the promotion of baby foods was less intensive in Tanzania than in some other African countries, and that a proportion of the baby-milk powder sold was used for adult consumption in the absence of other forms of milk.

[19] The design of these houses, involving a central corridor with rooms on each side with kitchen and ablutions in a courtyard at the back, enabled individual rooms to be let separately. In the early 1970s the NHC was not prepared to admit that multi-occupancy was a relevant consideration, and this design was discontinued.

[20] Jill Wells—personal communication.

[21] Marjorie Mbilinyi has elaborated this point in a series of papers, including 'Peasants' Education in Tanzania', *African Review*, Vol. VI No. 1 (1976); 'Basic Education: Tool of Exploitation or Liberation?', Research Report No. 21, Bureau of Resource Assessment and Land Use Planning, University of Dar es Salaam, 1977; and 'The Arusha Declaration and Education for Self-Reliance' in Coulson (ed.), *African Socialism* . . . , pp. 271–27. An earlier critique of *Education for Self-Reliance* was K. Hirji, 'School, Education and Under-development in Tanzania', *Maji Maji*, No. 12 (1973), p. 1–22.

[22] *Economic Survey 1970–1*, p. 112.

[23] Ibid., p. 113.

[24] This was achieved with some use of force or threats of force against parents who did not wish their children to go to school (see D. Williams 'Authoritarian Legal Systems and the Process of Capitalist Accumulation in Africa', Paper for the Southern Africa Social Sciences Conference, Dar es Salaam, 1979, p. 4).

[25] Not all the information was actually useful; there was a real danger, especially in agriculture, of giving over-simplified advice which would not be valid in all situations.

[26] See the special issue of *Geografiska Annaler* (Uppsala) on 'Soil Erosion and Sedimentation in Tanzania', 54. 3–4 (1972), including articles by P. Temple, A. Rapp, L. Berry, V. Axelsson, D. Murray-Rust, and J. Watson.

[27] *The Third Five-Year Plan* (1978) laid more stress on shallow wells and small dams, but even so budgeted to spend nearly 5.5 per cent of the total plan investment on water development (pp. 10 and 65).

[28] Maintenance remained a problem, however, and even a World Bank financed maintenance unit had difficulty keeping up with the deterioration of the surfaces.
[29] Little has been published on transport. But see R. Hofmeir *Transport and Economic Development in Tanzania* (Munich: Weltforum Verlag, 1973), and K. Hirji 'Political Economy of Transport', *Maji Maji*, No. 32 (1978), pp. 32–40.
[30] H. Chase 'The Zanzibar Treason Trial', *Review of African Political Economy*, No. 6 (1976), pp. 19–33; *The Daily News*, 26 and 27 October 1976; 'Nyerere Releases Death Cell Detainees', *The Guardian* (London), 27 April 1978.

CHAPTER 21, APPENDIX 1.

[1] From Nyerere's speech reprinted in *Freedom and Unity*, p. 307.
[2] See also Chapter 19.
[3] The paper was later republished by the Tanzania Publishing House, along with some comments on it (I. Shivji, *The Silent Class Struggle*, 1972) and reprinted in Cliffe and Saul (eds.), *Socialism in Tanzania*, Vol. 2 (1973), pp. 304–30.
[4] Rodney returned to Guyana in 1973 and helped to found a political party, the Working People's Alliance. He was assassinated in June 1980.
[5] For a critique of this viewpoint see John Saul's review of this book 'Nationalism, Socialism and Tanzanian History' reprinted in Cliffe and Saul (eds.) *Socialism in Tanzania*, Vol. 1 (1972), pp. 65–75.
[6] See Saul 'High Level Manpower for Socialism', pp. 280–81 for an account written as early as 1968.
[7] The student's manifesto, and a short explanation produced after the demonstration were reproduced in a 'briefing' in the *Review of African Political Economy*, No. 10 (1978), pp. 101–5.

CHAPTER 22

[1] Nyerere has often extended the scope of the Swahili language by using new words.
[2] Nyerere remained in touch with the Fabian Colonial Bureau well after independence.
[3] Little is known about the 'spontaneous' schemes. There is a brief discussion by L. Cliffe and S. Cunningham in a paper ('Ideology, Organisation and the Settlement Experience in Tanzania') in Cliffe and Saul (eds.), *Socialism in Tanzania*, Vol. 2(1973), pp. 132, 137–9.
[4] ʹⁿ Freyhold's study *Ujamaa Villages in Tanzania: Analysis of a Social Experiment* (Heinemann Education Books, 1979) argues that ujamaa could have succeeded, givem sympathetic responses by central government.
[5] This figure underestimates the number, since many practising villages were not recognized by the government for various reasons (M. von Freyhold—personal communication).
[6] M. von Freyhold dedicated her book *Ujamaa Villages in Tanzania*...to John Ngairo of the Ruvuma Development Association and Bernardo Kilonzo of Mbambara 'whose personal tragedy was part of the history of *Ujamaa*'.
[7] Von Freyhold, *Ujamaa Villages in Tanzania* and Sender 'Some Preliminary Notes...' Three other village reports were not included in the published version of von Freyhold's book.
[8] An unpublished typescript by Marja-Liisa Swantz.
[9] Villagers in Mtwara had an additional incentive to live in villages—to provide defence in case of incursions by the Portuguese army who were fighting FRELIMO guerrillas in nearby Mozambique.

[10] Tanganyika African National Union, *Siasa ni Kilimo* (Politics is Agriculture), policy paper, Government Printer, 1972. There is no official English translation.

[11] Militia groups are led by professional soldiers and keep their weapons in army stores. It is ironic that the militia should be the most outwardly visible manifestation of the 1971 *Mwongozo*, a Declaration which stressed the need for democractic control of the Party and the parastatals (English translation in Coulson (ed.), *African Socialism* . . . , pp. 36–42).

[12] Marja-Liisa Swantz, unpublished typescript.

[13] The officials referred to here, Divisional Secretaries (*Katibu Tarafa*) and Ward Secretaries (*Katibu Kata*) were officials both of Party and of Government, in the same sense as Regional Commissioners at Regional Level and Area Commissioners in the Districts.

[14] In the late 1960s and 1970s McKinsey and Company Inc., the American management consultancy, saw the potential for work in state corporations. In Britain alone they were involved with reforming the structure of local government, reorganization of the National Health Service, the British Steel Corporation, the BBC, the Bank of England, and many lesser public authorities. Tanzania became a training ground for some of the staff used on these contracts. The first Tanzanian consultancy was for the National Development Corporation (1968), discussed in Chapter 23. Then followed the State Trading Corporation (discussed in the Appendix to that chapter). Their last big Tanzanian contract was for the 'decentralization'; it involved separate consultancies for each central government ministry as well as the newly strengthened regions. Their work was eventually terminated when it became apparent that it was potentially never-ending.

[15] Nyerere continued to argue this way, e.g. in *The Arusha Declaration Ten Years After* (1977).

[16] Hence the title of her 1975 article, 'Ujamaa: African Socialist Productionism . . .'

[17] A useful discussion of the potential economies of scale in communal production is in von Freyhold *Ujamaa Villages* . . . , pp. 22–8.

[18] As late as October 1978 only one village in the country had been registered in this second stage (*The Daily News*, Regional Round-Up, 20 Oct. 1978).

[19] As René Dumont realized on his visit in 1979. See also United Republic of Tanzania, 'The Threat of Desertification in Central Tanzania', background paper (prepared by H. A. Fosbrooke) for the United Nations Conference on Desertification, August–September 1977.

[20] Swantz, unpublished typescript.

[21] Cholera reached East Africa for the first time in 1976.

[22] There were reasonable rainfulls in March 1974 in most parts of the country other than Arusha, Moshi, and Tanga Regions. See *The Daily News*, 2 Apr. 1974 ('Take Advantage of Rain—Plea') and 3 April 1974 ('Central Areas get Most Rain').

APPENDIX TO CHAPTER 22

[1] This appendix is a shortened version of a paper by A. Coulson, 'The Ruvuma Development Association 1961–1969', which will appear in H. Bernstein and D. Bryceson (eds.), *The Agrarian Question in Tanzania* (forthcoming), which in turn draws heavily on an unpublished typescript by Ralph Ibbott. Unless otherwise indicated, all quotations are from this typescript.

[2] B. Egero and R. Henin (eds.), *The Population of Tanzania: An Analysis of the 1967 Population Census*, Census Volume VI, Bureau of Resource Assessment

and Land Use Planning, University of Dar es Salaam and Bureau of Statistics, 1973, Table 11.3, p. 181.

CHAPTER 23

[1] C. D. Msuya, MP, Minister of Finance, 'Proliferation of Public Institutions in Tanzania: its Impact on the Economy'. Speech to the Economic Society of Tanzania, 22 February 1974, mimeo, p. 12.

[2] In Tanzanian official statistics a parastatal is defined as a corporation in which the State owns a majority of the shares. Ed. Clark in *Socialist Development and Public Investment in Tanzania* (University of Toronto Press, 1978) rightly extends the definition to include smaller shareholdings.

[3] The other investment bank, Investment Promotion Services (Tanzania), was controlled by the Aga Khan. By 1971 it had 15 investments, mostly for medium-sized industries owned by members of the Ismailia community. (C. Barker and D. Wield, 'Notes on International Firms in Tanzania', *Utafiti*, 3.2 (1978), p. 338).

[4] See Chapters 22 and 24.

[5] Its shareholders were the Commonwealth Development Corporation (British), Deutsche Gesellschaft für Wirtschaftliche Zusammenarbeit (West German), Nederlandse Overzeese Financierings-Maatschappij (of the Netherlands), and NDC.

[6] For notes on McKinsey's Tanzanian consultancies see Chapter 22, fn. 14. Reg Green comments: 'Tanzania's NDC under George Kahama had a clear revealed preference for maximizing group size and the scope of new ventures and a very low one indeed for raising internally generated group cash flow.' ('Public Directly Productive Units/Sectors in Africa and Political Economy', typescript n.d. (?1975), p. 13.)

[7] Turnkey projects and management agreements can prove very expensive if the holding company concerned is short of expertise. They are also obviously vulnerable to corruption. See below.

[8] For a study of the agricultural parastatal see P. Packard 'Corporate Structure in Agriculture...: A Study of the National Agricultural and Food Corporation', in Coulson (ed.) *African Socialism...*, pp. 200–13. For the construction parastatal see Appendix 2 to this chapter. Research on investment in tourism is being conducted by S. C. Curry at the University of Bradford.

[9] For example an automatic car-washing machine was imported, and electronic control equipment in new grain mills and the automated bakery. There was nothing that could be called a 'technology policy'.

[10] The 1977 World Bank mission recommended dismantling many of the controls, but their advice was contradicted by 1978 ILO Mission which produced the report *Towards Self-Reliance: Development, Employment and Equity Issues in Tanzania*.

[11] *The Nationalist*, 9 Oct. 1969, quoted in H. Mapolu (ed.), *Workers and Management* (Tanzania Publishing House 1976) p. 208. The purposals were put in concrete form in Nyerere's *Presidential Circular No. 1 of 1970* issued in Jan. 1970 and reprinted in Mapolu (ed.) *Workers and Management*, pp. 153–9.

[12] The *Mwongozo*, English translation in Coulson (ed.) *African Socialism...*, pp. 36–42.

[13] *The Daily News*, 7 June 1973.

CHAPTER 23, APPENDIX 1

[1] See also I. Resnick 'The State Trading, Corporation: A Casualty of Contra-

dictions, in Mapolu (ed.), *Workers and Management*, pp. 71–89.
[2] Tanzania *Second Five Year Plan*, Vol. 1, p. 142.
[3] See also Chapter 21, Appendix 2, p. 232.
[4] For more information on McKinseys, see Chapter 22, fn. 14.

CHAPTER 23, APPENDIX 2

[1] An earlier version of this appendix formed part of an article headed 'Blood-Sucking Contracts' which appeared in Mapolu (ed.), *Workers and Management* (Tanzania Publishing House, 1976), pp. 92–7.

CHAPTER 24

[1] *Freedom and Socialism*, p. 241.
[2] See Chapter 19.
[3] In the sense of C. Y. Thomas, *Dependence and Transformation* (Monthly Review Press, 1973), Chapters 4, 6 and 8; or J. Rweyemamu *Underdevelopment and Industrialization in Tanzania* (Oxford University Press, 1973), pp. 177–92.
[4] As stressed by the Chinese, for example, when they speak of the village of Tachai which dammed a river and terraced land while refusing offers of central government assistance.
[5] For a summary of this plan see A. J. Van der Laar, 'Tanzania's Second Five Year Plan' in L. Cliffe and J. Saul (eds.), *Socialism in Tanzania*, Vol. 2, pp. 71–81.
[6] Many of the changes made were cosmetic, e.g. 'fishing villages' in the draft became 'ujamaa fishing villages' in the final version, without any discussion of the problems of organizing an ujamaa fishing village.
[7] The planners were particularly anxious to discredit the selective approach but their discussion of the frontal approach was not well defined, and was later used to show that the Plan was consistent with villagization—i.e. everyone moving into villages. This was certainly not what most of the planners had in mind when writing about the frontal approach.
[8] *Second Five Year Plan*, Vol. 1, p. 65; Vol. 2, p. 77. The Plan also recognized (Vol. 1, p. 62) that 'A central concern... will be the fashioning of a longer term industrial strategy... which will provide the framework for detailed preparation of the Third Plan.' A new strategy was eventually prepared on the basis of industrial studies by consultants from the Harvard Advisory Services, but remained an uneasy compromise. See below.
[9] Loxley, 'Financial Planning...', pp. 56, 60–3; *Second Five Year Plan*, Vol. 1, pp. 2, 13.
[10] Discussed in Chapter 20, above and the first appendix to Chapter 23.
[11] IBRD, *Tanzania: Basic Economic Report, 1977*, p. 169.
[12] Calculated from the Balance of Payments figures in *Bank of Tanzania Economic and Operations Report*, June 1978, Table 20. For a contrary view which stresses the influence of those who lent, see M. von Freyhold 'The World Bank and its Relationship to Tanzania', Public Lecture, University of Dar es Salaam, 20 November 1975.
[13] The Arusha Declaration (*Freedom and Development*, p. 239) and the article 'Public Ownership in Tanzania' published a week later (*Freedom and Development*, p. 336).
[14] The clearest statement of Tanzanian foreign policy is Nyerere's speech of 16 October 1967, reprinted as 'Policy on Foreign Affairs' in *Freedom and Socialism*, pp. 367–84. See also J. Karioki, *Tanzania's Human Revolution* (Pennsylvania State University Press, 1979), p. 189 f.

348 NOTES FOR PAGES 306–316

[15] J. S. Saul, *The State and Revolution in Eastern Africa* (Monthly Review Press and Heinemann Educational Books, 1979). Chapters 1–3 are concerned with Mozambique, but see especially pp. 44–52.

[16] Ibid., pp. 110–19. Tanzanian policy was certainly not Chinese policy: the Chinese supported movements that did not receive support from the USSR, to the extreme of supporting the conservative US-backed FLNA in Angola.

[17] United Republic of Tanzania, *Tanzania Government's Statement on the Recognition of Biafra* (13 April 1968), (Government Printer, 1970); J. K. Nyerere, *The Nigeria–Biafra Crisis*, statement prepared for an OAU summit meeting, 4 September 1969.

[18] *The Treaty for East African Cooperation* (East African Common Services Organization, 1967). For a different interpretation see A. Hazelwood, *Economic Integration: The East African Experience* (Heinemann Educational Books, 1975). pp. 108–17.

[19] David Martin, *General Amin* (Sphere Books, 1974, revised and updated 1978), Chapters 10 and 11.

[20] Martha Honey, 'Tanzania Faces Food Shortage' *The Guardian* (London) 18 March 1980. A $260 million loan from the IMF was negotiated in August 1980, but almost exhausted by March 1981.

[21] United Republic of Tanzania, *Third Five Year Plan for Economic and Social Development 1976–1981* (3 volumes, National Printing Company, Dar es Salaam, 1978).

[22] Ibid, Vol. 1, Table 1.

[23] See note 3 above.

[24] In Thomas's argument, the 'basic industries' are derived from examination of the input–output tables of developed countries. Where possible, local raw materials are to be used to produce them. Where this is not possible, it may be practicable to substitute other products; otherwise raw materials should be imported in the cheapest possible form (e.g. pelletized iron ore).

[25] Alternatively a socialist power might be willing to transfer most of its process technology, on the basis of long-term credits. China might have been willing to do this in the early 1970s, but not in the 1980s.

[26] For a discussion of some of the difficulties of the strategy see the review article of Thomas's book by A. Coulson in *Utafiti*, Vol II No. 1 (1977), pp. 111–18.

[27] There would also be a role for less sophisticated technology and improvisation to minimize foreign exchange expenditure on capital goods. See D. Phillips 'Industrialization in Tanzania: The Case of Small Scale Industries', in Kim, Mabele and Schultheis (eds.). *Papers on the Political Economy of Tanzania*, pp. 78–94. For a paper by the Harvard term which describes their methods see M. Roemer, G. Tiddrick, and D. Williams, 'The Range of Strategic Choice in Tanzanian Industry' *Journal of Development Economics*, Vol. III No. 1 (1976), pp. 257–76.

[28] IBRD, *Tanzania:Basic Economic Report, 1977*, Annex 5, pp. 11–21. The Harvard Advisory Services' consultants also warned against expecting much from a strategy of processing agricultural products before export.

[29] In Oct. 1980 it was announced that 'Agrico [a subsidiary of Williams Companies of Oklahoma] will build $450 plant for Tanzania' (*Financial Times*, 30 Oct. 1980). This would be an ammonia fertilizer plant, based on the Songo Songo gas field on an island off the coast near Kilwa.

[30] e.g. Edgett Smith, op. cit.

[31] G. Tschannerl, 'Tanzania and the World Bank' (mimeo, n.d. (1975?), pp. 10–14.

[32] The move of the capital to Dodoma was announced at the TANU conference in October 1973(the same conference at which it was made public that villagization would be compulsory all over the country). The cost then was estimated at 3,710 million shillings, spread over ten years, but this was before detailed design and survey work had started. A 'master plan' was produced by the Canadian consultants Project Planning Associates. Water for a city of 100 000, it was later announced, could be found locally, but after that water would have to come from the Ruaha river, 144 kilometres distant. An elaborate bureaucracy was created, houses and flats were built, and TANU headquarters, the Prime Minister's Office, and some small government departments moved, but no major donor would get involved and the move lost momentum from mid-1975. The desirability of a new city in central Tanzania is hard to dispute, but Dodoma always seemed an odd choice, with its semi-desert environment and shortages of water. Iringa, in the highlands 200 kilometres to the south, with better road communications and plentiful water, would have been more logical. Dodoma was chosen because of its centrality, its acceptability to both Muslims and Christians, and as a response to a pledge of the President to help the Gogo people. (*The Daily News*, 'Capital to Move from Dar to Dodoma', 2 October 1973; 'Six Ministries will be in Dodoma by 1980', 25 June 1975.)

CHAPTER 25

[1] From an address to the diplomatic corps in Dar es Salaam, summarized in Nyerere's 'Guest Column' in *The Guardian* (London), 17 March 1980, p. 10.

[2] e.g. the papers and discussion at the NDC Group Managers' Conference in Dodoma, October 1971. George Kahama's paper (reprinted in *Mbioni*, VI, 11, 1972) makes the position clear: 'While power remains fairly and squarely in the hands of management, workers are being given more responsibility so that they may learn to exercise it with discretion ... Tanzania's present policy is designed to educate the worker in the responsible exercise of power.' (p. 17.)

[3] This is von Freyholds definition ('The Post-Colonial State and its Tanzanian version', *Review of African Political Economy* No 8 (1977), p. 85), though she has adopted a Poulantzian framework, and the definition refers to a 'governing class'. Compare Issa Shivji *Class Struggles in Tanzania*, p. 64. Another definition is that of 'leader' in the Arusha Declaration (*Freedom and Socialism*, p. 249) already quoted on p. 178.

[4] A closer comparison would be with the vision of the UK held by Fabian socialists.

[5] See the *Mwongozo* (in Coulson (ed.) *African Socialism* ..., pp. 36–42) Clauses 11–16, 27, 28–30.

[6] The theory also has problems in relation to the metropoles; there is no clear distinction between ruling and governing classes.

[7] This is to return to some of the points made in Chapter 2 but neglected in the detailed analysis which followed.

[8] W. A. Lewis, *The Emergence of the International Economic Order* (Princeton University Press, 1978).

[9] Hence Hamza Alavi's 'over-developed state' ('The State in Post-Colonial Societies', *New Left Review*, No. 74, July/August 1972).

[10] Hence the media promotion and involvement of politicians such as Edward Heath in the Brandt Report (Independent Commission on International Development Issues, *North-South: A Programme for Survival*, Pan Books, 1980).

[11] Nyerere published a pamplet (*Tujisahishe* ['Let us correct ourselves']) in 1962, advocating self-criticism, but it was never taken very seriously.

[12] As in Shivji's work.

[13] As Pratt gets close to doing.

[14] A demoralization and loss of efficiency, associated with a cynicism about socialism and an increase in petty corruption, set in after the food and foreign exchange shortages of 1975, and intensified in the difficult months following the 1979 invasion of Uganda.

[15] A. Stepan, *The State and Society: Peru in Comparative Perspective* (Princeton University Press, 1978), pp. 26–45.

[16] Up to 1977 the University of Dar es Salaam was an unusually free and creative institution, where it was possible to discuss the implementation of government policies openly. But thereafter most of this discussion was suppressed, and in 1978 more than 400 students were sent down for marching in support of the Arusha Declaration at a moment when the government was flouting it by raising MPs' and ministers' salaries. See Chapter 21, Appendix 1.

[17] Probably involving both private capital and state capital, local and foreign, in both urban and rural areas, and smaller civil service and parastatal sectors. There is no certainty that such a policy would lead to faster growth.

[18] It would also be necessary to control parastatal costs. Ellis ('Agricultural Pricing Policy...' p. 35f., reporting on research still in progress) writes of a 'Law of Rising Parastatal Marketing Costs'. Cashewnut production fell between 1973/4 and 1978/9 but overheads rose at nearly 20 per cent per annum, with the result that the share of cashewnut growers fell from 70 per cent of the export earnings to 35 per cent. The share of cotton producers fell from 70 per cent of the export earnings in 1969/70 to 45 per cent in 1978/9, while coffee producers received 80 per cent at the beginning of the decade but only 40 per cent in 1978/9. Similar cost increases without associated production increases were almost certainly associated with other parastatals.

FURTHER READING

CHAPTER 1: NYERERE'S TANZANIA

Collections of Nyerere's speeches have been published by Oxford University Press as *Freedom and Unity* (1966) for the years 1952–65, *Freedom and Socialism* (1968) for 1965–7, and *Freedom and Development* (1973) for 1969–73. A short collection, *Essays on Socialism* (1968), includes the important 1967 papers such as the *Arusha Declaration* and *Education for Self-Reliance*. The long essay *The Arusha Declaration Ten Years After* (Government Printer, 1977) shows Nyerere at his most self-critical, and is included in the collection of papers edited by Andrew Coulson (*African Socialism in Practice: The Tanzanian Experience*, Spokesman Books, 1979). An earlier collection of papers was edited by Lionel Cliffe and John Saul, (*Socialism in Tanzania*, East African Publishing House and Heinemann Educational Books, 2 volumes, 1972 and 1973). Issa Shivji's path-breaking *Class Struggles in Tanzania* (Tanzania Publishing House, and Heinemann Educational Books, 1975) is an attempt at a Marxist analysis, although neither Shivji nor most of his readers would claim it as a mature work.

CHAPTER 2: TANZANIA AND THE INTERNATIONAL ECONOMY

The framework for this chapter follows J. Forbes Munro, *Africa and the International Economy 1800–1960* (Dent, 1976), which may be compared with W. Rodney, *How Europe Underdeveloped Africa* (Bogle l'Ouverture and Tanzania Publishing House, 1972) and E. A. Brett, *Colonialism and Underdevelopment in East Africa* (Heinemann Educational Books, 1973). The best short history is still I. Kimambo and A. Temu (eds.), *A History of Tanzania* (East African Publishing House 1969, reprinted by Heinemann Educational Books), but for scholarly purposes this is now superseded by John Iliffe's *A Modern History of Tanganyika* (Cambridge University Press, 1979), which covers the period up to 1960.

CHAPTER 3: THE INTERIOR

This chapter draws on Helge Kjekshus's provocative study *Ecology Control and Economic Development in East African History* (Heinemann Educational Books, 1977). Earlier work, for example the seven studies edited by Andrew Roberts (*Tanzania Before 1900*, East African Publishing House, 1968), emphasized political rather than economic history. There is a mass of detail in Iliffe's *A Modern History of Tanganyika*, Chapters 2 and 3. For discussions of trade and trade routes R. W. Beachey, 'The East African Ivory Trade in the Nineteenth Century' (*Journal of African History*, VIII, 2 (1967)) is helpful; also Robert's article on the Nyamwezi in R. Gray and D. Birmingham (eds.), *Precolonial African Trade* (Oxford University Press, 1970).

CHAPTER 4: ZANZIBAR AND THE COAST

Material for this chapter has been drawn from an unpublished doctoral thesis by Abdul Sheriff ('The Rise of a Commercial Empire: An Aspect of the Economic History of Zanzibar 1770–1873', London University, 1971). The archaeological and other evidence from the coast is reviewed by Neville Chittick in *The Cambridge History of Africa*, Volume 3 (edited by Roland Oliver, 1977). See also Norman R. Bennett, *A History of the Arab State of Zanzibar* (Methuen, 1978) and M. Lofchie, *Zanzibar Background to Revolution* (Princeton University Press, 1965).

CHAPTER 5: THE GERMAN CONQUEST

The main argument again derives from Kjekshus, who was influenced by John Ford, *The Role of the Trypanosomiases in African Ecology* (Clarendon Press, Oxford, 1971). See also Iliffe, *A Modern History . . .*, Chapter 4 (The German Conquest), Chapter 5 (the ecological crisis), Chapter 6 (the Maji Maji rebellion), and Chapter 8 (including a section on World War I). A more nationalist perspective on the Maji Maji is Gilbert Gwassa's chapter in *A History of Tanzania* (ed. Kimambo and Temu, East African Publishing House, 1968). For an interesting chapter on the First World War by one who took part and was later to play a decisive role in shaping British policy in Tanganyika, see Philip Mitchell, *African Afterthoughts* (Hutchinson, 1954). The argument that reduced levels of population led to regression in agriculture provides interesting support for Ester Boserup's thesis in *The Conditions for Agricultural Growth* (Faber, 1965).

CHAPTER 6: THE GERMANY COLONY

The standard interpretations by John Iliffe are *Tanganyika Under German Rule* (Cambridge University Press, 1969) and his more recent *A Modern History . . .* (1979). The political events are summarized in J. Taylor, *The Political Development of Tanganyika* (Stanford University Press, 1963). On the Asian traders see J. S. Mangat, *A History of the Asians in East Africa* (the Clarendon Press, Oxford, 1969). On education see J. Cameron and W. Dodd, *Schools, Society and Progress in Tanzania* (Pergamon, 1970), and on health R. M. Titmuss and others, *The Health Services of Tanganyika* (Pitman Medical Publishing, 1964).

CHAPTER 7: AGRICULTURAL PRODUCTION UNDER THE BRITISH

John Iliffe's pamphlet *Agricultural Change in Modern Tanzania* (East African Publishing House, 1971), provides an excellent summary. For an interpretation sympathetic to the Government see Hans Ruthenberg, *Agricultural Development in Tanganyika* (Springer Verlag, 1964). There is a short description of the Groundnuts Scheme in an essay by S. H. Frankel in *The Economic Impact on Underdeveloped Countries* (Harvard University Press, 1953), but see also Alan Wood, *The Groundnut Affair* (Bodley Head, 1950). On agricultural change by rules and regulations see R. Young and H. Fosbrooke, *Land and Politics among the Luguru of Tanganyika* (North-Western University Press, 1960) and Lionel Cliffe's 1964 article 'Nationalism and the Reaction to Enforced Agricultural Change during the Colonial Period', reprinted in the reader edited by him and John Saul, *Socialism in Tanzania*, Volume 1 (East African Publishing House, 1972, pp. 131–40).

CHAPTER 8: AGRICULTURAL MARKETING AND CO-OPERATIVES

The co-operative movement is treated from a nationalist perspective by Iliffe in his chapter 'The Age of Improvement and Differentiation' in Kimambo and Temu (eds.), *A History of Tanzania*, and by John Saul, 'Marketing Co-operatives in a Developing Country. The Tanzanian case' in Cliffe and Saul (eds.), *Socialism in Tanzania* Volume 2. Regional studies that contributed to the chapter are: Susan Rodgers, 'The Kilimanjaro Native Planters' Association: Administrative Responses to Chagga Initiatives in the 1920s', *Transafrican Journal of History* (Nairobi), IV, 1/2 (1974); P. M. Redmond, 'The NMCMU and Tobacco Production in Songea', *Tanzania Notes and Records*, 79/80 (1976); R. A. Austen, *Northwestern Tanzania under German and British Rule* (Yale University Press, 1968); and Andrew Maguire, *Towards 'Uhuru' in Tanzania* (on the Sukuma) (Cambridge University Press, 1969).

CHAPTER 9: NON-INDUSTRIALIZATION

The issues are discussed in E. A. Brett, *Colonialism and Underdevelopment in East Africa . . . 1919–39* (Heinemann Educational Books, 1973) and J. Rweyemamu, *Underdevelopment and Industrialization in Tanzania* (Oxford University Press, 1973). See also Martha Honey, 'Asian Industrial Activities in Tanzania', *Tanzania Notes and Records*, 75 (1974).

CHAPTER 10: EDUCATION AND IDEOLOGY

Information about colonial educational policies can be found in D. R. Morrison, *Education and Politics in Africa: the Tanzanian Case* (Hurst and Co., 1976) and J. Cameron and W. Dodd, *Schools, Society and Progress in Tanzania* (Pergamon, 1970). See also articles by Marjorie Mbilinyi, in particular 'African Education in the British Colonial Period', the (1975) revised version of a paper for the 1974 Morogoro teachers' conference, 'The Evolution of Tanzanian Educational Policy' (University of Dar es Salaam, Department of Education, 1973), and her Ph.D. dissertation, 'The Decision to Educate in Rural Tanzania' (University of Dar es Salaam, 1972).

CHAPTER 11: INDIRECT RULE

The best detailed account of indirect rule policies in the 1920s and 1930s is R. A. Austen, *North-Western Tanganyika under German and British Rule* (Yale University Press, 1968), but see also Iliffe, *A Modern History*..., Chapter 10. Dundas's, Mitchell's, and (to a lesser extent) Cameron's memoirs are interesting (C. Dundas, *African Crossroads*, Macmillan, 1955; P. Mitchell, *African Afterthoughts*, Hutchinson, 1954; D. Cameron, *My Tanganyika Service and Some Nigeria*, Allen and Unwin, 1939). Lugard, *The Dual Mandate in British Tropical Africa* (William Blackwood, 1921, 5th edition 1965) is still worth reading. Charlotte Leubuscher was among the first to count the economic cost of subordination to Kenya: *Tanganyika Territory: A Study of Economic Policy under Mandate* (Oxford University Press, 1944).

CHAPTER 12: THE NATIONALISTS

The origins of nationalism have been explored by Iliffe. See 'The Age of Improvement and Differentiation' in Kimambo and Temu (eds.), *A History of Tanzania*; 'The Dockworkers of Dar es Salaam', *Tanzania Notes and Records*, 71 (1970) (reprinted in R. Sandbrook and R. Cohen (eds.), *The Development of an African Working Class*, Longmans, 1975); his biography of Martin Kayamba in *Modern Tanzanians* (East African Publishing House 1973); and *A Modern History of Tanganyika*, Chapters 12 and 13.

CHAPTER 13: THE INDEPENDENCE 'STRUGGLE'

Much of Nyerere's early writing is in *Freedom and Unity* (Oxford University Press, 1966); the introduction is particularly revealing, as is part of the introduction to his second book of speeches and writings, *Freedom and Socialism* (1968). The definitive study of this period is, however, *The Critical Phase in Tanzania 1945–1968: Nyerere and the Emergence of a Socialist Strategy* by R. Cranford Pratt (Cambridge University Press, 1976). An earlier account by Judith Listowel, *The Making of Tanganyika* (Chatto and Windus, 1965), is interesting in that much of it was based on interviews with Nyerere and other politicians. There is no good biography of Nyerere, but a picture and atmosphere is conveyed by William Edgett Smith, *We Must Run While Others Walk* (Random House 1971), revised as *Nyerere of Tanzania* (Gollancz, 1973, and Transafrica Publishers, Nairobi, 1974). On the co-operatives see G. Hyden (ed.), *Cooperatives in Tanzania: Problems of Organisation* (Tanzania Publishing House, 1976). On the Trades Unions see W. H. Friedland, *Vuta Kamba: the Development of Trade Unions in*

Tanganyika (Hoover Institution Publication 84, Stanford Institution Press, 1969).

CHAPTER 14: THE PEACEFUL TRANSITION

Pratt's *The Critical Phase in Tanzania* ... also covers this period in depth. Earlier studies are Henry Bienen, *Tanzania: Party Transformation and Economic Development* (Princeton University Press, 2nd edition, 1970) and W. Tordoff, *Government and Politics in Tanzania* (East African Publishing House, 1967). Extracts from some of the most important documents of the period are reprinted in Hadley E. Smith (ed.), *Readings on Economic Development and Administration in Tanzania* (Institute of Public Administration, Study No. 4, Oxford University Press, 1966). *The Economic Development of Tanganyika* (Johns Hopkins for the IBRD, 1961) is still accessible in many libraries.

CHAPTER 15: ZANZIBAR

The standard work (with a slight tendency to present an ASP point of view) is *Zanzibar: Background to Revolution* by M. F. Lofchie (Princeton University Press, 1965). See also his 1967 reconstruction of the 1964 revolution, 'Was Okello's Revolution a Conspiracy?', reprinted in L. Cliffe and J. Saul (eds.), *Socialism in Tanzania*, Volume 1. The most recent book-length history is N. R. Bennett, *A History of the Arab State of Zanzibar* (Methuen, 1978), but there is a useful summary in a pamphlet, *The 1948 Zanzibar General Strike*, by Anthony Clayton (Scandinavian Institute of African Affairs, Research Report No. 32, Uppsala, 1976).

CHAPTER 16: THE EARLY YEARS

Most of the accounts of this period also cover the run-up to independence, and have been referred to in the notes to Chapters 13 and 14. W. Friedland (*Vuta Kamba* ...) includes an interesting appendix on the 82-day rail strike in 1959. The 1965 General Election is the subject of Lionel Cliffe (ed.) *One Party Democracy* (East African Publishing House, 1967). See also Nyerere's speeches, and the papers in the two-volume collection *Socialism in Tanzania* (eds. Lionel Cliffe and John Saul).

CHAPTER 17: AGRICULTURAL POLICY 1961–1967

Informative papers by Awiti, Raikes, Saul, Migot-Adholla, Collinson, Ellman, and others are included in the collection *Rural Co-operation in Tanzania* (edited by L. Cliffe and others, Tanzania Publishing House, 1975). The settlement scheme policy is discussed by Cliffe and Cunningham (in *Socialism in Tanzania*, Volume 2), by Hans Ruthenberg, *Agricultural Development in Tanganyika* (Springer Verlag, 1964) and in the collection edited by him, *Smallholder Farming and Smallholder Development in Tanzania* (Springer Weltforum, 1968). On government staff, see the chapter with that heading in Michaela von Freyhold, *Ujamaa Villages in Tanzania: Analysis of a Social Experiment* (Heinemann Educational Books, 1979), H. U. Thoden van Velsen, 'Staff, Kulaks and Peasants' (in Saul and Cliffe (eds.), *Socialism in Tanzania*, Volume 2); and R. Hulls, 'An Assessment of Agricultural Extension in Sukumaland Western Tanzania' (Paper 71.13 Economic Research Bureau, University of Dar es Salaam, 1971). On intercropping see D. Belshaw and M. Hall, 'The Analysis and Use of Agricultural Experimental Data', *East African Journal of Rural Development*, V, 1/2 (1972).

CHAPTER 18: INDUSTRY BEFORE THE ARUSHA DECLARATION

The standard work on this period is Justinian Rweyemamu's *Underdevelopment and Industrialization in Tanzania* (Oxford University Press, 1973), more convincing than Ann Seidman's *Comparative Development Strategies in East Africa* (East African Publishing House 1972) although this also covers the East African dimension. On the Asian community see Martha Honey 'Asian Industrial Activities in Tanganyika', *Tanzania Notes and Records* 75 (1974). Information on the ownership of the biggest companies operating in Tanzania is compiled in C. Barker and D. Wield, 'Notes on International Firms in Tanzania', *Utafiti* (Dar es Salaam), Vol. 3, No. 2 (1978).

CHAPTER 19: THE ARUSHA DECLARATION

Nyerere's papers and speeches of the period (in *Freedom and Socialism* (1968) and *Freedom and Development* (1972)) are essential reading. The background to the Arusha Declaration is covered in depth in the last part of Pratt's book, while Edgett Smith conveys the atmosphere of 1967. For a contrary interpretation see Issa Shivji, *Class Struggles in Tanzania* and his earlier *The Silent Class Struggle* (Tanzania Publishing House, 1972, reprinted in Volume 2 of *Socialism in Tanzania* edited by L. Cliffe and J. Saul, which includes several other relevant papers.)

CHAPTER 20: PRODUCTION AND INCOME DISTRIBUTION

Up-to-date statistical material is published in the annual *Economic Surveys* (Government Printer) and in the quarterly *Bank of Tanzania Economic Bulletins*. The main trends were reviewed in the ILO Report, *Towards Self-Reliance: Development, Employment and Equity Issues in Tanzania* (1978) and in the IBRD, *Tanzania: Basic Economic Report 1977*. The ILO discussion of income distribution is challenged by Frank Ellis, 'Agricultural Pricing Policy in Tanzania 1970–1979 . . .' (Economic Research Bureau, University of Dar es Salaam, 1980). Earlier work is by R. Sabot, (*Economic Development and Urban Migration: Tanzania 1900–1971*, Oxford University Press, 1979). See also S. Rwegasira, 'Inflation and Monetary Expansion: The 1966–73 Tanzanian Experiences', in K. Kim, R. Mabele, and M. Schultheis (eds.)

Papers on the Political Economy of Tanzania (Heinemann Educational Books, 1976), and Y. Huang, 'Distribution of Tax Burden in Tanzania' (*Economic Journal*, March 1976). On foreign aid, Pratt (*The Critical Phase . . .*) is well informed up to 1969. Statistics for the food crisis of 1974 and 1975 are available in the *Data Report on the Food and Nutrition situation in Tanzania 1972/3—1976/7* (Tanzania Food and Nutrition Centre, 1978). Nyerere's reaction to the poor performance of the 1970s is in *The Arusha Declaration Ten Years After* (1977).

CHAPTER 21: SOCIAL CLASS AND SOCIAL SERVICES

On women's studies, see papers by Debbie Bryceson and Marjorie Mbilinyi, and in particular their joint paper, 'The Changing Role of Tanzanian Women in Production: From Peasants to Proletarians', presented at a Conference at the University of Sussex in September 1978. On health, see Malcolm Segall, 'The Politics of Health in Tanzania' in J. Rweyemamu *et al.* (eds.), *Towards Socialist Planning* (Tanzania Publishing House, 1972), the paper 'To Plan is to Choose' by John Yudkin of the Faculty of Medicine, University of Dar es Salaam (1978), and the BBC TV documentary film, *A Fair Share of What Little We Have* (1976). On housing, see the chapter by A. Macarenhas in the 1967 *Population Census*, Volume 6 (edited by B. Egero and R. Henin), and R. E. Stren, 'Urban Development in Kenya and Tanzania: A Comparative Analysis', IDS (Nairobi) Working Paper 147 (1974). On education and water supplies respectively see the papers by Marjorie Mbilinyi and Gerhard Tschannerl in the collection edited by Coulson (and elsewhere). There is little on transport more up-to-date than R. Hofmeir's *Transport and Economic Development in Tanzania* (Munich, 1973). On the law in Tanzania see papers by David Williams, notably 'Authoritarian Legal Systems and the Process of Capital Accumulation in Africa', Faculty of Law, University of Dar es Salaam, 1979.

CHAPTER 22: UJAMAA AND VILLAGIZATION

A discussion of ujamaa must take account of Nyerere's writing. The 1967 papers are in the short collection *Essays in Socialism* (Oxford University Press, 1968); later papers, including *Freedom and Development* (1968) and *The Arusha Declaration Ten Years After* (1977), are in A. Coulson (ed.), *African Socialism in Practice: The Tanzanian Experience* (Spokesman Books, 1979), which also includes case studies of ujamaa/villagization by von Freyhold (Tanga), Hill (Dodoma), De Vries and Fortmann (Iringa), Parkipuny (Maassailand), and Mwapachu (Shinyanga). Earlier case studies and commentaries are in Cliffe L. *et al.* (eds.), *Rural Co-operation in Tanzania* (Tanzania Publishing House, 1975)—including studies of Mbambara village by Wisner and others, Ismani by Awiti, and the policy as a whole by Ellman. An accessible review of a large body of empirical research is G. Hyden 'Ujamma, Villagization and Rural Development in Tanzania', *Overseas Develop-*

ment Institute Review, No. 1 (1975). The most profound study to date is M. von Freyhold, *Ujamaa Villages in Tanzania: Analysis of a Social Experiment* (Heinemann Educational Books, 1979). But see also P. Raikes, 'Ujamaa and Rural Socialism', *Review of African Political Economy*, No. 3 (1975), D. Leonard, 'Bureaucracy, Class and Inequality in Tanzania and Kenya', a paper presented to a conference on Inequality in Africa, Mount Kisco, New York, 1976; J. Boesen, 'Tanzania: From Ujamaa to Villagization', Institute for Development Research, Copenhagen, 1976; D. McHenry, *Tanzania's Ujamaa Villages: The Implementation of a Development Strategy* (University of California, 1979); and especially L. Fortmann, 'Peasants, Officials and Participation in Rural Tanzania: Experience with Villagization and Decentralization', Cornell University, 1980.

CHAPTER 23: PARASTATALS AND WORKERS

Several papers on parastatals are in the collection edited by Andrew Coulson (*African Socialism in Practice*...), including the *Mwongozo* (1971) and other documents, and five case studies of particular parastatals (NAFCO—a holding company—by Ph. Packard; LIDEP—an integrated rural development project by R. Matango; the fertilizer factor and the automated bread factory, by A. Coulson; and the Tanzania Publishing House by R. Hutchinson). There are studies by I. Resnick (on the State Trading Corporation) and I. Shivji (on management agreements) in H. Mapolu (ed.), *Workers and Management* (Tanzania Publishing House, 1976). The Dar es Salaam students' papers on tourism, the first public criticism of policy on parastatals, were published as I. Shivji (ed.), *Tourism and Socialist Development* (Tanzania Publishing House, 1973). There are articles on NDC (by Eric Svendsen) and the financial parastatals (by John Loxley) in Saul and Cliffe (eds.), *Socialism in Tanzania*, Volume 2 (1973). Michaela von Freyhold's 'The Workers and the Nizers' regrettably remains unpublished, but her brief 'Notes on Tanzanian Industrial Workers' in *Tanzania Notes and Records,* 81/82 (1977) is very valuable. See also Pascal Mihyo, 'The Struggle for Workers' Control in Tanzania' (*Review of African Political Economy* No. 4, 1975), and Issa Shivji's interpretation in *Class Struggles in Tanzania*.

CHAPTER 24: DEVELOPMENT STRATEGY AND FOREIGN RELATIONS

For material on Tanzanian foreign policy the starting-point is the writing of President Nyerere, e.g. the paper 'Policy on Foreign Affairs' in *Freedom and Socialism* (1968), the pamphlet *The Nigeria–Biafra Crisis* (1969), papers in *Freedom and Development (1973)* and relevant sections of *The Arusha Declaration Ten Years After* (1977).

The literature on Tanzanian planning includes papers on the First Plan (by Colin Leys and Cranford Pratt) and on the Second (by Brian van Arkadie) in Saul and Cliffe (eds.), *Socialism in Tanzania*, Volume

2 (1973). Justinian Rweyemamu (*Underdevelopment and Industrialization in Tanzania*, Oxford University Press, 1973) describes a basic industry strategy, and may be compared with the more abstract work by C. Y. Thomas (*Dependence and Transformation*, Monthly Review Press, 1973) and an article by Thomas in C. Widstrand (ed.) *Multinational Firms in Africa* (African Institute for Economic Development and Planning, Dakar, and Scandinavian Institute of African Studies, Uppsala, 1975.) The decision-making of the Third Plan is described by M. Roemer *et al.*, 'The Range of Strategic Choice in Tanzanian Industry' (*Journal of Development Economics*, III, 1, 1976).

On participation in development projects, see Tschannerl's paper on water supply in the Coulson collection, and papers produced by the University of Dar es Salaam Decentralisation Research Unit, notably D. Leonard and others, 'Decentralisation and the Issues of Efficiency, Effectiveness and Popular Participation' (1975), and S. S. Mushi, 'Popular Participation and Regional Development Planning in Tanzania: The Politics of Decentralized Administration', *Tanzania Notes and Records*, No. 83 (1978).

CHAPTER 25: THE TANZANIAN STATE

The discussion in this chapter owes much to Issa Shivji (*The Silent Class Struggle* and *Class Struggles in Tanzania*), to work by W. Olle and W. Schoeller, e.g. 'World Market, State and National Average Conditions of Labour' (Occasional Paper 77.1, Economic Research Bureau, University of Dar es Salaam, 1977), and to a book on Peru (Alfred Stepan, *The State and Society: Peru in Comparative Perspective*, Princeton University Press, 1978). These may be compared with papers by John Saul (in *The State and Revolution in Eastern Africa*, Monthly Review Press and Heinemann Educational Books, 1979). An article by von Freyhold ('The Post-Colonial State and its Tanzanian Version', *Review of African Political Economy*, No. 8, 1977) draws on the debates between Poulantzas, Miliband, and Alavi. A defence of the Tanzanian state (and a subtle attempt to rescue modernization theory) is Goren Hyden's *Beyond Ujamaa in Tanzania: Underdevelopment and an Uncaptured Peasantry* (Heinemann Educational Books, 1980).

BIBLIOGRAPHY*

ADAMSON, A. D. AND ROBBINS, S. R. (1975) *The Market for Cloves and Clove Products in the United Kingdom*. Report G93, Tropical Products Institute, London.

ALLAN, W. (1965) *The African Husbandman*. Oliver and Boyd: reprinted by Greenwood Press (Westport, Conn.), 1977.

ALLEN, C. (1977) 'Radical Themes in African Social Studies: A Bibliographic Guide', in Gutkind, P. and Waterman, P. (eds.) *African Social Studies: A Radical Reader*, Heinemann Educational Books.

ALPERS, E. (1969) 'The Coast and the Development of the Caravan Trade' in Kimambo and Temu (eds.) (1969) 32–56.

AMEY, A. (1976) 'Urban-Rural Relations in Tanzania: Methodology, Issues and Preliminary Results'. University of East Anglia Development Studies Discussion Paper No. 15, and University of Dar es Salaam Economic Research Bureau Paper 76.12.

ANGWAZI, J. AND NDULU, B. (1973) 'An Evaluation of Ujamaa Villages in the Rufiji Area, 1968–1972'. Social Science Conference, Dar es Salaam, December.

ARMITAGE-SMITH, SIR S. (1932) *Report on a Financial Mission to Tanganyika*. Cmd. 4182, HMSO.

ARNOLD, D. (1974) 'External Factors in the Partition of East Africa'. History Teachers Conference, Morogoro.

ARRIGHI, G. AND SAUL, J. (1973) *Essays on the Political Economy of Africa*. Monthly Review Press.

AUSTEN, R. A. (1968) *Northwestern Tanzania under German and British Rule*. Yale University Press.

AWITI, A. (1972a) 'Ismani and the Rise of Capitalism' in Cliffe *et al.* (eds.) (1975) 51–78.

AWITI, A. (1972b) 'The Development of *Ujamaa* in Ismani' in Cliffe *et al.* (eds.) (1975) 418–25.

BAKER, E. (1934) *Report on Social and Economic Conditions in the Tanga Province*. Government Printer.

BARKER, C., BHAGAVAN, M., VON MITCHKE-COLLANDE, R., AND WIELD, D. (1976) 'Industrial Production and Transfer of Technology in Tan-

---

* This bibliography is restricted to sources containing material specifically on Tanzania which were consulted during the preparation of this book.

zania: The Political Economy of Tanzanian Industrial Enterprises'.
Mimeo, Institute of Development Studies, University of Dar es
Salaam. To be published by Zed Press (London).

BARKER, C. *et al.* (1977) 'The Structure and Balance of Industrial Production in Tanzania'. *Utafiti* (Dar es Salaam) II, 1 81–98.

BARKER, C. AND WIELD, D. (1978) 'Notes on International Firms in Tanzania'. *Utafiti* (Dar es Salaam), III, 2 316–41.

BATES, M. L. (1957) 'Tanganyika under British Administration', unpublished D. Phil. thesis, Oxford.

BEACHEY, R. W. (1967) 'The East African Ivory Trade in the
Nineteenth Century'. *Journal of African History* VIII, 2 269–90

BECK, R. S. (1963) *An Economic Study of Coffee-Banana Farms in the
Machame Central Area, 1961.* USAID, Dar es Salaam.

BELSHAW, D. AND HALL, M. (1972) 'The Analysis and Use of Agricultural Experimental Data'. *East African Journal of Rural Development* V, 1/2 39–71.

BENNETT, N. (1978) *A History of the Arab State of Zanzibar.* Methuen.

BERNSTEIN, H. AND BRYCESON, D. (eds.) *The Agrarian Question in Tanzania* (in preparation).

BERRY, L. (ed.) (1971) *Tanzania in Maps.* University of London Press.

BIENEN, H. (1967, 2nd edition 1970) *Tanzania: Party Transformation
and Economic Development.* Princeton University Press.

BIENEFELD, M. (1970) 'Manpower Planning and the University: The
Position in Education, Arts and Social Science'. Paper 70.2, Economic Research Bureau, University of Dar es Salaam.

BIENEFELD, M. (1975) 'Socialist Development and the Workers in Tanzania', in Sandbrook and Cohen (eds.) (1975) 239–60.

BOEREE, R. M. (1972) 'Report to the Government of Tanzania on the
Economics and Planning of Irrigation'. Technical Assistance Report
TA 3096, FAO, Rome.

BOESEN, J. (1976) *Tanzania: from Ujamaa to Villagisation.* Institute for
Development Research, Copenhagen, Paper A76.7.

BOESEN, J., MADSEN, B. S. AND MOODY, T. (1977) *Ujamaa: Socialism
from Above.* Scandinavian Institute of African Studies, Uppsala.

BOESEN, J. AND MOHELE, A. T. (1979) *The 'Success Story' of Peasant
Tobacco Production in Tanzania.* Scandinavian Institute of African
Studies, Uppsala.

BOMANI, P. (1966) 'Planning for Rural Development'. *Mbioni* (Dar es
Salaam) II, 11 16–27.

BOWLES, B. (1974) 'The Political Economy of Colonial Tanganyika 1939–
61'. Teachers' Conference, Morogoro.

BOWLES, B. (1976a) 'Export Crops and Underdevelopment in Tanganyika 1929–1961'. *Utafiti* (Dar es Salaam) I, 171–85.

BOWLES, B. (1976b) 'The Political Economy of Zanzibar, 1945–1964'.
History Teachers' Conference, Morogoro.

BOWLES, B. (1979) 'Colonial Control and Cooperatives in Tanganyika
1945–1952'. Unpublished manuscript.

362

BIBLIOGRAPHY

BRETT, E. A. (1973) *Colonialism and Underdevelopment in East Africa*. Heinemann Educational Books.

BRYCESON, D. F. (1978) 'Peasant Food Production and Food Supply in Relation to the Historical Development of Commodity Production in Pre-Colonial and Colonial Tanganyika'. Service Paper, Bureau of Resource Assessment and Land Use Planning, University of Dar es Salaam.

BRYCESON, D. F. AND MBILINYI, M. (1978) 'The Changing Role of Tanzanian Women in Production: From Peasants to Proletarians'. Conference on Women and the Processes of Development, University of Sussex, September.

BUKENYA, A. (1972) *A People's Batchelor*. East African Publishing House.

CAMERON, SIR D. (1939) *My Tanganyika Service and Some Nigeria*. George Allen and Unwin.

CAMERON, J. AND DODD, W. (1970) *Schools, Society and Progress in Tanzania*. Pergamon.

CASTLE, E. B. (1966) *Growing up in East Africa*. Oxford University Press.

Chama cha Mapinduzi (Party of the Revolution) (1977). CCM Constitution (in English). *Mbioni* (Dar es Salaam) XIII, 6.

CHASE, H. (1976) 'The Zanzibar Treason Trial'. *Review of African Political Economy* 6, 15–33.

CHIDZERO, B. T. (1961) *Tanganyika and International Trusteeship*. Oxford, The Clarendon Press.

CHITTICK, H. N. (1977) 'The East African Coast, Madagascar and the Indian Ocean' in Oliver, R. (ed.) *The Cambridge History of Africa*, Vol. 3, Cambridge University Press, 183–231.

CLARK, W. E. (1978) *Socialist Development and Public Investment in Tanzania 1964–73*, University of Toronto Press.

CLAYTON, A. (1976) *The 1948 Zanzibar General Strike*. Research Report No. 32, Scandinavian Institute of International Affairs, Uppsala.

CLIFFE, L. (1964, postscript 1970) 'Nationalism and the Reaction to Enforced Agricultural Change in Tanganyika during the Colonial Period'. Reprinted in Cliffe and Saul (eds.) (1972) 17–24.

CLIFFE, L. (ed.) (1967) *One Party Democracy*. East African Publishing House.

CLIFFE, L. AND CUNNINGHAM, G. (1968) 'Ideology, Organisation and the Settlement Experience in Tanzania'. Reprinted in Cliffe and Saul (eds.) (1973) 131–40.

CLIFFE, L. *et al.* (1968) 'An Interim Report on the Evaluation of Agricultural Extension'. Rural Development Paper No. 5, Rural Development Research Committee, University of Dar es Salaam.

CLIFFE, L. AND SAUL, J. (1972) 'The District Development Front in Tanzania' in Cliffe and Saul (eds.) (1972) 302–28.

CLIFFE, L. AND SAUL, J. (eds.) (1972) *Socialism in Tanzania: An Interdisciplinary Reader, Volume 1*. East African Publishing House and Heinemann Educational Books.

CLIFFE, L. AND SAUL, J. (eds.) (1973) *Socialism in Tanzania: An Inter-disciplinary Reader, Volume 2*. East African Publishing House and Heinemann Eductional Books.

CLIFFE, L. *et al.* (eds.) (1975) *Rural Cooperation in Tanzania*. Tanzania Publishing House.

COE, R. L. (1964) 'Public Corporations in East Africa'. Maxwell School, Syracuse University.

COLLIER, P. (1977) 'Labour Market Allocation and Income Distribution'. Annex III, *Basic Economic Report, 1977*. International Bank for Reconstruction and Development.

COLLINS, P. (1972) 'The Working of Tanzania's Rural Development Fund: A Problem in Decentralisation'. *East African Journal of Rural Development* V, 1/2 141–62.

COLLINSON, M. (1962, 1963a, 1963b, 1964) Farm Management Survey Reports Nos. 1–4. Western Research Centre, Ukiriguru, Tanzania.

COLLINSON, M. (1970) 'An Example of Farm Survey Work directed towards the Solution of a Policy Problem: The Comparative Economics of Growing Aromatic or Virginia Tobacco on Small Family Farms in the Tabora Area of Tanzania'. Economic Research Bureau Paper 70.7, University of Dar es Salaam.

COLLINSON, M. (1972a) 'The Economic Characteristics of the Sukuma Farming System'. Paper 72.5, Economic Research Bureau, University of Dar es Salaam.

COLLINSON, M. (1972b) *Farm Management in Peasant Agriculture*. Praegar.

CORNEVIN, R. (1969) 'The Germans in Africa before 1918', in Duignan and Gann (eds.) Volume 1, 383–419.

COULSON, A. (1975a) 'Peasants and Bureaucrats'. *Review of African Political Economy* 3, 53–8.

COULSON, A. (1975b) 'Decentralisation and the Government Budget'. Paper 75.6, Decentralisation Research Project, University of Dar es Salaam.

COULSON, A. (1975c) 'Contradictions of Merchant Capital in East Africa'. East African Social Sciences Conference, Nairobi.

COULSON, A. (1976) 'Blood-Sucking Contracts' in Mapolu (ed.) (1976) 90–108.

COULSON, A. (1977a) 'Tanzania's Fertilizer Factory'. *Journal of Modern African Studies* XV, 1 119–25. (Reprinted in Coulson (ed.) *African Socialism . . .* 184–90).

COULSON, A. (1977b) Review of *Dependence and Transformation* by C. Y. Thomas. *Utafiti* (Dar es Salaam) II, 1 111–18.

COULSON, A. (1977c) 'Crop Priorities for the Lowlands of Tanga Region'. *Tanzania Notes and Records* 81/82, 43–54.

COULSON, A. (1978a) 'Agricultural Policies in Mainland Tanzania 1946–1976'. *Review of African Political Economy*, 10, 74–100. (Reprinted in Heyer, Roberts and Williams (eds.) (1981).

COULSON, A. (1978b) 'The Silo Project'. *IDS Bulletin* X, 1. (Reprinted in Coulson (ed.) *African Socialism* ... 175–8).

COULSON, A. (ed.) (1979b) *African Socialism in Practice: The Tanzanian Experience*. Spokesman Books, Nottingham, England.

COULSON, A. (1982) 'The State and Industrialization in Tanzania' in M. Fransman (ed.) *Industrialisation in Africa*. Heinemann Educational Books.

DE VRIES, J. AND FORTMANN, L. (1979) 'Operation *Sogeza* in Iringa Region' in Coulson (ed.) *African Socialism* ... 128–35.

DE WILDE, J. and others (1967) *Experiences with Agricultural Development in Tropical Africa*, 2 Volumes. Johns Hopkins University Press.

DUGGAN, W. R. AND CIVILLE, J. R. (1976) *Tanzania and Nyerere: A Study of Ujamaa and Nationhood*. New York: Orbis Books.

DUIGNAN, P. AND GANN, L. (eds.) *Colonialism in Africa 1870–1960*
Vol. 1 (1969) *The History and Politics of Colonialism 1870–1914*;
Vol. 2 (1970) *The History and Politics of Colonialism 1914–1960*;
Vol. 3 (1971) (edited by Victor Turner) *Profiles of Change: African Society and Colonial Rule*;
Vol. 4 (1975) *The Economics of Colonialism*
Vol. 5 (1973) *A Bibliographic Guide to Colonialism in Sub-Saharan Africa*.
Hoover Institution Publications.

DUNDAS, C. (1955) *African Crossroads*. Macmillan.

East African Common Services Organisation (1967) *Treaty for East African Cooperation*.

East African Statistical Department (1963) *The Gross Domestic Product of the Protectorate of Zanzibar 1957–1961*. (An extract is reprinted in H. Smith (ed.) (1966) 66–79).

EDGETT SMITH, W. E. (1971, 1973) *We Must Run While Others Walk*, Random House, 1971; updated as *Nyerere of Tanzania*, Gollancz, London, 1973, and Transafrica Publishers, Nairobi, 1974.

ELLIS, F. (1979a) 'A Preliminary Analysis of the Decline in Tanzanian Cashewnut Production: Causes, Possible Remedies and Lessons for Rural Development Policy'. Paper 79.1, Economic Research Bureau, University of Dar es Salaam.

ELLIS, F. (1979b) 'Marketing Costs and the Processing of Cashewnuts in Tanzania: An Analysis of the Marketing Margin and the Potential Level of the Producer Price'. Paper 79.2, Economic Research Bureau, University of Dar es Salaam.

ELLIS, F. (1980) 'Agricultural Pricing Policy in Tanzania 1970–1979; Implications for Agricultural Output, Rural Incomes, and Crop Marketing Costs'. Seminar on Development, Employment and Equity Issues, University of Dar es Salaam, 21–5 July.

ELLMAN, A. (1971) 'Development of the *Ujamaa* Policy in Tanzania' in Cliffe *et al.* (eds.) (1975), 312–45.

ERLICH, C. (1964) 'Some Aspects of Economic Policy in Tanganyika 1945–1960'. *Journal of Modern African Studies*, II, 2 265–7.

ERLICH, C. (1965) 'The Uganda Economy, 1903–1945', in Harlow, V.

and Chilver, E. M. (eds.) *History of East Africa Volume II*. Oxford, The Clarendon Press, 395–475.

ERLICH, C. (1976) 'The Poor Country: The Tanganyikan Economy from 1945 to Independence', in Low, D. A. and Smith, A. (eds.) *History of East Africa Volume III*. Oxford, The Clarendon Press, 290–330.

FEIERMAN, S. (1972) 'Concepts of Sovereignty among the Shambaa'. Unpublished D. Phil. thesis. Oxford University.

FEIERMAN, S. (1974) *The Shambaa Kingdom: A History*. Madison University Press.

FELDMAN, R. (1971) 'Custom and Capitalism: A Study of Land Tenure in Ismani, Tanzania'. Paper 71.14, Economic Research Bureau, University of Dar es Salaam.

FINLAY, R. (1974) 'Intercropping Soyabeans with Cereals'. Regional Soyabean Conference, Addis Ababa, October.

FORD, J. (1971) *The Role of the Trypanosomiases in African Ecology: A Study of the Tsetse Fly Problem*. Oxford, The Clarendon Press.

FORTMANN, L. (1980) 'Peasants, Officials and Participation in Rural Tanzania: Experience with Villagization and Decentralization'. Report No. 1, Special Series on Rural Local Organization, Rural Development Committee, Cornell University.

FRANKEL, S. H. (1950) 'The Kongwa Experiment: Lessons of the East African Groundnuts Scheme'. *The Times*, 4 and 5 October 1950, reprinted in Frankel, S. H. (1953), *The Economic Impact on Underdeveloped Countries*. Harvard University Press.

FRANSMAN, M. (ed.) (1981) *Industrialisation in Africa*. Heinemann Educational Books.

FRIEDLAND, W. H. (1969) *Vuta Kamba: the Development of Trade Unions in Tanganyika*. Hoover Institution Publication 84, Stanford Institution Press.

FUGGLES-COUCHMAN, N. R. (1964) *Agricultural Change in Tanganyika 1945–1960*. Stanford Research Institute.

GARDNER, B. (1963) *German East*. Cassel.

Geografiska Annaler (Uppsala) (1972) Special issue on 'Soil Erosion and Sedimentation in Tanzania', Vol. 54, No. 3–4.

GEORGULAS, N. (1963) 'An Approach to the Economic Development of Rural Areas in Tanganyika with Special Reference to the Village Settlement Program'. Maxwell School, Syracuse University.

GILMAN, C. (1942) 'A Short History of the Tanganyikan Railways'. *Tanganyika Notes and Records* 13, 14–56.

GOTTLEIB, M. (1973) 'The Extent and Characterisation of Differentiation in Tanzanian Agricultural and Rural Society'. *The African Review* (Dar es Salaam) III, 2 241–62.

GRAHAM, J. D. (1976) 'Indirect Rule: The Establishment of "Chiefs" and "Tribes" in Cameron's Tanganyika'. *Tanzania Notes and Records* 77/78, 1–9.

GRAY, R. AND BIRMINGHAM, D. (eds.) (1970) *Pre-colonial African Trade*. Oxford University Press.

Great Britain (1955) *East African Royal Commission 1953–5, Report.* Her Majesty's Stationery office.

GREEN, R. AND SEIDMAN, A. (1968) *Unity or Poverty? The Economics of Pan-Africanism.* Penguin.

GROENEVELD, S. (1968) 'Traditional Farming and Cattle-Coconut Schemes in Tanga Region', in Ruthenberg (ed.) (1968) 219–47.

GUILLEBAUD, C. W. (1958) *An Economic Survey of the Sisal Industry of Tanganyika.* Nisbet.

GULLIVER, P. M. (1955) *Labour Migration in a Rural Economy.* East African Studies No. 6, East African Institute of Social Research, Kampala.

GWASSA, G. C. (1969) 'The German Intervention and African Resistance in Tanzania' in Kimambo and Temu (eds.) *A History of Tanzania*, 85–122.

HAILEY, LORD (1942) *Native Administration and Political Development in British Tropical Africa.* HMSO.

HAILEY, LORD (1943) *The Future of Colonial Peoples.* Oxford University Press for the Royal Institute of International Affairs.

HAILEY, LORD (1950) *Native Administration in the British African Territories, Part I.* HMSO.

HAILEY, LORD (1952) 'A Turning Point in Colonial Rule'. *International Affairs* XXVIII, 2 177–83.

HALL, R. AND PEYMAN, H. (1976) *The Great Uhuru Railway.* Gollancz.

HARLOW, V. AND CHILVER, E. M. (eds.) (1965) *History of East Africa Volume 2* (General Editors R. Oliver and G. Matthew). Oxford, The Clarendon Press.

HARRISON, E. (1937) *Soil Erosion.* HMSO.

HART, R. (1977) 'Maternal and Child Health Services in Tanzania'. *Tropical Doctor* 7, 179–85.

HATCH, J. C. (1976) *Two African Statesmen: Kaunda of Zambia and Nyerere of Tanzania.* Secker and Warburg.

HAWKINS, H. G. C. (1965) *A Survey of Wholesale and Retail Trade in Tanganyika* (a report prepared by the Economist Intelligence Unit, and originally published in 1962). Praegar, New York.

HAZELWOOD, A. (1975) *Economic Integration: The East African Experience.* Heinemann Educational Books.

HENDERSON, W. O. (1965) 'German East Africa, 1884–1918', in Harlow, V. and Chilver, E. M. (eds.) *History of East Africa* Volume 2. Oxford, The Clarendon Press, 123–62.

HEYER, J., ROBERTS, P. AND WILLIAMS, G. (eds.) (1981) *Rural Development in Tropical Africa.* Macmillan.

HILL, F. (1975) 'Ujamaa: African Socialist Productionism in Tanzania' in Desfosses, H. and Levesque, J. (eds.) *Socialism in the Third World.* Praegar 1975, 216–51 (An extract from this is in Coulson (ed.) *African Socialism . . .*, 106–113).

HIRJI, K. (1973) 'School, Education and Underdevelopment in Tanzania'. *Maji Maji* (Dar es Salaam) 12, 1–22.

HIRJI, K. (1974) 'Colonial Ideological Apparatuses in Tanganyika under the Germans'. History Teachers' Conference, Morogoro.

HIRJI, K. (1978) 'Political Economy of Transport'. *Maji Maji* 32, 32–40.

HITCHCOCK, SIR E. (1959) 'The Sisal Industry of East Africa', *Tanganyika Notes and Records*, 52, 4–17.

HOFMEIR, R. (1973) *Transport and Economic Development in Tanzania*. Weltforum-Verlag (Munich).

HONEY, M. (1974) 'Asian Industrial Activities in Tanganyika'. *Tanzania Notes and Records* 75, 55–69.

HORNBY, G. (1962) 'A Brief History of Tanga School up to 1914'. *Tanganyika Notes and Records* 58/9, 148–50.

HORNBY, G. (1964) 'German Educational Achievement in East Africa'. *Tanganyika Notes and Records* 62, 83–90.

HUANG, Y. (1976) 'Distribution of Tax Burden in Tanzania'. *Economic Journal* 86, 73–86.

HULLS, R. H. (1971) 'An Assessment of Agricultural Extension in Sukumaland, Western Tanzania'. Paper 71.13. Economic Research Bureau, University of Dar es Salaam.

HUTCHISON, R. (1973) 'Neo-Colonial Tactics: The Tanzania Publishing House' in Coulson (ed.) *African Socialism* . . . 228–36.

HYDEN, G. (1975a), '"We Must Run While Others Walk": Policy-Making for Socialist Development in the Tanzanian-Type of Polities' in Kim *et al.* (eds.) *Papers on the Political Economy of Tanzania*, pp. 5–13.

HYDEN, G. (1975b) 'Ujamaa, Villagisation and Rural Development in Tanzania'. *ODI Review* No. 1, 53–72.

HYDEN, G. (ed.) (1976) *Cooperatives in Tanzania*. Studies in Political Science No. 4, Tanzania Publishing House.

HYDEN, G. (1980) *Beyond Ujamaa in Tanzania: Underdevelopment and an Uncaptured Peasantry*. Heinemann Educational Books.

IBBOTT, R. (n.d.) 'The Ruvuma Development Association'. Unpublished typescript.

ILIFFE, J. (1969a) 'The Age of Improvement and Differentiation' in Kimambo and Temu (eds.) 123–60.

ILIFFE, J. (1969b) *Tanganyika under German Rule*. Cambridge University Press.

ILIFFE, J. (1969c) 'Tanzania under German and British rule' in Ogot, B. A. and Kieran, J. A. (eds.) *Zamani: A Survey of East African History* (East African Publishing House, and Longmans); also included in Cliffe and Saul (eds.) Vol. 1 (1972) 8–17.

ILIFFE, J. (1970) 'A History of the Dockworkers of Dar es Salaam' *Tanzania Notes and Records* 71, 119–48; reprinted in Sandbrook, R. and Cohen, R. (eds.) (1975) 49–72.

ILIFFE, J. (1971) *Agricultural Change in Modern Tanzania*. East African Publishing House.

ILIFFE, J. (ed.) (1973) *Modern Tanzanians: A Volume of Biographies*. East African Publishing House.

ILIFFE, J. (1979) *A Modern History of Tanganyika*. Cambridge University Press.

INGLE, C. (1972) *From Village to State in Tanzania: The Politics of Rural Development*. Cornell University Press, 1972.

International Bank for Reconstruction and Development (World Bank) (1961) *The Economic Development of Tanganyika*. Johns Hopkins University Press, Baltimore.

International Bank for Reconstruction and Development (World Bank) (1977) *Tanzania: Basic Economic Report, 1977*.

International Labour Office (1978) *Towards Self-Reliance: Development, Employment and Equity Issues in Tanzania*. ILO (Addis Ababa and Geneva), Jobs and Skills Programme for Africa.

JAPHET, K. AND SEATON, E. (1967) *The Meru Land Case*. East African Publishing House.

JELLICOE, M. (1969) 'The Turu Resistance Movement'. *Tanzania Notes and Records*, No. 70.

Jenga (Dar es Salaam). Magazine of the National Development Corporation.

JERVIS, T. (1939) 'A History of *Robusta* Coffee in Bukoba'. *Tanganyika Notes and Records* 8, 47–58.

JIDDAWI, A. M. (1951) 'Extracts from an Arab Account Book 1840–1851'. *Tanganyika Notes and Records* 31, 25–31.

JONES, G. (forthcoming) *Technology and Self-Reliance in Tanzania*. Tanzania Publishing House.

KAHAMA, G. (1972) 'Participation in Tanzania: The Role of the National Development Corporation'. *Mbioni* VI, 11 6–35.

KARIOKI, J. (1979) *Tanzania's Human Revolution*. Pennsylvania State University Press.

KAWAWA, R. (1966) 'New Approaches to Rural Development'. *Mbioni* II, 114–15.

KAYAMBA, M. (1948) *African Problems*. Africa's Own Library, No. 18, Lutterworth Press.

KIERAN, J. A. (1970) 'Abushiri and the Germans' in Ogot, B. A. (ed.) *Hadithi 2*. East African Publishing House.

KIM, K. S., MABELE, R. AND SCHULTHEIS, M. (eds.) (1979) *Papers on the Political Economy of Tanzania*. Heinemann Educational Books.

KIMAMBO, I. AND TEMU, A. (eds.) (1969) *A History of Tanzania*. East African Publishing House and Heinemann Educational Books.

KIMAMBO, I. (1969) *A Political History of the Pare of Tanzania*. East African Publishing House.

KJAERBY, F. (1979a) 'Agricultural Productivity and Surplus Production in Tanzania: Implications of Villagization, Fertilizers and Mixed Farming'. Mimeo, Bureau of Resource Assessment and Land Use Planning, University of Dar es Salaam.

KJAERBY, F. (1796b) 'The Development of Agro-Pastoralism among the Barabaig in Hanang District'. Research Paper No. 56, Bureau of Resource Assessment and Land Use Planning, University of Dar es Salaam.

KJAERBY, F. (1980) 'The Problem of Livestock Development and Villagization among the Barabaig in Hanang District'. Research Report No. 40, Bureau of Resource Assessment and Land Use Planning, University of Dar es Salaam.

KJEKSHUS, H. (ed.) (1976) *The Party: Essays on TANU*. Studies in Political Science No. 6, Tanzania Publishing House.

KJEKSHUS, H. (1977) *Ecology Control and Economic Development in East African History*. Heinemann Educational Books.

KJEKSHUS, H. (ed.) (1977) *Labour in Tanzania*. Studies in Political Science No. 6, Tanzania Publishing House.

KOCH, R. (1898) 'Report on West Usambaras from the Point of View of Health', translated and reprinted in *Tanganyika Notes and Records* 35 (1953) 7–13.

KODA, BERTHA (1978) 'Liberation of Women in Tanzania'. *Maji Maji* (Dar es Salaam) No. 35, 54–61.

KRIESEL, H. *et al.* (1970) *Agricultural Marketing in Tanzania*. USAID, Dar es Salaam, and Department of Agricultural Economics, Michigan State University.

LAWRENCE, P. (1971) 'Plantation Sisal: The Inherited Mode of Production in Cliffe *et al.* (eds.) (1975) 103–30.

League of Nations. *Report by His Majesty's Government in the U.K. . . . to the Council of the League of Nations on the Administration of Tanganyika Territory*. Annually, 1918–38.

LEONARD, D. WITH HYDEN, G., MAEDA, J. AND MUSHI, S. (1975) 'Decentralisation and the Issues of Efficiency, Effectiveness and Popular Participation'. Mimeo, Decentralisation Research Project, University of Dar es Salaam.

LEONARD, D. (1976) 'Bureaucracy, Class and Inequality in Kenya and Tanzania'. Conference on Inequality in Africa, Mount Kisco, New York, October.

LEUBUSCHER, C. (1944) *Tanganyika Territory: a Study of Economic Policy under Mandate*. Oxford University Press.

LEYS, C. (1969) 'The First Tanzanian Five Year Plan' in C. Leys (ed.) *Politics and Change in Developing Countries*, Cambridge University Press, 1969, pp. 267–75; also in Cliffe and Saul (eds.) Vol. 2 (1973) 5–10.

LEYS, C. (1972) *Underdevelopment in Kenya*. Heinemann Educational Books.

LEYS, C. (1978) 'Capital Accumulation, Class Formation and Dependency: The Significance of the Kenyan Case', in R. Miliband and J. Saville (eds.) *The Socialist Register 1978* Merlin Press, 241–66.

LISTOWEL, J. (1965) *The Making of Tanganyika*. Chatto and Windus.

LITTLE, ARTHUR D., Inc. (1961) *Tanganyika Industrial Development. Government Printer, Dar es Salaam*.

LIVINGSTONE, I. (1970) 'Results of a Rural Survey: The Ownership of Durable Goods in Tanzanian Households and some Implications for Rural Industry'. Paper 70.1 Economic Research Bureau, University of Dar es Salaam.

LIVINGSTONE, I. (1971) 'Production, Price and Marketing Policy for Staple Foodstuffs in Tanzania'. Paper 71.16, Economic Research Bureau, University of Dar es Salaam.

LOFCHIE, M. (1965) *Zanzibar: Background to Revolution*. Princeton University Press.

LOFCHIE, M. (1967) 'Was Okello's Revolution a Conspiracy?' *Transition* (Kampala) 33, 39–42; reprinted in Cliffe and Saul (eds.) Vol. 1 (1972) 31–8.

LOFCHIE, M. (1978) 'Agrarian Crisis and Economic Liberalism in Tanzania'. *Journal of Modern African Studies* XVI, 3 451–75.

LORD, R. F. (1963) *Economic Aspects of Mechanised Farming at Nachingwea in Tanganyika*. HMSO.

LOXLEY, J. (1966) 'Development of the Monetary and Financial System of the East African Currency Area'. Unpublished Ph.D. thesis, University of Leeds.

LOXLEY, J. (1972) 'Financial Planning and Control in Tanzania', in J. Rweyemamu and others (eds.) *Towards Socialist Planning*. Tanzania Publishing House, 50–72.

LOXLEY, J. (1973) 'Structural Change in the Monetary System of Tanzania' in Cliffe and Saul (eds.) Vol. 2, 102–11.

LOW, D. A. AND SMITH, A. (eds.) (1977) *A History of East Africa, Vol. 3, 1945–1961*. Oxford, The Clarendon Press. (General editors R. Oliver and G. Matthew.)

LUGARD, LORD (1921) *The Dual Mandate in British Tropical Africa*. William Blackwood and Sons, Edinburgh. (4th edition, 1929; 5th edition Frank Cass and Co., 1965.)

LUGARD, LORD (1933) *Foreword* to Strickland (1933).

LUNING, H. AND VENEMA, L. (1969) 'An Evaluation of the Agricultural Extension Service'. Rungwe District Research Project, Afrika-Studiecentrum, Leyden, Netherlands.

LWOGA, C. M. (1978) 'Bureaucrats, Peasants and Land Rights: A Tanzanian Case Study'. Mimeo, Department of Sociology, University of Dar es Salaam.

MCHENRY, D. E. (jr.) (1979) *Tanzania's Ujamaa Villages: The Implementation of a Rural Development Strategy*. University of California, Research Series No. 39.

MCLOUGHLIN, P. (1967) 'Tanzania: Agricultural Development in Sukumaland'. Chapter 6 of de Wilde J. C. (ed.) *Experience with Agricultural Development in Tropical Africa, Volume II*, Johns Hopkins Press, Baltimore.

MAGUIRE, G. A. (1969) *Towards 'Uhuru' in Tanzania*. Cambridge University Press.

Maji Maji (Dar es Salaam). Journal of the Tanu Youth League, University of Dar es Salaam.

MALIMA, K. (1971) 'The Determinants of Cotton Supply'. Paper 71.4, Economic Research Bureau, University of Dar es Salaam; reprinted in Kim, Mabele and Schultheis (eds.) (1979) 223–7.

MALIMA, K. (1978) 'Planning for Self-Reliance; Tanzania's Third Five Year Plan'. Paper 78.1 Economic Research Bureau, University of Dar es Salaam.

MAMDANI, M. (1976) *Politics and Class Formation in Uganda.* Heinemann Educational Books.

MANGAT, J. S. (1969) *A History of the Asians in East Africa c. 1886 to 1945.* Oxford, The Clarendon Press.

MAPOLU, H. (1972) 'Labour Unrest: Irresponsibility or Workers' Revolution?' *Jenga* (Dar es Salaam) 12, 20–3. ,.

MAPOLU, H. (1973) 'The Workers' Movement in Tanzania'. *Maji Maji* (Dar es Salaam) 12, 31–43.

MAPOLU, H. (ed.) (1976) *Workers and Management.* Tanzania Publishing House.

Marketing Development Bureau, Dar es Salaam (1974). 'A Strategic Grain Reserve Programme for Tanzania'. Mimeo.

Marco Publications (Nairobi) (1968) *Who's Who in East Africa,* 3rd edition.

MARO, P. S. AND MLAY, W. I. (1978) 'People, Population Distribution and Employment', *Tanzania Notes and Records* 83, 1–19.

MARTIN, D. (1974, revised edition 1978) *General Amin.* Sphere Books.

MARTIN, R. (1974) *Personal Freedom and the Law in Tanzania.* Nairobi: Oxford University Press.

MASAO, F. T. (1974) 'The Irrigation System in Uchagga: An Ethno-Historical Approach'. *Tanzania Notes and Records* 75, 1–8.

MASEFIELD, G. B. (1955) 'A Comparison between Settlements in Villages and Isolated Homesteads'. *Journal of African Administration* VII, 2, 64–8.

MASCARENHAS, A. (1973) 'Urban Housing in Mainland Tanzania', in Egero, B. and Henin, R. (eds.) *The Population of Tanzania: An Analysis of the 1967 Population Census.* Census Volume 6, Bureau of Resource Assessment and Land Use Planning, and Bureau of Statistics, 98–118.

MASCARENHAS, A. AND MASCARENHAS, O. (1976) 'Man and Shelter: An Overview and Documentation on Housing in Tanzania'. Research Paper No. 45, Bureau of Resource Assessment and Land Use Planning, University of Dar es Salaam.

MATANGO, R. (1975) 'Operation Mara: Paradox of Democracy'. *Maji Maji* (Dar es Salaam) No. 20 17–30.

MATANGO, R. (1976a) 'The Role of Agencies for Rural Development in Tanzania: A Case Study of the Lushoto Integrated Development Project'. Paper 76.3, Economic Research Bureau, University of Dar es Salaam. Revised version in Coulson (ed.) *African Socialism...* 158–72.

MATANGO, R. (1976b) 'Peasants and Socialism in Tarime District'. Unpublished M.A. dissertation, University of Dar es Salaam.

MBILINYI, M. (1972a) 'The Decision to Educate in Rural Tanzania'. Unpublished Ph.D. thesis, University of Dar es Salaam.

MBILINYI, M. (1972b) 'The "New Women" and Traditional Norms in Tanzania'. *Journal of Modern African Studies* 10, 57–72.

MBILINYI, M. (1973) 'Education for Rural Life or Education for Socialist Transformation?' East African Social Science Conference, Dar es Salaam, December.

MBILINYI, M. (1975) 'African Education in the British Colonial Period'. A revised version of a paper presented to the History Teachers' Conference, Morogoro, June 1974.

MBILINYI, M. (1976) 'Peasants' Education in Tanzania'. *African Review* (Dar es Salaam) VI, 1.

MBILINYI, M. (1977a) 'Basic Education: Tool of Exploitation or Liberation?' *Prospects*, December. Also Research Report No. 21, Bureau of Resource Assessment and Land Use Planning, University of Dar es Salaam.

MBILINYI, M. (1977b) 'Economic Independence and Liberation of Women'. Conference on Women and Development, Maseru, Lesotho, April.

MBILINYI, M. (1979) 'The Arusha Declaration and Education for Self-Reliance' in Coulson (ed.) *African Socialism* . . . 217–27.

MBILINYI, M. (ed.) (forthcoming) *Who goes to School in East Africa?* East African Literature Bureau.

MBILINYI, S. (ed.) (1973) *Agricultural Research for Rural Development.* East African Literature Bureau.

Mbioni (Dar es Salaam). Monthly journal of Kivukoni College.

MEEK, C. I. (1953) 'Stock Reduction in the Mbulu Highlands'. *Journal of African Administration* V, 4 158–66.

MESAKI, S. (1975) 'Operation Pwani, Kisarawe District: Implementation Problems, Prospects'. Unpublished M.A. dissertation, University of Dar es Salaam.

MIGOT-ADHOLLA, S. (1969a) 'The Politics of a Growers' Cooperative Organisation', in Cliffe *et al.* (eds.) (1975) 221–53.

MIGOT-ADHOLLA, S. (1969b) 'Power, Differentiation and Resource Allocation: The Cooperative Tractor Project in Maswa District', in Hyden (ed.) (1976) 39–57.

MIHYO, P. (1975) 'The Struggle for Workers' Control in Tanzania'. *Review of African Political Economy*, 4, 62–85.

MITCHELL, SIR P. (1954) *African Afterthoughts*. Hutchinson.

MKUFYA, W. E. (1977) *The Wicked Walk*. Tanzania Publishing House.

MOLLOY, J. (1971) 'Political Communication in Lushoto District, Tanzania'. Unpublished Ph.D. thesis, University of Kent.

MOODY, A. (1970) 'A Report on a Farm Economic Survey of Tea Smallholders in Bukoba District'. Paper 70.8, Economic Research Bureau, University of Dar es Salaam.

MORGAN, W. T. (ed.) (1968, 2nd edition 1972) *East Africa: Its People and Resources*. Oxford University Press (Nairobi).

MORRIS-HALE, W. (1969) 'British Administration in Tanganyika from 1920 to 1945'. Unpublished Ph.D. dissertation, University of Geneva.

MORRISON, D. R. (1976) *Education and Politics in Africa: the Tanzanian Case*. C. Hurst and Co.

MSEKWA, P. (1974) 'Decision-making in Tanzania: A Study of the Changing Relationship between the NEC of TANU and the National Assembly since 1945'. Unpublished M.A. dissertation, University of Dar es Salaam.

MSUYA, HON. C. D. (1974) 'Proliferation of Public Institutions in Tanzania: Its Impact on the Economy'. Address to the Economic Society of Tanzania, 22 February.

MUNRO, J. FORBES (1976) *Africa and the International Economy 1800–1960*. Dent.

MUSHI, S. S. (1978) 'Popular Participation and Regional Development Planning: The Politics of Decentralised Administration'. *Tanzania Notes and Records* 83, 63–97.

MUTHANA, A. Z. (1968) 'The Political Impact of the Cooperative Union in Dodoma District'. In Hyden (ed.) (1976) 21–8.

MWANSASU, B. AND PRATT, R. C. (eds.) (1979) *Towards Socialism in Tanzania*. University of Toronto Press.

MWAPACHU, H. B. (1976) 'The Restructuring of Public Enterprises for Improved Performance'. *Mbioni* (Dar es Salaam) VIII, 1.

MWAPACHU, J. V. (1976) 'Operation Planned Villages in Rural Tanzania'. *African Review* VI, 1 1–16. Reprinted in Coulson (ed.) (1979) 114–27.

National Development Corporation, Dar es Salaam. *Annual Reports* 1965–.

NELLIS, JOHN R. (1972) *A Theory of Ideology: The Tanzanian Example*. Oxford University Press.

NELSON, ANTON (1967) *The Freemen of Meru*. Oxford University Press.

NEWIGER, N. (1968) 'Village Settlement Schemes: The Problems of Cooperative Farming', in Ruthenberg (ed.) (1968) 249–73.

NIBLOCK, T. (1972) 'Aid and Foreign Policy in Tanzania'. Unpublished D. Phil. thesis, University of Sussex.

NYERERE, J. K. (1958) 'National Property'. See Nyerere (1966) 53–8.

NYERERE, J. K. (1962a) *Ujamaa—the Basis of African Socialism*. Included in Nyerere (1966) 162–71.

NYERERE, J. K. (1962b) 'President's Inaugural Address'. See Nyerere (1966) 176–87.

NYERERE, J. K. (1962c) *Tujisahihishe* ['Let us correct ourselves']. Government Printer.

NYERERE, J. K. (1963) 'Democracy and the Party System'. See Nyerere (1966) 195–203.

NYERERE, J. K. (1966) *Freedom and Unity: A Collection from Writings and Speeches 1952–62*. Oxford University Press.

NYERERE, J. K. (1967a) *The Arusha Declaration*. See *Freedom and Socialism* (1968). 231–50.

NYERERE, J. K. (1967b) 'Public Ownership in Tanzania' in *Freedom and Socialism* (1968) 251–6.

NYERERE, J. K. (1967c) *Education for Self-Reliance*. See *Freedom and Socialism* (1968) 267–90.

NYERERE, J. K. (1967d) *Socialism and Rural Development*. See *Freedom and Socialism* (1968) 337–66.

NYERERE, J. K. (1967e) 'Policy on Foreign Affairs' in *Freedom and Socialism* (1968) 367–84.

NYERERE, J. K. (1968a) *Freedom and Socialism: A Selection from Writings and Speeches 1965–1967*. Oxford University Press.

NYERERE, J. K. (1968b) *Essays on Socialism*, Oxford University Press.

NYERERE, J. K. (1968c) *Freedom and Development*. Reprinted in *Freedom and Development* (1973) 58–71, and in Coulson (ed.) (1979) *African Socialism in Practice: the Tanzanian Experience* 27–35.

NYERERE, J. K. (1969) *Presidential Circular No. 1 of 1969*. Reprinted in Cliffe et al. (eds.) (1975) 27–34.

NYERERE, J. K. (1970) *Presidential Circular No. 1 of 1970: The Establishment of Workers' Councils, Executive Boards and Boards of Directors*. Reprinted in Mapolu (ed.) *Workers and Management* 153–9.

NYERERE, J. K. (1973b) *Freedom and Development: A Selection from Writings and Speeches 1969–1973*. Oxford University Press.

NYERERE, J. K. (1975) 'Report to the TANU National Conference'. *Daily News*, 24 September 1975.

NYERERE, J. K. (1977) *The Arusha Declaration Ten Years After*. Government Printer, Dar es Salaam. Reprinted in Coulson (ed.) (1979) *African Socialism in Practice: The Tanzanian Experience* 43–71.

OKELLO, J. (1967) *Revolution in Zanzibar*. East African Publishing House.

OLIVER, R. (1952, 2nd edition 1965) *The Missionary Factor in East Africa*. Longmans.

OLIVER, R. AND MATTHEW, G. (eds.) (1963) *History of East Africa Vol. 1 Up to 1900*. Oxford, The Clarendon Press. (Vol. 2 eds. V. Harlow and E. Chilver, 1965, covers 1890–1945; Vol. 3, eds. D. A. Low and A. Smith, 1976, covers 1945–61.)

OLIVER, R. (ed.) (1977) *The Cambridge History of Africa, Vol. 3, from c. 1050 to c. 1600*. Cambridge University Press.

OLLE, W. AND SCHOELLER, W. (1977) 'World Market, State and National Average Conditions of Labour'. Occasional Paper 77.1, Economic Research Bureau, University of Dar es Salaam.

ORDE-BROWNE, Major St. J. (1946) *Labour Conditions in East Africa*. London: HMSO.

Overseas Food Corporation (1956) *Annual Report and Statement of Accounts for the Year ended 31 March 1955*. HMSO.

PACKARD, Ph. (1972) 'Corporate Structure in Agriculture and Socialist Development in Tanzania: A Case Study of the National Agricultural and Food Corporation'. *East African Journal of Rural Development* V, 163–82. A revised version is in Coulson (ed.) (1979) 200–13.

PARKIPUNY, L. (1976) 'Some Crucial Aspects of the Maasai Predicament'. In Coulson (ed.) (1979) 136–57.

PHILLIPS, D. (1974) 'The Need for the Development of the Food Industry through Small-scale Production'. Mimeo, Small Industries Development Organisation, Dar es Salaam.

PHILLIPS, D. (1976) 'Industrialisation in Tanzania: The Case of Small Scale Production', in Kim, Mabele and Schultheis (eds.) (1979) 78–94.

PRATT, R. C. (1967) 'The Administration of Economic Planning in a Newly Independent State: The Tanzanian Experience 1963–66'. *Journal of Commonwealth Political Studies* V, 1 (38–59); reprinted in Cliffe and Saul (eds.) Vol. 2 (1973) 11–24.

PRATT, R. C. (1976) *The Critical Phase in Tanzania 1945–1968: Nyerere and the Emergence of a Socialist Strategy.* Cambridge University Press.

RAIKES, P. (1971) 'Wheat Production and the Development of Capitalism in North Iraqw', in Cliffe *et al.* (eds.) (1975) 79–102.

RAIKES, P. (1972) 'Differentiation and Progressive Farmer Policies'. Paper presented to the East African Agricultural Economics Society, Kampala, June.

RAIKES, P. (1976a) 'Coffee Production in West Lake Region, Tanzania'. Paper A.76.9 Institute for Development Research, Copenhagen.

RAIKES, P. (1976b) 'Sugar Production in West Lake Region, Tanzania'. Paper A.76.10, Institute for Development Research, Copenhagen.

RAIKES, P. (1976c) 'Tea Production in West Lake Region, Tanzania'. Paper A.76.11, Institute for Development Research, Copenhagen.

RANGER, T. (1969) 'The Recovery of African Initiative in African History'. Inaugural Lecture No. 2, University of Dar es Salaam.

RAUM, O. F. (1940) *Chagga Childhood.* Oxford University Press.

RAUM, O. F. (1965) 'German East Africa: Changes in African Tribal Life under German Administration' in Harlow, V. and Chilver, E. (eds.) *History of East Africa Volume 2.* Oxford, The Clarendon Press, 163–208.

REDMOND, P. (1972) 'A Political History of the Songea Ngoni from the Mid-Nineteenth Century to the Rise of the Tanganyika African National Union'. Unpublished Ph.D. thesis, University of London.

REDMOND, P. (1976) 'The NMCMU and Tobacco Production in Songea'. *Tanzania Notes and Records* 79/80, 65–98.

RESNICK, I. (ed.) (1968) *Tanzania: Revolution by Education.* Longmans.

RESNICK, I. (1976) 'The State Trading Corporation: A Casualty of Contradictions' in Mapolu (ed.) (1976) 71–89.

Review of African Political Economy (1977) 'Briefings: Tanzania Students Protest Politician's Spoils', No. 10, 101–5 (June 1978).

RIGBY, P. (1971) 'Politics and Modern Leadership Rules in Ugogo' in Turner (ed.) 393–438.

ROBERTS, A. (ed.) (1968) *Tanzania before 1900.* East African Publishing House.

ROBERTS, A. (1970) 'Nyamwezi Trade', in Gray, A. and Birmingham, D. (eds.) (1970) *Pre-colonial African Trade*. Oxford University Press.

RODGERS, S. F. (1974) 'The Kilimanjaro Native Planters' Association: Administrative Responses to Chagga Initiatives in the 1920s'. *Transafrican Journal of History* IV, 1/2, 94–114.

RODNEY, W. (1972) *How Europe Underdeveloped Africa*. Bogle L'Ouverture (London) and Tanzania Publishing House (Dar es Salaam).

RODNEY, W. (1973) 'Policing the Countryside in Colonial Tanganyika'. Paper 51, East African Social Science Conference, Dar es Salaam, December.

ROEMER, M., TIDDRICK, G. AND WILLIAMS, D. (1976) 'The Range of Strategic Choice in Tanzanian Industries'. *Journal of Development Economics* III, 1 257–76.

ROEMER, M. (1978) 'Dependence and Industrialisation Strategies'. Development Discussion Paper No. 37, Harvard Institute for International Development.

ROTENHAN, D. von (1968) 'Cotton Farming in Sukumaland', in Ruthenberg (ed.) (1968) 51–85.

ROUNCE, N. V. (1946) *The Agriculture of the Cultivation Steppe*. Longmans (Cape Town).

RUTHENBERG, H. (1964) *Agricultural Development in Tanganyika*. Springer-Verlag.

RUTHENBERG, H. (ed.) (1968) *Smallholder Farming and Smallholder Development in Tanzania*. Springer-Weltforum.

RWEGASIRA, D. (1976) 'Inflation and Monetary Expansion: The 1966–73 Tanzanian Experiences' in Kim, Mabele and Schultheis (eds.) (1979) 143–54.

RWEYEMAMU, J. (1969) 'Some Aspects of the Turner Report'. Paper 69.20, Economic Research Bureau, University of Dar es Salaam.

RWEYEMAMU, J. et al. (eds.) (1972) *Towards Socialist Planning*. Tanzania Publishing House.

RWEYEMAMU, J. (n.d. ?1972) 'The Silent Class Struggle in Retrospect' Mimeo, Department of Economics, University of Dar es Salaam.

RWEYEMAMU, J. (1973) *Underdevelopment and Industrialization in Tanzania*. Oxford University Press.

SABOT, R. (1979) *Economic Development and Urban Migration: Tanzania 1900–1971*. Oxford, The Clarendon Press.

SANBERG, A. (1974) 'The Impact of the Steigler's Gorge Dam on the Rufiji Flood Plain'. Service Paper 74.2, Bureau of Resource Assessment and Land Use Planning, University of Dar es Salaam.

SANDBROOK, R. AND COHEN, R. (eds.) (1975) *The Development of an African Working Class*. Longman.

SAUL, J. (1968) 'High Level Manpower for Socialism' in I. Resnick (ed.) *Tanzania: Revolution by Education*, reprinted in Cliffe and Saul (eds.) Vol. 2 (1973) 275–82.

SAUL, J. (1970a) 'Radicalism and The Hill'. *East African Journal* (Nairobi) 7, 12 reprinted in Cliffe and Saul (eds.) Vol. 2 (1973) 289–92.

SAUL, J. (1970b) 'The Reorganisation of the Victoria Federation of Cooperative Unions', reprinted in Cliffe et al. (ed), (1975) 212–20.

SAUL, J. (1971a) 'Nationalism, Socialism and Tanzanian History' in Cliffe and Saul (eds.) Vol. 1 (1972) 65–75.

SAUL, J. (1971b) 'Marketing Co-operatives in a Developing Country. The Tanzanian Case'. Reprinted in Saul and Cliffe (eds.) Vol. 2 (1973) 141–52.

SAUL, J. S. (1979) The State and Revolution in Eastern Africa. Monthly Review Press and Heinemann Educational Books.

SAYLOR, G. (1970a) 'Variation in Sukumaland Cotton Yields and the Extension Service'. Paper 70.5, Economic Research Bureau, University of Dar es Salaam.

SAYLOR, G. (1970b), 'An Opinion Survey of Bwana Shambas in Tanzania'. Paper 70.15, Economic Research Bureau, University of Dar es Salaam.

SAYLOR, G. (1973) 'A Social Cost/Benefit Analysis of Agricultural Extension and Research Services among Small-holder Coffee Producers in Kilimanjaro District', in V. F. Amann (ed.) Agricultural Policy Issues in East Africa. Makerere University Printery, 263–73.

SAYLOR, G. (1974) 'Farm Level Cotton Yields and the Research and Extension Services in Tanzania'. East African Journal of Rural Development VII, 1/2 46–60.

SCHEFFLER, W. (1968) 'Tobacco Schemes in the Central Region', in Ruthenberg (ed.) (1968) 275–305.

SEGALL, M. (1972) 'The Politics of Health in Tanzania' in Rweyemamu et al. (eds.) (1972) 149–65.

SEIDMAN, A. (1972) Comparative Development Strategies in East Africa. East African Publishing House.

SENDER, J. (1974) 'Some Preliminary Notes on the Political Economy of Rural Development in Tanzania'. Paper 74.5, Economic Research Bureau, University of Dar es Salaam.

SENDER, J. (1975) 'The Development of Capitalist Agriculture in Tanzania'. Unpublished Ph.D. thesis, University of London.

SHERIFF, A. M. (1971) 'The Rise of a Commercial Empire: An Aspect of the Economic History of Zanzibar 1770–1873'. Unpublished Ph.D. thesis, University of London.

SHERIFF, A. M. (1976) 'The Peasantry in Zanzibar under Colonial Rule'. Maji Maji 28, 1–32.

SHIVJI, I. G. (1972) The Silent Class Struggle. Tanzania Publishing House. Reprinted in Cliffe and Saul (eds.) Vol. 2 (1973) 304–30.

SHIVJI, I. G. (ed.) (1973) Tourism and Socialist Development. Tanzania Publishing House.

SHIVJI, I. G. (1975) Class Struggles in Tanzania. Heinemann Educational Books (London) and Tanzania Publishing House (Dar es Salaam).

SHORTER, A. (1973) 'Interlacustrine Chieftainship in Embryo'. Tanzania Notes and Records 72, 37–50.

SMITH, A. (1963) 'The Missionary Contribution to Education (Tanganyika) to 1914'. *Tanganyika Notes and Records* 60, 91–109.

SMITH, H. E. (ed.) (1966) *Readings on Economic Development and Administration in Tanzania.* Institute of Public Administration, University of Dar es Salaam, Study No. 4, Oxford University Press.

SOUTHALL, A. (1980) 'Social Disorganisation in Uganda: Before, During and After Amin'. *Journal of Modern African Studies*, 18, 4 627–56.

SPERLING, D. (1976) 'Village Trial Experience of Tanzanian Maize Research Programme'. Mimeo, Ilonga Research Station, Tanzania.

STEPHENS, H. W. (1968) *The Political Transformation of Tanganyika 1920–1967.* Praegar.

STERLING, HON L. (1977) 'Speech by the Minister for Health . . . for the Financial Year 1977/78'. Mimeo, Ministry of Health, Dar es Salaam.

STREN, R. (1974) 'Urban Development in Kenya and Tanzania: A Comparative Analysis'. IDS (Nairobi) Working Paper No. 147.

STRICKLAND, C. (1933) *Co-operation for Africa.* Oxford University Press.

SUTTON, J. (1970) 'Dar es Salaam: A Sketch of a Hundred Years'. *Tanzania Notes and Records* 71, 1–19.

SUTTON, J. (1973) 'Engaruka and its Waters'. Seminar Paper, Department of History, University of Dar es Salaam, 20 February.

SVENDSEN, K. E. (1968) 'Decision-making in the National Development Corporation', in Cliffe and Saul (eds.) Vol. 2 (1973) 89–96.

SWANTZ, M.–L. and others (1975) 'Socio-Economic Causes of Malnutrition in Moshi District'. BRALUP Research Paper No. 39, University of Dar es Salaam.

SWANTZ, M.–L. AND BRYCESON, D. F. (1976) 'Women Workers in Dar es Salaam'. Research Paper No. 43, Bureau of Resource Assessment and Land Use Planning, University of Dar es Salaam.

Tanganyika African National Union (1971) *The Mwongozo* (TANU Guidelines 1971), Government Printer. English version in Coulson (ed.) *African Socialism* . . . 36–42.

Tanganyika African National Union (1972) *Siasa ni Kilimo* ('Politics is Agriculture'), policy paper, Government Printer.

Tanganyika, Government of. *Annual Report of the Administration,* annually (1919–60); *Annual Report of the Department of Agriculture* (1923–60); *Annual Report of the Department of Education* (1923–1960); *Annual Report of the Medical Department* (1918–60); *Annual Report of the Labour Department* (1927–31; 1939–64); *Annual Report on Cooperative Development* (1948–64).

Tanganyika, Government of. *Report by His Majesty's Government . . . to the League of Nations on the Administration of Tanganyika Territory,* annually.

Tanganyika, Government of (1933) *The Recruitment, Employment and Care of Government Labour.* Government Printer, 2nd edition.

Tanganyika, Government of (1938) *Report of the Committee Appointed to Consider and Advise on Questions Relating to the Supply and Wel-*

fare of Native Labour in the Tanganyika Territory. Government Printer.

Tanganyika, Government of (1940) *Report of the Central Development Committee*. Government Printer.

Tanganyika, Government of (1944) *An Outline of Post-War Development Proposals*. Government Printer.

Tanganyika, Government of (1946) *A Ten-Year Development and Welfare Plan for Tanganyika Territory*. Government Printer.

Tanganyika, Government of (1953) *Report of the Sample Census of African Agriculture 1950*. East African Statistical Department.

Tanganyika, Government of (1961) *Development Plan for Tanganyika 1961/2 to 1963/4* (the Three-Year Plan). Government Printer.

Tanganyika, Republic of (1964) *The Tanganyika Five Year Plan for Social and Economic Development July 1964–June 1969* (the First Five-Year Plan). Government Printer.

Tanzania, Bank of. *Economic Bulletin* (quarterly) and *Economic and Operations Report* (annually).

Tanzania Food and Nutrition Centre (1978) 'Data Report on the Food and Nutrition Situation in Tanzania 1972/3–1976/7'. Mimeo.

Tanzania, United Republic of. *The Economic Survey*. Annually, Government Printer. (The 1967 and 1968 surveys were entitled *Background to the Budget: An Economic Survey*.)

Tanzania, United Republic of. *The Annual Plan*. Government Printer.

Tanzania, United Republic of. *Industrial Directory*. Annually. Ministry of Commerce and Industries.

Tanzania, United Republic of. *Annual Manpower Report to the President*. Ministry of Manpower Development.

Tanzania, United Republic of. (1966) *Report of the Presidential Special Committee of Enquiry into Cooperative Movement and Marketing Boards*. Government Printer.

Tanzania, United Republic of (1967 ff.) *The Population of Tanzania*. 6 Volumes, Bureau of Statistics.

Tanzania, United Republic of (1967) *Background to the Budget*, see Tanzania, United Republic of *The Economic Survey*, Supra.

Tanzania, United Republic of. (1969) *Tanzania Second Five Year Plan for Economic and Social Development July 1969–June 1974*. 4 Volumes. Government Printer.

Tanzania, United Republic of (1971, 1972) *1969 Household Budget Survey*, 3 Volumes, Bureau of Statistics, Dar es Salaam.

Tanzania, United Republic of (1970) *Tanzania Government's Statement on the Recognition of Biafra* (13 April 1968). Government Printer.

Tanzania, United Republic of (1972) *Survey of Employment and Earnings*. Bureau of Statistics.

Tanzania, United Republic of (1974) *Analysis of Accounts of Parastatals 1966–73*. Bureau of Statistics.

Tanzania, United Republic of (1977) 'The Threat of Desertification in Central Tanzania', a technical paper prepared for the United Nations Conference on Desertification, August–September 1977, by H. A. Fosbrooke.

Tanzania, United Republic of (1978) *Third Five Year Plan for Economic and Social Development*, 3 Volumes. National Printing Co.

TAYLOR, J. C. (1963) *The Political Development of Tanganyika*. Stanford and Oxford University Presses.

TEMPLE, P. H. (1972) 'Soil and Water Conservation Policies in the Uluguru Mountains, Tanzania'. *Geografiska Annaler* 54, 3–4 110–23.

THODEN VAN VELSEN, H. V. (1973) 'Staff, Kulaks and Peasants...' in Cliffe and Saul (eds.) (1973) 153–79.

THOMAS, C. Y. (1973) *Dependence and Transformation*. Monthly Review Press.

THOMAS, C. Y. (1975) 'Industrialization and the Transformation of Africa: An Alternative Strategy to MNC Expansion' in C. Widstrand (ed.) *Multinational Firms in Africa*, African Institute for Economic Development and Planning, Dakar, and Scandinavian Institute of African Studies, Uppsala, pp. 325–60.

THOMAS, IAN (1979) 'Population Policy in Tanzania', Development Studies Discussion Paper No. 51, University of East Anglia.

TITMUSS, R. M. *et al.* (1964) *The Health Services of Tanganyika: A Report to the Government*. Pitman Medical Publishing Co., London.

TORDOFF, W. (1967) *Government and Politics in Tanzania*. East African Publishing House.

TOROKA, S. (1968) 'Education for Self-Reliance: The Litowa Experiment' in Cliffe and Saul (eds.) Vol. 2 (1973) pp. 264–70.

TSCHANNERL, G. (1973) 'Rural Water Supply in Tanzania: Is Politics or Technique in Command?' Bureau of Resource Assessment and Land Use Planning, reprinted in Coulson (ed.) *African Socialism*... 86–105.

TSCHANNERL, G. (1974) 'Periphery Development and the Working Population in Tanzania'. *Utafiti* (Dar es Salaam) I, 1.

TSCHANNERL, G. (n.d.) 'Tanzania and the World Bank'. Mimeo.

TURNER, V. (ed.) (1971) *Colonialism in Africa 1870–1960, Vol. 3 Profiles of Change*. Hoover Institution Publications. (General editors P. Duignan and L. Gann.)

TUROK, B. (1971) 'The Problem of Agency in Tanzania's Rural Development: Rufiji Ujamaa Scheme' in Cliffe *et al.* (eds.) (1975) 396–417.

United Nations Trusteeship Council, Visiting Missions to Trust Territories in East Africa, *Report on Tanganyika and Related Documents*, 1948 (T/218), 1951 (T/1032), 1954 (T/1169), 1957 (T/1401), and 1960 (T/1550). United Nations, New York.

United Republic of Tanzania. See Tanzania, United Republic of.

Utafiti (Dar es Salaam). Journal of the Faculty of Arts and Social Science, University of Dar es Salaam.

VAN ARKADIE, B. (1969) 'Planning in Tanzania' in Cliffe and Saul (eds.) Vol 2 (1973) 25–39.

Van Der Laar, A. (1969) 'Towards a Manpower Development Strategy in Tanzania' in Cliffe and Saul (eds.) Vol. 2 (1973) 224–45.

Van Hall, L. le (1979) 'Transfer Pricing: The Issue for Tanzania' in Coulson (ed.) *African Socialism* . . . 191–9.

Van Hekken P. and Van Velsen, H. U. Thoden (1972) *Land Scarcity and Rural Inequality in Tanzania: Some Case Studies from Rungwe District.* Mouton (The Hague).

von Freyhold, M. (1972) 'Government Staff and Ujamaa Villages'. East African Social Science Conference, Nairobi.

von Freyhold, M. (1975) 'The World Bank and its Relationship to Tanzania'. Public lecture, University of Dar es Salaam Economic Association, 20 November.

von Freyhold, M. (1977a) 'On Colonial Modes of Production'. History seminar, University of Dar es Salaam, 25 August.

von Freyhold, M. (1977b) 'Notes on Tanzanian Industrial Workers'. *Tanzania Notes and Records* 81/82, 15–21.

von Freyhold, M. (1977c) 'The Post-Colonial State and its Tanzanian Version'. *Review of African Political Economy* 8, 75–89.

von Freyhold, M. (1979) *Ujamaa Villages in Tanzania: Analysis of a Social Experiment.* Heinemann Educational Books.

von Freyhold, M. (n.d.) 'The Workers and the Nizers'. Unpublished typescript.

Wangwe, S. M. (1977) 'Factors Influencing Capacity Utilisation in Tanzanian Manufacturing'. *International Labour Review* 115, 1 65–77.

Whiteley, W. (1969) *Swahili*, London.

Williams, D. (1975) 'National Planning and the Choice of Technology in Cotton Textiles'. Seminar paper, Economic Research Bureau, University of Dar es Salaam.

Williams, D. V. (1979) 'Authoritarian Legal Systems and the Process of Capitalist Accumulation in Africa'. Southern African Social Sciences Conference, Dar es Salaam, June.

Wisner, B., Kassami, A. and Nuwagaba, A. (1971) 'Mbambara: The Long Road to *Ujamaa*'. In Cliffe *et al.* (eds.) (1975) 370–91.

Wood, Alan (1950) *The Groundnut Affair.* Bodley Head.

Yaffey, M. H. (1970) *Balance of Payments Problems of a Developing Country.* Springer-Weltforum (Munich).

Yoshida, M. (1972) 'Agricultural Survey of the Lower Rufiji Plain'. Mimeo. Report to the Ministry of Water Development and Power.

Young, R. and Fosbrooke, H. (1960) *Land and Politics among the Luguru of Tanganyika.* North-Western University Press, Chicago.

Yudkin, J. (1978) 'To Plan is to Choose: The Burning Question of People's Health: A Critical Analysis of the Health Question in Tanzania'. *Maji Maji* (Dar es Salaam) 34, 12–40.

INDEX

accumulation of capital, 324–6, 331
Adamson, A. D. and Robbins, S. R.,
199, 199 fn. 9, 200 (table)
administrative systems, 18, 41–2
Adu, A. L., 121, 121 fn. 8
Advisory Council on Native
Education, 101
African Association, 101, 113–14, 114
fn. 6, 127
African Welfare and Commercial
Association, 104
Afro-Shirazi Party, 130–3, 201
Afro-Shirazi Union, 130
agriculture, 6, 6 fn. 1, 9 (map), 10,
15–16, 18, 35–40, 43–59, 70, 120,
145–67, 177, 180, 188–190, 237–8,
245, 249, 256, 260, 300, 301, 313,
326–7, 330.
    extension workers, 52, 55, 147,
    152–7, 166, 203
    processing industries, 63–4, 71, 72,
    73–4, 76–7, 168, 173, 190, 313
    research, 42, 54, 166
    see also famine, food, mechanization,
    and specific crops (i.e. cashewnuts,
    cotton, etc.)
aid, see foreign capital
Aga Khan, 89, 169–70
Alavi, Hamza, 326 fn. 9
Allan, W., 70 fn. 2
Alpers, E. A., 21
Amin, Idi, 285, 307, 309–310
Angwazi, J. and Ndulu, B., 247
Aquinas, Thomas, 329
Arabs, 22–6, 28, 123–33
Aristotle, 329
Armitage-Smith, Sir S., 73, 75, 76–7
army, British, 113, 140
    German, 27–32
    King's African Rifles, 113–14

Tanzania People's Defence Force,
140, 310
Arnold, David, 34 fn. 2
Arusha, 146, 307, 318
Arusha Declaration (1967), 1, 5,
176–83, 229, 272, 274, 299–301, 325,
328, 329–330
*The Arusha Declaration Ten Years
After* (1977), 256 fn. 15, 328
Asian community:
    in agricultural production, 45
    crop purchasing, 39–40, 60–9
    education, 84–6, 89
    housing, 212
    in industry, 71, 78, 79, 169–70, 203
    and nationalization, 179 fn. 13, 275,
    315
    in politics, 112–13, 115, 119
    retail trade, 66, 121, 203, 290–1, 292,
    321
    on Zanzibar, 12, 23, 24, 124–5, 127
Austen, R. A., 77, 94, 95, 353, 354
Awiti, Adhu, 58, 163–4, 163 fn. 17,
249

Babu, Abdulrahman, 131, 182, 182 fn.
17, 223
baby foods, 210, 210 fn. 18
Baker, E., 46
bakery, automated, 281
balance of payments, 185, 186–7, 283,
300; see also trade
Bank of Tanzania, 275
banks, 178, 201, 275–6, 277, 301, 314
bao, 206
Barclay's Bank, 179, 275–6
Barker, Carol, and Wield, David, *et
al.*, 172, 172 fn. 3, 174, 174 fn. 5 and
6, 274, 274 fn. 3, 280–1, 356
Barongo,Peter, 266

basic industry strategy, 311–13, 311 fn. 24, 316
Bata Shoe Company, 178, 179
Bates, Margaret, 94
Batson, E., 128 fn. 2
Bayi, Filbert, 206
Beachey, R. W., 24, 352
Beck, R. S., 155
Belshaw, D. and Hall, M., 155, 356
Bennett, N. R., 123, 124 fn. 1, 352, 355
'Biafra', 306, 306 fn. 17
Bienefeld, M., 227
Bienen, Henry, 182 fn. 17, 355
Bismarck, 33–4
Boeree, Robert, 161
Boesen, Jannik, 157, 252, 358
Bomani, Paul, 67, 119, 143–4, 239
Boserup, Ester, 352
Bowles, Brian, 49, 52, 59, 64–9, 64 fn. 5, 78, 78 fn. 7, 127, 130, 132, 132 fn. 4
Brett, E. A., 13 fn. 4, 48, 73, 75, 77, 351, 353
breweries, 74, 168, 171, 172, 178
bride-price, 83, 204
British-American Tobacco Company, 159, 169, 178, 286–7
British Government,
  agricultural policy, 43–5, 48–9, 50–2, 62–9
  indirect rule, 94–7
  industrial policy, 76–9
  mandate in Tanganyika, 44–5, 78, 94, 96, 111
  relations after independence, 140–3, 315
  transfer of power, 110–12, 118–22
  and Zanzibar, 24, 123
Bryceson, Debbie, 19, 48, 204 fn. 7, 357
Bryceson, Derek, 119
Bukenya, Austin, 207 fn. 14
Bukoba, 17, 27–8, 36, 63, 155
  Bukoba Bahaya Union, 63
  Bukoba Coffee Control Board, 64–5
  Bukoba Co-operative Union, 65–6, 152 fn. 11
bureaucratic bourgeoisie, 4, 321–2, 326–7, 329–31
Bushiri, 29–30
Bwana Heri, 29–30
Byatt, Sir Horace, 94, 95

Cameron, Sir Donald, 43, 47, 61, 71, 76, 94–6, 110, 333, 354
Cameron, J. and Dodd, W. A., 41, 83, 88, 88 fn. 9, 89, 90, 92, 352, 353
Canada, 137, 277, 301
capacity utilization, 192
capital, see foreign capital
capital city, see Dar es Salaam, Dodoma
capital goods, 13, 175, 283, 325
capitalism, 10–14, 55–9, 69, 145, 146, 148, 162–7, 168–75, 179, 237, 316, 324–7
cashewnuts, 9, 10, 58, 165, 173, 190, 260, 313, 331 fn. 18
Castle, E. B., 83
cattle, see livestock
cement factory, 168, 172, 178, 190, 281, 283
Chagga tribe, 16 fn. 3, 30–1, 61–2, 89, 119
Chama cha Mapinduzi (CCM), 201
Chamwino village, 248
Chandaria family, 170, 288
Chande Industries, 170
Chase, Hank, 223 fn. 30
chiefs, 15, 16–17, 18, 19, 24, 34, 35, 36, 52, 61, 63, 81, 82–3, 88, 88 fn. 8, 94–7, 115, 119, 327
China, People's Republic of, 141, 142–3, 160, 173, 201, 218, 231–4, 282, 291–2, 306 fn. 16, 312 fn. 25
Chittick, H. Neville, 21, 21 fn. 1, 25, 352
cholera, 259, 259 fn. 21
Christianity, see missions
Chunya, 249
civil service, 83, 88, 103–4, 110–11, 112, 114, 118, 120, 121, 124, 125, 136, 183, 198, 203, 172, 320, 321–2
Clark, Edmund, 179, 179 fn. 12 and 13, 272 fn. 2, 279 (table), 280–1
classes, 176–7, 202–4, 215, 230, 235, 317–324, 329–31.
class struggles, 4, 91–3, 97–8
Clayton, A., 124, 126, 127, 128, 355
Cliffe, Lionel, 52, 137 fn. 6, 143, 154, 238, 238 fn. 3, 315, 351, 353, 355, 357
'closer union', 96, 103
cloves, 12, 22–3, 25, 26, 123–4, 126–7, 131, 199–201
coal, 70, 233, 313

coastal trade, 10–11, 12
coffee, 16–17, 36, 47, 58–9, 63–5, 74, 155, 165, 173, 190, 249, 331 fn. 18
Collier, P., 196, 197–8, 202
Collinson, Michael, 54, 155, 156
colonization, 12, 28–32, 33–42
Committee on Constitutional Development, 112–13, 114
Commonwealth Development Corporation, 276
communal labour, 16, 38, 239–46, 257, 265, 319
community development, 147, 157–8, 161
compensation, 178, 179, 221
compulsion, 35, 38, 48, 49, 52–5, 69, 125, 149, 161, 217 fn. 24, 221–2, 242–3, 249–53, 256–7, 266
Compulsory Marketing Orders, 149
Conference of Berlin, 34
construction industry, 168, 233, 278, 283, 295–8
consumer goods, 71–3, 78, 168–75, 211–2, 309
Consumer Supply Association of Tanganyika (COSATA), 290
contraception, 205, 205 fn. 9, 305
co-operatives, 60–9, 95, 98–9, 107–8, 115–16, 121, 144, 147, 148–52, 180, 180 fn. 14, 264, 273, 278, 290, 320, 321
Co-operative Development Division, 68, 107, 150
corruption, 150–1, 221, 281–2, 350 fn. 14
cost of living index, see retail price index
cotton, 37, 38, 47–8, 49, 58, 64–5, 66–7, 68, 74, 156, 157, 190, 260, 331 fn. 18; see also textiles
Coulson, Andrew, 156, 281, 351, 357, 358
credit, 24, 55, 147, 150, 152, 159–60, 277
Credit to Natives (Restriction) Ordinance, 61
crop authorities, 278; see also marketing boards
crops, see agriculture, food, and specific crops (cashewnuts, coffee, etc.)
culture, 83, 206–7

currency, xv; see also banks, monetary system

Daily News, see newspapers
Dar es Salaam, 10, 26, 35, 101, 106, 199, 203–4, 212–14, 219, 221
decentralization of Government, 252, 254–5, 319–20, 345 fn. 14
Defence Forces, Tanzania People's, see army
democracy, 4, 136, 137, 137 fn. 6, 143–4, 177, 177 fn. 4, 322–3
Democracy and the Party System, 136 fn. 3, 137 fn. 6
demography, see population
dependency theory, 4, 6–14, 20, 26, 27–8, 32, 43, 316, 324–7, 330–1
development planning,
pre-independence, 78, 78 fn. 6, 90, 112
three-year plan, 121
first five-year plan, 141–2, 147–8, 161–2
second five-year plan, 291, 300–1
third five-year plan, 311–13, 343 fn. 27
De Vries, J. and Fortmann, L., 250–1, 259
De Wilde, J. et al., 54, 166
District Councils, 113, 136
District Development Corporations, 278, 318, 320
Divisional Secretaries, 254, 254 fn. 13
divorce, 205
dockers, 104–7, 128
Dar es Salaam Dockworkers and Stevedores Union, 106–7
Dodoma, 113, 248, 289, 316, 316 fn. 32, 319
drama, 206, 207, 268
drugs, 73, 209–11
Duggan, W. R. and Civille, J. R., 114 fn. 7
Dumont, René, 259 fn. 19
Dundas, Charles, 61–2, 95, 354

East African Common Market, 73, 121, 170, 307–9
East African Common Services Organization, 121, 138–9, 307
East African Community, 278, 307–9. See also Kenya, Uganda

East African Currency Board, 274–5
East African Royal Commission, 92
ecology, 6, 10, 15–16, 238, 258–9
The Economic Development of Tanganika, 120, 147; *see also* International Bank for Reconstruction and Development
Edgett Smith, W. E., 114 fn. 7, 140, 141, 181–2, 182 fn. 17, 183, 222, 226, 354, 356
education, 41, 81–93, 97–8, 112, 142, 180–2, 203, 214–17, 224–30, 267–9, 323.
Education for Self-Reliance, 1, 86, 178, 214–16
Egero, B. and Henin, R., 267 fn. 2
elections, 115, 117, 119, 130–2, 137; *see also* democracy
Ellis, Frank, 188 fn. 3, 190 fn. 5, 196, 197 (table), 331 fn. 18, 356
Ellman, A., 240
employment, 72 (table), 74, 78–80, 79 (table), 125–7, 137, 146–7, 173, 196, 196 (table), 279 (table), 280; *see also* inequality, migrant labour, trade unions, wages, workers
Engaruka, 16
Ente Nazionale Idrocarburi (ENI), 172
equality, *see* inequality, leadership conditions
Erlick, C., 39
erosion, *see* soil erosion
European settlement, *see* settlers, plantations
exchange control, 275
exploitation, 176–7
exports, *see* trade
extension workers, *see* agricultural extension workers

Fabian socialism, 115, 237, 237 fn. 2, 322 fn. 4, 327–8, 329
Family Planning Association of Tanzania, 205 fn. 9
famine, 19, 29, 31, 48, 156–7, 188, 247
Faudon, M. J., 141
Feldman, Rayah, 163, 163 fn. 17
fertilizer, 92 fn. 10, 155–6, 166, 190, 235, 257–8.
fertilizer factory, 281, 313 fn. fn. 29
Fiah, Erika, 104–5
finance, *see* monetary system, taxation

Finlay, Richard, 154
firearms, 17–18, 19, 20, 27, 29–30
First World War, 29, 31, 71–3
five-year plans, *see* development planning
focal point approach, 55
food, food crops, 16, 37, 48, 49, 59, 127, 149, 163, 188, 260–1, 265, 315–6
forced labour, 35–6, 48, 52–5
Ford Foundation, 121, 121 fn. 8
Ford, John, 32 fn. 2, 259, 352
foreign capital, 2, 120, 142–3, 168–75, 177, 180, 186, 193, 194, 201, 228, 321–4, 260–1, 277, 299–306, 307, 309, 312, 312 fn. 25, 313–6
Foreign Investment Protection Act, 173
foreign policy, 137, 141, 142–3, 304–11, 304 fn. 14
Fortman, Louise, 250–1, 259, 358
Fosbrooke, H. A., 53, 259 fn. 19, 353
Frankel, S. H., 50–2, 353
Freedom and Development, 242–3, 262
Freedom of expression, 176, 206, 221–2, 342–3
FRELIMO, 226, 248 fn. 9, 306, 306 fn. 15
Friedland, W.H., 107 fn. 8, 137, 138, 354–5
Friendship Textile Mill, 282
frontal approach (to ujamaa), 300, 300 fn. 7
Fuggles-Couchman, N. R., 50 fn. 4, 165

Galbraith, J. C., 179 fn. 11
Gardner, B., 71
General Superintendence Company, 283
General Tyre Company, 296
Germans, 24, 27–32, 33–42, 73
Federal Republic of Germany, 142, 213, 301
German Democratic Republic, 141, 142, 201
German East Africa, 13, 34, 82–3
German East Africa Company, 35, 273
Geografiska Annaler, 217 fn. 26
Georges, Chief Justice, 220
Gesellschaft für Deutsche Kolonisation, *see* Society for German Colonization

Gogo tribe, 18, 30, 348–9
gold, 11, 21, 48
Gottlieb, M., 203 fn. 5
Grain Storage Department, 68
Great Depression, 34
Great Uhuru Railway, 218, 231–4; see also China, People's Republic of
Green, Reg, 278 fn. 6
Groeneveld, S., 157
gross domestic product, 146, 170, 185–6, 188–91
gross material product, 186, 188, 188 fn. 3
groundnuts, 40
Groundnut Scheme, 50–2, 50 fn. 5
Gulliver, P. M., 45 fn. 3
Gwassa, Gilbert, 352

Hadimu tribe, 22–3, 125, 126
Hailey, Lord, 101, 110, 274
Hall, R. and Peyman, H., 231–3
Hanga, Kassim, 222
Harvard Advisory Service, 300 fn. 8, 312 fn. 27
Hatch, J. C., 114 fn. 7
Hawkins, H. C., 61, 121 fn. 7
health, 42, 199, 205, 207–11, 259, 259 fn. 21, 267
Helgoland, 35
Henderson, W. O., 37, 40
Heri, Bwana, 29–30
Hill, Frances, 248, 256, 256 fn. 16
Hirji, Karim, 41, 81, 93, 215 fn. 21, 219 fn. 29
Hitchcock, E., 37
Hizbu l'Watau l'Riaia Sultan Zanzibar, 129
Hofmeir, R., 219 fn. 29, 357
Honey, Martha, 74, 78, 169–70, 311 fn. 20, 353, 356
Hornby, G., 41, 83
hospitals, see health
housing, 211–14, 259, 266, 276
Huang, Yukon, 193, 357
Hulls, Robert H., 154, 356
Hussain, Abdallah, 207 fn. 14
Hyden, G., 354, 357–8, 359

Ibbott, Ralph, 263–4, 263 fn. 1, 269
ideology, 5, 81–93, 319, 328–9, 330
Iliffe, John, 16 fn. 1, 17 fn. 4, 31, 35–40, 35 fn. 3, 42, 45, 45 fn. 3, 47,

61 fn. 2, 64, 81 fn. 1, 82, 84, 94, 95, 97, 101–8, 101 fn. 2, 102 fn. 2, 104 fn. 5, 105 (table), 106, 106 fn. 8, 204 fn. 6, 206, 247, 351, 352, 353, 354
import licences, 275, 283
import substitution, 13, 73–4, 77, 78, 168–75, 192
improvement approach, 120, 147, 148–58
incremental capital output ratios, 192
independent weighing scheme, 66–7
Indians, see Asian community
indirect rule, 94–9, 110, 333
industrialization, 13–4, 19, 70–80, 121, 168–75, 177, 180, 190–2, 269–70, 300, 300 fn. 8, 301, 312–3; see also Arusha Declaration, Asian community, multinational corporations, nationalization, parastatals, private sector
inequality, 58, 69, 148, 152, 163–5, 195–9, 202–3, 203 fn. 5, 216
inflation, 105–6, 127, 186, 195–6, 300
Ingle, C., 245
insurance, 178, 274, 276
intellectuals, 177 fn. 4, 330
inter-cropping, 18, 154–5
intermediate goods, 175, 311, 325
International Bank for Reconstruction and Development (the World Bank), 13, 120, 121, 147–8, 173, 214, 231, 257, 274, 277, 283 fn. 10, 301, 301 fn. 12, 304, 313, 314–16
international economic order, 2, 326
International Labour Office, 203 fn. 3, 283 fn. 10, 356
International Monetary Fund, 13, 311 fn. 20, 348 fn. 20
International Trading Association of Tanzania (INTRATA), 276, 290–1
Investment Promotion Services, 169, 274 fn. 3, 287
Iringa, 58, 163–4, 248–9, 250–1, 259, 316 fn. 32
Iringa Dipping Scheme, 53, 54
iron production, 15, 17, 18, 19, 313
irrigation, 16, 16 fn. 3, 38, 148, 160–1, 247
Islam, 21, 81–2, 204, 204 fn. 6, 205
Ismani, 58, 163–4, 248–9
Italy, 172–3, 281
ivory, 11, 12, 17–8, 21, 23–4, 27

Jamal, Amir, 119
Japhet, Kirilo and Seaton, Earle, 111
  fn. 3
Jellicoe, Marguerite, 333
Jervis, T., 17
Jiddawi, A. M., 82
jiggers, 29
Jones, G., 71 fn. 3
judiciary, 220–1
Jumbe, Aboud, 201

Kaduma, Ibrahim, 225, 228–30
Kahama, George, 119, 278, 278 fn. 6,
  319 fn. 2
Kahe Irrigation Scheme, 160
Kambona, Oscar, 112, 119, 136, 140,
  143, 182–3
Kaplinsky, R., 171 fn. 2
Karimjee family, 169
Karioki, J., 304 fn. 14
Karume, Abeid, 2, 126–7, 133, 142,
  199, 222–3
Kaunda, Kenneth, 232
Kawawa, Rashidi, 107, 116–17, 119,
  135–7, 139, 141, 159, 181, 225, 239,
  248, 309
Kayamba, Martin, 96, 102–4, 102 fn.
  3, 103 fn. 4
kenaf, 281
Kenatco, 309
Kenya,
  'closer union' with, 96, 103, 138–9
  industrialization in, 14, 73–6, 96,
    169–72, 307, 325
  Mombasa port, 74–6, 292
  settlers in, 47, 61, 73, 76, 170–1
  trade with, 74, 75 (table), 77–8, 292,
    307–9, 308 (table)
  see also East African Common Market
Kiembe Samaki village, 129
Kigoma, 28, 38, 40, 43, 249
Kiiza, Klemenz, 63–4
Kilimanjaro, 16, 16 fn. 3, 30, 36, 47,
  89, 146, 165, 203
  Kilimanjaro Native Co-operative
    Union, 62, 152 fn. 11
  Kilimanjaro Native Planters'
    Association, 61–2, 95
Kilonzo, Bernardo, 244
Kilwa, 10, 11, 19, 22, 25, 31
Kimambo, Isaria, 18, 351
kipande system, 45–6

Kitching, Gavin, 108 fn. 9
Kivukoni College, 112, 263
Kjaerby, Finn, 16 fn. 2, 32 fn. 2, 54,
  164 fn. 18
Kjekshus, Helge, 17, 18, 19, 27–32, 32
  fn. 2, 43, 247, 249, 351, 352
Klerruu, Wilbert, 248–9
Koch, Robert, 42
Kriesel, Herbert et al., 149
kulaks, 55, 58, 69, 116, 163–7, 203, 320
Kwetu, 101, 104

labour, see compulsion, employment,
  inequality, migrant labour, trade
  unions, wages, workers.
  Department of Labour, 107–8
Lancaster House Conference, 146, 146
  fn. 2, 275
land tenure, 43, 46–7, 92, 111–12, 127,
  136, 155, 164, 221, 320
law, 220–3, 224
Lawrence, Peter, 47
leadership conditions (of the Arusha
  Declaration), 177–8, 198
League of Nations, 44–5
Leonard, David, 257, 358, 359
Leubuscher, Charlotte, 73 fn. 4, 75,
  78, 354
Lewis, W. Arthur, 326 fn. 8
Leys, Colin, 108 fn. 9, 171 fn. 2
liberation movements, 137, 143, 226,
  306, 315
Lint and Seed Marketing Board, 68
Listowel, Judith, 84, 87 fn. 7, 88, 88
  fn. 9, 95, 111 fn. 3, 112, 114, 115,
  116, 118 fn. 1, 140, 354
literacy, 20, 81, 217 fn. 25
Litowa village, see Ruvuma
  Development Association
Little, Arthur D., Inc., 121
livestock, 10, 16, 16 fn. 2, 18–19, 28–9,
  31–2, 53, 54, 129, 258, 301
Livingstone, Ian, 163 fn. 15, 211, 212
  (table)
local government, see decentralization,
  District Councils, indirect rule
lock-outs, 286–8
Lofchie, Michael, 124 (table, 127–33,
  127 (table), 128 fn. 2, 130 fn. 3, 260,
  352, 355
Lonrho, 171, 172, 219, 231, 278, 340
  fn. 3

Lord, R. F., 159
Loxley, John, 146 fn. 2, 179, 273, 274–6, 300 fn. 9
Lugard, Lord, 94 fn. 2, 97–8, 354
Lule, Yusufu, 310
Luning, H. and Venema, L., 157
Lushoto Integrated Development Project, 279
Lwoga, C. M., 250

Maasai, 18, 29, 36, 251
McHenry, Dean, 252, 358
McKinsey and Company, Inc., 255, 278, 292–4, 345 fn. 14
Macleod, Iain, 110, 120
Macmillan, Sir Harold, 120
Macnamara, Robert, 315, 316
Madhvani family, 170, 174
Maguire, G. A., 52–3, 67 fn. 6, 353
maize, 16, 44, 49, 58, 59, 149, 156–7, 163, 165, 257, 260 (table), 261 (table), 265–6
Maji Maji revolt, 31, 38
Makerere University, 87, 90–1, 103, 112, 113, 114
Malima, Kighoma, 166 fn. 19
malnutrition, 199, 207; see also famine, food, health
management agreements, 278, 283, 295–8
mandate, see British Government, mandate in Tanganyika
Mangat, J. S., 39, 352
manpower planning, 142, 203 fn. 3
Mapolu, Henry, 284–7, 284 fn. 11, 358
maps, ix, 41
Marealle, Chief, 36
Marketing Boards, 60, 64–9, 273; see also co-operatives, crop authorities
markets, see trade
Maro, P. S. and Mlay, W. I., 205 fn. 8
Marriage Act, 204–5
Martin, David, 310 fn. 19
Martin, R., 220
Masao, F. T., 16 fn. 3
Mascarenhas, Adolpho, 211, 213 (table), 214, 357
Masefield, G. B., 258
Master and Servant Ordinance, 45
Matango, Reuben, 251
Matetereka village, see Ruvuma Development Association

Mbambara village, 238, 243–4
Mbarali Irrigation Scheme, 160
Mbeya, 149, 160, 165, 233, 249
Mbilinyi, Marjorie, 84 fn. 4, 86, 86 fn. 5, 202, 204 fn. 7, 215, 215 fn. 21, 353–4, 357
Mboya, Tom, 107, 116
Mbulu, 58, 164
    Mbulu Development Scheme, 53, 54
Meat Rations Ltd., 76–7
mechanization, 50, 51, 58, 150–1, 157, 157 fn. 12, 164–5
medical services, see health
Meek, C. M., 53, 119, 136
merchants, 12, 20, 23, 24, 39
    merchant capital, 108 fn. 9
    see also trade
Merinyo, Joseph, 61–2
Meru Citizens' Union, 111
Meru Land Case 111–12, 111 fn. 3, 114, 164
Migot-Adholla, Shem, 150–1, 152 fn. 11
migrant labour, 36, 37, 38, 125–7
    see also labour, urbanization
Mihyo, Pascal, 287, 358
militia, 251–2, 252 fn. 11, 329
milling, grain, 74, 171, 172, 178, 265–6
Millinga, Ntimbanjayo, 263–4
minerals, see raw materials; also basic industry strategy, coal, gold, salt, Williamson's Diamonds
minimum wage, see wages
mining, 188; see also coal, gold, salt, Williamson's Diamonds
missions, Christian, 41, 81, 82–3, 90, 102, 114, 124 fn. 1, 204, 204 fn. 6, 205, 208, 209
Mitchell, Sir Philip, 95–6, 103, 352, 354
Mkufya, W. E., 207 fn. 14
Mkwawa, Chief, 30
modernization theory, 55, 92–3, 92 fn. 10, 152, 159–60, 161–2, 238, 322, 329
Mogadishu Agreement, 310
Molloy, Judith, 53
monetary system, 273, 274–6, 283
Moody, A., 157
Morogoro, 36, 38, 250
Morrison, D. R., 84, 85 (table), 90 (table), 181 fn. 16, 224, 225, 227, 353
motor vehicles, 78, 170, 171, 190, 219–20, 309

Mount Carmel Rubber Company, 174, 287–9, 319
Msekwa, Pius, 225, 229
Msuya, Cleopa D., 272, 272 fn. 1, 274, 277, 300
multinational corporations, 13, 78–9, 169, 171–3, 178, 277–8
Mumford, W. B., 88 fn. 8
Munro, J. Forbes, 6, 10, 351
Mushi, Samuel S., 319–20, 359
Muslim faith, see Islam
Musoma Resolutions, 228
mutiny, 140
Mwananchi Development Corporation, 273, 295
Mwananchi Engineering and Construction Company(MECCO), 273, 295–8
Mwanza, 47, 106, 183, 208, 258
  Mwanza African Traders' Co-operative Society, 67, 321
  Mwanza Textile Mill, 282
Mwapachu, Juma V., 252, 255
Mwinyi Mkuu, 22
Mwongozo ('TANU Guidelines 1971'), 252 fn. 11, 262, 284–6, 329

National Agricultural and Food Company (NAFCO), 346 fn. 8
National Bank of Commerce, 179, 292, 296
National Development Corporation (NDC), 274, 277–8, 283, 291, 295–6, 297–8, 319 fn. 2, 345 fn. 14
National Housing Bank, 276
National Housing Corporation (NHC), 213–14, 213 fn. 19
National Insurance Corporation, 276
National Provident Fund, 276
National Service, 181–2, 225, 251
National Union of Tanganyika Workers (NUTA), see trade unions
nationalism, 92, 101–8, 166–7, 170, 226 fn. 5, 235, 322
  see also Arusha Declaration, ideology, nationalization
nationalization, 2, 121, 136, 136 fn. 5, 139, 178–80, 272–83, 300, 322, 325
Native Authorities, 113, 136
  Native Authority Schools, 87–8, 89
Nellis, J. R., 5, 96
Nelson, Anton, 111 fn. 3

newspapers, 206–7
  The Daily News, 206–7, 229–30, 288–9
  Kwetu, 101, 104
  Mwongozi, 129
  The Nationalist, 182, 273
  The Standard, 171, 206 fn. 13, 226
  Uhuru, 273
Ngoni tribe, 18, 30
  Ngoni-Matengo Co-operative Marketing Union, 62–3
Nigerian Civil War, 306, 306 fn. 17
'nizers', 203–4, 321–2
Njombe District, 258–9
Northern Provinces Wheat Scheme, 49–50
novels, 207 fn. 14
Nyamwezi tribe, 12, 18, 28, 30, 119
Nyerere, Mwalimu Julius K.
  early life, 113–15
  ideology, 5, 95, 103, 327–31, 335 fn. 10
  independence campaign, 107, 109, 113–15, 118–20
  independence to the Arusha Declaration, 135–41
  1967 papers, 1, 86, 176, 180–3, 351
  post-Arusha policies, 5, 185, 206, 224–5, 230, 235–8, 248–50, 255–7, 264, 266, 270, 271, 284, 284 fn. 11, 309, 313–16, 354
  and Zanzibar, 130, 133, 222–3

Obote, Milton, 285, 309, 310
oil companies, 179–80.
  oil refinery, 168, 172–3, 179
Okello, John, 133, 133 fn. 6
Oliver, Roland, 82, 82 fn. 3
Olle, W. and Schoeller, W., 324–5, 359
one-party democracy, see democracy
'operations', see villagization
Orde-Browne, St. J., 49
Organization of African Unity, 137, 143, 306, 310
Overseas Construction Company, 295–8
Overseas Food Corporation, 50–2, 159
oxen, see mechanization
Oxfam, 266

Packard, Philip, 346 fn. 8
paddy, see rice

parastatals, 272–83, 272 fn. 2, 285–7, 299, 301, 317, 321, 331 fn. 18; see also Arusha Declaration, nationalization
Parkipuny, L., 54, 251
Party, the, see Chama cha Mapinduzi, Tanganyika African National Union
pastoralists, 10, 16, 32, 54
peasant production, 38–40, 55–9, 60–7, 92–3, 125, 147, 163–7, 180, 247–9, 250–3, 255–6, 259, 261, 262, 318–19, 320
Pemba, 21, 22, 23, 123–33, 145
pensions, 143, 143 fn. 8, 275; see also National Provident Fund
Permanent Mandates Commission, see British Government, mandate in Tanganyika
Peters, Karl, 34, 35
petty bourgeoisie, 81, 91–2, 108, 320–1
Phelps-Stokes Committee, 86
Philips Electronics, 169, 174, 174 fn. 5
Phillips, David, 312 fn. 27
planned villages, see villagization
planning, see development planning
plantations, 13, 33, 36, 37, 146, 318; see also sisal, tea
population, 10, 102, 124, 205 fn. 8
Portuguese, 11, 21–2, 285
Poulantzas, N., 319 fn. 3, 324
Pratt, R. Cranford, 4, 5, 91 (tables), 109, 112, 113, 114, 115, 118 fn. 1, 135, 136, 137 fn. 6, 139, 140, 141, 142, 143, 177 fn. 4, 180, 180 fn. 15, 183, 226, 277, 315, 354, 355, 356, 357
Presidential Circular No. 1 of 1969, 240–3
Presidential Circular No. 1 of 1970, 284 fn. 11
Presidential Planning Teams, 248
Presidential Special Committee of Enquiry into Co-operative Movement and Marketing Board, 149 fn. 9, 150, 150 fn. 10
Preventive Detention Act, 140, 220, 221–3
preventive medicine, see health
prices, 48, 49, 58–9, 66, 69, 149, 195, 197, 317, 331 fn. 18
primary products, see prices, raw materials, trade
Prime Minister's Office, 254, 319, 349

private sector, 121–2, 168–75, 203, 203 fn. 4, 277, 279–80, 301, 318
processing, see agricultural processing industries
productivity, 4, 188–9, 192, 280–1, 324–5
property, nationalization of, 179, 179 fn. 13, 315
protection, see tariffs
public, corporations, see parastatals

radio, 206
Raikes, Philip, 58, 155, 157, 164, 358
railways, 36, 38, 40, 47, 74–6, 218–20, 231–4
rainfall, 7, 8, 50–1, 260, 260 fn. 22
Raisman Commission, 121, 121 fn. 9
Ranger, Terrance, 226
Raum, O. F., 37, 83
raw materials, 11, 12, 13, 33, 44, 70–1, 71 fn. 3, 110, 121, 175, 233
Rechenberg, Governor, 38–9, 40
Redmond, P. M., 17, 18, 35, 62–3, 62 fn. 3, 353
Regional Commissioners, 136, 136 fn. 4, 220, 252–4, 254 fn. 13
regional planning, 314
Registrar of Co-operative Societies, 62, 64, 99, 149
religion, see Islam, missions
reserves, foreign exchange, see balance of payments, banks, foreign capital
resistance to the German conquest, 28, 29–31, 31 fn. 1, 81
Resnick, Idrian, 290 fn. 1
retail price index, 105, 195 (table), 197 (table); see also inflation
Revolutionary Council (of Zanzibar), 133, 141, 222–3
rice, 16, 49, 149, 163, 165, 247, 261
rinderpest, 28–9, 30
riots, 64, 65, 127–8, 129
roads, 41, 153 (map), 173, 218–20, 218 fn. 28, 219 fn. 29
Robert, Shabaan, 206
Roberts, Andrew, 15, 16, 28, 82, 352
Rodgers, Susan, 61 fn. 2, 95, 353
Rodney, Walter, 226, 226 fn. 4, 228, 351
Roemer, Michael et al., 312 fn. 27, 359
Roman Catholic Church, see missions
Rotenhan, D. von, 54

Rounce, N.V., 52
rubber, 37, 49, 74, 174, 287–9
Rufiji valley, 6, 38, 242, 247–8, 271
ruling class, *see* class
rupees, xv
rural development, *see* agriculture
Ruthenberg, Hans, 55–8, 152, 157, 159, 353, 355
Ruvuma Development Association, 238–9, 243, 262, 263–71, 319
Rwegashora, A. G., 60
Rwegasira, S., 356
Rweyemamu, Justinian, 147 fn. 4, 168–9, 299 fn. 3, 311, 353, 359

Sabot, R., 107, 203 fn. 1, 356
salaries, *see* inequality, wages
salt, 17, 19, 273, 281
Sandberg, A., 247
Saul, John, 151–2, 225, 226, 227 fn. 5 and 6, 306 fn. 15 and 16, 351, 353, 359
Saylor, G., 54, 157, 165
Scheffler, W., 159
Second World War, 48–50, 90, 105–6, 110, 113
Seers, Dudley, 185 fn. 2
Segall, Malcolm, 208, 357
Seidman, Ann, 170, 172 fn. 3, 356
self-criticism, 136, 327, 327 fn. 11
self-reliance, 2, 71–3, 177, 180, 299–300, 319
semi-pastoralists, 10
Sender, John, 58, 154, 163 fn. 16, 244–6, 245 fn. 7
services, productive, 185–6, 189
services, social, 41–2, 81–93, 185–6, 194, 202–20, 256–7, 326–7; *see also* education, health, housing, motor vehicles, railways, roads, water supplies
settlement schemes, 147, 148, 159–61, 238–9, 264, 270
settlers, white, 36, 39, 40, 45, 47, 49, 59, 61, 64, 95, 115, 119, 136, 146, 318
Sewji, Jairam, 24
Seyyid Said, 22
Sheriff, Abdul, 23–6, 28, 125, 352
Sheriff, Othman, 222
Shivji, Issa, 4–5, 179 fn. 13, 226, 226 fn. 3, 228, 287, 321, 321 fn. 3, 351, 356, 358, 359

Shorter, Aylward, 15, 18
Siasa ni Kilimo ('Politics is Agriculture'), 249, 249 fn. 10
sisal, 37–8, 45, 49, 74, 142, 146–7, 178, 179, 190, 244, 276
site and service schemes, 214
slaves, 11, 12, 24–6, 125–6
sleeping sickness, *see* tsetse fly
smallpox, 29
Smith, A., 83, 93
Smith, Hadley E., 355
Social and Revolutionary Army, 264–5
socialism, 2, 145, 146, 235–62, 263–71, 284–9, 317–31
    Socialism and Rural Development, 1, 146, 179, 239–40
    see also agriculture, ideology, Fabian socialism, nationalization, Nyerere, ujamaa, villagization
social services, *see* services, social
Society for German Colonization, 34
Sodefra, 282
soil conservation, 16–7, 43, 48, 52–5, 69, 112, 166, 217, 217 fn. 26, 258–9, 259 fn. 19
Songea, 35, 43, 62–3, 149, 263, 270
Songo Songo gas field, 313, 313 fn. 29
sorghum, 16, 257
Southern Africa, *see* liberation movements
Soviet Union, 141, 177 fn. 4, 306, 306 fn. 16, 322
Sperling, David, 156
spontaneous settlement schemes, 238–9
squatters, 13, 126
The Standard, see newspapers
Standard Bank, 275–6
state, the, 108, 176, 289, 316, 317–31
state corporations, *see* parastatals
state farms, 201, 300
State Trading Corporation (STC), 276, 290–4, 345 fn. 14
steel industry, 233, 313
Stepan, A., 330 fn. 15, 359
Stren, R. E., 357
Strickland, C. F., 62, 98
strikes, *see* trade unions
students, *see* University of Dar es Salaam
sugar, 79, 281, 313
Sukumaland, 52–3, 67, 76–7, 164–5, 252; *see also* Mwanza

Sultan of Zanzibar, *see* Zanzibar
Sutton, John, 26, 212
Svendsen, K. Eric, 277
Swahili, 42, 83, 204, 235 fn. 1,
  Swahili house, 212, 213, 213 fn. 19
Swainson, Nicola, 171 fn. 2, 172 fn. 3
Swantz, Marji-Liisa, 203, 248 fn. 8, 252
  fn. 12, 259
Sweden, 218, 219, 248, 277, 301

Tabora, 19, 24, 28, 40, 47
Tabora School, 87, 114
Tanga, 36, 37, 38, 157, 281
Tanganyika African Association, *see*
  African Association and 337 fn. 6
Tanganyika African National Union
  (TANU), 1, 104, 109–17, 135–7, 201,
  249, 253, 255, 262, 270–1, 284–5, 300,
  323–4.
  Central Committee, 248, 253, 270–1
Tanganyika Agricultural Corporation,
  273, 274
Tanganyika Development
  Corporation, 274
Tanganyika Development Finance
  Company Ltd. (TDFL), 274, 277, 277
  fn. 5, 287, 289
Tanganyika Federation of Labour,
  107, 116–17, 139
Tanganyika Packers Ltd., 79, 273, 278
Tanganyika Railway African Union,
  107, 137–9
Tanganyika Territory African Civil
  Services Association, 104
TANU Guidelines, *see Mwongozo*
TANU Youth League (TYL), 238,
  244, 263
Tanzania Food and Nutrition Centre,
  199 (table), 207 fn. 15, 260 (table),
  357
Tanzania Housing Bank, 214
Tanzania Investment Bank, 277, 314
Tanzania Rural Development Bank,
  277, 314
Tanzania Zambia Railway Authority
  (TAZARA), 218, 278, 291–2, 307
  309
tariffs, 74, 76, 96, 169
taxation, 18, 22, 30–1, 35, 40, 45, 48,
  65, 89, 193–5, 300, 329–30
Taylor, J. C., 40, 42, 352
tea, 74, 157, 190, 276, 315

technology policy, 283 fn. 9
television, 206
Temple, Paul, 54, 55, 343 fn. 26
Temu, Arnold, 229, 351
terraces, 53–5
textiles, 11, 12, 19, 23, 27–8, 79, 168,
  170, 190, 281–2, 313, 326
Thomas, Clive Y., 299 fn. 3, 311–13,
  311 fn. 24, 359
Thomas, Ian D., 10
Titmuss, Richard, 42, 208 fn. 16, 352
tobacco, 62–3, 149, 156, 157, 165, 190,
  266, 270; *see also* British-American
  Tobacco Company
Tordoff, William, 117, 137, 140 fn. 7,
  355
Toroka, Suleiman, 268
towns, *see* urbanization
tractors, *see* mechanization
trade
  colonial, 33–40, 43–4, 48, 56–7
  (table), 58–9, 60–9, 74–5, 121
  post-colonial, 145–6, 145 (table),
  162–3, 169–70, 179, 186–7, 187
  (tables), 276, 290–4, 300, 307–9, 308
  (table)
  pre-colonial, 10–14, 17–18, 21–6,
  27–8
  traders, 39–40, 60–1, 121, 149, 321
  trading companies, 24, 171, 178
trade unions, 4, 80, 105–8, 116–7,
  127–8, 135, 137–40, 273–4, 284–9,
  296, 318–9; *see also* wages, workers
transfer pricing, 281, 283
transformation approach, 120, 147–8,
  159–61, 162
Treaty for East African Co-operation,
  73, 307
Trusteeship Committee (of the United
  Nations), 90, 111, 113
Tschannerl, Gerhard, 218, 316, 316 fn.
  31, 357, 359
tsetse fly, 10, 18–9, 27, 31–2, 164
Turnbull, Sir Richard, 117, 119, 135
turn-key projects, 278, 281
Turok, Ben, 242
twelve treaties, 34
Twining, Sir Edward, 109, 111–13, 115

Uganda, 285, 307–10
ujamaa, 2, 221, 235–62, 257 fn. 18,
  263–71, 300, 328

Ujamaa—the Basis of African Socialism, 146, 235–8
Ujamaa Villages Act, 257, 319
see also villagization
Uluguru mountains, 53–5, 249
Umma Party, 131, 132, 133
Umoja wa Wanawake wa Tanzania (UWT), 205, 205 fn. 10, 222
underdevelopment, *see* dependency theory
unemployment, *see* labour, workers
Union of Soviet Socialist Republics, *see* Soviet Union
Union with Zanzibar, 2, 133, 140–1, 199–201
United Africa Company, 50, 171
United Kingdom, 322–3; *see also* British Government
United Nations, 111, 112, 148; *see also* Trusteeship Committee
United States of America, 13, 24, 121, 143, 173, 260–1, 277, 301, 305
United Tanganyika Party, 115
universal primary education, 216–7
University of Dar es Salaam, 5, 89, 181–2, 224–30, 230 fn. 7, 279, 328, 330 fn. 16
urbanization, 10, 41, 74, 101–2, 102 (table), 203, 196 (table)
see also employment, inequality, workers
Usambara mountains, 16, 30, 36, 53
Uvinza salt works, *see* salt

van Arkadie, Brian, 300
van der Laar, A. J., 224, 300 fn. 5
van Velsen, Thoden, 154, 221, 356
Vasey, Sir Ernest, 119, 120, 136
Victoria Federation of Co-operative Unions, 67, 99, 151, 152 fn. 11
Victoria, Lake, 30, 36, 309; *see also* Sukumaland
villages, 4, 18, 103, 241
village settlements, *see* settlement schemes
villagization, 4, 4 fn. 4, 217, 221, 237–62, 316, 319
Visram, Allidina, 39
von Freyhold, Michaela, 157, 158, 204, 240 fn. 4 and 5, 244–6, 244 fn. 6, 245 fn. 7, 252, 256 fn. 17, 301 fn. 12, 321–2, 321 fn. 3, 324, 330, 356, 358, 359

wages, 45, 46 (table), 105–6, 237, 139, 181–2, 195–9, 195 (table), 201; *see also* employment, inequality, trade unions, urbanization, workers
Wallerstein, I., 10 fn. 2
Wangwe, Mwita, 192
water supplies, 51, 212, 213, 217–18, 218 fn. 27, 266, 301
Webb, Sydney, 62
West Germany, *see* Germany, Federal Republic of
West Lake, *see* Bukoba
wheat, 49–50, 58–9, 146, 164, 260 (table), 261 (table)
Whiteley, W., 206
Wicken, Joan, 112
Williams Companies of Oklahoma, 313 fn. 29
Williams, David, 217 fn. 24, 220–2, 235, 357
Williamson's Diamonds Ltd., 41, 273, 278, 283
Wisner, Ben, *et al.*, 238, 243–4
women, 128, 147, 157–8, 204–5, 204 fn. 7, 206, 207
Wood, Alan, 50–2, 353
workers, working class, 4, 35–6, 45–6, 71, 105–7, 127–8, 129, 177 fn. 4, 203–4, 236, 284–9, 296, 318–19, 319 fn. 2, 321, 328–9
Workers' Committees, 284, 287
Workers' Councils, 285
see also employment, trade unions
Workers' Development Corporation, 274
World Bank, *see* International Bank for Reconstruction and Development

Yoshida, M., 247
Young, R. and Fosbrooke, H., 53, 353
Yudkin, J., 209–10

Zambia, 172–3, 231–4
Zanzibar, 2, 12, 21–6, 28, 78, 123–33, 140–1, 142, 199–201, 199 fn. 8, 222–3, 337 fn. 6, Ch. 13
Sultans of Zanzibar, 12, 22, 23, 24, 25, 26, 34, 123–4, 125, 129, 130
Zanzibar National Party, 129–32
Zanzibar and Pemba People's Party, 130–2
Zanzibar Revolution, 132–3
Zimbabwe, 11, 143, 315